BECKETT IN THE THEATRE

BECKETT IN THE THEATRE

The Author as practical Playwright and Director

Volume 1: From *Waiting for Godot* to
Krapp's Last Tape

by

DOUGALD McMILLAN
AND
MARTHA FEHSENFELD

JOHN CALDER · LONDON
RIVERRUN PRESS · NEW YORK

First published in 1988 in Great Britain by
John Calder (Publishers) Ltd
18 Brewer Street, London W1R 4AS

and in the U.S.A. by Riverrun Press Inc.,
1170 Broadway, New York, NY 10001

Copyright © Dougald McMillan and Martha Fehsenfeld 1988

British Library Cataloguing in Publication Data
McMillan, Dougald
 Beckett in the theatre.
 Vol. 1
 1. Beckett, Samuel — Stage history
 I. Title   II. Fehsenfeld, Martha
 792.9'5   PR6003.E282Z/

 ISBN 0-7145-3952-X

American Library of Congress Cataloging-in-Publication Data
Fehsenfeld, Martha.
 Beckett in the theatre.

 Bibliography: p. 265
 Includes index.
 1. Beckett, Samuel, 1906—   —Sources
I. McMillan, Dougald.   II. Title.
PR6003.E282Z6514   1988   848'.91409   86-13813
ISBN 0-7145-3952-X

Typeset in Baskerville by Maggie Spooner Typesetting, London
Printed in the USA by Maple-Vail, Binghamton, NY

Contents

5

List of Illustrations

Acknowledgements

More than most books this one was made possible by the help of others. Actors, directors, researchers, technicians, translators, librarians, colleagues, authors, researchers, typists, students, friends of Beckett, and others not so easily categorised all contributed. The names of those we remember so well for their help are so many, that to list them here would seem more like ostentation than thanks. But if the appearance of this volume recalls pleasant associations for each of them as it does for us, they will know our gratitude and affection. Four played special parts. Patrick Magee and lighting technician Duncan Scott first introduced us backstage at The Royal Court Theatre. Those contacts proved invaluable as we continued our work. As we assembled and prepared our text, we had the indispensable assistance of Beverly Brown, and Maggie Spooner's patient and creative help was more an act of editing than typesetting.

Reading University Library for *Regiebuch* of *Warten auf Godot, Eleuthéria, Mime du Rêveur, Avant fin de partie, Magee Monologue,* Director's Notebooks of *Endspiel* and *Das letzte Band*.

Washington University Library for the Production Script of *Endspiel*.

Ohio State University Library for the two act version of *Fin de partie*.

University of Texas Humanities Research Center for typescripts of *Krapp's Last Tape*.

Lilly Library of Indiana University for the Production Script of *La dernière bande*.

Preface

'If they did it my way they would empty the theatre,' Beckett once said while discussing the possibility of a new production of *Waiting for Godot*.[1] An entry in his production notebook for *Godot* calls for Estragon and Vladimir to be offstage 'long enough for empty stage to carry'. While many of his interpreters have occupied themselves with 'emptiness', 'the void', 'nothingness' in an abstract way, Beckett has displayed more interest in the stage itself as space to be used. Shown the tiny stage of the Théâtre de Petite d'Orsay for the first time Ionesco said, 'Well, I guess I'll have to cut my lines in half.' When Beckett was shown the stage, he paused to observe it and then remarked, 'I think you could do something with that space.'[2] His drafts, annotated texts, and director's notebooks reveal him making changes and additions as he found ways to make his plays work onstage. In rehearsals he has given explicit indications of his way of doing it without insisting that it is the only way. Much more than the philosophical problems or even traditional examinations of character and motivation, his pragmatic concerns disclose how the plays are conceived by their author.

In spite of the fact that he has been remarkably open about these pragmatic concerns, the view still persists that Samuel Beckett is rigidly secretive and silent about his work. It is fostered by anecdotes, like those making much of his refusal to attend openings of his plays (even those he has directed), and of his embarrassment at requests to appear onstage as author. Even though true, these anecdotes have been repeated until they have gained a disproportionate significance. Beckett is a private man. By his own account he has given only one official interview, 'which', as he says, 'I regret'. He does not as a rule respond to or read even the best known criticism of his works. And he has persistently refused to talk about the meaning and philosophical implication of them or to reduce them to paraphrase. Like many contemporary authors, he is a part of what Nathalie Sarraute called the 'age of suspicion' — an age characterised by a belief that the substance of literature cannot be conveyed by the author or accepted by the public in a few direct generalizations. But Beckett is not a gloomy recluse totally unwilling to answer questions about his work. Nor is he deliberately deceptive or unusually elusive. The reclusiveness he does display is not a result of cultivated mystery or arrogant withdrawal. It arises from a practical need to preserve a private existence, giving himself time to write in face of the overwhelming demands of scholars and the intrusions of modern journalism.

Within his own limits and in his own way, Beckett has had a great deal to say about theatre and about his own works. His early parody, now lost, of Corneille's *Le Cid* and his 'jettisoned' plays *Human Wishes* and *Eleuthéria* are all significant comments on dramatic form and theatrical conventions. He has been notably generous and helpful to many scholars, answering their written enquiries about specific facts, changing his schedule to facilitate discussions with them, and giving permission to quote unpublished material which he sometimes provides. He has made statements about his plays and their production more frequently than is generally recognised. Some of these statements have been reported in published accounts, but because they are often in French or German or have appeared in newspapers, or theatre programmes difficult to obtain, they are not widely known. Even when scholars have tracked these down, they have usually quoted only small fragments relative to specific points in their own arguments.

He has also made unpublished drafts of the plays and copies of his production notebooks available through libraries. There are Beckett collections at Trinity College Dublin, Washington University at St. Louis, The Ohio State University, The University of Texas, Dartmouth College, Yale University, Harvard University and Boston University. Most notably he has given and continues to give manuscripts and other materials to the Beckett Archive established by James Knowlson at Reading University. This collection is unsurpassed by any other available for a living author of Beckett's stature. And he has shared portions of his production notebooks with the general public by selecting important, representative pages for theatre programmes and exhibitions.

In addition to published statements and the evidence of unpublished written material in libraries, Beckett's previously unrecorded remarks to translators, directors, actors, production assistants, stage and costume designers and technicians with whom he has worked closely, also provide an important body of commentary. In rehearsals, Beckett speaks frequently of the need to 'get it right' and in the course of achieving this aim, his remarks point out with great precision the way he sees his plays onstage.

The plays have undergone nearly constant alteration from the first stages of composition through the productions which he has helped others to direct or has directed himself. Beckett spoke of this process in terms implying a continuing organic growth. 'Well, I hope they are not stillborn.'[3] This evolution of the plays from the original concept to more and more refined forms worked out in performance is the subject of this book.

Our guiding principle has been to present Beckett's own statements and choices as free from extraneous commentary as possible. Secondary interpretation has been held to a minimum so that the most immediate evidence of Beckett's own hand could remain paramount. Moreover, there has been no attempt to provide a continuous narrative where direct statements speak for themselves. But readers should keep in mind that words here attributed to Beckett were, with rare exceptions, not spoken as public commentary or verified by him. They represent Beckett as reported by others — frequently in translation. Even the most scrupulous attempts to remember and to render faithfully what was said cannot always succeed in quoting exactly one who uses language so sparingly and precisely.

The focus of the book is on the plays themselves and not the personality of the author or even his development as a practical dramatist. Inevitably, however, his personality does emerge in the accounts of those who worked closely with him. And although not presented as a chronicle, his development from a sometimes tentative, sometimes implacable consultant at the early Roger Blin productions of the 1950s to unofficial assisting director in the Patrick Magee/Jack MacGowran *Endgame* in 1964, and later to the confident accomplished director of the internationally successful 1975 Schiller-Theater Berlin *Warten auf Godot* is clear and impressive. The effect of his direction on the later works is also discernible in his increasing attention to visual form and the manipulation of technical control.

The works considered include all of the theatrical forms — plays and scripts for television and film. The radio plays and mimes which he has written have not been included because Beckett has had little to do with the actual production of them, and their difficulty requires more secondary interpretation than is consistent with the aims of this book. Elmar Tophoven's account of Beckett's cooperation in translating his own works, and the account of Pierre Chabert's production of Robert Pinget's *L'Hypothèse* — the one time Beckett assisted in the direction of a play other than his own — are included because of the light they shed on production choices characteristic of Beckett.

The chapters vary in size and content depending on the nature and availability of material relative to each play. There is, for example, no attempt to deal with all states of composition of each play. Only those textual emendations important for production are discussed. In some cases accounts of rehearsals were available and could be included without further comment. In other cases only the brief remarks of numerous participants were available and had to be incorporated into a more formal discussion. It was thus impractical to impose a consistent format.

Some sections are concerned with details of text and production — changes of single words, stage diagrams, light and sound cues — which might at first seem intended only for specialists. That is not the case. For Beckett, these details give his plays their shape, which is so important to him. It is the discovery of that shape for each of the plays that we hope to make possible.

Dougald McMillan
Martha Fehsenfeld

Beckett on Theatre: General Statements

Beckett has had little to say about the meaning and background of his plays. The few general remarks he has made when questioned by journalists and critics are almost exclusively denials that there is a philosophical system behind the plays and explicit refusals to reduce them to codified interpretations. For him, the plays are attempts to depict the 'confusion', 'distress', and 'impotence' of humanity in basic dramatic forms which work effectively on stage. It is the realization of the plays themselves rather than the elaboration of an ideology which concerns him most. The following quotations are revealing.

> Tragedy is not concerned with human justice. Tragedy is the statement of an expiation, but not the miserable expiation of a codified branch of a local arrangement, organized by the knaves for the fools. The tragic figure represents the expiation of original sin, of the original and eternal sin of having been born (*Proust* John Calder Ltd. 1965, p. 67)

> Once Beckett was asked if his system was the absence of system. He replied,
> 'I'm not interested in any system. I can't see any trace of any system anywhere.'
> (To Israel Shenker, 'Moody Man of Letters', *New York Times*, May 6, 1956, Section 2, p. 1)

> The key word in my plays is 'perhaps'.
> (Beckett to Tom F. Driver, 'Beckett By The Madeleine', *Columbia University Forum* IV, Summer 1961, p. 23)

> If pessimism is a judgement to the effect that ill outweighs good, then I can't be taxed with same, having no desire or competence to judge. I happen simply to have come across more of the one than the other.
> (Letter to Professor Tom Bishop of New York University, 1978)

> . . . The Kafka hero has a coherence of purpose. He's lost, but he's not spiritually precarious, he's not falling to bits. My people seem to be falling to bits. Another difference. You notice how Kafka's form is classic, it goes on like a steamroller — almost serene. It seems to be threatened the whole time —

but the consternation is in the form. In my work, there is consternation behind the form, not in the form.
(To Israel Shenker, 'Moody Man of Letters', p. 3)

There will be new form, and this form will be of such a type that it admits the chaos and does not try to say that the chaos is really something else. The form and the chaos remain separate. The latter is not reduced to the former. That is why the form itself becomes a preoccupation, because it exists as a problem separate from the material it accommodates. To find a form that accommodates the mess, that is the task of the artist now.
(To Tom F. Driver, 'Beckett by the Madeleine', p. 23)

The more Joyce knew the more he could. He's tending toward omniscience and omnipotence as an artist. I'm working with impotence, ignorance. I don't think impotence has been exploited in the past. There seems to be a kind of esthetic axiom that expression is an achievement — must be an achievement. My little exploration is that whole zone of being that has always been set aside by artists as something unusable — as sounding by definition incompatible with art.

I think anyone nowadays who pays the slightest attention to his own experience finds it the experience of a non-knower, a non-can-er (somebody who cannot). The other type of artist — the Apollonian — is absolutely foreign to me.
(To Israel Shenker, 'Moody Man of Letters', p. 3)

Two Questions
> I. When *Endspiel* was performed for the first time ten years ago a large part of the public was left with the feeling of bewilderment. One felt that the audience had been given riddles whose answers the author himself did not know. Do you believe that *Endspiel* presents the audience with riddles?
>
> II. Are you of the opinion that the author should have a solution for the riddle at hand?

Two Answers
> 1. *Endspiel* is pure play, nothing less. Of riddles and solutions there is therefore no thought. For such earnest matters there are universities, churches, Chambers of Commerce and so forth.
>
> 2. Not the author of this play.

(*Materialien zu Beckett's Endspiel*; Suhrkamp Verlag, Frankfurt am Main, 1967. Authors' translation)

When it comes to journalists I feel the only line is to refuse to

be involved in exegesis of any kind. And to insist on the extreme simplicity of dramatic situation and issue. If that's not enough for them, and it obviously isn't, it's plenty for us, and we have no elucidations to offer of mysteries that are all of their making. My work is a matter of fundamental sounds (no joke intended) made as fully as possible, and I accept responsibility for nothing else. If people want to have headaches among the overtones, let them. And provide their own aspirin.
(Letter to Alan Schneider, December 29, 1955, *Village Voice Reader*, p. 185.)

I produce an object. What people make of it is not my concern . . . I'd be quite incapable of writing a critical introduction to my own works.
(To Colin Duckworth, *En attendant Godot*, edited by Colin Duckworth, George C. Harrap, London, 1966, p. xxiv)

Theatre for me is a relaxation from work on the novel. You have a definite space and people in this space. That's relaxing.
(To Michael Haerdter during rehearsals of *Endspiel*, Berlin, 1967. Authors' translation)

When I was working on *Watt* I felt the need to create for a smaller space, one in which I had some control of where people stood or moved, above all of a certain light. I wrote *Waiting for Godot*. (To Rosette Lamont Paris 1983 when asked 'how he started to write for the stage.' *Other Stages* June 16, 1983, p. 3)

. . . One must make a world of one's own in order to satisfy one's need to know, to understand, one's need for order . . . There for me, lies the value of the theatre. One turns out a small world with its own laws, conducts the action as if upon a chessboard . . . Yes, even the game of chess is still too complex.
(To Michael Haerdter, Berlin, 1967)

. . . I am panting to see the realisation and know if I am on some kind of road, and can stumble on, or in a swamp.
(Letter to Alan Schneider, October 15, 1956.)

Sorry I wasn't of more help about the play but the less I speak of my work the better. The important thing was for you to see the production.
(Letter to Alan Schneider, October 26, 1957.)

The use of stage space is primary in dramatic construction.
(To Jean Reavey, August 1962; Journal in her possession)

When I write a play I put myself inside the characters, I am also the author supplying the words, and I put myself in the audience visualising what goes on onstage.
(To Jean Reavey, Paris, August 1962)

You should visualise every action of your characters. Know precisely in what direction they are speaking. Know the pauses.
(To Jean Reavey, August 1962)

Producers don't seem to have any sense of form in movement. The kind of form one finds in music, for instance where themes keep recurring. When in a text, actions are repeated, they ought to be made unusual the first time so that when they happen again — in exactly the same way an audience will recognize them from before. In the revival of *Godot* [in Paris] I tried to get at something of that stylised movement that's in the play.
(To Charles Marowitz *Encore* IX March-April 1962, p. 44.)

Beckett believes there is an inevitable sort of correspondence between word and movement; certain lines simply cannot be delivered from certain positions and without compatible 'actions'. Isn't this a matter of each producer's interpretation? I asked. Yes, but within the limits of a specified text the producer has plenty of scope for interpretation. But in a lot of cases, producers go directly contrary to what is intended.
(Marowitz p. 44.)

I never write a word without first saying it out loud.
(To Jean Reavey, August 1962)

Drama is following music.
(To Jean Reavey, August 1962)

Not for me these Grotowskis and Methods . . . the best possible play is one in which there are no actors, only the text. I'm trying to find a way to write one.
(To Deirdre Bair, *Samuel Beckett: A Biography*, New York, 1978, p. 513)

CHAPTER ONE

Clearing the Stage for Godot:
Le Kid, Human Wishes and Eleuthéria

Three unpublished plays preceded *En attendant Godot*. All three were comic commentary in the form of parody on the inadequacy of existing dramatic methods and conventions: *Le Kid* (1931), *Human Wishes* (1937), and *Eleuthéria* (1947) and thus three important steps in preparation for *Godot*.

Though only a collegiate *jeu d'esprit*, *Le Kid* is an early indication of his general attitude toward the existing dramatic tradition and method which presages his later work. In *Human Wishes*, his fragment of an abortive drama of psychological explanation of 'Dr Johnson in love', Beckett extended his questioning of the tradition to include psychological realism, comedy of manners, and even Shakespeare. And finally he questions any drama dependent upon dialogue. Beckett's rejection of dramatic traditions culminated in *Eleuthéria*. Its exhaustive parody of existing dramatic elements, conventions, and techniques constitutes Beckett's discourse of method. (In the action of the play the characters in conventional roles are expelled from the stage space of the protagonists's bare room and the set of the bourgeois drawing room which they inhabit is literally 'swept into the pit'.) Only after such a clearing of the stage did Beckett write *Godot*.

LE KID

Beckett's first writing for the stage was done while he was lecturer at Trinity College, Dublin. *Le Kid* was an 'irreverent burlesque' of scenes loosely based on Corneille's *Le Cid*. Written in French in collaboration with Georges Pelorson, exchange lecturer at Trinity from *L'École Normale Supérieure*, it was performed February 19, 1931 at the Peacock Theatre on the same bill with *La Souriante Madam Beudet* by Denys Amiel and André Obey, and *La Quema* by Serafin and Joaquin Quintero as part of the Trinity College Modern Language Society's annual presentation of foreign drama. The inclusion of a parody of Corneille was a departure from the Society's tradition of presenting an example of European classics each year. *Le Kid* had been preceded the previous year by Molière's *Misanthrope* and the year before that by Racine's *Andromaque*. There are no known copies of the text still extant.

The anonymous review of the evening in the *Irish Times* (20 Feb. 1931) gives a sense of the context in which Beckett's first theatrical work appeared and some of the details of the lost text. According to Maureen O'Brien Flegg[1] who played in *Le Kid*, Beckett, himself, had a hand in the portion of the review dealing with *La Quema* and *La Souriante*.

Peacock Theatre
Three Foreign Plays

Last night the Dublin University Modern Language Society presented three plays at the Peacock Theatre. The first play, *La Quema*, by the Brothers Quintero, is a light but effective one-act comedy with a discreet element of melodrama. Valentin, the hero, is a rich young man who is embarrassed by the pertinent curiosity of his *fiancée* Teodora, a wise and witty widow. He is on the point of burning his love letters when Teodora arrives and insists on reading them. The examination of all the mementoes of Valentin's former love affairs, including an ambiguous photograph of Valentin as a child, leads to emotional difficulties, which are eventually smoothed out in a deliberately conventional ending. Mr. M.L. Ferrar played the part of Valentin, the *blasé* and rather stupid Don Juan, with a polished suavity. Miss Moira Gamble's interpretation of the caustic and temperamental Teodora was completely convincing. Miss Conan was adequately pert as the maid, Delfina.

The politely frivolous 'Quema' was followed by the politely ruthless 'Souriante Mme. Beudet'. Its hard tolerance was most effectively communicated by the Society and the inconclusiveness admirably suggested of a *dénouement*, that might more adequately be described as a *renouement*. Miss Travers interpreted Mme. Beudet with intelligence and restraint and succeeded in transmitting the weariness and disgust that are only articulate within the limits of an exasperated decency. Mr. Chalmers, as the typical rough diamond, Gaillard, to the point of cruelty constructed a really excellent study of boisterous provincial ferocity. The more sympathetic Lebas, willing to admit what he cannot understand, was played with appropriate sobriety by Mr. Skeffington. The pretentious decadence of Danzat was quietly and efficiently stated by Mr. Mandy. The treatment of the minor roles at the hands of the Misses Gress, Gamble, Gore-Grimes and Gwynn achieved the unity of what in every respect was a painstaking and praiseworthy performance.

Le Kid described as a Cornelian nightmare, provided an amusing climax to the programme. Here we had classicism held up in the distorting mirror of expressionism. The heroes of Corneille suddenly assumed grotesquely comic shapes. Don Diègue beats his sword into an umbrella. The King becomes a figure of tragic bathos in a bathchair, the Infanta drifts vaguely across the stage in mute Cartesian bewilderment. The men are in modern dress. The 'Kid' in flannel trousers is a mocking echo of Hamlet in plus fours. The comic symbols of balloons and rattles, and the 'Time, Gentlemen, Time,' of a barman who dismisses the actors, complete this modernist variation on a classical theme. A silent figure seated on a ladder and smoking a cigarette turns the hands of a great clock to 'match his wristwatch' while Don Diègue rushes through his soliloquy. In all *Le Kid* is an excellent *jeu d'esprit*. The chief parts are most capably acted by Mr. Sam Beckett, M. Georges Pelorson, Miss Maureen O'Brien and Mr. Wynburne. The pace needs to be quickened up and the actors should play with a more intense seriousness.

Dr. and Mme. Starkie, who were responsible for the production of *La Quema*, and M. Georges Pelorson, the producer of *La Souriante Mme. Beudet* and *Le Kid*, are to be congratulated on a most interesting and varied dramatic entertainment.

Mrs. Flegg, who played the principal female role of Chimène recalls the performance of *Le Kid*, under the direction of Pelorson, as 'under-rehearsed and untidy,' almost an improvisional set of skits. The characters and general subject matter were, however, taken directly from Corneille. The cast of characters included Chimène; her suitor Don Rodrigue, the Cid (played by Victor Wynburne); her father Don Gomès (played by Mr. Beaumont); the Cid's father, Don Diègue (played by Beckett himself); Doña Urraque, The Infanta; and numerous soldiers.

Pelorson[2] remembers the play as an attempt to ridicule the conventions of classical French theatre; the unities of time, place and action; the absence of violent physical action on stage; heroic grandeur; and careful preparation for every exit and entrance.

In parodying the concern for the unities, *Le Kid* not only made fun of Corneille's play, it also mocked the controversy between Corneille and Georges Scudéry which was finally submitted to the *Académie Française following the great public success of Le Cid*. Many of the aspects and details of *Le Cid* parodied in *Le Kid* were those which Scudéry had pointed out in letters arguing that in spite of its great popular success *Le Cid* should not be accepted as a masterpiece because it 'shocked the principles of poetic drama.'[3] Among Scudéry's main points were that the events of *Le Cid* were too vast to be contained in the time allotted for it; in the actual production the stage space had not been defined specifically enough because one scene had been used to represent several places; some of the scenes, particularly those concerning the Infanta, bore no direct relation to the major action between Chimène and Don Rodrigue.

The whole concept of unity was ridiculed by having the characters disparately dressed in costumes of different countries and different eras left over from previous Trinity theatrical productions — some in Tudor outfits, some in German Army uniforms of World War I, and others in modern street attire.[4] The preoccupation with unity of time and Corneille's obvious and unconvincing attempts to accommodate deaths, battles, duels, changes of social station and changes of heart to a two-day time span by referral to the passing of the hours was mocked by having a tall student standing on a ladder synchronising his watch with a tall cardboard clock. But instead of changing his wristwatch, the actor moved the hands of the clock counter-clockwise to bring the two timepieces into accord. Beckett, himself, in the role of Don Diègue, played a character haunted by time. During his soliloquies he fell asleep, was awakened by a large alarm clock, and then resumed speaking.

The concern for unity of place was mocked by a set that indicated no recognisable scene. Instead of conventional realistic backdrops, the stage was simply draped with curtains and the characters leaned against or perched on large cubes representing nothing in particular.[5]

Unity of action was ridiculed by a portrayal of the Infanta even more arbitrary than that in Corneille (which Scudéry characterised as 'the extravagance of the superfluous child'). Dressed like the famous Velasquez' portrait she drifted on and offstage to the accompaniment of Ravel's 'Pavanne for a Dead Princess'.

Corneille had peopled his play with supernumeraries who functioned both as friends visiting Don Rodrigue and then conveniently as the army with which he defeats the Moors. In *Le*

Kid the stage was unaccountably filled with soldiers swarming about in pointed German Army helmets and large coats. Ultimately, mock violent action erupted on stage as balloons invaded the stage from the house, and *Le Kid* jumped up to puncture them with a large wooden sword in samurai fashion.

The heroic grandeur of the classical French stage was reduced to comedy as Beckett as Don Diègue in modern dress with an umbrella (instead of a sword) lifted his bowler hat reverently each time the king was mentioned. The whole air of respect for an ancient tradition and language was ridiculed by deliberate, exaggerated mispronunciation which caricatured Old French. (Scudéry had also objected that all of Corneille's characters spoke with the same air of Spanish bravado.)

Le Kid was dismissed condescendingly in the review in T.C.D. *Miscellany*.

> To be truthful, it made us laugh, but with a rather bitter laughter, and it was not at Corneille we were laughing. Really, wasn't it rather naive? . . . unless you happened to hate Corneille very, very heartily it was a strain on the digestion. The name of the author, or rather adaptor, did not appear on the program, but we have a theory that it was the work of Guy de Maupassant — his very last work, if not indeed posthumous. None of the actors was outstanding, but all were capable.[6]

This review evoked a response from Beckett in the form of another dramatic burlesque — a one-page contribution to *A College Miscellany* of March 12, 1931, entitled 'The Possessed':

The Possessed
[*We are given to understand that the following is a reply to our reporter's criticism of the M.L.S. Plays; as such we publish it.* — Ed. *T.C.D.*]
LADIES AND GENTLEMEN!
  On my left, torturing his exquisite Pindaric brolly, the Divine Marquis of Stanfor (cries of 'What?' 'Whom?' 'Never!'). On my right and slightly to my fore, ineffably manipullulating his celebrated tipstaff, his breastfallen augs sorrowfully scouring the arena for two snakes in the grass, Professor Giovannino Allcon, direct from the Petites Maisons. Order gentlemen please! This is a respectable stadium. These are two honest boys. Ladies! Ladies! This unprecedented contest — shall I say competition? — is timed to begin from one minute to another. Silence for the mal sacré. Now please.
STANFOR: Telephus and treachery!
ALLCON: I spy a Guy
    with the G.P.I.
    passing woeful
    in a B.A. shroud.

21

S. (*rending stays from his umbrella, torn by the violence of his epileptical intimations*):
How square, O Lord, how square!
Kiss me Stanley,
Tom's in his hedge
creeping and peeping.
Doom in a desert!

A. (*clenching the caduceus*):
I am from the North,
from Bellyballaggio
where they never take their hurry
minxing marriage in their flaxmasks
omygriefing and luvvyluvvyluvving and wudiftheycudling
from the fourth or fifth floor of their hemistitched hearts
right and left of the Antrim Road.
That's why I like him
Ulster my Hulster!
Daswylyim! (*Weeps.*)

S. (*Postponing inarticulation*)
In the chiarinoscurissimo
I was unable to distinguish the obvious balloons.
The Infanta might have cantered
like a shopwalker
through the Dämmerung
but she was not in training.
The Cid (or hero, whose death, we understand, occurred in 1199)
could have been transmitted with a seriousness
more in keeping with the spiritual ancestor of the centre-forward.
A production, Professor,
from every centre of perspective
vox populi and yet not
platotudinous
cannot entertain
me.

A. (*bravely sustaining the impact of his refracted imaginings*):
O saisons! o châteaux!
I will play now a little song on my good grand.
I will be very, very heartily
too, too fascinating
on my sickroom aelopantalion
Purchè por —
ti la gonnel —
la
or a Godsent Dumka at prima vista
inspired in the early morning
by the Marquise de Brinvilliers.
O the bitter giggle and the grand old cramp
of a cold heart and a good stomach!
O saisons! o châteaux!

S. What barley beans lentiles millet fitches.
A. Shall we prepare our bread therewith?
S. When the cows come home
when the cows come home.
A. And consider the case of a lesser known author?

The piece written in mock-elevated style is full of multi-lingual Joycean portmanteau words, recondite allusions, and topical references to figures around Trinity. The major concerns can, however, be traced. *The Possessed* is both a response to the *Miscellany* review and the form as a contest between two disputants in an august forum with an authoritative moderator probably derived from the exchange of letters between Corneille and Scudéry edited by Voltaire in his preface to *Le Cid*. Voltaire's notes couched in authoritative editorial language were nonetheless quite partial to Corneille.

In *The Possessed* an unidentified professorial voice announcing the 'unprecedented contest' in a 'respectable stadium' tries to re-establish the decorum in an audience that is over-excited — a parody of both the unruly performance and the exaggerated reaction to it. Cries of 'What?' 'When?' 'Who?', references to 'two snakes in the grass' followed by the assurance that the combatants are 'two honest boys' reflect the dismay that two respected scholars like Beckett and Pelorson had betrayed the traditions of the Modern Language Society. Then the two contestants, Professors Stanfor and Allcon (based in part on W.B. Stanford and John Allcon, student editors of the Mis-cellany), vie to see who can express the most dismay at *Le Kid*. Stanfor begins by calling the two authors 'Telephus and Treachery' (Telephus' birth in the temple of Athena was a defilement bringing pestilence. Beckett and Pelorson treach-erously brought a similar defilement to the learned, proper halls of Trinity College.) Allcon accounts for the incident as undergraduate madness — General Paralysis of the Insane in 'a BA shroud'. Stanfor next notes the unwholesome influence of T.S. Eliot: 'Tom in his hedge creeping and peeping . . . doom in a desert.' As in *The Wasteland*, the great Western cultural tradition has been presented in a debased and lifeless modern form.

Allcon continues by saying, sorrowfully, that he likes the author and understands him because he is from Ulster where there is also a non-classical, popular poetic tradition dealing with conflicted love affairs ('omygriefing and luvvyluvvyluvving and wudiftheycudling'). Stanfor turns to a discussion of the particulars of the performance — the balloon-popping battle scene, the arbitrary entrances and exits of the Infanta, the use of inappropriate German costumes, the indecorous presentation of *Le Cid*, and the lack of a 'centre of perspective'.

Pedantically, Stanfor asserts that the Cid died in 1199,

implying that so great a literary figure could not be done in by a burlesque in 1931. In the spirit of Queen Victoria's 'we are not amused', he declares that a production which is *'vox populi'* but not 'platotudinous' (i.e. an expression of popular taste not adhering to a classical ideal and offering sententious wisdom) 'cannot entertain me.' (This is probably also a reference to Scudéry's observation that it was for presenting characters like Chimène without condemnation that Plato had banished all poets from his Republic.)

Allcon goes beyond concern with the death of the Cid to announce that the play will bring his own melodramatic demise. After quoting Rimbaud's line *'O saisons, o châteaux!'* the beginning of the farewell to poetry in *Une saison en enfer*, he says he will fade away to the accompaniment of his own 'sick room' music or take poison which will produce 'a bitter giggle' and 'a grand old cramp' (like the 'bitter laughter' and 'indigestion' in the Miscellany review.) The contest concludes with a ceremonial meal as the combatants agree finally to 'prepare our bread' with the odd assortment of grains and gas-producing beans presented to them. They will, it seems, have to stomach the fare they've been given even though it is not of their choosing and may have unpleasant effects.

Beckett's main point in *The Possessed* is that reviewers and professors have made too much of an obvious spoof. Their preoccupation with heroic grandeur, focused on a character who is 'the spiritual ancestor of the centreforward', and mechanical adherence to conventions keep them from seeing that classicism might also be palatable in new form. The final question, 'And consider the case of a lesser known author?' is probably a direct reference to Scudéry whose case against Corneille, though ridiculous in its own right, did point out much in *Le Cid* that Beckett and Pelorson also found objectionable. It is possibly also a reference to Joyce, whose *Portrait of the Artist* also contained an undergraduate accused of suffering from 'G.(eneral) P.(aralysis) of the I.(nsane)' and in whose style the piece is written. His modern use of classical material and tradition, Beckett had pointed out two years earlier in his essay 'Dante . . . Bruno. Vico . . . Joyce', was still largely unaccepted in Ireland in 1931 but deserved to be recognised.

Both *Le Kid* and *The Possessed* are at best hastily written examples of collegiate humour. They do, however, show the background in which some of Beckett's most important ideas about drama developed. His own characters are in part a reaction against an ideal of heroism which appeared ridiculous in a modern world. The mixture of tragedy and comedy in his work is a rejection of the tradition of pure genres and the decorous seriousness of classical French drama. The action in his plays is a conscious departure from elaborate plots based on large casts, grand exploits, preoccupation with conflicted love and noble deaths. Still it would be wrong to see in *Le Kid* only the rejection of classical conventions. The mockery in *Le Kid* of the unquestioning reverence for the unities, does not mean that Beckett had no respect for the unities themselves. No modern playwright is more classical than Beckett in presenting single, unified action concentrated in one stage space uncomplicated by changes in set. And none has compacted the events of his characters' entire lives into the short time span of the action itself as performed on stage.

HUMAN WISHES

In his Trinity College lectures on Racine, Gide and Balzac given in the same year as *Le Kid* and his unpublished autobiographical novel *Dream of Fair to Middling Women*, Beckett developed his ideas of characterisation, plot, and audience expectation. In both one can observe the development of the aesthetic position that Beckett would express more exhaustively in his drama. His Trinity lectures stressed the problems of rendering what he called 'human reality'. He was particularly opposed to the 'snowball act', a plot gathering reason after reason for the motivation of the characters in each action depicted, as it moves predictably and relentlessly toward one great conclusion. And in those lectures he also compared the characters of literature to individual atomic particles which operate unpredictably outside the laws of physics governing collective matter.[7]

The central problem addressed by Beckett in all of his consideration of drama and convention up to and including *Eleuthéria* was the conflict between the complex and indeterminant nature of 'human' experience and the reductive and intrusive mechanisms of existing literary forms. He found his own antithesis in Balzac. As he wrote in *Dream of Fair to Middling Women*:

> [Balzac] can write the end of his book before he has finished
> the first paragraph, because he has turned all his creatures

into clockwork cabbages and can rely on their staying put wherever needed or staying going at whatever speed in whatever direction he chooses . . . we all love and lick up Balzac, we lap it up and say it is wonderful, but why call a distillation of Euclid and Perrault Scenes from Life? Why *human* comedy?[8]

Beckett's second attempt at drama pointed out even more directly than *Le Kid* the inability of existing dramatic methods to portray the human condition. In 1936 he had made extensive biographical notes for a long realistic psychological study of Dr. Johnson in love. The play was to have been entitled *Human Wishes* leaving his audience to supply the commentary of Dr. Johnson's own title *Vanity of Human Wishes*. In it he would 'explain what has never been explained, i.e. his grotesque attitude toward his life and Mrs. Thrale.'[9] But the more universal question raised by Dr. Johnson himself of the general possibility of human happiness was also in the foreground. The play was thus of a personal psychological response to the universal human condition. Johnson was, as Beckett wrote to his friend Thomas McGreevy, 'spiritually selfconscious, was a tragic figure, i.e. worth putting down as part of the whole of which oneself is part . . .'[10]

Beckett abandoned *Human Wishes* after writing only a brief opening exposition scene. That scene, however, is an integral work which Beckett has allowed to be published and performed.[11] It is the first of Beckett's 'dramaticules' — pointing out the impossibility of realistic psychological drama for him.

Human Wishes begins as familiar theatrical exposition. Three women talk in a drawing room defining their situation in Dr. Johnson's household at Bolt Court. They are identified by their backgrounds, and minor conflict brings out their character differences. Predictably at this point a new character is introduced so that the question of the possibility of human happiness may receive more focused attention. Levett, Dr. Johnson's apothecary, whose drunkenness has already been suggested as a possible surrogate for happiness, enters. As he staggers through the room without saying a word or acknowledging the presence of the three women, he is, like Victor Krap in Act I of *Eleuthéria*, a figure in pantomime to be revealed by the commentary of others. Already in his first serious attempt at playwriting, as later in the fragment *Avant fin de partie*, *Eleuthéria* and the more recent *Catastrophe*, Beckett juxtaposed mimed action to the failure of conventional dialogue and characterisation. At this point the attempt to provide understanding through commentary breaks down.

No longer content to fill their role as members of a bourgeois household and part of a conventional exposition, the three women — one reading, one blind and absorbed in meditation, and one knitting — become more like three Parcae who rebel against revelation and withhold explanation. In contrast to *Eleuthéria* in which the characters are only too eager to seek explanation from the protagonist, Levett is 'ignored ostentatiously', then 'surveyed with indignation' and finally after his exit the women exchange looks and make gestures of disgust. The play begins to acknowledge its own inadequacy.

> Mrs. W. Words fail us.
> Mrs. D. Now this is where a writer for the stage would have us speak no doubt.
> Mrs. W. He would have us explain Levett.
> Mrs. D. To the public.
> Mrs. W. To the ignorant public.
> Mrs. D. To the gallery.
> Mrs. W. To the pit.
> Miss C. To the boxes.

The play next moves beyond the acknowledgement of its own inability to explain to the assertion that whole dramatic traditions are no longer viable. Three contemporary playwrights (all with associations in the Johnson household which might have given them information and insight with which to construct explanations) are linked with the 'ignorant public'. Explanation would also be demanded for Mr. Murphy, Mr. Kelly, and Mr. Goldsmith. Arthur Murphy (who did write a biography of Johnson) is dealt with first. A pun on the phrase 'debt to nature' is used to allude to his death and to assess his artistic achievement. It is pointed out that 'the dear doctor's debt to nature is discharged these seven years', i.e. he is dead. But it is also observed that his debt to nature was 'not a very large one'. Further play upon the title of Murphy's monograph *Animated Nature* again disparages his ability to render reality. The artificiality and didacticism of the comedy of manners embodied in his works is no longer a live tradition. Murphy, and by extension what he represents, is 'D-E-A-D. Expired. Like the late Queen Anne and the Rev. Edward ——.'

Also dead is the playwright Hugh Kelly — 'the creator of *False*

Delicacy, a sentimental comedy of manners in which he maintained overtly that art was a vehicle for moral instruction. (Dr. Johnson said of the piece that it was 'totally devoid of character'.) But Mrs. D.refuses at first to admit that he is dead and ends by asserting that if he has died and it has escaped her notice, she would 'regret it bitterly' and the advocate of dead forms exits weeping, closing the door softly behind her.

Goldsmith remains undiscussed by the women, but by implication even his greater talent does not restore to the comedy of manners the status of a vital tradition. We are invited to question whether even Goldsmith might not be dead.

To dismiss the comedy of manners is widesweeping, but *Human Wishes* goes much further in its attack upon dramatic tradition. Mrs. W. who pronounces the death of Murphy and Kelly 'at the top of her lungs', also responds to Shakespeare. Before her exit, Mrs. D., the adherent of Murphy and Kelly, makes an allusion from *Hamlet* to death as 'that undiscovered country . . .'. Mrs. W. pounds on the floor with her stick as she says, 'None of your Shakespeare to me, Madam. The fellow may be in Abraham's bosom for aught I know or care . . .' The ability of even Shakespeare to explain and deal with death is questioned. And the grammatical ambiguity of 'fellow' invites the suggestion that Shakespeare is also among the dead. The death of Shakespeare as a live tradition remains in question for Beckett and if it is a fact, he is at least accorded a place of honour and permanence in the bosom of Abraham after his demise.

The fragment ends with the suggestion that it is not drama, at least as seen in prevailing modes, which can present the human predicament. The ubiquity and indifference of death to the particulars of circumstance or attitude defy the explanation of drama. But they are expressed in another form. Miss C. begins to read aloud. 'Death meets us everywhere, and is procured by every instrument and in all chances and enters in at many doors . . .' Mrs. W. begins to dismiss this formulation as she dismissed the dramatists. 'What twaddle is this, Miss Carmichael?' But as the balanced periodic sentences begin to delineate the omnipresence of death even in the duality of opposites,' 'by the aspect of a star and the stink of a mist . . . by a full meal or an empty stomach; by watching at wine or watching at prayer, by the sun or the moon; by a heat or cold; by sleepless nights or sleeping days; by water frozen or water thawed . . .', she urges 'Continue, continue'. And Miss Carmichael reads on to an account of the determination of human existence closer to that presented in *Godot* than that implied in the opening dramatic scene of this fragment. Death enters 'by a hair or a raisin; by violent exertion or by sitting still; by severity or dissolution; by God's mercy or God's anger; by everything in Providence and everything in manners, by everything in nature and everything in chance.'

At the conclusion Mrs. W. tries eagerly to ascertain the author. Is it Brown, she asks. 'Brown or black, Madame, it is all one to me.' Miss C. replies unhelpfully, but finally turns to the title page and reads the name: 'Taylor'. The work that set out to be a realistic dramatic explanation of the psychology of Dr. Johnson ends by abandoning dramatic presentation of personal psychology to quote the balanced prose of Jeremy Taylor's *Rule and Exercises of Holy Dying*.

Beckett explained to Deirdre Bair in 1972 that he abandoned *Human Wishes* because he was unwilling to deal with the disparity between the 'awful jargon' he 'put in the mouths' of the other characters and the 'proper language of the period' which he would have to write for Dr. Johnson. Seen in the light of the fragment he did produce, this explanation reveals more than an unwillingness to undertake the hard work of reconciling one style of dialogue with another. Even before starting to write the lines for Dr. Johnson, he had found in Taylor's prose, 'the proper language of the period', a formulation which for the time being was more satisfactory than the dramatic dialogue he had set out to produce. Until he could find dramatic means the equal of Taylor's prose, he could not go on.

ELEUTHÉRIA

Although *Human Wishes* makes a complete commentary, it is still a fragmentary work. Only with *Eleuthéria* did Beckett complete a full-length play. In it he continued to question the ability of existing drama to represent humanity. It was thus the culmination of his examination of the dramatic tradition of which he was a part. If we do not have for Beckett a direct manifesto like Corneille's *First Discourse on the Uses and Elements of Dramatic Poetry*, Strindberg's prefaces to *Miss Julie* and *Dream Play*, Zola's preface to *Thérèse Raquin*, or Brecht's *Short Organum for the Theatre* we do have in *Eleuthéria*[12] Beckett's own full statement on dramatic method — a statement which clearly influenced his later plays.

Gogo and Didi did not spring onto the stage full blown from Beckett's brow. Though couched in the humorous language of dramatic parody, *Eleuthéria* contains the serious theoretical underpinnings of the new kind of drama Beckett was to initiate in *Godot*. Many passages in it contain the seeds of Beckett's later work. The holograph bears Beckett's notation 'Prior to *Godot*'. At the time of its composition Beckett clearly regarded *Eleuthéria* as a serious work to be considered along with *Godot*. He offered both plays to Roger Blin in 1951 in hopes that Blin would produce both. He left Blin the choice between them if only one could be produced. One of the many suggestions for the title of *Godot* may have come from *Eleuthéria*. Throughout *Eleuthéria* the audience witnesses the search for a play which would provide a more suitable dramatic vehicle for the humanity represented by its protagonist Victor Krap. The purpose of the play is described three times by its characters in the same phrase: to *'amuser les badauds'* ('amuse the gawkers'). The need to satisfy an inappropriate audience is thus emphasised as a major source of the failings of the dramatic tradition. In *Waiting for Godot* which contains so many performances and places, so much emphasis on the characters' being properly observed, one aspect of the figure anticipated by Gogo and Didi may be a better audience. The name for that figure may be associated with the audience through a bilingual pun on 'good' and 'bad'. They await a 'good' audience, a 'Godot', to replace a 'bad' one, 'les badauds'. That audience would be capable of heeding the command given at the climactic moment of *Eleuthéria*: *'En attendant mieux!'* ('Wait for better').

As its Greek title suggests, *Eleuthéria* is the assertion of 'freedom' from the constraints of dramatic precedents reaching back into classical antiquity. Freedom for the protagonist Victor Krap to absent himself from the family of Kraps and Piouks. This includes first the freedom of the play from the necessity of trying to provide an artificial catharsis in drama which is not available in life. As he had written in his essay on Proust:

> Tragedy is not concerned with human justice. Tragedy is the statement of an expiation, but not the miserable expiation of a codified breach of a local arrangement, organized by the

knaves for the fools. The tragic figure represents the expiation of original sin, of the original and eternal sin of having been born.

For such a guilt there is no catharthis; the purgation is endless. The title also includes the freedom of Victor Krap not to assume a pre-existing social or theatrical role. *'Il est peut-être temps que quelqu'un soit tout simplement rien'* ('Perhaps it is time that someone were simply nothing') he says (p. 62). And in a line adumbrating the opening of *En attendant Godot*, he defines the liberty which he defends as the freedom *'pour rien faire'* (p. 68).

Much of the freedom demanded in *Eleuthéria* is achieved through destructive humour. The play is, among other things, a very sophisticated and funny burlesque catalogue of particular plays or traditions. By placing Victor Krap in scenes which parody existing types of drama, Beckett shows the comic absurdity of previous attempts to render the human condition dramatically. Gross parallels link Victor with Hamlet, Oedipus, and Oswald Alving. Like Alfred Jarry, Victor's father writes in the genre *'merdre'*. In the true fashion of Artaud's Theater of Cruelty, the script is tossed aside before a Chinese torturer is brought in to interrogate Victor. Victor hides from Madame Meck under his bed *'comme du temps de Molière* (p. 52). As if he were a character out of Yeats' *Purgatory* something is causing Victor to *'tourner et à girer comme une âme en peine'* (to turn and gyre about like a soul in pain') (p. 92). The list is exhaustive. There are parodies or allusions from Sophocles, Shakespeare, Molière, Corneille, Shaw, Zola, Ibsen, Hauptmann, Pirandello, Yeats, Symbolism, Surrealism, Artaud, Jarry and Socialist Realism to name only the most evident. As the Glazier, who functions as a kind of stage manager, says near to the end of the play: *'Pour un tour d'horizon. C'est un tour d'horizon.'*

Ostensibly the plot of *Eleuthéria* is the unsuccessful attempt of members of the Krap family to persuade Victor Krap to return to his former life. Victor is a young writer who has 'lost his taste for life' and abandoned his family and fiancée for a minimal existence in a boarding house room with only a bed. The conflict between Victor and his family is made clear by a dual set and dual actions. The stage is divided into the Krap drawing room and Victor's room so that both are visible to the audience but separate and invisible to each other. The set revolves so that the action is seen from a different perspective in each act. In the first two acts there is an *'action principale'* and an *'action marginale*' which takes place during a pause in the principle action.

In Act I the principle action takes place in the Krap drawing room and the marginal action in Victor's room when the landlady announces Victor's mother and he leaves before she arrives. In Act II the principal action is in Victor's room and the marginal action in the Krap household. These actions are brief and contain only a single line of dialogue in each case. They highlight in nearly wordless pantomime the two major concerns of the play: Victor's absence from the family circle in the first case and the necessity that he give an explanation of that absence in the second case. By the beginning of Act III the set has revolved so that the Krap household set has disappeared and all of the action is in Victor's room. *Eleuthéria* thus presents physically to the audience an image of a complete dramatic revolution. The drawing room drama of the Krap household which is parodied in Act I is literally swept away in Act III to be '*mangé par la fosse*' ('devoured by the pit'). '*Drame Bourgeois*' as Beckett subtitled the play, is consigned to the pit, dumped back into the lap of the audience which demanded it.

The center of the well-made plot is the action of Dr. Piouk, Victor's uncle newly married into the family who arrives from abroad at the beginning of the play. Reputedly a Scandinavian and formerly a specialist in venereal disease, he functions like one of Ibsen's catalytic agents who define alternatives and present choices which will establish the attitude and destiny of the protagonist. When Victor's father demands to know what role he plans to take in 'the comedy', he assures him that he will be useful. To the amazement of the elder Krap, he asserts that '*il y a des choses à faire*' to '*régler la situation du genre humain*' ('there are things to be done [to] order the situation of human kind') (P. 33). Because the members of the Krap household find it intolerable that 'nothing' is done and refuse to allow Victor to exist in a state of 'sordid inertia', Dr. Piouk will initiate action. The action he initiates is an example of the 'snowball act' which Beckett rejected in Balzac. Everything will be settled by one single action. He will offer Victor the opportunity to commit suicide by taking a tablet of morphine. This will force him to choose between the 'grand refusal' or re-entry into life. Victor will be defined and his destiny determined once and for all.

The outcome of Dr. Piouk's plan might be either a recognisable tragedy or comedy. The play would end in tragic death or comic restitution with Victor reunited with his fiancée, and restored to the family and society he has abandoned. In the end the resolution of the play into a familiar generic formula is not successful. As an Aristotelian tragic hero modelled upon Oedipus, Victor is a complete failure. He does not achieve tragic grandeur by committing suicide. And as he points out, he is not one of those who has 'paid the price' so that 'accountability is maintained'. He is called upon repeatedly to give an accounting which he fails to make and the play ends with him still owing the landlady for the right to inhabit his room. He fails to disclose his 'unique error'. He fails to arouse pity and terror in his fellow men as other social misfits do. And the *'broche'* which is to serve as a catheter for his own catharsis is never employed.

Victor turns out to be no better a representation of a traditional comic protagonist than a tragic one. He doesn't swallow the morphine but he refuses to be reunited with his fiancée and family. Unlike the young comic lovers of Molière, Ben Jonson, and the Restoration stage, he is totally indifferent to the reading of his father's will and any legacy that might confer the ability to begin domestic life. (As it turns out, he has no part whatsoever in the comic pattern of transmission of life from one generation to the next. He receives no legacy and is not even mentioned in the will.) As the play ends, he refuses to join the others in the conventional celebratory banquet of comedy. His fiancée Olga Skunk exits with the doctor for their heralded meal without Victor, and it is Dr. Piouk who in satisfying his appetite for oysters will celebrate the life-force of comedy.

That the central action devised by Dr. Piouk is contrived and superfluous is demonstrated by the blatant sexual overtones of the preparation for it. The obligatory scene between Victor and Dr. Piouk is part of a mechanistic three part structure of arbitrary anticipation: approach and withdrawal, building to a climax. It is twice delayed, first by Victor's absence when Piouk comes to his room and then by Dr. Piouk's failure to appear at the appointed hour because he has suffered a crisis in the night and lost his memory. Predictably, it is only on the third attempt, after the appetite of the audience has been whetted for it, that Dr. Piouk gets to carry out his plan. When he does finally attempt to burst onto the stage at the climax of the play, he actually impedes discovery and the door must be barred against his entry in order to allow the Glazier and the Spectator to finish interrogating Victor. '*Pelotez-vous encore un peu! En attendant mieux!'* ('Go pet a little more! While you're waiting!') (p. 121), the Glazier tells Dr. Piouk and Olga Skunk as they try to break through the door into Victor's room. And when they do enter to enact the anticipated scene, it is anticlimactic because Victor has already revealed all that he can to the other characters.

This action is only a kind of palliative to satisfy the demands of the audience for neat explanations and solutions. Dr. Piouk offers Victor two small white tablets saying *'La liberté!'* and Victor reads on them the words *'Aspirine du Rhône'*. Piouk hastily explains that he has made a mistake, the aspirins are for himself and he swallows them. Victor will be given the real morphine. The aspirins for Dr. Piouk are of the same kind that Beckett prescribed for journalists who demanded from *Waiting for Godot* something other than the fundamental simplicity he had presented on stage (See his letter to Alan Schneider, director of the American première, on page 15).

This plot centred on Dr. Piouk is obviously not meant to be taken at face value. The characters of *Eleuthéria* are more than stage representations of 'real' people. They are caricatures of stage devices and their actions dramatise their shortcomings. Each of the acts explores a different dramatic method. Act I presents the absurdity of trying to reveal central characters through ancillary ones. In the primary action the group assembled in the Krap drawing room provide an example of classical exposition in the style of Scribe and Ibsen. They talk of the absent Victor in order to provide the audience with the facts of his situation and the family reaction to it. As in *Human Wishes* this kind of exposition is reduced to ridicule by the overt references to what is transpiring. As the characters dominate the scene in turn in order to develop their special perspective on Victor, they are invited to move to the seat at the table most central and directly under the light. The occasion for retelling recent events to Madam Krap's sister is described variously by the other characters who each refer to her recent arrival from a different place. The constant interruption of the conversation by the entry and exits of the servants whose special knowledge will be so important later, approaches slapstick in its comic repetition. When the mother leaves the scene to make her unsuccessful plea to Victor to return home, her husband announces that her long absence occasioned by some mysterious urge is without dramatic significance. He adds that they all thought she had been unusually long in the toilet. The use of other characters to provide an initial understanding of the protagonist, the presence at the outset of characters who will be a credible source of fuller relevation later on, and the presentation of both in the context of a situation designed to maintain interest while the facts are being established are basic to the introductory scenes of most of Western drama. But Beckett reduces them to a set of awkward contrivances.

In Act II the conventional methods of direct self-revelation are called into question when the scene shifts to Victor's room. They fare no better at Beckett's hand than the indirect methods of Act I. In an obvious parody of the soliloquies in *Hamlet*, Victor begins the act by stepping to the front of the stage, contemplating the audience, trying to speak but not doing so, walking away and then finally returning to address the audience: '*Il faut que je dise . . . Je ne suis pas*' ('It is necessary for me to say . . . I am not'), he begins but breaks off unable to say more than that (p. 50). Later in the act after fending off a group of intruders from the Krap household who demand explanations for his conduct, he again approaches the 'ramp' and wants to speak but cannot and '*fait un geste d'impuissance, sort avec des gestes fous*' ('makes a gesture of powerlessness, exits with gestures of madness') (p. 74).

As even Shakespearean soliloquy is being called into question, the text draws attention to the difficulties of breaking with tradition. Just following his first unsuccessful attempt to address the audience directly, Victor remarks '*Impossible de rien casser*' ('It is impossible to break anything'). He has thrown a shoe through the window through which he might be observed by others and a Glazier has appeared immediately to repair it. Like the Glazier in Strindberg's *Dream Play* who with his diamond opens the door concealing the central character Victoria, this glazier has as his major function the task of revealing Victor by evoking from him an explanation of his motivation. In both cases what waits to be revealed is finally described as 'nothing'. With the entry of the Glazier it is clear that the old windows into character — exposition by the dialogue of others and conventional soliloquising — must be replaced. He brings a set of tools including the diamond which like the one that allowed the Glazier of *Dream Play* to reveal Victoria is presumably the ultimate dramatic device which will allow him to reveal Victor. Beckett's Glazier, however, misplaces his diamond and departs asking Victor and the landlady to look for it.

The Glazier has not only come to repair the window, he returns the shoe Victor hurled through it. And Victor comments on the inability to divest himself of anything, '*On ne peut rien perdre non plus*' ('And one can't lose anything either'). In the end Victor cannot divest himself of his shoe which like Gogo's boots seem to indicate his involvement in a physical universe. But he does lose his '*veston*', his superficial outer covering. While this loss suggests the possibility of removing superficial attributes in order to achieve a true revelation, the play makes it clear that this is still only a possibility. When Dr. Piouk arrives to present Victor with the choice that will force him to define himself, the Glazier tells him that Victor has lost his 'coat'. The announcement prompts Dr. Piouk to break incongruously into a song and dance:

> *Il a perdu son pantalon*
> *Tout en dansant le Charleston*

Victor may be exposed and ready for the great moment of revelation which the doctor has prepared, but it is all part of a theatrical routine not to be taken seriously.

Having dispensed with indirect presentation through others in Act I and conventional conscious self-revelation in Act II, Beckett opens Act III by questioning the method of unconscious self-revelation in the tradition of the expressionistic dream play. It is past 4.00 pm and Victor is still asleep. He dreams of diving into the profundity of the sea, '. . . *a marée basse — mer basse — profonde.*' And then in a parody of the blatant sexual imagery with literary overtones of Strindberg's dream plays, he goes on, '*Là les yeux — mille navires — les tours — circoncisés — feu — feu.*' ('The eyes, a thousand ships, the towers, circumcised, fire, fire.') For the Glazier this plunge beneath the surface is of no interest. It will not be enough to see Victor through his dreams. '*Les tours circoncisés feu feu! Eh bien! C'est du joli! Debout cloaque! . . . Le soleil se couche. Votre père est en terre. Et vous voilà vautré dans vos rêves lubriques!*' (Circumcised towers, fire, fire! Oh that's fine! A filthy beginning! . . . The sun is setting. Your father is buried. And there you are wallowing in your wet dreams!) Still later in the act when Victor and the Glazier are all alone and the Glazier has abandoned all his other tools and is looking for his diamond, he has another opportunity to learn what Victor's recurrent dream of diving into the sea among rocks might reveal about him. This is the one subject Victor seems eager to discuss. But ironically the character drawn from *Dream Play* vehemently rejects the methods of that play. Like Vladimir he does not want to hear of dreaming. '*Non, non, ne le dites pas, je déteste les histoires de rêves.*' (p. 120). ('No, no, don't tell me, I hate the stories of dreams.') Victor continues on despite this objection, but the Glazier shows only perfunctory interest and Victor changes the subject.

As a Pirandellian examination of drama, *Eleuthéria* might be described as eight characters in pursuit of another. Running counter to the imposed well-made plot of Dr. Piouk's plan to restore Victor to his family, is Beckett's own plot of Victor Krap's struggle to expel the series of intruders who enter his room. Madame Krap, Madame Meck, The Spectator, Jacques, The Glazier, Dr. Piouk, Olga Skunk, and Madame Karl all make threats, demands, or suggestions which would deprive Victor of his freedom not to be a familiar stage entity. In some way each of them intrude upon the set of his room in attempts to get him to assume theatrical roles he rejects. It is all done for the benefit of the audience. Victor has '*tombé dans le domaine public*' ('fallen into the public domain') and has become '*La proie d'inconnus*' ('The prey of those unknown') (p. 112).

The persistence and ability of these characters to force their way into Victor's room suggest that they represent more than just familiar stage roles. They are the embodiment of more fundamental elements of drama and only with the greatest difficulty can they be excluded.

Madame Krap, Victor's mother is (like the mother of Pirandello's *Six Characters in Search of an Author*) the embodiment of the reality of a personal history with emotional content. It is she who makes the first appeal to Victor to re-enter the Krap household, for only by being a part of a realistic context could such a personal history exist. When she arrives a second time at Victor's room in the company of the other members of the Krap household, Victor has departed briefly to escape from the intruders. She dominates the scene with her show of grief and tears for her missing son. In the end she is not to have a second opportunity to appeal to his emotions. She is sent home while the others remain to deal with Victor. Just as she was the first to come, she is the first to go. The direct realistic portrayal of emotional relationships, once the very staple of drama, is no longer essential. The Glazier acknowledges that what was formerly central is now inconsequential background. After the distraught Madame Krap has been 'pushed gently outside' by Dr. Piouk, he complains, '*Le temps qu'on perd avec les figurants!*' ('The time we waste with these background figures') (p. 78). Not surprisingly, after creating the more abstract characters of *Waiting for Godot, Endgame*, and *Happy Days*, when Beckett did present a character with a full realistic personal emotional history, that character bore the name of Krapp.

The first visible encounter of Victor with one of the characters in pursuit of him is with Madame Meck. She is the embodiment of the conventional reasoneur. A friend of the family, she is, as her name (which means 'pimp') implies, only an agent with no direct part in even the contrived action of the Krap household.* She is the aging holdover from the previous era. The elder Krap counsels her to take a less active role: '*Autant rester assise, ma pauvre Jeanne, que tergiverser debout, ployé sous le poids de votre équipment. Elle domine la scène, ma foi, elle qui n'a rien à y voir!*' ('Better remain seated, my poor Jennie, than hop about, under the weight of your equipment. She dominates the scene but my God she's got nothing to do with it!') But she refuses to relinquish her role, and replies '*sur une ton de pythonisse*' ('hissing'): '*Je ne suis qu'une vieille femme, laide malade et seule. Pourtant le jour veindra où tous vous m'envierez*' ('I am only an old woman, ugly, sick, and alone. But the day will come when you will envy me.') In a burst of comic understatement Dr. Piouk comments, '*Elle a peut-être une fonction que vous ne soupçonnez pas.*' ('Perhaps she has a function which you do not suspect') (p. 29). As a purely theatrical device designed only to ask questions and provide answers for the audience, Madame Meck is the most flagrant threat to Victor's freedom. The crude mechanism of any kind of *raisoneur*, even the most modernised version, is pointed out by the fact that Madame Meck arrives at Victor's room with a gigantic ex-wrestler and a chauffeur educated in mechanics to take Victor back home by force. To stress the dogged tenacity of creating characters whose sole purpose is to reveal others, the wrestler has a purple mark on his nose where he was bitten by another wrestler trying to force him to release a hold. Victor makes an active defense against Madame Meck by driving her from his

---

* ('*mec*') often means pimp, but is also used in the same way as 'guy' in American. But Beckett may well have had Madame von Meck, the dominating patronesse of Tchaikowsky, Mussorgsky and other artists in mind as well.

room with an umbrella. She is the first in the series of characters to be dispatched by Victor from his room into the corridor.

The next character to be forcibly expelled from the scene into the corridor is the Spectator. Bored and unsatisfied, he has watched the play in a state of fascinated frustration. He describes his reaction in a passage which is unmistakably the germ of *Endgame*:

> *Non, si je suis toujours là c'est qu'il y a dans cette histoire quelque chose qui me paralyse littéralement et me remplit de stupeur. Comment vous expliquer ça? Vous jouez aux échecs? Non. Ça ne fait rien. C'est comme lorsqu'on assiste à une partie des échecs entre joueurs de dernière catégorie. Il y a trois quarts d'heure q'ils n'ont pas touché à une pièce, ils sont là comme deux couillons à bayer sur l'échiquier, et vous aussi vous êtes là, encore plus couillon qu'eux, collé sur place, dégoûté, ennuyé, fatigué, emerveillé par tant de bêtise. Jusqu'au moment où vous n'y tenez plus. Alors vous dites, mais faites ça, faites ça qu'est-ce que vous attendez, faites ça et c'est fini, nous pourrons aller nous coucher.*
> (p. 103)*

No longer able to stand Victor's refusal to reveal himself and assume a recognisable shape, he enters the stage from the audience bringing with him a Chinese torturer with a cang to force Victor to speak. (From the time of his early poem 'Casket of Pralines for a Mandarin's Daughter' written in the period he was consciously developing his own theories of character, Beckett had used the stylised formality of Chinese art and music as emblematic of the arbitrary and reductive imposition of artifice upon experience. In *Dream of Fair to Middling Women* he had written of the reduction of his protagonist's fluid experience to a static image as a 'cang of emblem'.) With the torturer to enforce his demands, the Spectator poses to Victor precisely the same choice between suicide and re-entry into life that Dr. Piouk will belatedly present when he arrives. Under this threat Victor does explain himself after a fashion. But as he warns them, such an explanation is a contrivance to meet the demands of an audience and is therefore not the truth, contradictory, and no sooner made than recanted. The Spectator is obviously an

---

* No, if I am still here it is because there is something in this story which literally paralyses me and fills me with stupor. How to explain that to you? Do you play chess? No? That's nothing. It's like when one is watching a game of chess between players of the worst kind. For three quarters of an hour they don't touch the pieces. They are there like two imbeciles, yawning over the board. And you are also there even more imbecile than they are, glued in place, disgusted, bored, tired, and amazed by so much stupidity. Until the moment you say, do it, do what you have been waiting for, do it and it will be finished and we can go to bed. (Authors' translation).

embodiment of the Pirandellian device of depicting audience reaction within the play itself. By acknowledging the presence of audience expectations and dealing directly with them, the play might identify contrivance and correct for it in the real audience.

The Spectator embodies more, however, than just the Pirandellian manifestation of the audience on stage. '*C'est tout ce qu'il fallait démontrer. Qu'au fond il n'y a que nous*' ('All we need to demonstrate is that there is only us.') he tells Victor. In an echo of Baudelaire's line '*hypocrite lecteur, mon semblable, mon frère*' ('hypocrite reader, my double, my brother') popularised by T.S. Eliot in *The Waste Land*, he calls Victor '*Mon frère*' and offers his hand. Victor ignores the gesture, but the Spectator is unperturbed. All that matters for him is the ability to see himself in Victor. Victor's aloofness suggests that in Beckett's drama the audience may still be presented with an image of itself but not as a parcel of familiar personality traits for facile identification. Both the necessity and the difficulty of removing from drama the direct identification of the audience with the protagonist is dramatised when the Glazier menacingly forces the Spectator to exit into the corridor like the others, rather than back into the auditorium from which he came. The removal from the stage of intrusive audience expectations is emphasised when the Glazier throws after the Spectator the chair which he has brought with him from the auditorium.

Jacques the servant is more deferential in his intrusion onto the set of Victor's room, but he too is dismissed if not driven out. He appears in Victor's room not to receive Victor's self-explanation. That has already taken place in the Krap household the previous evening. In his function as a receiver of confidences he is notably inept — unable to repeat what Victor has told him, capable only of expressing a fawning gratitude for Victor's telling them about the life he leads and explaining his motives. His purpose in coming to Victor's room is to offer him information: '*J'ai pensé qu'il fallait que Monsieur sache — Que vous sachiez dans quel état se trouve la famille . . .*' ('I thought Monsieur should know — that you should know the state of the family') (p. 95). Even if the drama rids itself of the contrived characters who actively manipulate the protagonist, the presence of some character other than the protagonist to provide and receive information and to react would seem indispensable. Jacques embodies that presence. The demands of the audience for other characters to interact with the protagonist are illustrated when

Jacques says *'Je dois m'en aller'* ('I must go') and the Spectator tells him vehemently, *'Asseyez-vous!'* ('Sit down!'). He then sits down with the Glazier on the bed with Victor between them so that the three make a little arranged tableau. When Dr. Piouk does not arrive, and the play appears about to dissolve in an air of 'fatigue and fatuity', Jacques raises his arms and lets them fall listlessly (p. 108). This gesture is to be the action of the Auditor in *Not I*. The serviceable Jacques may reappear later in the greatly reduced and abstracted role of Auditor, but the presence of another actor, however unobtrusive, is not after all indispensable for the portrayal of Victor Krap. Monologue and mime may suffice as dramatic methods. Sensing that he is no longer needed, the servant rises to depart in peace. *'Laissez-moi partir'* and asks Victor one more time, *'Monsieur ne désire rien?'* Victor makes no response. Jacques is dismissed by the Glazier who confirms *'on n'a plus besoin de lui'*. He turns sadly to Victor, repeats the gesture of raising his arms and letting them fall, and departs (p. 99).

The Glazier, like the stage manager in Pirandello's *Six Characters in Search of an Author*, represents an authorial presence, there to mediate between audience and the representation on stage. He calls himself a poet, accepts responsibility for producing a play that will *'tenir debout'* ('hold up') and a characterisation of Victor that will make the play acceptable. As he says in telling Victor why he should explain himself, '. . . *Il faut qu'on sache à peu près pourquoi. Sinon on va le vomir. Et nous autres avec. A qui croyez-vous que nous avons à faire? A des esthètes?'* ('It's necessary that they know approximately why. Otherwise they will vomit you up. And the rest with you. Who do you think we are dealing with? Esthetes?') (p. 86). When Dr. Piouk asks him, *'C'est vous l'auteur de cette plaisanterie de lycéen?'* ('Are you the author of this school amusement?'), he makes no denial but simply responds *'Faut bien amuser les badauds'*. Pointed reference is made to his resemblance to the deceased elder Krap — *'Homme de lettres'* who prefers the genre *'merde'*, and is a member of *'l'Institut'*, supervises the actions of the other characters in Act I, and brings the act to a close by calling out *'Rideau'*. The Glazier's task of repairing the broken window in Victor's room obviously represents the attempt to provide an adequate dramatic method to reveal Victor. His tools are the mastic which holds things together, the measure for assessing character and situation, the hammer and scissors with which he forcibly does away with unnecessary elements like the wrestler. In addition,

41

he ridicules or curtails actions which he regards as uninteresting or irrelevant and suggests to the other characters lines of action which might produce an acceptable play. And most importantly, he prevents Victor's attempts to escape from the play entirely. He is unsuccessful in nearly all that he attempts. He never employs his diamond. He leaves with the window still unfixed and the door still lacking the lock he promised to keep out the intruders. Contrary to his earlier assertion that once he set his hand to repairing the window pane he would not stop until it was fixed, he announces that he won't return tomorrow. To Victor's *'Vous avez fait du beau travail'* ('You've worked in vain'), he responds simply *'Oui'*. In defeat, lacking the heart to pick up his tools, he leaves them, except for the diamond which is lost, in disarray on the floor for Victor to sell to pay the rent. Later as the play approaches a classical melodramatic ending of narrowly avoided expulsion for non-payment (the play is several times referred to as turning to melodrama), the gift of the tools does allow Victor the choice to stay on in his room. Somehow humanity will not be driven off the stage. In leaving his tools with Victor, who has himself been a writer, he relinquishes to him the role of the authorial presence. In Beckett's later works that role is also left to the protagonists who deliver lines of ironic self-commentary on the play directed toward the audience. In departing, the Glazier leaves his business card in case Victor should desire his services in the future, but Victor seems to think that unlikely and passes the card on to his landlady, Mrs. Karl.

Dr. Piouk and Olga Skunk, Victor's fiancée, make their exit as a pair. Piouk's role of 'King Catalyst', as the Glazier proclaims him, has already been pointed out. That he should remain on stage until the very last, determining and dominating action which has become patently redundant, illustrates the difficulty of constructing a play without perceptibly structured action. The characters who serve for exposition are more expendable than he is. As the stage directions point out, Victor's condition is evident from his movements alone. *'Ses mouvements pour être vagues, n'en suivant pas moins un rythme et un dessin de sorte qu'on finit par savoir à peu prè sa situation sans avoir à le regarder'*. (Although vague, his movements nevertheless have a rhythm and pattern so that one knows his situation approximately without having to see it.') (p. 2). Dr. Piouk's voluntary departure to preside over the traditional comic feast of celebration comes at the conclusion of the play when his function of providing the plot and action has been fully carried out. His part seems permanent. He leaves one theatrical scene to preside at another. He suffers crises but survives them. His memory fails but is restored and he recalls vividly his former days on stage. For Beckett some kind of plotted action — as opposed to arbitrary disruption of plot through devices like Gide's *'Acte gratuit'* or Brecht's epic scenes — seems an essential element of drama.

Olga Skunk's presence is nearly as persistent as Dr. Piouk's. Her naive, realistically portrayed responses are in contrast with those of the other characters and provide the few brief moments of verisimilitude in the play. She embodies the underlying reality of an actual experience. In Act II when she enters his room to plead for his return to her, Victor admits that he did once express love for her, but that now that has changed and he wishes her to go away for ever. In Act III she does exit with the doctor after Victor elects to remain in his room alone rather than join her 'to face life hand in hand'. But this is not necessarily a permanent parting. Victor leaves open the possibility that he will change his mind and agrees to give her a sign if he does. It remains to be seen whether humanity can be represented on stage without in some way acknowledging the power of romantic love even if it is what Beckett called in *Echo's Bones* a 'spoilt love'.

The last to leave Victor's room is his landlady Madame Karl. Many details associate her with socialist realism. Her name recalls Karl Marx and Karl Radek, the official Soviet proponent of socialist realism. She is the keeper of a boarding house, the classical locus of much naturalistic fiction and drama (cf. Balzac, Ibsen's *Wild Duck*, and Gorky's *The Lower Depths*). Her daughter is named Thérèse like Zola's model of naturalism, Thérèse Raquin. She is preoccupied with material circumstances. The other characters make remarks to her about the red colour of garments as if this otherwise gratuitous information would have significance for her. The Glazier complains of her, *'C'est un moment historique et vous venez nous assommer avec vos histoires de garni'* (It is a historic moment and you put us asleep with your tales of the boarding house'), and scolds her for interrupting Victor's meditations (p. 100). She nevertheless has her followers. *'J'en ai ma claque, moi'* she asserts. But like the others, Madame Karl also represents an aspect of theatre more fundamental than any specific tradition or movement. The question raised by her presence, or rather by Victor's presence in her space, is whether those in control of the economic and physical realities of the theater are willing to make a place for the humanity Victor represents. Mrs. Karl is the keeper of the door. She wants to know whether Victor is staying or going. If he is staying, she wants her bill paid. First two, then three others are waiting to replace him if he can't meet expenses or finds the room unsuitable. Beckett seems as doubtful about the present and future material conditions for dramatising humanity as he does about the suitability of the previous dramatic methods. It seems likely that regard for performances which meet the old public expectations and so pay the rent will prevail. It is Madame Karl who is left ultimately with the Glazier's old tools and his card. Victor will stay on temporarily with his landlady. The arrangement, however, is like those of *Godot* and *Endgame* — inextricable but unsatisfactory. Their relationship is not at the final point of termination, but demonstrably fails to provide satisfaction. Victor's final interaction with a fellow creature is to request a blanket. Madame Karl responds by telling him spring will come and offering him a bowl of soup instead. (As one might imagine a later Beckett character paraphrasing 'Our Saviour', 'I was naked and you gave me bread, I was hungry and you clothed me.') The final words of the play come from Madame Karl: '*Ce n'est pas moi qui pourrai vous soigner. (Silence) Quelle pitié! (Elle sort).* ('It is not I who will care for you . . . What a pity!').

The play ends with a short mime and Victor free at last from the intruders. The devices of convention have been systemically excluded the stage. With great difficulty Victor moves his bed as far as possible from the broken window. The direction of that movement is not, however, away from the audience but to the very front of the stage. He sits on the bed and '*Il regarde le public avec application, l'orchestre, le balcon (le cas échéant), à droite, à gauche. Puis il se couche, le maigre dos tourné à l'humanité*' ('He looks intently at the public, the orchestra, the balcony . . . to the right, to the left, then he lies down, his thin back turned towards humanity').* This final gesture is ambiguous. If his posture implies rejection of the audience, he has previously acknowledged them. And his posture does not preclude his being seen and understood for

* The similarity of the theme of *Eleuthéria* with much of Beckett's post-war prose of the same period, especially *First Love*, written at about the same time, will be obvious to many readers.

what he is. Even in that thin back huddled in its bed in recoil from a life offering no acceptable solace, the audience may perceive a stage image of humanity.

Eleuthéria in its enumeration and elimination of the unsuitable elements of dramatic tradition defines a freedom *from* something more than a freedom to *do* something. The freedom to present a character who is 'nothing' in conventional terms is clearly articulated. But the methods of a drama which might do that are only adumbrated. *Eleuthéria* was preparation — a clearing of the set. Only in writing *Godot* did Beckett discover the methods which would allow him to present 'human' reality. But without an exploration of dramatic method like the one accomplished in *Eleuthéria*, the new beginning in *Godot* would have been impossible.

CHAPTER TWO

Waiting for Godot

ORIGINS: 'NOTHING TO BE DONE'

In the first place . . . the source of the dialogue between the boy and Vladimir is to be found in the unpublished play *Eleuthéria.** He then added, 'If you want to find the origins of *En attendant Godot*, look at *Murphy*.'
(Colin Duckworth, *En attendant Godot*, London, 1966, pp. xlv, xlvi.)

Dear Sighle Kennedy,
I don't have thoughts about my work [. . .] If I were in the unenviable position of having to study my work my points of departure would be the 'Naught is more real . . .' and the '*Ubi nihil vales . . .*' both already in *Murphy* and neither very rational.
Bon courage quand même.

Sincerely
(signed) Sam. Beckett
(Sighle Kennedy, *Murphy's Bed*, Bucknell University Press, 1971, p. 300.)

The very opening line is *Rien à faire.*' Sam has translated this as, 'Nothing to be done . . .', but in French this is a colloquialism, and can be thrown away with a sigh as just a little exclamation of tedium. In the original Dublin production I changed it to 'It's no good,' because I felt that it was more colloquial and less significant. However, I subsequently discussed it with Sam, and he was most emphatic that he wished it to be spoken as 'Nothing to be done.'
(Alan Simpson, *Beckett and Behan and a Theatre in Dublin*, London, 1962, p 95.)

Was Beckett uninterested in economics, did he never treat problems, such as how his characters earned their livings? 'My characters have nothing,' he said, and let the matter drop.
(Israel Shenker, 'Moody Man of Letters,' *New York Times*, May 6, 1956, Sec. 2, p. 3.)

* The extract overleaf from *Eleuthéria*, written in 1947, unpublished and unperformed, is reproduced here for the first time by the courtesy of Mr. Beckett.

47

Vitrier	Quel âge as-tu?
Michel	Dix ans, papa.
Vitrier	Dix ans. (*Silence*) Et tu ne sais pas ce que ça veut dire, heureux?
Michel	Non papa.
Vitrier	Tu sais quand il y a quelque chose qui vous fait plaisir. On se sent bien, n'est-ce-pas?
Michel	Oui papa.
Vitrier	Eh bien, c'est à peu près ça, heureux. (*Silence*) Alors, tu es heureux?
Michel	Non, papa.
Vitrier	Et pourquoi?
Michel	Je ne sais pas, papa.
Vitrier	C'est parce que tu ne vas pas assez à l'école?
Michel	Non, papa, je n'aime pas l'école.
Vitrier	Tu voudrais jouer avec tes petits camarades?
Michel	Non, papa, je n'aime pas jouer.
Vitrier	Je ne suis pas méchant avec toi?
Michel	Oh non, papa.
Vitrier	Qu'est ce que tu aimes faire?
Michel	Je ne sais pas.
Vitrier	Comment, tu ne sais pas? Il doit y avoir quelque chose.
Michel	(*Après réflexion*) J'aime quand je suis dans le lit, avant de m'endormir.
Vitrier	Et pourquoi?
Michel	Je ne sais pas, papa. (*Silence*)
Vitrier	Profites-en.
Michel	Oui papa. (*Silence*)
Vitrier	Viens que je t'embrasse. (*Michel avance. Le Vitrier l'embrasse*) Tu aimes quand je t'embrasse?
Michel	Pas beaucoup, papa.
Vitrier	Et pourquoi?
Michel	Ça me pique, papa.
Vitrier	Tu vois, tu sais pourquoi tu n'aimes pas quand je t'embrasse.
Michel	Oui papa.
Vitrier	Alors dis pourquoi tu aimes quand tu es dans le lit.
Michel	(*Après réflexion*) Je ne sais pas, papa. (*Silence*)
Vitrier	Tu as encore faim.
Michel	Oui papa.
Vitrier	(*Lui donnant le sandwich*) Tiens, mange ça.
Michel	(*Hésitant*) Mais c'est à toi, papa.
Vitrier	(*Avec force*) Mange! (*Silence*)
Michel	Tu n'as pas plus faim, papa?
Vitrier	Non.
Michel	Et pourquoi? (*Silence*)
Vitrier	Je ne sais pas, Michel. (*Silence*)

RIDEAU [End of Act II]

48

V. How old are you?
M. 10 years old, papa.
V. 10 years old. (*silence*) And you don't know what it means to be happy?
M. No, papa.
V. You know when something gives you pleasure. You feel good, right?
M. Yes, papa.
V. Good, it's a lot like that. (*silence*) Well, are you happy?
M. No, papa.
V. Why not?
M. I don't know, papa.
V. Is it because you haven't been to school enough?
M. No, papa, I don't like school.
V. Don't you want to play with your little friends?
M. No papa, I don't like to play.
V. I'm not mean to you?
M. Oh no, papa.
V. What is it you like to do?
M. I don't know.
V. Why don't you know? There must be something.
M. (*after reflecting*) I like it when I am in my bed, before I go to sleep.
V. Why is that?
M. I don't know, papa (*silence*)
V. Make the most of it [Profites-en.]
M. Yes, papa.
V. Come here let me give you a kiss, (*Michael goes to him. The Glazier kisses him*) Do you like it when I kiss you?
M. Not very much, papa.
V. Why?
M. It's prickly, papa.
V. You see, you know why you don't like it when I kiss you.
M. Yes, papa.
V. Well then, tell me why you like it when you are in your bed.
M. (*after reflecting*) I don't know papa. (*silence*)
V. Are you still hungry?
M. Yes, papa.
V. (*handing him a sandwich*) Here, eat this.
M. (*hesitating*) But that's for you, papa.
V. (*forcefully*) Eat!
(*silence*)
M. Are you still hungry, papa?
V. No.
(*silence*)
M. Why not?
(*silence*)
V. I don't know, Michael.
(*silence*)

CURTAIN [End of Act II]

(Authors' translation)

The large question of the possibility of human happiness first addressed in *Human Wishes* is here linked for the first time in Beckett's drama to a state of repose and reverie indifferent to the external world and volition. The state

Democritus: 'Naught is more real . . .'

The protagonist of Beckett's first novel *Murphy* plays a game of chess with a mental patient named Endon. At the end of the game, Murphy experiences a moment in which he 'sees nothing.' To define this state of consciousness Beckett refers directly to the quotation 'Naught is more real . . .' from the pre-Socratic Greek atomist, Democritus, which he pointed out in his letter to Sighle Kennedy. The description also contains other phrases, echoes, and concepts from Democritus and his atomist world view. The relevant passages from Democritus are noted here in the text of *Murphy* and translated below.

> . . . Murphy began to see nothing, the colourlessness which is such a rare postnatal treat, being the absence (to abuse a nice distinction) not of *percipere* but of *percepi*. His other senses also found themselves at peace, an unexpected pleasure. Not the

---

described by the boy is like that of Victor Krap at the end of *Eleuthéria*. It is comparable to the moments Vladimir recalls when he considers if he has ever known happiness (see p. 53 below). It is a condition like the one toward which Estragon tends constantly and also defines as the source of happiness (cf. his 'If I could only sleep' and 'Why will you never let me sleep? . . . I was dreaming I was happy.') It may be seen again in the posture of the protagonist at the end of *Act Without Words I*. It is the state of rest implied for the 'wearyish old man' Krapp who sings a hymn imploring 'Jesus give the weary calm and sweet repose'. And it is the state that Joe in *Eh Joe* and the speaker of *A Piece of Monologue* are trying to achieve when they are interrupted by the intrusion of painful memories. Most significantly the most explicit expectation Vladimir and Estragon have of Godot, and the one reason given for waiting for him, is that he might provide such a state. For his Schiller-Theater production Beckett restored a passage of dialogue contained in the first French edition not translated by Beckett for the Faber and Grove editions. For that passage Vladimir and Estragon consider whether it is worth waiting for Godot. The passage in the French text occurs just after Vladimir and Estragon think they have heard Godot shouting at his horse (Fp.19; Gp13R.). Estragon says they should leave; Vladimir counters with the idea that something more specific than the pending answer to their 'vague supplication' is worth waiting for:

E.	Allons-noüs-en.	(Let's go)
V.	Ou? *Un temps*. Ce soir on couchera peut-être chez lui au chaud, au sec, le ventre plein, sur la paille. Ça vaut la peine qu'on attende. Non?	(Where? Tonight we will sleep perhaps with him, warm, dry, our stomachs full, in the straw. That's worth the trouble of waiting. No?)
E.	Pas toute la nuit.	(Not all night)
V.	Il est encore jour.	(It is still day.)

numb peace of their own suspension, but the positive peace*
that comes when the somethings give way, or perhaps add up,
to the Nothing† than which in the guffaw of the Abderite§
naught is more real. Time did not cease, that would be asking
too much, but the wheel of rounds and pauses** did, as
Murphy with his head among the armies (i.e. the chessmen)
continued to suck in,‡ through all the posterns of his
withered soul, the accident-less one-and-only§ § conveniently called Nothing. Then this also vanished, or perhaps simply
came asunder, in the familiar variety of stenches, asperities,
ear-splitters, and eye-closers, and Murphy saw that Mr.
Endon was missing. (*Murphy*, Calder edition, London 1977, p.
138.)

---

* There are two forms of knowledge, one genuine, one obscure. To the
obscure belong all of the following: sight, hearing, smell, taste, feeling. The
other form is the genuine. Whenever the obscure way can no longer see, hear,
smell, taste or touch . . . the true way of knowledge which possesses a finer
organ of perception supercedes it. (*Fragmente der Vorsokratiker*, Herman Diels,
Frag. 11 p. 140) (Authors' translation from German.)

† 'The Nothing (*Meden*) exists as surely as the something.' (*Den*) (Frag. 1
p. 178.) Also translated 'The Aught has no more reality than the Naught.' (*The
Pre-Socratic Philosophers*, Kathleen Freeman, Oxford 1953, p. 304.)

§ By 'den' and 'meden' Democritus refers respectively to the vortex of atoms
which constitute corporeal reality and the void in which they move. According
to another fragment 'only atoms and the void are real.' (*Source Book in Ancient
Philosophy*, ed. Charles M. Bakewell, Scribners, N.Y. 1939 p. 66)

** Democritus of Abdera was commonly called 'The Laugher' because he
mocked the folly of human beings in their foolish desires. (Freeman, p. 292)
eg. 'The Hippocratic Letters' tell a story of how the Abderites apply to
Hippocrates to cure Democritus of his madness and his laughter at mankind;
Hippocrates after consultation with Democritus is convinced that Democritus
alone has the wisdom and sanity which is taken by the rest of the world for
madness. (Freeman, p. 325)

‡ cf Democritus' depiction of the physical world as a circular membrane out
of which a vortex of 'manifold forms' is separated. (Freeman, p. 302)
[Democritus saw] respiration as the boundary with which life was coterminous.
It was . . . the tendency of the encircling atmosphere to cause contraction in
the animal body and to expel those atomic forms, which, from never being at
rest themselves, supply animals with movement. This tendency, however, was
counteracted by the reinforcements deprived from the entrance from outside
in the act of respiration of new atoms of a similar kind. These last in fact . . . as
they united to repel the compressing and solidifying forces prevented those
atoms already existing in animals from being expelled from them: and life . . .
continued so long as there was strength to carry on this process. (Aristotle, *De
Anima*, I, 2 quoted in Bakewell, p. 60)

§§ Everything happens according to necessity; for the cause of coming into
being of all things is the whirl which [Democritus] calls necessity.' (*The
Presocratic Philosophers*, ed. G.S. Kirk and J.E. Raven, Cambridge, 1957,
p. 412)
(Beckett could not have used all of the texts cited here, but his view of
Democritus would have been based on the same fragments and similar
commentary by other philosophers.)

The states of consciousness which Murphy distinguishes here are two different 'nothings'. First the positive one which comes when sensual perception gives way and he perceives the void. It is designated as 'nothing' with a small 'n' and as 'naught'. And then is the negative one associated with the whirling vortex of atoms, sensual perception, and finally with the life process itself; it is designated 'Nothing' with a capital 'N'.

The 'guffaw of the Abderite' is in this context a reference to the word play of Democritus in his statement affirming the reality of the void. To make his point Democritus used a new term. The word '*meden*', nothing, (the void) already existed in Greek, but his term for substance (the atoms) '*den*' was a neologism created by dropping the negative prefix '*me*' from '*meden*'. By deriving the word 'something' from 'nothing', the formulation implies that it is a secondary, lesser entity. Beckett's own formulation is also a complex piece of word play relegating 'somethings' to secondary importance. The statement that 'somethings add up to the Nothing . . . than which naught is more real' reflects the usual English translation of Democritus' '*meden*' and '*den*', as 'naught' and 'aught'. The external circular motion of the material world is equated with the round mathematical symbol, 'aught', zero. The negation of 'aught', 'naught', is 'more real' than it is.

The 'guffaw of the Abderite' is also an allusion to the popular epithet *Gelasînos* (Laugher) bestowed on Democritus because he mocked the folly of humanity in its struggles to achieve earthly desires. Both his cosmology and his general attitude deprive 'real' life of the primary value placed on it by others. Murphy shares Democritus' disdain for 'real' life. He continues to breathe in the atoms that sustain life and he remains sentient. But head down among the chessmen left over from the abandoned game, he knows how to evaluate the external world that goes on about him and the life process it maintains in being. This external existence is 'conveniently called Nothing'.

His evaluation does not, however, mean that he can escape from what he rejects. In the end Murphy not only continues to breathe in the atoms, he is again caught up in the greater whirl of perception — 'the familiar variety of stenches, asperities, ear-splitters, and eye-closers'.

The characters in *Godot* are sentient, and have desires and entangling relationships, and do not achieve Murphy's 'nothing', the 'naught'. Estragon attempts to escape from existence by sleeping, but in his sleep he sees the visions of his dreams and not the nothing of the void. In the first French edition Vladimir did approach Murphy's vision of nothingness. Early in Act II (Faber p. 59; Grove p. 38) Vladimir speaks of being happy when Estragon is absent. Estragon questions, 'Happy?' and Vladimir responds, 'Perhaps it's not quite the right word.' But the kind of moment Vladimir associates with contentment is shown in the dialogue that followed in the first edition:

> '. . . when I close my eyes (closes eyes and covers them with his hands for more security) I feel . . . yes . . . that the light abandons me. (He opens his eyes) Now, there you are (he closes his eyes and concentrates) Now I feel myself becoming all black inside.' (*En attendant Godot, Éditions de Minuit*, Paris, 1953, p. 99, Authors' translation.)

This passage was crossed out in Beckett's prompt script for the original 1953 production of *Godot* and deleted in subsequent editions and translations. Even the temporary release to the kind of nothing Murphy experiences is removed as a possibility in *Godot*. The 'Nothing to be done' which opens the play, and the nothing that 'happens' throughout is the other 'Nothing' — the circular activity of corporeal existence which Murphy rejects.

Geulincx: '*Ubi Nihil*'

The second quotation, *Ubi nihil vales, ibi nihil veles*, cited by Beckett in his letter to Sighle Kennedy is rendered in *Murphy* as 'want nothing where [you are] worth nothing.' This formulation keeps the balance and alliteration of 'the beautiful Belgo-Latin' original. However, the Latin verb '*valere*' is more expressive of capability than worth. And the passage in which this sentence occurs stresses the inability of our actions to alter our fundamental condition: 'Where you *can* do nothing, there *wish* to do nothing.'

The sentence is from a footnote to the first chapter of the *Ethica* of the seventeenth-century Catholic philosopher Arnold Geulincx. For Geulincx this statement is the starting point of the whole ethical system given in his second chapter. In March, 1936 Beckett read that chapter at the library of Trinity College Dublin and was so impressed that he recommended Geulincx enthusiastically to his friend Arland Ussher.*

* Note overleaf

The passage in Geulincx reads:

> *Where you can do nothing, there wish nothing*, or in other words
> *Nothing is to be done for naught* . . . . [This is] the highest principle
> of ethics, from which easily follows each and every obligation,
> the obligations which make up the pages of my *Ethica*. For if
> nothing ought to be done in vain, one ought not to struggle
> against God's calling us and releasing us from the human
> condition. Which is the first obligation. [i.e., To accept death
> and make no effort to elude it.] And if nothing ought to be
> done in vain, one ought not to struggle against God's bidding
> us still to live, detaining us in the human condition. Which is
> the second obligation [i.e., To accept life and make no effort to
> escape from it.]
>
> And if these things are so, therefore food ought to be
> sought. Which is the third obligation [i.e., To perpetuate
> existence during the period of life ordained by God.]
>
> And if these things are so, there is some occupation to be
> followed, etc.[1]

The remaining obligations of the *Ethica* are grouped here by
Geulincx under the heading of 'occupation . . . etc.' The fourth
is to 'follow some purpose of life', the fifth is to 'do and endure
many things', the sixth is to 'relax the spirit' in order to be able
to continue, and the seventh is to accept humbly the fact of our
birth.

The passage in *Murphy* quoting Geulincx deals with Murphy's
attempt to renounce the useless struggle of the external world,
'the occasions of fiasco', by suppressing desire.

> "I am not of the big [external] world, I am of the little
> [interior] world" was an old refrain with Murphy, and a
> conviction, two convictions, the negative first. How should
> he tolerate, let alone cultivate the occasions of fiasco having
> once beheld the beautiful idols of his cave? In the beautiful

---

*

He recommended Geulincx in general, the *Ethica* especially, and called particular
attention to the second section of the second chapter of the first tractate in which
Geulincx discussed his fourth cardinal virtue, Humility. He supplied the Latin of
Geulincx's definition of Humility: *contemptus negativus sui ipsius*. The Latin of Geulincx's
definition of humility translates literally 'a negative contempt of one's own self'. But the
phrase is more complex than this literal English translation indicates. As Beckett would
have been aware, in the Latin the *negativus* truly modifies *contemptus* rather than just
intensifying it. And he would also have been aware of a wider context of reference in *sui
ipsius* to the entire personal circumstances — all that attaches to onself — rather than just
the immediate person. The *contemptus negativus* of the Latin thus describes a complex
attitude which places no great positive value on the things which make up the
circumstances of one's existence but is negative in the sense that it does not totally reject
them either. Vladimir and Estragon 'are not saints' but they exhibit this complex form of
contemptus mundi so admired by Beckett.

Belgo-Latin of Arnold Geulincx: *Ubi nihil vales, ibi nihil veles.*
(*Murphy*, p. 101.)

The attempt is, however, not entirely successful. 'But it was not enough to want nothing where he was worth nothing.' Murphy still has urges which keep him divided between the big world and the little one — 'witness his deplorable susceptibility to Celia, ginger, and so on.'

Like Democritus, Geulincx represents for Murphy primarily a rationale for escape into a solipsistic 'microcosm'. The characters in *Godot*, Estragon and Vladimir, in contrast, retain more of a 'deplorable susceptibility' to external urges and so are more entangled in the futile struggle Geulincx warns against. The condition of their waiting and many of their activities suggest a connection with the obligations and the visual metaphors of Chapter II of the *Ethica* as illustrated in the following juxtaposed quotations from the *Ethica* and *Godot*: (Some of these passages from the *Ethica* are also relevant to *Endgame*.)

> I know my condition; it remains to be considered how I arrived in it. I am at a loss, I don't know, nor do I have another thing to say except, "I do not know." [. . .] I introduced no judgement of my own will [. . .] I did not come here at my own initiative, neither did the one who so miraculously placed me here ask me at any time whether it pleased me to be here. (*Ethica*, p. 35)

> [. . .] I lay myself under obligation [. . .] I was born, brought here. I approve that He brought me. I am departing from here. I wish to go when He says. I do not wish to go when He does not say. (*Ethica*, p. 57)

> [From the inspection of myself] I can see my first obligation. It is, when God calls me away from the living and bids me return, not to refuse or tarry for a long time but rather to be ready at once. (*Ethica*, p. 37)

> E: Let's go.
> V: We can't.
> E: Why not?
> V: We're waiting for Godot.
> E: Ah!

> [My second obligation is] not to go unless called and not to leave my station — my post in life — without a summons from that highest Commander. [Imperator] (*Ethica*, p. 38)

> E: . . . we were to wait.
> V: He said by the tree.

My third obligation is [. . .] to restore my body, to eat, to drink, to sleep, but to do all these things in moderation; to wait for hunger, thirst, sleep, not to summon or anticipate these things, rather to overcome those which are at hand when they have taken possession of me. (*Ethica*, p. 44)

E: . . . Funny, the more you eat the worse it gets.
V: With me it's just the opposite.
E: In other words?
V: I get used to the muck as I go along.

[The fourth obligation] bids that I learn some skill, that I embrace a condition of life and purpose and after I have embraced it, that I empty myself into it with diligence and not spit it out or reject it even though there is an opportunity for changing it or even though I have selected badly — that I cling to it doggedly as if my way of life and my life itself were intermingled. [. . .] (*Ethica*, p. 48)

V: . . . Come, let's get to work! . . . In an instant all will vanish and we'll be alone once more, in the midst of nothing-ness!

I should choose some province that is not only suitable for me, but to which I am equal. I ought not to choose some [task] so that borne away by my indifference or my insolence, as by a storm, I cling to it as though to a rock. Am I endowed with a strong body but have a mind that is dulled and a weak spirit? I shall serve as a craftsman or a porter. Am I weak in body and mind but have a good natured spirit? I should be a merchant . . . (*Ethica*, p. 49)

(cf. Estragon's stone* and his constant tendency to return to it; Lucky, who Beckett originally conceived of as dressed as a railway porter; and Pozzo's physical dependence, failing memory, desire to please, and traffic in the market place.)

God enjoins a purpose for me but not an outcome. He wished [the purpose] to be in my control but its achievement is not subject to my obligation and not within my power. If, therefore, you wish to obey God, and wish this alone (as you ought to do), what is it, my soul, that torments you? (*Ethica,* p. 50)

The fifth obligation . . . bids us do many things, endure many things in order to serve without interruption and with equanimity a course of life once resolved upon, or at some point to change it that is necessary. [. . .] one must freeze, labors must be endured, weariness must be swallowed before

---

* In all productions with which he has been associated Beckett has insisted that Estragon be seated on a stone with which he is identified rather than the 'low mound' of the English text.

one will make even modest progress in any skill or discipline whatsoever to which one lends his name. What if I think about the summit of wisdom, in order to be of assistance to others? Hard and difficult things will await me; ... the criticism of others will lash me, the envy of others will gnaw at me, even the powerlessness of others will restrain and undermine me. (*Ethica*, p. 50)

(cf. Estragon: 'I'm cold'; Vladimir: 'He is tired' [in 1978 production text]; the hostile response to Lucky's speech, Vladimir's peripatetic discourse on the need to give aid in Act II and the fall of Vladimir and Estragon as they are pulled to the ground when they attempt to help Pozzo get up.)

> The sixth obligation is the law of relaxing the soul on occasion, lest it be broken in unceasing struggle. One ought to make propitiation gratuitously once in a while; one ought to walk, one ought to wander or stroll; one ought to indulge in jokes, stories, and dancing with friends, one ought to banquet, one ought to drink ... one ought to indulge in trifling (I almost said one ought to be silly, but in the proper place) [. . .] Let the soul recede back now and then to these sports, so that then, when one's strength has been restored and one has been stirred up as though by a race, one can return to serious matters all the more vigorously and with a longer stride. The bow with which we contend can be stretched even more after it has been relaxed.
>
> V: Our elevations.
> E: Our relaxations.
> V: Our elongations.
> E: Our relaxations.

(cf. the joke of the Englishman in the brothel, and Vladimir: 'How time flies when one has fun!')

> The soul ought to be allowed to relax as much as is necessary for it to contend better, one ought to indulge his natural inclinations enough to break through the torpor, sadness, and the other obstacles which ensnare us in the net of our responsibilities. To seek anything further than that is to seek oneself again and to leap down from the edifice of Virtue ... (*Ethica*, pp. 51–52)

(cf. the title of Lucky's dance, 'The Net', Estragon's dream of 'falling ... on top of a —' and the reference to leaping 'hand in hand from the top of the Eiffel Tower ...')

> The seventh obligation is the 'Law of humility'. Namely, that I take in good part, be satisfied with, my nativity; lest even I

curse it or complain about it. Lest I come at any time to that degree of powerlessness, that I regret that I was born. Lest I levy a curse against those who begat me; not to mention levying a curse against Him (a thing I am not able to say without horror) who sent me into my body and, by joining me so miraculously with it, brought it about that it was mine. Lest I share the opinion of fools (though to the people, because they rave differently and more splendidly, they appear wise): it is best not to be born; next best to this is to die as soon as possible. (*Ethica*, p. 54)

V: Suppose we repented.
E: Repented what? [. . .]
E: Our being born?

If I know another law about which there is a question as to whether it comes from God, or if I only suppose it comes from God, or if I believe others who claim that it did or if I make it up out of my own desire . . . I will be obeying not God but my own opinions, levity, and foolishness. I shall be revering not God but a rock from the sepulchre in place of God . . . or I shall be scratching at a wound given to me by others . . . [because] What He wishes to be done by me He intones in a voice appropriate to a master. I hear it well enough except when I myself in the midst of his words make a noise importunately with the rattling and rustling of desires. . . . He does not carry on his transactions with me through an interpreter or through a messenger. . . . That servant is useless and demented who . . . undertakes to do something which he dreamed at night that his Lord commanded him to do; or dances and makes mischief in the market place because some idle swaggerer said that the Lord desired this, . . . He is a worthless fellow and deserves a beating. (*Ethica*, p. 57)

(cf. E's attention to the wound received from Lucky; 'All the dead voices . . . They rustle;' The Boy with the message that 'Mr. Godot told me . . . he won't come this evening but surely tomorrow,' and Lucky's dance at Pozzo's command, 'Dance, misery'.)

THE SHAPE THAT MATTERS

St Augustine

'I am interested in the shape of ideas even if I do not believe them. There is a wonderful sentence in Augustine. I wish I could remember the Latin. It is even finer in Latin than in English. "Do not despair; one of the thieves was saved. Do not presume one of the thieves was damned." That sentence has a wonderful shape. It is the shape that matters.'* (To Harold Hobson, 'Samuel Beckett — Dramatist of the Year,' *International Theatre Annual*, 1956, 1, pp. 153–155.)

Scholars have been unable to locate the exact sentence to which Beckett refers. In an interview with the authors in 1979, Beckett said he thought it was in the *Confessions*, but no sentence there has the form he described. The closest approximation appears in *Epistola* XLVIII: *Tres cruces in loco uno erant: In una latro liberandus: in alia latro damnandus: in media christus: alterum liberatur: alterum damnatur.*

Critics have said that 'Godot's' structure and message left the author free to lay down his pen at any moment. Beckett disagrees: 'One act would have been too little and three acts would have been too much.' (Israel Shenker, 'Moody Man of Letters,' *New York Times*, 6 May, 1956, sec. 2, p. 3.)

THE CHARACTERS IN GODOT

'I think of my characters as thin. They're ghosts and I don't want to see them mangled.'
(Beckett to Barney Rosset, editor of Grove Press; Authors' Interview 1978)

Godot

Beckett has refused to limit the identification of Godot himself to any single source of interpretation. And from the manuscript through productions he has made choices which leave the question 'Who is Godot?' as open as possible. As he said to Alec Reid, the critics and public were busy interpreting in allegorical or symbolic terms a play which 'strove at all costs to avoid definition.'[2] In answer to the actor Jack MacGowran, Beckett was emphatic in denying the most popular association of Godot with God:

Because Godot begins with g–o–d, people have got the idea that he's referring to God. But he categorically states that that is not the point at all, that it doesn't mean God at all. † The whole play's about waiting.[3]

An abandoned title, *En Attendant* — without *Godot* — for the French version shows that Beckett originally contemplated

---

* As early as October 1935 Beckett had heard Carl Jung speak in his third Tavistock lecture of the importance of the two thieves as scapegoats and redeemers of mankind (See *Analytical Psychology in Theory and Practice*: Routledge 1975, p. 109).
† The suggestion that God might be *one* of the associations of Godot is retained in Beckett's own pronunciation of the word. Even with American actors he insists that it be pronounced 'God oh', with the stress on the first syllable.

directing attention away from the enigmatic character awaited, to the act of waiting itself. His deletion of 'wir' from the original title *Wir Warten auf Godot* (*We Wait for Godot*) in the German translation of Elmar Tophoven also placed the emphasis upon the act of waiting rather than upon the characters who wait.[4]

Beckett has responded to attempts by others to find a single source for the name Godot with whimsy and denial. He said to Roger Blin that the name came from the French words for boot, *godillot, godasse*, but Blin regards this answer as only a bit of Irish humour.[5] When Alan Schneider asked, 'Who or what does Godot mean?' Beckett replied, 'If I knew, I would have said so in the play.'[6] And he showed amused approval of Schneider's list of over a hundred identifications of Godot.

Godot's human existence was made less definite by the deletion of a portion of the manuscript which refers to a piece of paper in Godot's own hand giving the time and place of the appointment. As Colin Duckworth points out:

> In the manuscript of the play this arrangement is not just verbal, as in the published text (p. 9) but *written down by Godot himself*:
> – Tu es sûr que c'était ce soir?
> – Quoi?
> – Notre rendez-vous.
> – Diable – (*Il cherche dans ses poches.*) Il l'a écrit. Qu'est-ce que tu lis?
> – 'Samedi soir et suivants.' Quelle façon de s'exprimer!
> – Tu vois!
> – (*rendant le papier*). Mais sommes-nous samedi?
>
> (– Are you sure that it was this evening?
> – What?
> – Our rendezvous.
> – The devil! (*He searches his pockets*) He wrote (*he pulls out a number of pieces of paper and hands one over*) What do you read there?
> – 'Saturday evening and the following.'
> – You see!
> – (*putting the paper back*) But is it Saturday?)

When Duckworth asked about two suggested sources, Beckett stated that he was not aware of either of them until after the play had been completed:

> It has been suggested that Beckett had in mind Balzac's play *Mercadet*. Mercadet has a business partner, Godeau, who never appears. All Mercadet's creditors are anxiously

awaiting the return of Godeau in order to retrieve embezzled funds. At the end, it is announced that Godeau has come back, a rich man from India — but the audience never sees him. The similarities are considerable; the situation will be saved by Godeau, as it will be by Godot. But the hypothesis is not exactly helped by the fact that Mr. Beckett assures me that he only came to know *Mercadet* after writing *Godot*, and that it had no influence on his own play whatsoever.

The second Godeau was (or is) a veteran racing cyclist. Therefore (according to Hugh Kenner) he 'typifies Cartesian Man in excelsis, the Cartesian Centaur, body and mind in close harmony . . . Cartesian Man deprived of his bicycle is a mere intelligence fastened to a dying animal.' As the effect of this theory is to reduce the play to the level of a recondite geometrical puzzle, it is just as well that Mr. Beckett informs me he was told after writing Godot about the story of the little crowd of bystanders still watching and waiting at the end of a cycle race. *'Qu'est-ce qu'on attend?'* they were asked. *'On attend Godeau.'*[7]

An additional bit of dialogue written for the original Blin production and inserted in the *Éditions de Minuit* reprint September, 1953 deliberately dissociated Godot from any particular activity or profession while emphasising the theme of nothingness. Questioned by Vladimir at the end of Act II about what Godot does, the boy replies, *'Il ne fait rien, Monsieur'* ('He does nothing, sir'). An addition to the 1976 Schiller production text adds the possibility that Godot's beard might be red as well as black or white widening the scope of interpretation by associating him with the red-haired prostitute and male homosexual prostitute of Estragon's joke about the Englishman in the brothel.

Place and time appointed by Godot are also left deliberately ambiguous. Duckworth, who found echoes of Dante's Purgatory in the setting and language of the manuscript, raised the question directly:

> When I mentioned the possibility (that the characters are in a Dantesque purgatory) to Mr. Beckett, his comment was characteristic: 'Quite alien to me, but you're welcome.'[8]

Jack MacGowran, who had the help of Beckett's suggestions for the role of Lucky, described the action as taking place in indefinite space and time.

> I just saw them (Estragon and Vladimir) as two men isolated in an area where people weren't about. I didn't play it in any futuristic sense; I played it as happening in the present time.[9]

61

Vladimir and Estragon

Speaking to Jack MacGowran, Beckett stressed the need for both opposition and interdependence between Vladimir and Estragon.

> 'Treat it as a movable force meeting an immovable object' (Vladimir being the movable force and Estragon being the immovable object). But, he said, 'They are interdependent; one needs the other'. Estragon has so many nightmares, he must have someone to talk to. And Vladimir could not bear to be alone, because he cannot find any answers to the questions he is seeking. He hopes Estragon will provide the answers.[10]

When Bert Lahr as Estragon in the American production insisted that he was 'top banana' and warned Tom Ewell as Vladimir, 'Don't crowd me,' the balance of the play was disturbed. Alan Schneider reported Beckett's response, 'Beckett assumes that Vladimir is his major character. He was upset that the play was taken away from his major character.'[11]

Estragon is like Lucky in embodying human decline. As Beckett wrote to Colin Duckworth, 'The second day boots are no doubt same as first and Estragon's feet wasted, pined, shrunk and dwindled in interval. There's exegisis for you.'[12]

Pozzo and Lucky

> The first entrance of Pozzo and Lucky reads in the manuscript: '*Entrent deux messieurs, un très grand et un petit.*' (Enter two men, one very large and one small.) They are then referred to as '*le grand*' and '*le petit*'. Pozzo is not given a name until he introduces himself (p. 16) — which he does in the manuscript with the [potentially ambiguous] words '*Je m'appelle Pozzo*' [literally 'I call myself Pozzo']13.

The manuscript reinforces the likeness of Pozzo and Lucky to a pair of comedians implied in this first description by having Vladimir and Estragon refer to the popular Russian comics Bim and Bom. † [14] The first edition retained the names and included political overtones by identifying them as '*les comiques staliniens*' (the Stalinist comedians). In the original production prompt script and later editions, this reference was changed to simply 'the circus', keeping the quality but allowing for a wider range of interpretation in the relationship of Pozzo and Lucky.

---

† References to Bom and Bim persist throughout Beckett's work: for instance as early as *Murphy* and as late as *How It Is* and *What Where*.

Pozzo

Although Pozzo's association with Godot as an enigmatic master was present in Beckett's early concept of the play, identification of the two has never been for Beckett more than a possibility or a suggestion. Duckworth describes Beckett's responses to his enquiry on this point:

> To my verbal question, 'Is Pozzo Godot?' Mr. Beckett replied, 'No. It is implied in the text, but it's not true.' However, when I visited him in Paris several months later, he opened the manuscript of Godot and said, 'It's a long time since I looked at this.' He glanced at the page where it had fallen open in his hands. 'This, for example' he went on, 'I'd completely forgotten about it: "*Suggérer que Pozzo est peut-être Godot après tout, venu au rendez-vous, et qu'il ne sait pas que Vladimir et Estragon sont Vladimir et Estragon. Mais le messager?*"' [15]*

Beckett removed an association of Pozzo and Godot as godlike figures who come from another place by excising two references in the first edition to Pozzo and Lucky as only passing through and thus different from Estragon and Vladimir who remain on the plateau. When Vladimir declares that they are no longer alone, Estragon disagrees:

> E: *Mais ils sont seulement de passage . . .*
> E: *Mais ils ne font que passer.*
> V: *Ce sera suffisant.***

When Beckett directed his 1976 Schiller-Theater production he gave Pozzo a less mysterious and more solid bourgeois character by having him speculate in a new bit of dialogue that he must have left his watch at home 'on the Steinway'.

Roger Blin as the original Pozzo played the part both with and without the white beard inviting identification with Godot as described by the boy in Act I. Later productions in which Beckett was involved omit Pozzo's beard.

Almost every aspect of Pozzo is enigmatic in the early stages of the text. A note in the manuscript has him merely dissembling blindness: '*Après départ deuxième acte de Pozzo et Lucky suggérer que celui-là fait seulement semblant d'être aveugle.*' [16] †

---

*('Suggest that Pozzo is perhaps Godot after all, come for the rendezvous but that he doesn't know that Vladimir and Estragon are Vladimir and Estragon. But the messenger?')

**E: But they are only passing through . . .
E: But they only pass by.
V: That is sufficient.

† 'After the beginning of the second act Pozzo and Lucky suggest that the former only pretends to be blind.' Simulated blindness is also a major characteristic of the master figure, X, in the unfinished draft *Avant fin de partie*.

In rehearsal comments Beckett has placed emphasis on Pozzo's overt deception but has indicated that the actor just play the part as if he were blind. Paul Curran, who acted the role at the Royal Court in 1964 under Beckett's co-direction, felt that there was to be no question about Pozzo's blindness.

> Obviously we queried and debated many alternatives in *Godot* — but the truth of Pozzo's blindness was not one of them. There is no doubt in my mind that he is blind nor, I am sure, is there any doubt in Sam's mind. I remember he gave me a note in rehearsal once that I was looking too directly at Vladimir; I must look further 'off' for if I didn't it gave him the impression that I could see Vladimir. Doesn't that seem to you conclusive?[17]

Lucky

While Beckett left the character of Pozzo like that of Godot open to many speculations and undefined possibilities, he conceived Lucky as a character clearly embodying the decline of human possibilities and hopes described in his speech. When Duckworth asked Beckett, 'Is Lucky so named because he has found his Godot?', he answered, 'I suppose he is lucky to have no more expectations.'[18]

Lucky's Dance

The changes of the titles of Lucky's dance in the manuscript, in the texts for the original production, in the English and German translations and in the text for the Schiller-Theater production indicate the importance of the dance in the play. And they point out Beckett's concern to establish in the dance a metaphor for human existence.

At the conclusion of the dance, Pozzo asks 'What do you think he calls it?' and Estragon and Vladimir each offer a title before Pozzo supplies the correct one. In the manuscript the title, given by Estragon, was simply *'la mort du canard'* ('the death of the duck', with a pun on the secondary meanings of *canard* as 'joke' or 'malicious lie'). Between manuscript and the published text this was changed to *'la mort du lampiste'* ('the death of the lamplighter'). The phrase refers to the lowliest employee in a French railway station. The lamplighter was first to come, the last to go, and performed the most menial tasks. He occupied a room next to the toilets in an outbuilding where the three doors were *'Hommes', 'Dames'* and *'Lampiste'*. This change of phrase in the text supplants the death of an animal, avid to live, with a human death that might be seen as a welcome end to a life of servitude and waiting. 'The Scapegoat's Agony' of Beckett's English translation, intensifies the suggestion of death as a relief from suffering. The title, *'Der Tod der armen Schlucker'*, ('the death of the poor wretch') in the German translation, with which Beckett was directly involved, also retains that suggestion. The title suggested by Estragon sets up death as the first item of a series that moves from finality to inconclusiveness.

The title suggested by Vladimir, is, *'Le cancer des Vieillards'* ('the cancer of the old men'). It was added after the manuscript to create the second stage of the progression: the protracted suffering of old age and disease. Beckett's English translation is an obvious departure from a literal equivalent of the original. 'The Hard Stool' (which Beckett assured Colin Duckworth was a reference only to constipation and not to a seat of penance[19]) retains the reference to human ailments and obliquely to aging since constipation is a frequent complaint of the elderly (cf. Krapp). But it lays much greater stress than the French on a process which is painful and difficult to bring to conclusion. The German, *'Das Krebsgeschwür der Greise,'* ('the cancer [sore] of the old men') presents the same disease as the French but includes the physically repugnant image of life as a running sore like the 'sanies' which Beckett had used in an image of the life process in his short story 'Yellow' from *More Pricks than Kicks, Echo's Bones* and *Eleuthéria.*

The final title, which Pozzo supplies, is essentially the same in all three languages — *'La Danse du Filet'*, 'The Net'* *'Der Netztanz'* — and has never been subjected by Beckett to changes in translation or in performance. It completes the progression: from the finality of death, to protracted suffering, to present entanglement which lacks even the implied conclusion of a terminal illness or passing of the hard stool.

It is noteworthy in this respect, that the dance itself is the first item of a three-part series of performances by Lucky which leads toward a conclusion that does not occur. Lucky dances first and 'thinks afterwards' in what Pozzo confirms is 'the natural order.' Pozzo also mentions earlier that Lucky can sing. Following the dance, the original French text contained a long passage in which Pozzo referred to occasions when Lucky disobeyed his commands by singing when he was told to dance or think or

---

*Beckett's choice of a serio-comic image of his protagonist caught in a net, may be a counter statement to the image of the ensnared hero in classical Greek tragedy.

vice-versa. This section of dialogue was cut in the 1953 prompt script and deleted from all latter editions. In his Royal Court and Schiller texts Beckett made further cuts at this point so that Vladimir's 'tell him to think' follows almost immediately the end of the dance, setting up an uninterrupted progression. The deletion of the passage from the French original did more than make the progression more immediate. The singing, which would complete Lucky's repertoire and fulfill the French proverb alluded to in *Endgame*, 'Everything ends in a song,' becomes an implied future conclusion to the progression rather than a past activity.* But in Act II, when Vladimir does request that Lucky sing, he is mute. The expected progression — dance, think, sing — is clear, but the conclusion in song is as elusive in *Godot* as it is in *Endgame*.

Although these changes are evidence of the importance of progression away from finality, that was not Beckett's exclusive concern. The *'lampiste's'* undignified location next to the toilets introduced oblique reference to the theme of 'alimentation and defecation' which Lucky mentions later in his speech. The German *'Schlucker'*, from the verb *'schlucken'* 'to swallow' or 'hiccup', also connotes ingestion and expulsion. The English 'hard stool' makes the theme explicit. In his 1953 prompt script Beckett marked through Vladimir's *'le cancer des vieillards'* and replaced it with *'Devant le buffet'* — an allusion to the French saying *'Danser devant le buffet'* ('To dance in front of the buffet') meaning to starve while others eat. This change combined the element of protracted suffering with a direct reference to alimentation. Unlike several other changes in that text, this one was not included in later editions. It does, however, show the importance of the process of eating and excretion as a metaphor for the whole life process. †

In the end, neither this metaphor nor the progression implied in the titles was paramount for Beckett. In preparing the text for the 1975 Schiller Theater production and later for the American adaptation of it by his associate Walter D. Asmus, he cut the alternative titles of Lucky's dance leaving 'The Net' as its only title. Beckett as director chose to focus attention on a single metaphor of a permanent state enacted in a simple clear, visual stage image.

* The inability to find a musical resolution is an important theme in Beckett appearing as early as 'Dortmunder' in *Echo's Bones* and prominently in *Fin de partie* and *Happy Days*. See page 175 below.

† This motif is extremely prominent in the early draft version of *Endgame*.

Lucky's Speech

Jack MacGowran, with whom Beckett worked most closely on the role of Lucky, laid great stress on Lucky's speech as a statement of human decline.

> Lucky's speech, you see, is divided into three sections — the constancy of the divine, the shrinkage of humanity, and the petrification of the earth ('the great cold, the great dark of old stones'). He's a relic of all human decency at the mercy of the bourgeois. He is all life finally lived, and his great speech is perhaps what goes through everybody's mind at the verge of death.[20]

Later when MacGowran was asked what sections of the play he discussed with Beckett, he again referred to Lucky's speech.

> We discussed the rhythm of Lucky's speech. The speech has always been a problem to most actors. Because I had access to Beckett — I got from him what it means and also the rhythms of the speech, which are terribly important. Every time I've seen *Godot*, Lucky's speech has been a jumble — you couldn't make anything out, it's delivered so quickly. But this needn't be the case. When Beckett was trying to explain the rhythms to me, he said, 'I can't explain what a rhythm is except that it's iambic pentameter or trochaic; outside that they are just specific rhythms of my own.' And I said, 'Well, the only way we can do it is if I hear them.' So he recorded Lucky's speech for me on a tape recorder and I listened to that many, many times. That is how I got the rhythm of the speech, and from those rhythms I could actually hear what was being said. It's really one long sentence that ends with the conclusion that man 'wastes and pines wastes and pines.'[21]

Beckett's close friend, A.J. Leventhal, told Donal Donnelly, who played Lucky in the 1955 Dublin production:

> Sam says that Lucky's long speech is like a phonograph record getting faster and faster and faster until it is out of control.[22]

Of Lucky's muteness in Act II Jack MacGowran said:

> I didn't find I had to talk to him very much about that. In the first act Lucky is an extremely damaged person mentally — hence his speech disintegrates because his mind is disintegrating. Pozzo says, 'I am bringing him to the fair, where I hope to get a good price for him.' They arrive back in the second act when Pozzo hasn't been able to get rid of Lucky because he's blind and he needs the halter to hold onto. But there can be no communication because Lucky has gone dumb and cannot answer; he has said all he has to say and can say no more. But they remain interdependent.[23]

PRODUCTIONS

The Original *Godot*, Roger Blin

Beckett had seen Roger Blin's production of Strindberg's *The Ghost Sonata* at the Gaité-Montparnasse in 1951, liked it, and concluded that Blin was a director with whom he could trust his play. Through his wife, Suzanne, he sent Blin *Eleuthéria* and *En attendant Godot*. Blin accepted *Godot* for production, arranged financing, agreed to direct and acted the role of Pozzo.

Roger Blin's Account of the Original Théâtre de Babylone Production:

> At the time *Godot* went into rehearsal Beckett did not yet have much experience in the theatre but he already had a very precise knowledge of the theatre as a spectacle — that is to say, as an event unfolding on a stage. (It must be noted that, unlike many other authors he has always refused to write about the theatre and especially about his own plays.) He did indicate in his text the motion, the timing he desired, but those indications were meant especially for the reader; once on the stage things change: it is necessary to take into account the imponderable personality of the actor, the material necessities, the expressive value of certain words. Beckett soon realised on the spot which things were intellectual and accepted my suggestions with good grace. Looking first and foremost for stylized action, he approved whenever its achievement required adjustment. He was not against motivations but insisted that they be organically and totally justified. Should I mention some suggestions he approved? Well, here are two. At the end of the first act, to stress the derisory character of the Pozzo-Lucky couple, I made them walk around and around, one dragging the other, as clowns would do in the circus. I had, moreover, imagined a semi-circular set like a circus ring which reinforced that idea. (A suggestion Beckett rejected as too obvious.) And again in the second act when Pozzo and Lucky are prostrate and Vladimir discusses with Estragon the possibility of picking them up, they walk around the set while talking and, at the time of Vladimir's great discourse, they step as if unaware on the bodies of Pozzo and Lucky, the words 'we are all mankind' being accompanied by vigorous steps on Pozzo's back. Beckett accepted that because here he saw a piece of stage business which was not contrived. The same is true of Lucky's costume: he had originally envisioned him dressed as a station porter, but yielded to my suggestions. He did not yet have the fussy desire for precision he has acquired since and while following the rehearsals actively, he left the director his share of freedom, as long as he did not impose on him anything he did not approve. Besides, the

attitude of the director towards the author must, to my way of thinking, be one of humility, but an active humility.

It is probable that while writing *Godot* Beckett was, as far as his four characters were concerned, under the influence of the great American comic actors of the time. When I was thinking of staging it, I was myself completely obsessed by them and I can say that one day I suddenly saw the characters such as I wanted them to be. They were, ideally, Charlie Chaplin for Vladimir, Buster Keaton for Estragon, and Charles Laughton for Pozzo. Because Pozzo must be played by a fat man, I have played it myself but it is not my part and from now on I shall play Estragon. Pozzo, an Italian once told me, is a thin man crying from a fat one. He is, in fact, the most miserable, a loud mouth and that is all.

Beckett did not want the Pozzo-Lucky couple to have social overtones: what Vladimir and Estragon see is the harnessing of exploitive social oppression; that is what comes across to them. But Beckett shies away when told he has said something he did not mean to say. Besides, he refused to express himself about his work.

I remember before *Godot* was played, we once gave the play on the radio and they interviewed Beckett on that occasion. All he said was that he did not know why he wrote *Godot*. It just happened, the only thing he was sure of was that his characters wore bowler hats. One should not forget there is often a hint of the practical joker in this former English lecturer at the school in the *rue d'Ulm* (*l'École Normale Supérieure*): thus the white beard on Mr. Godot, which he did not have in the first version, perhaps in order to send the interpretation of Godot on a false direction, just as he said as a joke that Godot came from 'godillot' because of Estragon's shoes. There is a great deal of Irish sense of humour in his theatre. For that reason it is a mistake to play it as a tragedy, Godot must not end on an impression of crucifixion, it must not be interpreted tearfully; it is not a theatre of tears but of cruelty, of humanity.

According to Beckett, *Godot* is a very active play, a kind of Western. Basically I believe he has tried to follow on the stage a lead parallel to the one he followed in his novels. Remember before *Godot* he published *Molloy* and afterwards *Malone Dies* and *The Unnamable*. His characters are progressively becoming paralysed. After *The Unnamable* Beckett found himself in a vicious circle and he himself told me 'I don't know what to do with the characters, I can no longer write novels. I still have something to say in the theatre but always in the same direction.'

(Pierre Mélèse, *Samuel Beckett*, Paris 1966, pp. 146-148. Authors' translation.)

In an interview in 1976 Blin also recalled other details of the Théâtre de Babylone production. Beckett approved touches of

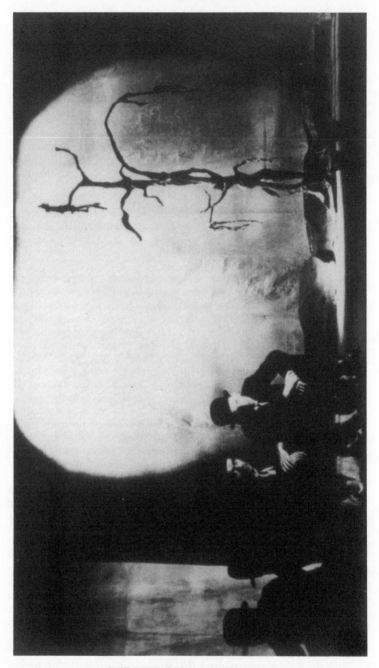

THE FIRST GODOT, PARIS 1953

realism in the costuming of the characters. Vladimir was a little like a professor dressed in the coat worn by Blin's father at his wedding. Other costumes and props were found at the flea market. Lucky wore black pants and a French vest. Pozzo was dressed like an English gentleman farmer, but Beckett insisted on bowler hats for all the characters.

Blin established the distinctive actions of each of the characters by associating them with their particular ailments. Estragon suffers from his feet and always tends to his stone where he may sit down to rest. Vladimir has urinary problems and is restless and peripatetic because he needs to piss. The corpulent Pozzo has heart troubles and therefore waddles about with recurrent involuntary constraints for which he compensates with verbal bluster. Lucky suffers from general decrepitude and tends to remain fixed but trembles constantly.

LUCIEN RAIMBOURG (ESTRAGON), PIERRE LATOUR (VLADIMIR), ROGER BLIN (POZZO), THÉÂTRE DE BABYLONE, 1953

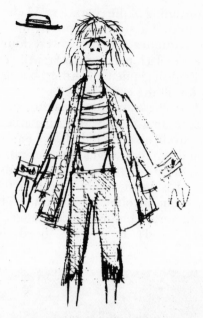

ROGER BLIN'S SKETCH FOR LUCKY

At an early stage Blin was thinking of playing Lucky himself. A notebook sketch by him shows Lucky dressed in livery with long dishevelled hair. In all but one production in which Beckett has been involved a white, fright wig has been part of Lucky's costume.

From the original performance Estragon had an oblong seat — rather than the 'low mound' of the text — later to become a rectangular stone which Beckett insisted upon in later productions. The tree in this production was simple but not the two-branched one Beckett envisioned in a sketch on the first page of his prompt script.[24]

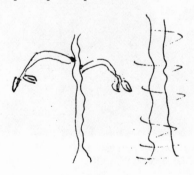

ROGER BLIN AS POZZO, THÉÂTRE DE BABYLONE, 1953

* When Beckett directed the San Quentin Drama Workshop in 1984 in preparation for their Australian tour billed as 'Beckett directs Beckett', he declared J. Pat Miller 'the best Lucky I've ever seen'. He has re-affirmed that assessment on several occasions. By the time Beckett observed him in the role, Miller had already developed in earlier rehearsals a presentation of Lucky in contradiction to that in the text. In place of 'long white hair' mentioned in the stage directions he had a completely smoothshaven head. After seeing a run-through of Miller in the role, Beckett accepted the change from his text without demur. Miller's innovation in costuming strengthened significantly the direction of Lucky as the prototype of inevitable human decline. In the scene just prior to Lucky's monologue obviously preparing for the theme of 'dwindling man', Pozzo points out Lucky's decline from the 'Grace, Beauty, perfect truth' for which he acquired him as a servant sixty years ago (F 33; G 22R). Pozzo vainly asserts his own immunity to the decline of age which has beset Lucky by ordering him to remove his hat to reveal the long white hair of an aged man and then removing his own hat to reveal his own head which is 'completely bald'. The comparison does not work as Pozzo intends: 'Compared to him I look like a young man, No?' No. Gray hair and baldness are both signs of aging. In spite of his bluster, Pozzo too 'shrinks and dwindles' In Miller's presentation, the universal prospect of decline is even more evident. Both men are bald. In at least one respect, Pozzo's physical condition is identical to Lucky's. If Lucky precedes him in other signs of decline, it is, as Vladimir asserts earlier of Lucky's physical infirmity, 'inevitable' and Pozzo too will reach the same state. The depiction of Lucky as the prototype of dwindling man had a reality in this production that neither Beckett nor Miller could have been aware of at the time. In another of the many tragic ironies with which Beckett's own personal experience seems unusually filled, Miller was already infected with AIDS, from which he died on Easter Sunday, 1985 shortly after the close of the Australian tour .

Pozzo's speech which intervenes between this exchange and Lucky's monologue can also be recognised as an earlier slightly less confused stage in the decline from 'perfect truth' to incoherence. The parallels between Pozzo's depiction of 'how it is on this bitch of an earth' and Lucky's treatment of the same subject are clear. Both begin like Genesis from a consideration of 'the firmament' to which they look for a concerned God. Pozzo begins by forcing his inattentive audience to look at the sky. In it they perceive nothing 'extraordinary' — no evidence of Divinity. Lucky begins by referring to an indifferent God who regards man from 'the heights of divine apathy', he moves on to a consideration of the intermittent calm of the blue sky sometimes inhabited by a 'personal God' who as the occasion dictates may or may not share the sufferings of humanity. This partial attentiveness is 'better than nothing'. Both speeches depict the universe in progressive states of decline. Pozzo describes the progression of the sky beginning in 'effulgence' growing 'ever a little paler' and finally ending in darkness. Lucky after describing the decline of man describes the earth already declined into darkness and

J. PAT MILLER AS LUCKY, SAN QUENTIN DRAMA WORKSHOP, 1984

cold to become the 'abode of stones'. The 'great cold' and 'great dark' overtakes first 'the air' [the subject of Pozzo's speech] and then 'the earth' [the focus of Lucky's speech]. Pozzo's speech does not yet centre upon 'dwindling man' as Lucky's does, or even refer directly to that topic. However, his delivery wavering between 'prosaic' and 'lyrical' exhibits momentary impairment. And his acknowledgement, 'My memory is defective', in apology for the faults of his speech confirms what the comparison with Lucky in the previous exchange had established: that he is already in the process of physical and mental decline. The verbal echo of Pozzo's single still cogent 'Qua sky' in Lucky's distorted stuttering fourfold 'quaquaquaqua' with no referent is an even more specific bit of evidence of the process of decline observable from Pozzo's oration to Lucky's. In the rehearsals Beckett concurred with J. Pat Miller's incorporation of gestures in Lucky's monologue similar to those of Pozzo in his to create a visual parallel between the two speeches. (This information from authors' observations and interviews with San Quentin cast during rehearsals at Riverside Studios, London, March 1984.)

Jean Martin's Account

In an interview in 1976 Jean Martin remembered Beckett's favourable reaction to his performance of Lucky, and Lucien Raimbourg in the role of Vladimir.

> When I played Lucky I was all white with red eyes. I put some red on my eyes because I remember my grandmother when she was very old and was always crying because she was very old, and the inside of the eye was always open, you know what I mean. And you can see the flesh too . . . I tried to fix my eyes like that . . . Also my mouth, it was red. You couldn't tell whether it was blood or flesh or what . . . I was always talking with half mouth closed and the other half open . . . drooling like this . . . I had just one or two teeth and talked that way, trembling all over. As if I couldn't control any of my movements at all.[25]

Beckett's Prompt Script

Even at the rehearsals of this first *Godot*, Beckett made textual changes and notations concerning the staging in his own prompt script — a copy of the *Éditions de Minuit*, first edition.[26] Numerous cuts in the dialogue tightened the action (See p. 154 below). Several additions and deletions strengthened or eliminated aspects of character as discussed above. The exchange of insults in Act II (F75, G48-R), which was indicated but not supplied in the original published text, was written out by Beckett in the margin.*

*	Andouille	Fool
	Tordu	Freak (literally twisted)
	Crétin	Cretin (etymologically Christian)
	Curé	Curate, priest (Irish slang for barman)
	Dégueulasse	Repugnant
	Micheton	Prostitute's client, 'manure'
	Ordure	Ordure
	Architecte	

According to Blin the culmination in 'architect' stemmed from an exchange of insults between taxi drivers which Blin had overheard in Brussels where post-war demolition and redevelopment was so unpopular that the term could be used as an insult. See p. 262 below for Elmar Tophoven's account of how the insults were similarly rendered in German. The terms which Beckett supplied in the text of the first English editions:

Moron!
Vermin!
Abortion!
Morpion! (crab louse)
Sewer-Rat!
Curate!
Cretin!
Crritic!

were as much determined by the repetition of sounds and cadences as by the meanings of the paired couplets as in the French original. But like the French and German which culminates in 'Ober . . . Forstinspektor' (Chief Forestry Inspector), it too culminates in a normally neutral occupation which has been transformed into a term of abuse.

JEAN MARTIN AS LUCKY, THÉÂTRE DE BABYLONE, 1953

There are a few marginal notes defining character or indicating important reactions. At the top of page one he wrote:

> Characteristic of Vladimir to establish at the outset: movement stopped abruptly by the effect of a thought.
> (PS, p. 11, Authors' translation)

When Estragon asks Pozzo for the bones, a note indicated greater emphasis on the bones by having Estragon act 'more embarrassed'. (PS p. 42).* At the end of the first act when Vladimir learns that Godot will not come today but surely tomorrow, Beckett wrote 'mark the blow more clearly' (*Marque le coup davantage*') (PS p. 85). The 'blow' is undoubtedly twofold. Not only will Godot not come today, but another day of anticipation and waiting is projected.

---

* At the outset Beckett was concerned with patterns of movement about the tree and downstage to Estragon's stone as evidenced by the drawing to the right of the sketch of the tree anticipating the detailed diagrams for movement in the *Regiebuch* of the Schiller production. Bones and stones are an important composite motif in Beckett's work. The added emphasis on the bones here in the first production shows Beckett's concern to establish indirectly an element of individualised personal suffering as a component of the universal situation depicted in *Godot*. In his unpublished short story *Echo's Bones*, and his early autobiographical poem sequence *Echo's Bones and Other Precipitates*, bones represent the symbolic white residue of painful memory of dead loves. In both these works as in Lucky's speech, bones are finally replaced by white stone which is the final less individual residue of memory as the past recedes. In *Godot* 'the bones belong to the carrier [Lucky] in theory'. And the final content of Lucky's 'think' is of the stones as he passes from the repeated refrain referring to the bones of 'the skull, the skull, the skull in Connemarra' to the 'shouted' ('howled' in both French and German versions) repetition of the words 'the stones', . . . 'the stones'. The pattern in Lucky's monologue was also that established by Beckett when he directed Jack MacGowran and Sian Phillips in *Eh Joe*. There Beckett also foregrounded the words 'the stones', . . . 'the stones' in a similar manner at the end of the play by having them repeated and spoken more intelligibly in an otherwise only partially intelligible text. In *Eh Joe* the stones are overtly connected with the memory of the details of the attempted suicide of Joe's dead love.

The bones which belong to the carrier in theory are taken in fact by Estragon and as in Beckett's earlier works they result in a wound. His assumption of the bones — which are for him 'like fishbones' that stick internally to cause pain — earns Estragon a kick from Lucky even as he tries to dry his tears. The kick produces a festering wound like the 'running sore' prominent on Lucky. These sores are like the running sore of a life haunted by dead love described in the poems 'Sanies I' and 'II' in *Echo's Bones* and the story 'Yellow' in *More Pricks than Kicks*. For Estragon, as for Beckett's autobiographical character Belacqua before him, life is the draining of a persistent if changing emotional wound. Estragon points this out in an allusive play upon Heraclitus' assertion that all things are flowing and his image of existence as a river which is constant but into which one cannot step twice. 'Everything oozes', he says. 'It is never the same pus from one second to the next.' (F60, G39L).

Many of the notes and additions are stage directions for a formalised style of acting similar to that he called for when he directed *Godot* in Berlin twenty-two years later. The principle of separation of speech and movement, a hallmark of his later direction, is instituted at the very beginning. The stage direction for Vladimir's first line, 'approaching with little steps', is marked out and replaced by specific indications of when Vladimir 'advances' between phrases throughout the text.

The technique of what he later called the 'approach by stages' is also evident in the addition of precise indications of the points at which Vladimir 'advances' and 'turns away' or remains immobile as he moves in on Estragon with each new piece of information about the two thieves (PS pps. 17-19).

There is nothing so structured as the '*Wartestelle*' ('moments of waiting') in which the characters freeze in the tableaux that he introduced in Berlin. However, vertical marks in the margin beside Vladimir's line 'How time flies when one has fun!' (PS p. 128), Pozzo's lines, 'Atlas, son of Jupiter!' (PS p. 50) and 'My memory is defective' (PS p. 62), all followed in Berlin by long freezes, at least indicate that these were points at which he desired a special action even in the first production. And in Lucky's speech he circled key words and drew lines leading to specific marginal stage directions for three listeners (PS p. 72-75). This is an anticipation of his even more detailed orchestration of the speech and the reaction to it in his Berlin production notebook (see p. 93 below). The addition of the stage direction '*petit tour*' ('little turn') when Estragon inspects the sky in answer to Pozzo's question 'What time is it?' (PS p. 145) shows that he was concerned from the first with the circular movements which pervaded the stage at the Schiller-Theater.

In at least one important instance when the performance deviated from the effect he wanted, he made his objections known to Blin in a letter.

> One thing troubles me, the pants of Estragon. I naturally asked Suzanne if they fell well, and she told me that he keeps them half on. He mustn't. He absolutely mustn't. It doesn't suit the circumstances. He really doesn't have the mind for that, then. He doesn't even realise that they're fallen. As for the laughter, which could greet their complete fall, there is nothing to object to in the great gift of this touching final tableau; it would be of the same order as the preceding scenes. The spirit of the play, to the extent to which it has one, is that nothing is more grotesque than the tragic. One must

express it up to the end, and especially at the end. I have a lot of other reasons why this action should not be tampered with but I will spare you them. Just be good enough to reestablish it as it is in the text and as we always foresaw it during rehearsals. And that the pants fall completely around the ankles. That might seem stupid to you but for me it's capital.[27]

The 1961 Odéon revival of *En attendant Godot*, in which Jean-Marie Serreau, Blin, and Beckett all shaped the direction, retained Jean Martin in the role of Lucky and Lucien Raimbourg as Vladimir. It also adhered to the severe simplicity of Blin's original production. There Beckett and Blin had agreed that it would be more effective to have the tree in Act II with just a few sparse leaves rather than 'covered with foliage' as described in the French text. For the Odéon production sculptor Giacomo Giacometti designed a tree which became a special emblem of the production. Martin recalled the mutual fascination it held for the author and the sculptor:

> This tree of Giacometti was so wonderful. It was made of plaster and thin wire and it was very flexible. Every night Sam and Giacometti came before the beginning of the play. Giacometti would change the position of a twig a little bit and then Sam would come later and he would change it. It was just as if it was the most important thing. And in fact it was a very important thing you know.
> (Interview, June 1976)

It was of this production that Beckett told Charles Marowitz, 'I tried to get at something of that stylized movement that is in the play.' (See p. xvi above).

Other *Godots*

From the earliest rehearsals Beckett had definite ideas about the staging of *Godot*. He told Alan Schneider who proposed to do the play in the round, 'I don't in my ignorance agree with the round and feel *Godot* needs a very closed box.'[28] Beckett elaborated later on this concept to Schneider saying he preferred a proscenium production because it retained the formal confrontation with the audience, allowed for clearly defined entrances and exits, and heightened the sense that the characters are 'all trapped'.[29]

Although he disavowed concern with success or failure at the public level, he did react to productions which he felt violated the spirit of the text. He was pleased with the overall economy

TREE BY GIACOMETTI, FOR *EN ATTENDANT GODOT*, ODÉON THÉÂTRE, 1961

and combination of the clownish and the tragic in Blin's original production. He reacted negatively to more elaborate and less balanced productions in which he took no part. He disagreed with Alan Simpson's view that the set by Sergio Gerstein for the original *Godot* at the Théâtre de Babylone was too amateurish. He preferred that set, in which the back and sides of the stage were simply draped in light green cloth, to Simpson's set for the Pike Theatre Dublin production in 1955 — which used backcloths daubed in black, green and brown to vaguely suggest an Irish bogland and gloomy sky.[30]

Peter Bull's account of the 1955 production, directed by Peter Hall at the Arts Theatre Club, indicates the disparity between the way Beckett envisioned *Godot* and the first London production.

> The author left his Montparnasse lair and visited us round about the hundredth performance and proved to be shy, modest and not frightfully helpful about the meaning of his play. We got the impression that he didn't care for the London production a great deal. He gave us a party, where we were all rather rude to him, but he took it in good part, and left for France telling us that he didn't think the pauses quite long enough. We told him that if they were any longer, not a customer would be left in the building.[31]

The actors did accept Beckett's suggestion that they adopt the technique of 'contrapuntal immobility', accompanying lines like 'let's go . . .' with complete stillness on the part of the speaker,[32] but the production was for Beckett still just 'wrong'.[33] Not only were the pauses too short, but Hall had filled the more important ones with a kind of heavenly music.[34] There was too much stress on farce without enough tragic balance.[35] And the set was also inappropriate. Beckett told Charles Marowitz, 'the text asks for a bare stage — except for this tree, and there the stage was so cluttered the actors could hardly move.'[36]

When the famous Czechoslovakian scenic artist Josef Svoboda created an elaborate baroque set implying bourgeois decadence for the Salzburg production in 1970, Beckett expressed his strong disapproval to his own designer, Matias.[37]

On several occasions Beckett has given active resistance to productions which departed from the basic simplicity and balance between comedy and tragedy established in Blin's original production. The subtitle 'a tragi-comedy in two acts' was a deliberate addition by Beckett for his translation of the first English editions. He refused to allow film rights to Bert

WAITING FOR GODOT LONDON PREMIÈRE, ARTS CLUB, 1955

Lahr who played Estragon in producer Michael Meyerberg's extension of the Miami premier billed as the 'laugh riot of two continents', because Lahr had introduced sight gags where the text explicitly indicated 'no gesture'. And when the Theatre Royal of Stratford advertised its 1962 revival in advance as 'the most uproarious comedy of the century', he tried unsuccessfully to block the performance before it opened.[38]

Deryk Mendel recalls being corrected by Beckett for eliminating Estragon's stone from the set when he directed *Warten auf Godot* in Berlin in 1965.

> We had started with a little stone large enough to sit on, but Estragon's discomfort was causing problems with the scene, so I decided to replace the stone with a stack of twigs as if the tree had been chopped. When Sam saw this heap of twigs and branches he explained that it had to be a stone to go along with the tree so that animal, mineral, and vegetable would all be onstage.[39]

Mendel's Berlin production also had a heaviness which ran counter to the spirit Beckett described to Alan Schneider as essential to his works. He called Schneider's attention to 'the

WARTEN AUF GODOT, SCHILLER-THEATER, 1965

need for laughter throughout the play', saying, 'All my plays should be played light and fast. I don't want to dwell upon their seriousness . . . my plays shouldn't be ponderous.'[40]

Mendel tells how he and Beckett attempted to restore comedy and simplicity to the production:

> When I was directing *Godot* in Berlin in 1965 I was having a terrible time. Beckett came over to help me. The whole production was unacceptable. There wasn't the slightest laugh. There wasn't any lightness. They were all doing A BECKETT PLAY in capital letters. Neither Sam nor I was satisfied. Sam said to 'relax above all'.
>
> When all the actors would cross the stage they would put all their weight on each foot and stop and look as if they were walking on stepping stones. Beckett said, 'No, no, you should walk right over'. As for the lines, Sam would never say, 'Say it like this', he would just say, 'A little quicker', or 'A little slower', or 'Lighter'.
>
> The actor playing Pozzo had his pipe, his bowler, his whip, his rope. It was just too complicated and Sam said there were far too many accessories anyway and that they were in the way. We didn't eliminate the accessories but we did try to minimise the prominence the actor had given them. He was overplaying his entrance. We had private rehearsals with him to try to keep him calm. To help him we would cut out gestures or cut them down and would say 'Well, don't do this, don't do that . . .' Sam would show what he meant by doing it for him. But we never did get it right. And finally Sam said, 'You won't do it my way. Just do it.'[41]

In the Royal Court Theatre revival of 1964, Anthony Page staged *Godot* with Beckett in attendance. Page incorporated many of Beckett's concepts of production. He relates that at eleven o'clock p.m. on Christmas Eve Beckett was still working with the actors on their lines 'in an extremely unassuming, creative, craftsman-like way'. Page found Beckett's active assistance a great advantage.

> He saved hours of floundering about. It is a very concentrated text and the phrases carry a great charge. His certainty about it wasn't a straitjacket but a great liberating force.
>
> *Godot* is very much about relationships between human beings. He said things like 'This moment should be an extremely tender moment of complete understanding between the two characters', and that at once made the line work. I don't think it's very easy in four weeks to co-direct, but I found it very exciting and a very good discipline for me to do it rather than procrastinating. If you ask him about a character

or a motivation, he'll just say 'I have no information about that'. But the thing that impressed me very much when he came to rehearsals was how absolutely definite he was about what a certain moment meant in terms of the relationship.[42]

John Fletcher saw this production and described it.

In the recent London Royal Court Theatre production, supervised by the author, the actors maintained during pauses the stance and attitude which they had adopted as the last words were being uttered: they did not fidget or budge, but stared before them, until the time allowed for the pause had elapsed. Not only was the tension palpable, but the play's characteristic rhythm was preserved: a burst of activity followed a still silence, in regular alternation.[43]

Fletcher's account again shows the continuity of Beckett's earlier ideas about staging *Godot* and the way it was staged when Beckett directed his own production of *Warten auf Godot* at the Schiller-Theater in Berlin in 1975.

CHAPTER THREE
Beckett's Godot

In 1975 after years of attending rehearsals and assisting in varying degrees of participation with productions of *Godot* officially directed by others, Beckett accepted the invitation by the Schiller-Theater to direct the play himself.* In this production the 'shape' inherent but not completely specified in Beckett's original text was realised and clarified. The *Regiebuch*, or Director's notebook, and related production documents which Beckett prepared to direct *Warten auf Godot* and the rehearsal diary of his assistant, Walter Asmus, provide an unusually detailed indication of how Beckett sees *Godot*.

THE SCHILLER-THEATER *REGIEBUCH*

The hardbound red *Regiebuch* which Beckett prepared for the Schiller production was preceded by notations in two paperback Suhrkamp editions of *Warten auf Godot*, and an earlier small green notebook. The *Regiebuch* is essentially a fair copy of the material in the green notebook with additional notes, made after rehearsals began, added in red ink and ballpoint pen. It is written in English in black ink in Beckett's 'public' hand.† According to his usual practice, the right-hand pages contain his primary analysis or directions, while the facing left-hand pages are reserved for additions, diagrams and other

---

* Although *Godot* was Beckett's first play, this was not his first Schiller-Theater direction. He had assumed the title of Director listed on the programme for the first time ever with the 1967 *Endspiel* and he had directed *Das letzte Band (Krapp's Last Tape)* in 1969 and *Glückliche Tage (Happy Days)* in 1971. These productions are treated at length in other chapters.

† Beckett's normal handwriting, difficult to read even by his regular correspondents, is tiny and individual, but his 'public hand' as evidenced by the illustrations in this volume are clear, large and careful, obviously intended to be legible by colleagues. These documents are in the Beckett Archives of Reading University Library designated by Reading as:

Regiebuch	RUL MS 1396/4/4
Suhrkamp *Warten auf Godot* 1	RUL MS 1481/1
Suhrkamp *Warten auf Godot* 2	RUL MS 1481/2
Green notebook	RU MS 1396/4/3

Parenthetical references below use R to refer to the Regiebuch and GN to refer to the Green Notebook.

secondary elucidating material. The small printed squares of the notebook allowed Beckett to locate accurately points onstage in the diagrams.

A title page, on page 36, and diagrams on pages 30, 31 and 37, were written in with felt pen to facilitate reproduction of pages selected by Beckett for the public exhibition in the foyer of the Schiller-Theater and in the programme.

This *Regiebuch* is Beckett's attempt to give form to a play which he considered undisciplined. He told his production assistant, Walter D. Asmus, that the play was 'a mess'. On the next to last page of the preliminary green notebook, he wrote in German, '*Der Konfusion Gestalt geben*' ('To give form to the confusion').

Beckett's first concern in the *Regiebuch* is with the larger structure of the play. The notebook opens with a division of the play into eleven sections:

A-1: (R2-5)	opening to 'People are bloody ignorant apes.'	(F9-13, G7L-9R)
A-2: (R6-9)	Estragon's inspection ('Rises painfully...') to entry of Pozzo and Lucky.	(F13-21, G9R-15L)
A-3: (R10-15)	The entrance of Pozzo and Lucky until Pozzo sits.	(F21-24, G15L-17L)
A-4: (R16-21)	From Pozzo sitting down to Pozzo: 'My memory is defective'.	(F24-38, G17L-25R)
A-5: (R22-27)	Estragon: 'In the meantime nothing happens.' to the exit of Pozzo and Lucky.	(F38-48, G26L-31R)
A-6: (R28-31)	Exit of Pozzo and Lucky to end of Act I.	(F48-54, G31R-35R)
B-1: (R32-33)	Opening to Vladimir: 'Ah! Que voulez-vous. Exactly.'	(F57-65, G37L-42L)
B-2: (R34-41)	Estragon: 'That wasn't a bad little canter.' to the entry of Pozzo and Lucky.	(F65-77, G42L-49R)
B-3: (R42-45)	Entry of Pozzo and Lucky to Vladimir: 'We are men.'	(F77-82, G49R-53L)
B-4: (R46-49)	Estragon: 'Sweet mother earth!' to exit of Pozzo and Lucky.	(F82-89, G53L-57R)
B-5: (R50-53)	Exit of Pozzo and Lucky to the end of Act II.	(F89-94, G57R-60R)

(English text of lines in German and page references to Faber and Grove editions supplied by authors. G7L designates left side of opening 7 of Grove edition which has only one page number per opening. References to pages in the *Regiebuch*, 'R2-5' etc., are Beckett's.)

These divisions are partly for designating convenient rehearsal segments, but they are also a guide to the structure of the play and the parallels between the two acts. A-1 is exposition. It establishes that there is an appointment with Godot and that until he arrives there is 'nothing to be done'. It associates Estragon with boots and stone, Vladimir with hat and tree, and introduces the important themes of suicide and the 'two thieves'. In A-2 the waiting assumes a more active form: both Estragon and Vladimir move about the stage to inspect the scene; they eat, piss, walk, and actually consider suicide instead of just talking about it. A-3 introduces the second couple, Pozzo and Lucky, establishing them as master and slave. A-4 is Pozzo's discourse as he attempts to impress Vladimir and Estragon. A-5 focuses on Lucky: his dance and 'think'. A-6 is the exchange with the boy and the fall of night.

In Act II, B-1 like A-1 defines the situation. Vladimir and Estragon question the time and place of their appointment with Godot and go through their first spontaneous caper to pass the time. B-2 — which opens with Estragon's 'What shall we do now?' — parallels A-2 in presenting assorted activities to pass the time: Estragon's radish meal, Vladimir and Estragon's promenades, the duel of insults, their playing of Pozzo and Lucky, their calisthenics, and the frantic circulation of the hat routine. Act II contains no parallel to A-3: the introduction of Pozzo and Lucky. B-3 is rather a reversal of A-4: Pozzo, who dominated Vladimir and Estragon with his discourse, is now on the ground crying for help, and it is Vladimir who dominates the scene with his rhetoric. In B-4 the physical action is centred on the rise of all four characters from their fallen state as Pozzo and Lucky prepare for their exit. As in A-5, the action of B-4 focuses on Lucky, a hapless victim, kicked by Estragon to rouse him to re-assume his burden. And Lucky is now more impaired than in the earlier scene. In this section there is only a reference to his former ability to dance and speak, and when Vladimir asks for him to sing, Pozzo announces that he is dumb.

In the directions in the *Regiebuch*, Beckett began by changing the opening and closing sections of both acts to create closer parallels and significant variants, just as he had done when he directed *Endspiel* at the Schiller-Theater eight years earlier. Both acts now open with tableaux. Vladimir no longer enters from offstage as in the published text. The opening directions in the *Regiebuch* read:

> E. on stone, still, bowed. Resumption of boot breaks spell. (W1)* (*Regiebuch* p. 3)

And a diagram facing page 1 shows Vladimir upstage left '½ in shadow'. The directions for the opening of Act II read:

> E. edge of shadow, bowed. V. back to audience, head raised, intent. (R. 33)

The spell is broken this time by Vladimir. Estragon's 'listening' is in contrast to Vladimir's 'looking'.

At the close of Act I Vladimir and Estragon cross upstage to assume briefly a tableau by the tree (as they do in the printed text); Estragon is stage right of the tree and Vladimir is stage left, but in the scene as indicated in the *Regiebuch* they cross back downstage to assume a new tableau sitting on Estragon's stone. The description on page 31 reads:

> Stone too short for 2. E. not moving up. V. half on half off . . . (R. 31)

Act II closes as it does in the published text with the couple again framing Vladimir's tree. Together, the closing tableau of Act I at the stone and that of Act II at the tree create a parallel with the opening of the play in which Vladimir is at the tree and Estragon at the stone. There is also a pattern of parallel and variation in the postures of Vladimir and Estragon in these opening and closing scenes. Originally, the *Regiebuch* notations for the final tableau in Act II called for Vladimir to be looking up and Estragon to be looking down as they were at the start of both acts and at the end of Act I. These directions were marked through in red so that at the end of the play Estragon and Vladimir stand together both looking forward. The end and the beginning are alike but there is also a perceptible difference.

After outlining the structure, Beckett turned to the details of the stage action. In 1962 he had told Jean Reavey that with *Godot* and partially with *Fin de partie* he had just written dialogue without seeing the stage movement in strict detail. In the later plays he had been aware of every movement of the actors even

---

* W.1. is Beckett's designation of *Warterstelle 1* (first waiting point). In speaking of these 'points' in English, he spoke of 'moments of stillness'. They are carefully chosen points in the text where all motion is suspended for special emphasis.

before he wrote the dialogue, and he knew which direction his actors would face before they spoke because what he made them say depended upon it. Sometimes he even said one character's lines aloud while making the movement of another.[1] The bulk of the *Regiebuch* — (the first 53 pages) — is devoted to providing detailed stage directions for the co-ordination of lines and movements in the parallel divisions of the play. In the green notebook Beckett broke the action down further into 109 units which might be called 109 ways of waiting. (See p. 92)

While Beckett seems to have made no systematic attempt to integrate these divisions with the directions in the *Regiebuch*, much of his commentary there does reflect the division of the play into these smaller segments. For nearly all of the 109 units, the notes on the right-hand pages of the *Regiebuch* designate the position of the actors on stage, the directions they face, the directions in which they move, and the cues for each movement or gesture they make. The control of the action is so precise that at places where ad-libbing of movement seemed appropriate it is indicated in the directions.

VISUAL ELEMENTS

Underneath the designation of the larger divisions of the play Beckett made an index to fifteen items treated under separate headings in the second half of the *Regiebuch*. The order (which Beckett changed when he copied out these sections from the green notebook) shows his preoccupation with giving the play a visual form. Beginning with Lucky, who has only one set piece of dialogue, the first six headings deal with each of the characters in turn, concentrating on the physical objects and postures associated with each of them.

Lucky's Moves

The first heading is 'Lucky's moves A-3'. It begins with a consideration of his 'Load: in R hand bag and stool, in L hand basket, over L arm horizontal coat' (R. 55). The 'moves' it details are almost exclusively an account of how Lucky sets down and reassumes objects that burden him as he obeys the commands of Pozzo. He is 'never a moment free of load except 1) to dance 2) to think 3) when fallen. Does not resume load after 2nd dance only because forbidden (A-5 23)' (R. 54).

① opening with ~~voice~~ / Eiffel Tower / open play /
V's hat / E's boot / 2 thieves
E inspects / doubts concerning place. time.

② appointment / E sits, sleeps / V inspects, wakes
E / V pisses off / Decide not to hang themselves / little turn / False alarm / E's
carrot / arrival of P/L

③,4,5 Meeting with P / P sits, eats / Inspection
of L / E & the bones / V scandalized /
P false depart / tobacco speech / P sits
again / Explanation why L does not put
down bags / L weeps / Kicks E / tears of
the world / Knuck / V reproaches ... P
P's breakdown / V reproaches L / P's recovery /
can't find pipe / charming evening / V pisses
off / V's anger / Pan steps / E helps P to sit /
P's sunset speech / Praised by V & E / L
dances / V puts L's hat on L's head / L thinks /
L downed / held up by V - E / P collects
bags / exeunt P/L

⑥ V questions P/L identity / arrival of
boy / E dozes off / dialogue V / Boy / Exit
boy / Moon rises V & E at tree ~~fork stone~~

Song / reproached by E / V - E ~~happy~~ /
Tree with leaves / E's bad memory / his angry
refusal to recognise place / denial of Breisgau /
Voices dialogue / thoughts dialogue / tree with
leaves / E denies place / E's legs & marks of
L's boot / E's ~~boots~~ not his / E tired / refuses
impossible radish / tries - keeps on boots / sits /
Lullaby / Nightmare / E's outburst / L's hat /
game with hats / V plays L / E tries to escape /
Watch out / Insults & reconciliation / Exercises /
arrival of P/L
Collapse of P/L / V & E conspire / little turn /
All born mad / V joins heap / E do. / P
crawls away / V - E up / help P up /
reeling trio / E time of day / E kicks
P, sits, dozes / L up / P's time speech /
P/L exeunt / E dozes off again / Boy
V wakes E / arrives / dial. V / boy / moon rises /
E wakes / hanging / end by tree

UNITS OF ACTION, GREEN NOTEBOOK, P. 97

Lucky's Think

The second heading, 'Lucky's think', lays down the structure, points of stress and 'main shocks' of the speech (See p. 94). It is an even more detailed organisation of mime responses to elucidate Lucky's monologue than similar stage directions included in the 1971 Faber and Grove texts.

Even this attention to verbal aspects is to facilitate organisation of the physical reactions of the three other characters which help to point out the form and meaning of Lucky's confused monologue. Following the identification of the five structural divisions of the speech is a list of the reactions at each division. Each of the sections evokes a reaction which portrays the condition discussed. While Lucky talks of 'an indifferent Heaven' in section 1, Pozzo is notably inattentive. As Lucky introduces the topic of 'dwindling man' in section 2, new 'shocks' make it more evident that his mental powers have diminished to the point of incomprehensibility. Vladimir and Estragon, who up to this point have concentrated on Lucky's speech, grow restive. By the time Lucky is discussing how man 'dwindles and shrinks' physically in 3, Vladimir gets up and moves away, and Pozzo puts his fingers in his ears and bows his head forward (R. 56). In section 4 in which Lucky discusses 'earth abode of stones', Estragon and Vladimir make co-ordinated exits and entrances which leave Lucky alone in the landscape and highlight his references to the deeps and stones. Estragon leaves the second time that Lucky repeats 'what is more' and returns when he mentions the 'great deeps'. Vladimir then exits at Lucky's fourth 'what is more'. He returns at Lucky's fourth repetition of the line 'I resume'. Estragon makes his second exit on this same line ('I resume') simultaneous with Vladimir's re-entry. Vladimir's second exit then comes with the fifth 'I repeat'. While they are both offstage Pozzo covers his head with his coat completing Lucky's isolation. Vladimir and Estragon re-enter together on the second repetition of 'skull in Connemara'. Shortly thereafter Pozzo puts the stool over his head. The eight repetitions of 'skull' are the 'last straw', and on the words 'Cunard Cunard' Estragon and Vladimir attack Lucky who finishes the 'cadenza' of his monologue, shouting from the ground.

In a change from the original plan, Pozzo does not join in the attack. His only response to Lucky's effort to please him is his steady progression of efforts to avoid hearing the speech.

L's Think   57

I

Opening — Willkommen ist
aber greifen wir nicht vor ⟧ Indifferent heaven

"Better than nothing — not so fast"

2

u. andererseits — Im Begriff
ist abzumagern

"What is more — wastes and pines"   ⟧ Dwindling man

3

u. zugleich parallel — die
Dinge sind so

"Simultaneously — facts are there"

4

u. wenn man andererseits — die
Dinge sind so man weiss nicht warum

"And considering — the facts are there but"   Earth abode of stones
                                                     ↲ cadenza

5

ich wiederhole zum folgenden   New elements Kopf (8) -
                                            Last straw - Tränen (1)
"I resume"   Skull (8)
                                                     Tears (1)

I

P attentive back ← forth to L ← V/E less to performance
than to their reactions
V/E concentrated in spite of earlier shock of Kwakwakwakwak
← kwakwa

2

Growing restiveness of V/E beginning with kakakaka -
popopopo till hope of better things with wird
deutlich dass der Mensch revives some attention.
P increasingly unhappy.

"It is established"

3

                                                          in der Luft
V/E some interest in Sportsarten till Hockey ~~in Lande~~
too much. audible protestations. On say Wiederhole 3
V↗. P fingers in ears bowed forward.

"physical culture till Hockey in the Air"

LUCKY'S THINK FROM *REGIEBUCH* PP. 57-61

Noch schlimmer ist 2   ⁴

" " ^ 4

"what is more"

grossen Tiefen

"great deeps"

Wiederhole 4

' " "

" 5

"I resume"

P increasingly huddled

E exit ←

V " →

behind L

E reappears

things no better

E reexit

V reappears

things no better

V reexit

On 18 [E exit schlimmer 2
       " enter Tiefen
       " exit wiederhole 4
       " enter Kopf 1] off 100

[words]

" 40 / Kopf in / Edinburg 2

"what is more" 2
"Deeps"
"I resume" 4
"Skull"

"Skull in Conemara" 2
[added in red]

On 16 [V exit schlimmer 4
       " enter Wiederhole 4
       " exit   " 5
       " enter Kopf 1] " 100

" 30 / Kopf in / Edinburg 2

V off 1 (schlimmer ist 4) – P gives up, turns away, fingers in ears

der Äther – Coat over head

der Bart – Stool " "

"what is more"
"The Air"
"The Beard"

[added in red]

der Kopf 1

Conard conard

⁵

V/E enter. Whistles – boos from
E, V P to have him put a stop to it
(all close in to down L
but P

["Not P" added in red]

STRESS
all research tandems

Poinçon - Waltmann 2
Testa - Conard 4
Fartov - Belcher 1
Steinweg - Petermann 2

die Hölle an den Himmel
aber greifen wir nicht vor 3
festgestellt 2
es ebenso klar erscheint
wird deutlich das der Mensch
abzumagern
kleiner zu werden
abzumagern einzulangen
die Dinge sind so 2
gut für die steine 3

"Hell to Heaven"
"But not so fast" 3
"Established" 2
"is established"
"wastes and pines"
"shrinks and dwindles"
"the facts are there" 2
"Abode of stones" 3

Main shocks

Kwa kwa kwa kwa
kwa kwa
a ka ka ka ka kademie
anthropopophometrie
gestellt ter
was folgt ter
Testu v. Conard 3 - 4
Hockey zu Land
Tennis auf Eis
ich wiederhole 3

ohne Schuhe in Oldenburg
Noch schlimmer 2
"   "   4
ich wiederhole 4
"   "   5
"   "   8

in der Luft

V starts to leave

Exit E
"   V
Reexit E
"   V
last straw

"Qua, qua, qua, qua"
"Ac ca ca ca ca de mie"
"Anthropometrie"
"Established"
"As a result"
"Testu and Coward" 3-4
"Hockey in the air"
"Tennis on ice"
"I resume" 3 [crossed through]
"stockinged feet in Conemara" [added in red]
"more grave" 2
"I resume" 4

96

Estragon's Feet

After Lucky's speech Beckett turned next to the two physical aspects which characterise Estragon. At the section 'E's feet' Beckett notes the times he holds out his feet, puts on his boots, exchanges kicks with Lucky, and walks in pain. (See p. 127)

Estragon's Sleep

The next section, 'E sleeps, drowses on stone', opens with the note, 'establishes posture' and goes on to give the times he assumes that posture, and makes two references to sleep when he is not on the stone. Three of the entries establish the immediate connection in the action between Estragon's sleep as relief from discomfort of his feet and waking as a return to it. A tabulation, however, shows that sleep affords only slightly better odds for happiness than the waking world: not counting his brief sleep on the ground, Estragon has three sleeps and two drowses which lead to 'two dreams of happiness and one nightmare of falling from a height'. (Two in five at best.)

Pozzo's Whip

Physical characterisation of Pozzo follows that of Lucky and Estragon. 'Whip' is the fifth section — a running account of its whereabouts and use in A-3 to A-5 and in B-3.

Vladimir's Tree

The survey of characters is completed by a section dealing with the tree associated with Vladimir: 'V/E and tree'. The contrast between their observation of the tree clearly establishes its connection with Vladimir as opposed to Estragon. In A-2 Estragon doubts that it is the 'right tree or one at all' (R. 71), while Vladimir is more in awe, insisting that if they were there before, Estragon 'could not have forgotten such a tree' (R. 71). At A-5 the tree is 'lost sight of in E's denial of place'.

Inspection of Place

The next item is 'Inspection place' — the first of a group of large structured stage movements which work as visual leitmotivs in the play. The four inspections of place are clockwise circuits around the perimeter of the stage exploring the physical possibilities confronting Vladimir and Estragon: the stone from which inspection begins, the offstage right area from which they thought they heard Godot arriving, the area offstage left from

INSPECTION PLACE

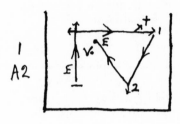

1
A2

1. *Lauschiges Plätzchen*
   "Charming spot"
2. *Heitere aussichten* ..
   Komm wir gehen
   "Inspiring prospects"
   "Let's go!"

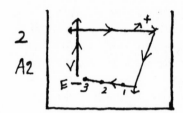

2
A2

1. Gogo
2. "
3. "

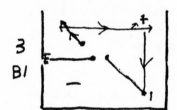

3
B1

1. Boots.
   Ein Hund kam ..
   "A dog came in . . ."

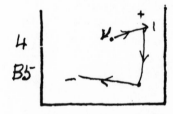

4
B5

1. Looks after receding P/L

Not *properly inspection*

INSPECTION PLACE, *REGIEBUCH*, P. 73

which Pozzo and Lucky enter and the boy enters and exits, and the inaccessible 'void' in the auditorium (See R73 p. 98). The place is the same for Vladimir as it is for Estragon in their two parallel inspections in A-2. And it does not change with time. When Vladimir makes his second inspection in a mime prologue before dialogue begins in Act II, the elements are as before — a few leaves are the only sign of change. And in B-5 when Vladimir makes a final shorter version of the circuit, the echo of the previous movements suggests that the limits of the physical situation defined early in the play also prevail at the end. But Vladimir's final assessment is 'not properly inspection' but a 'Simplified version' (GN 104).He is by the end of the play inured to the situation. He only looks in the direction in which Pozzo and Lucky have departed; he does not pause to look at the tree; and he does not even turn his attention to the opposite wing from which they at first thought they heard the approach of Godot.

Divided Circles: Arcs and Chords

In the green notebook, 'Inspection place' was listed a second time and bracketed together with two other large patterns of movement, 'Little turns' and 'Approach by stages', under the heading 'RECURRENCES' in capital letters. These recurrent patterns are a major structural device of Beckett's *Godot*.

The two 'clockwise' movements of the section headed 'Little turns' are part of a series of related circular and linear approaches to the tree and the stone. They are examples of the kind of 'subliminal stage imagery' which Beckett described to Michael Haerdter when directing *Endspiel* at the Schiller-Theater eight years earlier. A coordinated set of arcs and chords forming halves of a divided circle suggest an existence which is endlessly repetitious. It also suggests the duality in contrasting, complementary but unintegrated parts of a greater whole.

The red *Regiebuch* contains no single heading drawing the stage imagery together, but the structure of the organised configuration of arcs and chords forming two halves of a circle is evident in numerous diagrams, cross-references, and notes. It is illustrated most graphically on pages, 30, 31 and 36 of the *Regiebuch* which Beckett chose for reproduction in the Schiller-Theater programme.

At six points in the play, three times in each act, Vladimir and Estragon take 'walks' that culminate in (or in the first instance, lead away from) tableaux where they wait by the tree or the stone. In Act I, two patterns of movement to and from the tree are followed by one ending at the stone. In Act II, two patterns leading to the stone are followed by one leading to the tree. Together the movements of Act I trace one half of a circle, those of Act II the other half. In Act I the first two movements are curvilinear and the third rectilinear. In Act II the first two movements are rectilinear and the third curvilinear. (See pp. 101-102)

The pattern of images is begun with the first 'little turn' in A-2 (R 8). It begins with Vladimir's line 'Nothing very definite' (F 18, G 13L) an explanation of what they have requested in their 'supplication' to Godot. He takes Estragon's arm and leads him away from the first tableau 'framing the tree'. They move in a large counter-clockwise semicircle past the stone, to a position opposite it downstage left. In A-6 near the end of Act I Vladimir and Estragon approach the tree for a second tableau (See diagram R 30, 31). Following Estragon's 'Pity we haven't got a bit of rope', (F 53, G 35L) they traverse the same semicircular path they had taken away from the tree in A-2, but this time in a clockwise direction towards it. Their walk ends when they separate on Estragon's line, 'How long have we been together all the time now?' as Estragon 'stops at his place', stage right of the tree and Vladimir 'stumbles on to his stage left of it'. (In both of these first two walks, Vladimir initiates the action by taking the more passive Estragon by the arm and leading him.)

Having traced the pattern of an arc in their movements together to and from the tree, Vladimir and Estragon complete the figure of a closed half-circle by tracing the chord in separate movements in straight lines back downstage to the stone for the final tableau of Act I. This action begins with Estragon's final 'wait' in response to Vladimir's 'Come on'. Originally their approach to the stone had a distinct four-part structure. Estragon began moving away from Vladimir halfway to the stone when he stopped, saying 'I wonder if we wouldn't have been better off alone'. Vladimir then moved halfway down to follow him, then Estragon moved the other half of the way to sit on the stone after the line 'We weren't made for the same road.' Finally, Vladimir moved silently the last half of the way to join him and sat on the stone beside him. In rehearsal, Vladimir's stop midway was eliminated so that he reaches the stone after Estragon in one move while Estragon reaches it in two movements. This created a link with the final approach to the

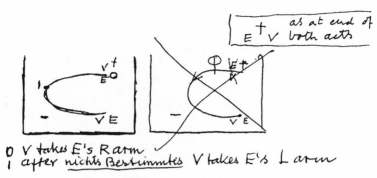

E † V as at end of both acts

O V takes E's R arm

1 after *nichts Bestimmtes* V takes E's L arm

Nothing very definite
(Descent from the tree A2 *Regiebuch* p. 8)

K. D. Friedrich

4/3
100/3

A Stoh for *Schade* ..
B " " *Hilf mir* ..
C " " *Wie lange*

} Still linked

With *Wie lange* E pulls his hand/arm free,
V stumbles on to D. With final *Komm*
V takes E's hand/arm again, E pulls
himself free & starts for stone.

(Approach to the tree A6 *Regiebuch* p. 30)

A Pity
B Help me
C How long

Komm / V takes E's left hand or arm
as far walks A 2 h , ~~B2 h~~ B2 h. , B3 h

Stone too short for 2.
E not moving up V
half on half off.
cf. lullaby B2 h.

A *Warte*
B *ich frage mich*
C *Wir waren* ~ Sits
D *Mich friert*
E ~~Silent~~
F " & Sits
~~G with E~~
~~DF " BC~~

D to F without vis after E sits

A wait
B I sometimes wonder
C we weren't made for the same road
D I'm cold
(Approach to the stone A6 *Regiebuch* p. 31)

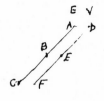

1 A - B Für mich -- passiert
2 B. Du hast -- gehört
3 D. Du hast -- mich
4 B Du hat -- singt
5 D - E. Man ist -- Launen.
6 E Ich fühl -- mal.
7 B - C. Siehst du -- da bin
8 E - F Du fehltest -- Zufrieden!
9 F Ist das nicht merkwürdig etc

1. A - B "For me it's over and done with
2.   B I heard you singing
3.   D That's right I remember
4.   B That finished me, . . . he sings
5. D - E One is not master of one's moods
6.   E All day I've felt in great form
7. B - C You see you piss better when I'm not there
8. E - F I missed you . . . I was happy
9.   F Isn't that a queer thing

(Approach to the stone B1 *Regiebuch* p. 32)

Each ⟶ a little nearer P/L

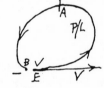

+

Wir wollen unsere Zeit
V talking E's Larm

"Let us not waste our time"

A Stop for Der Ruf .. ganze Menscheit. Photo
B Was sagst du . E may pull his arm free
here (unspoken hör auf ich bin müde) ⌐ sit,
rising for Was haben sie bloss , and V on ⟶ al
with Sicher ist

A "To all mankind . . . those cries"
B "What do you say?"
(unspoken "Leave off I'm tired")
rising for "What's the matter with you all?"
with "All I know"
("Second little turn" B3 *Regiebuch* p. 43)

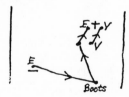

(Approach to tree B5 *Regiebuch* p. 50)

tree at the end of the play. There Vladimir reaches the tree first in one move and Estragon joins him in two moves.

The close juxtaposition in A-6 of these two approaches — one curved and one in a straight line — established visually the contrast implied by the dialogue: Vladimir tends towards the tree in a curved path drawing a resisting Estragon with him; Estragon tends towards the stone in a straight line moving away from Vladimir who follows him. Like arc and chord in a geometry exercise, these two contrasting patterns of movement connect the cardinal points of tree and stone and define the boundaries of a closed, circular universe and exhibit the differing tendencies of Vladimir and Estragon.

Although this world is circular and repetitious, it is also divided and incomplete. The configuration traced by the 'walks' in Act I is only a half-circle. The other half is not provided until the second act. But even in the half-circle apparent in Act I the contrast of movements and the shape itself express graphically the fact that Vladimir and Estragon are separate, opposed, and yet complementary.

The second half-circle is delineated in Act II by a pattern of walks which is the reverse of the pattern in Act I. In Act II the chord precedes the arc. Very near the beginning, following their reunion and brief embrace, Vladimir and Estragon approach the stone in a movement 'echoing the walk ending A-6'. (See diagram R32) The dialogue is again of separation and incompatibility.*

The arc is not supplied until B-3 by the second 'little turn'. Vladimir draws Estragon with him like a portable audience and arm-in-arm they promenade around Pozzo and Lucky who are lying in a cruciform pattern on the ground. (GN 58). (See diagram p. 115) The movement has two parts. First they make a counter-clockwise semicircle upstage towards the tree, pass it, and stop upstage centre for Vladimir's 'To all mankind these cries of help are addressed . . . All mankind is us.' With this line the second half-circle, corresponding to the configuration at the end of Act I is complete.

* 1. A - B For me its over and done with
  2.   B I heard you singing
  3.   D That's right I remember
  4.   B That finished me, I said to myself. He's all alone, he thinks I'm gone forever and he sings.
  5. D - E One is not master of one's moods
  6.   E All day I've felt in good form
  7. B - C You see you piss better when I'm not there
  8. E - F I missed you . . . and at the same time I was happy
  9.   F Isn't that a queer thing

The second part of this 'little turn' is another semicircle. Estragon and Vladimir continue downstage here to the stone. Estragon pulls free just before reaching it with an 'unspoken "Leave off. I'm tired",' (R. 43) and sits. Vladimir continues on alone in a circle past the stone and then provides the chord by moving in a straight line to stage left near the place he and Estragon had reached at the end of the first 'little turn' in Act I. This part of the 'walk' is a recapitulation of the first half of the circle presented in Act I with the variation of Estragon's stop at the stone. The two parts of the second 'little turn' thus present in one large action both halves of the complete circle. In the first there is a reluctant union; the second is marked by separation.

The third approach of Act II brings Vladimir and Estragon to the tree again for the final tableau concluding the play. In a change from the text, Vladimir, rather than Estragon, again initiates the final movement towards the tree. Estragon approaches Vladimir from downstage left, stops beside him and Vladimir then draws him upstage in a straight line. Vladimir moves first to his place stage left of the tree, and Estragon completes the pattern by moving to his place stage right of it. The pattern of the movements echoes the approach to the stone at the conclusion of Act I: Estragon reaching his goal in two stages, Vladimir in one. But this time Vladimir arrives first at the tree just as Estragon had arrived first at the stone. The linear form is that earlier associated with the approach to the stone; and it is Vladimir who moves away from Estragon. This tableau itself, however, is like the first one near the beginning of the play. The change in the approach only serves to highlight by contrast the essentially unchanging quality in their predicament of waiting. This final straight ascent also balances the initial curved descent in A-2.

The movements of the moon and the boy in each act echo the arcs and chords laid out in the approaches to the stone and tree and integrate them structurally in the play. A change in the exits of the boy at the end of each act introduced two striking instances of the form, this time displayed vertically against the backdrop. In both acts instead of turning to run offstage as in the text, the boy moves backward from Vladimir in two stages and then finally 'calmly backward off' — the straight line of a chord. The moon rises simultaneously in a perfect arc and comes to a stop as the boy leaves the stage, disappearing into

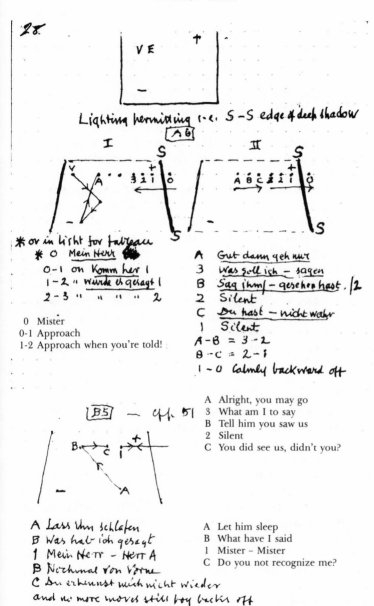

28

Lighting herniating i.e. S-S edge of deep shadow

A B

I   S   II   S

* or in light for tableau
* O Mein Herr
  0-1 on Komm her!
  1-2 " wurde ch gesagt!
  2-3 "   "   "   2

  0 Mister
  0-1 Approach
  1-2 Approach when you're told!

A Gut dann geh nur
3 was soll ich – sagen
B Sag ihm – gesehen hast . /2
2 Silent
C Du hast – nicht wahr
1 Silent
A-B = 3-2
B-C = 2-1
1-0 Calmly backward off

B5 — off 51

A Alright, you may go
3 What am I to say
B Tell him you saw us
2 Silent
C You did see us, didn't you?

A Lass ihn schlafen
B Was hab ich gesagt
1 Mein Herr – Herr A
B Nochmal von Vorne
C Du erkennst mich nicht wieder
and no more moves still boy backs off

A Let him sleep
B What have I said
1 Mister – Mister
C Do you not recognize me?

ENTRANCE AND EXIT OF BOY *REGIEBUCH*, P. 28

'the edge of deep shadow' to be created by lighting (R. 28).*

Together, the exits present a complex of images connecting the conclusion of each act with the themes of completion and incompletion, unity and separation presented in the approaches. The nearly perfect symmetry of the dialogue and action in the two scenes with the boy is itself a kind of closure. At its second occurrence it will signal for the audience the approaching end of an act and of the play. But the repetition of the action suggests a kind of endless circulation. The rising full moon is a perfect circle bringing the day to a close. The boy's straight line leads off to an indeterminate, unseen point, infinity perhaps. The arc and the chord present both parts of a recognisable figure but that figure is again only half of a larger one. And the simultaneous but separate appearance of arc and chord in sequence on one line makes it evident that they don't coincide — even the half-circle is open and incomplete. The responses of Vladimir and Estragon illustrate both union and separation. In Act I Vladimir and Estragon both look as the moon rises, but Estragon looks at Vladimir while Vladimir looks at the moon; in Act II Vladimir looks at the moon but Estragon sleeps. In Act I Vladimir exclaims, 'At last,' as the moon appears and all action stops for a marked silence. His expression of fulfilled expectation is absent in Act II and the action does not stop.

Empty Crosses

A second set of large stage movements in Act II establishes the stage imagery of three crosses. Already in the original version of the play just after the introduction of the theme of the two thieves very early in Act I (F13, G9R) the directions for Estragon's actions clearly indicate a cruciform pattern followed by a salient reference to the tree. The scene in A-2 parallels and adumbrates the scene in B-2 in which Vladimir and Estragon first gaze into the wings and then contemplate the auditorium and disparage the audience. Following the line 'People are bloody ignorant apes' (for believing that one of the thieves was saved) Estragon 'rises painfully', limps to 'extreme left', gazes into the wing, goes to 'extreme right' and gazes into the other wing, then 'moves to centre' with back to audience, turns and 'advances to front'. There he delivers his first 'Let's go' which is

---

* For a description of the 'moon machine' by which the scenic effect of a perfect arc was achieved see p. 151 below.

met with Vladimir's first announcement that they are 'waiting for Godot' whom they were to meet 'by the tree'.

Beckett's directions for A-2 in the *Regiebuch* (R p. 6 and 7) replace Estragon's cruciform movement with his first 'Inspection of Place'. The visual imagery of the cross was thus eliminated from Act I and concentrated in Act II.

Two crosses, each with an empty centre, are indicated in the *Regiebuch* directions for B-2. On page 40 Beckett diagrammed the movements for the scene in which Vladimir and Estragon hear a noise off stage. (See diagram p. 108) The parallel with the two thieves is pronounced at this point. Vladimir announces prematurely, 'It is Godot! We're saved! Let's go and meet him.' Estragon has just declared himself 'accursed' and equally prematurely announces, 'I am in Hell'. From a point just slightly right of centre stage they rush in straight lines upstage to look out the wings. Estragon heads in his usual direction and exits stage right while Vladimir goes stage left and remains onstage.

The diagram next indicates three movements to and from centre stage in straight lines along what Beckett called in the original French text *'l'axe de la route'*. First Estragon and Vladimir return to reunite stage centre. Then they move apart again. Vladimir, who thinks Godot is approaching, takes Estragon's arm to lead him stage right, on the line 'We're saved . . . Let's go and meet him'. But Estragon, who fears an onslaught of attackers, breaks away and exits toward the opposite side of the stage. Vladimir exits to stage right. For one brief climactic moment the stage is empty. Finally, to complete the triad of movements they return from the wings to meet again midstage.

The double exit was only one of three possibilities entertained by Beckett:

1) E. hardly off when on again. V not off.
2) Both hardly off when on again.
3) Both off enough for empty stage to carry. (R 40)

The diagram illustrates the first possibility, not the one finally chosen (1 and 3 are marked-through in red) but the basic figure of the triad of movements is ultimately the same: They form a horizontal axis composed of two separate parts meeting at a central point like the two arms of an unfinished cross. The moment of emptiness at the centre of the action provides a

40

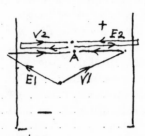

ihm entgegengehen
A V takes E's arm for ← E breaks away for →
    "to meet him"
3 Possibilities
    1. E turned off when on again, V not off
    2 Both   "   "   "   "   "
    3 " off long enough for empty stage to carry

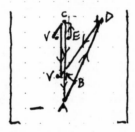

C Idiot V takes hold of E and draws him part of
    way to A . A - B backward   B to shelter of V
B Du willst nicht   after hintern Baum V with E
D Rühr dich nicht   to tree
D - V Den Baum Kann man   behind the tree

C Imbecile
B You won't
D Don't move
D-V Decidedly this tree

climax which gives structure to the section. The double exit reinforces the symmetry of the configuration. Though more brief than the third possibility, the one chosen still allows the empty stage 'to carry' to establish visually the major theme of the play — the absence of its central figure.

Estragon's three attempts to find a place to hide, which follow immediately, establish the vertical axis of the cross. As diagrammed on page 40 of the *Regiebuch*, he moves first to the most extreme point upstage centre. Then Vladimir takes his arm and they both move in straight parallel lines towards downstage centre, facing the auditorium. Vladimir stops short about two thirds of the way and Estragon continues the rest of the way downstage alone completing the cross. This second direction of escape is no better than the first. Estragon recoils backwards from it and then turns to 'the shelter of Vladimir'. After reflecting briefly, Vladimir directs him on to the third potential hiding place. In a unified depiction of its controlling image, the section concludes with action centred on the tree: 'Quick! Behind the tree,' exclaims Vladimir and they rush to it. The tree, 'pale and stark as a skeleton,' with two drooping branches is a ludicrously inadequate refuge. The section which began with the noise they heard off-stage closes as they move to midstage on the path between tree and stone with Vladimir's line, 'Decidedly this tree will not have been of the slightest use to us.'

The movements creating two horizontal arms are recapitulated almost immediately to begin the formation of a second cross. This time it is Estragon who initiates and controls the action by drawing Vladimir upstage right and positioning him to 'scan the horizon' for an arrival while he goes upstage left to assume watch in the opposite direction. 'Back to back like in the good old days', filling the lateral positions of the two thieves, they alternate between looking at each other and looking into the wings. The space at the centre of the stage which their brief exits earlier had left vacant 'long enough to carry' remains vacant. At this point the absence of the central figure is emphasised not by a totally empty stage but by the dialogue and its mode of delivery. Although there is no indication of it in the *Regiebuch*, Estragon's line 'Do you see anything coming?' and Vladimir's 'You must have been mistaken' ('You must have had a vision' in Beckett's English translation) were chanted antiphonally in the Berlin production and the American adaptation of it. The echo of the Mass suggests a manifestation of Divine presence.

Following a long silence in which there is neither arrival nor vision, they decide to 'abuse' each other. As they begin, they move to the centre in a precisely delineated 'approach by stages' and face each other 'nose to nose'. Had Beckett diagrammed this second cross as he did the first, the diagram of lateral actions with return to the centre would have looked nearly identical.

In the Gospel account it is 'Our Saviour' who is 'abused' by one of the thieves. In the absence of a saviour to abuse for not saving them, Gogo and Didi must self-consciously resort to abusing each other. And the ensuing reconciliation is equally provisional — only a human waltz to the tune of *The Merry Widow* rather than divine assurance 'This very day thou shalt be with me in Paradise.'

Like the figure of the circle, the figure of this second cross remains uncompleted until B-3, where the 'Trio' of Vladimir and Estragon staggering downstage in a straight line with Pozzo suspended between them on each arm provides the vertical axis. (See diagram p. 111) That scene also provides a third cross and a single unified, if inadequate, image of three forms suspended with outstretched arms.

On page 46, Beckett diagrammed actions completing the second cross and creating the third. As before, the two lateral components are presented first. After rising from the 'heap' in B-4, Estragon and Vladimir pick up Pozzo who has crawled upstage centre. He 'sags between them, his arms round their necks' (F84, G54R), then they move away from him — Estragon in a short counter-clockwise parallel figure to his right, and Vladimir in a mirroring movement moves clockwise in a parallel figure to his left. The horizontal arms of a cross are thus presented again. Pozzo falls. They raise him up again and the three stagger straight downstage from upstage centre. Part way there, Pozzo falls a second time, 'bowed down as L. A-5 p. 25'. Again 'they raise him up again and stagger forward . . .', the two more stages to the front of the playing area completing the vertical axis of the cross.

'Breaks' preceding them gave emphasis to seven lines of dialogue which establish the connection with the Crucifixion of Christ:

> The reference to thieves in 'You are not highwaymen?'
> The discussion of being forsaken in 'Don't leave me.'

46

ct. 10al/3

TRIO

after	ich bin blind	stoh stagger
"	denn Freunde	fall "
"	spät ist es	less "
"	moment schwankte	full "
"	Karyatiden	less "
"	früher als gestern	stop "
"	ich gehe	full "
"	Ablenkung nenn't	less "
"	Er stinkt so	P greifs V with RH
"	die augen nicht von mir	V/P ↝ tc E/L

/ ich frage sie, ob es
ganz auf einmal gekom-
men ist

Before	Sind sie keine Räube	short break
"	Lassen sie mich nicht allein	" "
"	Wie spät ist es	" "
"	Sie sagten etc	" "
"	Wo sind wir etc	" "
"	Wo ist mein Knecht	" "
"	Was ist eigentlich passiert	" "

(Unrealizable)

After I am blind
 " Your friend
 " What time is it?
 " For a moment
 " Caryatids
 " ~~Yesterday~~ All of a sudden
 " I'm going
 " Some diversion
 " He stinks so
 " Eyes off me

Before You are not highwaymen?
 " Don't leave me alone
 " What time is it?
 " You said, etc.
 " Where are we, etc.
 " Where is my menial?
 " What exactly has happened?

POZZO'S STAGGER *REGIEBUCH*, P. 46

> The discussion of premature darkness stemming from the
> question 'What time is it?'
> The echo of Christ's 'You have said it' in Vladimir's
> challenging 'You said your sight used to be good.'
> And the three summary questions — 'Where are we?';
> 'Where is my menial?'; 'What happened exactly?' — inviting
> a general appraisal of the scene and the fates of those involved
> in it.

Estragon's lines 'How much longer are we to cart him around?
[. . .] We are not caryatids!' by asserting that they are not
recognisable figures of Classical Greek culture — the remnants
of a defunct religion still supporting the Parthenon — invite
comparison to other recognisable figures.

This scene completing the vertical axis of the cross begun in
B-2 is unmistakably linked with the scene establishing the
horizontal axis by the same chanted delivery of the Latin line
Memoria praeteritorum bonorum 'memory of past happiness'
(which Dante defines as the greatest torment of the damned).
The chanted Latin words make the allusion to the Mass even
more apparent and establish clearly the Christian overtones of
the configuration. But if Pozzo does fill the centre of the
previously empty crucifixion scene, he is a woefully inadequate
saviour who constantly issues cries for help (which Beckett
referred to in the *Regiebuch* as 'SOS' calls) and must be rescued
from his fallen state and supported by others.

In performance the stylized movement 'failed' and Beckett
crossed through the 'Trio' and wrote 'unrealisable' at the
bottom. In the American adaptation, the section of dialogue
accompanying the staggering downstage was cut to shorten the
scene, but the basic form of the action as described in the
Regiebuch was retained.

As early as the green notebook, Beckett diagrammed two
figures offering alternate possibilities for linking the circular
patterns of the approaches to stone and tree with the
corresponding set of crosses made by the movements in
Act II.

The scene involved occurs just following Lucky's speech. (See
diagram p. 114) After he is attacked by the others, Lucky falls.
Estragon and Vladimir raise him up and support him — as they
do Pozzo in B-4. Pozzo's actions mark the key points of the
movement. He shouts commands, 'Don't let him go,' 'Don't
move,' 'Hold him tight,' etc., and reloads Lucky first with the
bag and then with the basket.

The scene as indicated in the *Regiebuch* expands the original. The movement itself is greater than that implied in the text. It is preceded by a better translation of the French original which calls attention to the importance of the direction of movement. Instead of asking, 'Will he be able to walk?' Vladimir asks, 'Will he be able to orientate himself' (vs. the correct 'orient' himself). And significantly Lucky's bag now falls on Estragon's foot (See list of textual changes, p. 153).

The first of the diagrams was ultimately rejected. It is of interest, however, for the indication it gives of the significance of clockwise and counterclockwise directions in Beckett's work. In it Estragon, Lucky and Vladimir stagger first in a decreasing oscillation clockwise up to a point where Lucky assumes the bag, then counterclockwise down to their starting point, then clockwise in a smaller arc back up to the point where Lucky drops the bag on Estragon's foot and counterclockwise down again to the starting point. Then they make a complete clockwise circle with Lucky assuming the basket at midpoint. The three clockwise motions are unmistakably associated with the assumption of burdens and suffering, the counterclockwise motions with the movement away from the points where burdens are assumed and pain inflicted. The association is strengthened by the fact that the oscillations of the first part echo the clockwise approaches to the tree and the counterclockwise descent from it which introduced the pattern in A-2.

In choosing the alternative represented in the second diagram, Beckett sacrificed the parallel with the approach to and descent from the tree in favour of a pattern which presents more clearly and exclusively two half-circles. In the second diagram the three stagger first counterclockwise in a semicircle, Lucky assuming his bag at midpoint. In a variation of the linear chord, they then make a loop up into the unfinished circle to change their direction for a second semicircle. At the peak of this loop, Lucky drops his bag on Estragon's foot. They complete the second half of the circle by moving clockwise, Lucky re-assuming the burden of his basket midway. (Although it is not indicated in the *Regiebuch*, in performance Lucky's arms were set swinging as he reassumes his burdens creating another highly visible set of semi-circular oscillations.) The presentation of the circular pattern in a scene so obviously parallel to the one in B-4 in which Estragon, Pozzo and Vladimir stagger to complete the configuration of the cross connects the two major visual motifs of the play and suggests their thematic interrelationship.

32

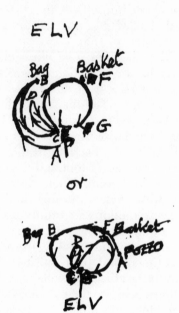

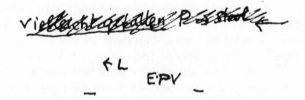

A "Don't let him go!"
B "Don't move!"
C "Hold him tight!"
D Bag falls on E's foot
C to F "Don't let him go!"
F to G "Hold him tight!" with ad-lib if required

LUCKY'S STAGGER *GREEN NOTEBOOK* P. 32

114

Approach by Stages

The last pattern of movement noted in the *Regiebuch* is 'Approach by stages' (R 101). Under that heading, Beckett listed places in the text where the characters come together and go apart. By separating dialogue and movement and by breaking each approach into distinct parts, usually triads, he created a visual motif which permeates nearly every action in the play. On page five of the *Regiebuch* at the first instance of 'Approach by stages' he laid down the principle behind the motif.

> Thus establishes at outset 2 caged dynamics,
> E sluggish, V restless,
> + perpetual separation and reunion of V/E.

In the green notebook (facing page one) he was more explicit about the comparison of Vladimir and Estragon to animals:

> Gen. effect of moves esp. V's though apparently motivated that of those in a cage.

And he even contemplated in a note — crossed out in the same pen —

> 'Faint shadow of bars on stage floor.'

Wartestelle

Smaller visual units are dealt with in the next section, entitled 'W' for '*Wartestelle*' — points of waiting (R 75). The play is broken at twelve points by silence during which the action ceases as the characters assume unmistakable tableaux. Beckett listed twenty points at which such pauses might occur (see overleaf). That is, in addition to those opening and closing each act, four other '*Wartestelle*' were to be chosen for each act. Red check marks beside the list indicate the four from each finally chosen: 2, 4, 6, 7 for Act I and 12, 13, 14, and 16 for Act II.

The tableaux of the opening and closing of each act discussed above seem to have been considered separately by Beckett. The remaining eight were taken up at rehearsals as two series of four. The four for Act I were chosen before rehearsals began. They define the circumstances pictorially. The first depicts Estragon and Vladimir in anticipation of Godot's arrival. At Vladimir's suggestion that Godot might shout at his horse (F19, G13R), they freeze in position looking at each other — caught in the realisation that the 'unidentifiable being' only hinted at earlier but now envisioned as a demanding master might actually be about to appear. Their waiting has become tangible. So has their fear. The second in the series presents their physical condition. Lucky stands midstage still burdened with his luggage, Estragon sleeps on his stone downstage left, Vladimir is upstage right, his back to the audience and his head up, his angry outburst having subsided. Pozzo is at his stool downstage right. He stops, declaiming with the words, 'Pan sleeps' (F36, G24L). They all pause to listen — engulfed in silence and fixed in a motionless minimal world surrounded by shadows. The third, following Pozzo's line, 'My memory is defective,' (F38, G25R) portrays confusion and disappointed anticipation. This comes as Vladimir is approaching Pozzo and Estragon is 'craning forward from stone' (GN28). They are intent on Pozzo, eager 'to receive confidence' (GN28) but, as Vladimir says later, 'Nothing

---

[At the] opening/close both acts (R 75) [and]
1. A 2 after 'In my opinion'
2. A2 after 'his horse' (R 9, W 2)
3. A2 after 'It is still day'
4. A4 after 'Pan sleeps.' (R 19, W 3)
5. A4 after 'Shall I tell you'
6. A4 after 'My memory is defective' (R 21, W 4)
7. A5 after 'Entangled in a net' (R 23, W 5) (see list of cuts, p. 154)
8. A5 before 'I don't seem to be able . . . to depart'
9. A6 (before 'That passed the time') (see cuts p. 154)
10. A6 after Moon up before E up (R 31, W 6)
11. B1 between 'Ah yes' and 'Things have changed since yesterday.' (R 37, X out)
12. B2 after 'lullaby, both on stone (R 39, W 9)
13. B2 after 'How time flies when one has fun.' (R 41 'W possible here')
14. B3 after 'We are men' (all fallen) (R 45, W 10)
15. B5 after exit of Pozzo and Lucky. (R 50, W 11 X out)
16. B5 after Moon up before E up (R 51, W 11)

Above all possible Most likely
A 2, 4, 6, 7 — 6 in all
B 11, 12, 14, 15, 16 — 6 in all
[11 X out, 16 added]*

* Lines from English text corresponding to those in German supplied by authors. Parenthetical references supplied by authors to indicate designations of *Wartestelle* in the pages of the *Regiebuch*. E.g. in the case of possibility 11. Beckett did on page 32 designate a *Wartestelle* as Estragon and Vladimir look at the tree, but crossed it out.

is certain . . .' in their world. Memories fail, confusion of facts abounds. The last of the series in Act I presents a picture of a hapless victim and a conspiratorial master. It follows Lucky's dance, a physical representation of the struggle against restrictions. Vladimir and Estragon are beside the stone, Lucky is midstage, Pozzo is at his stool. 'He thinks he's caught in a net,' (F40, G27L) says Pozzo, 'leaning toward V. and E. confidential aside, hand screening from L. with final finger on lips' (GN29).

These frozen silences are, as Beckett's German term for them indicates, tangible instances of waiting. They lead directly into four key references to waiting. The first two references define specific expectations. The last two register unfulfilment. After mentioning Godot's horse, Vladimir, in a line restored from the French, describes the comfort which Godot might provide — 'We may sleep tonight in his loft, snug and dry with our bellies full, in the hay. That's worth waiting for. No?' To which Estragon responds, 'Not all night.' and Vladimir rejoins: 'It's still day' (See list of textual additions p. 153). After Pozzo's 'Pan sleeps' as the landscape assumes a nocturnal quiet, Vladimir cries out, 'Will night never come?' When Pozzo's memory fails and his discourse breaks down, Estragon complains because the diversion has ceased, 'In the meantime nothing happens.' After Pozzo's explanation for Lucky's dance, a long section is cut so that Estragon's impatience for the promised second part of Lucky's performance, his 'Think', erupts: 'Nothing happens, nobody comes, nobody goes, it's awful' (See list of cuts, p. 153). The series establishes the conditions, expectations, and disappointments that are central to the play: Estragon and Vladimir anticipate in an alien, essentially life-less world, amidst confusion, the arrival of a deceptive master.

The four *Wartestelle* of Act II concentrate on the ambiguous relationship between Estragon and Vladimir. Entries in both the green notebook and the *Regiebuch* indicated that Beckett still had not made his final selection until after rehearsals began. Like the actions of the 'Approach by stages', the series he finally chose presents their contrasting temperaments and constant comings together and goings apart in alternating images of union and separation, stasis and activity. The first of this series presents Estragon and Vladimir passive together on the stone. Vladimir's lullaby has put Estragon to sleep, Vladimir remains with his arm about him in a touching but comic picture of interdependence and inadequate consolation. In the second they are active and apart. Upstage slightly right of centre, just after a moment of reconciliation leading to a 'waltz', they actively recoil and stand apart looking at one another for Vladimir's line, 'How time flies when one has fun!' Activity and approach are at best a brief respite, not a solution to their predicament. After a momentary silence, Estragon asks petulantly, 'What do we do now?' Vladimir responds, 'While waiting.'* In the third, they are part of a configuration depicting both their inextricable union in a common fate and their separate existences within that fate. 'Who are you?' Pozzo asks. 'We are men,' replies Vladimir.

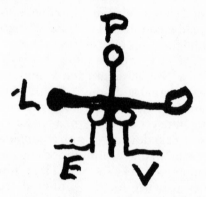

CRUCIFORM "HEAP" *GREEN NOTEBOOK* P. 58

At this point all four characters are on the ground, 'all fallen.' Pozzo's body lies at right angles across Lucky's forming a cross. Estragon occupies the lower stage right quadrant of the cross and is facing stage right, Vladimir is in the lower stage left quadrant and faces stage left. The last of the series comes in B-5 when Pozzo and Lucky have left, the boy has just made his exit, and the moon has risen. Estragon sits on a stone, facing the audience, head down, dozing. Vladimir stands near his tree, back to the audience, head up contemplating the moon. For a moment they seem to lead separate existences. Each is alone at

---

* This is a change from the English translation. See list of textual additions below p. 153.

opposite parts of the stage, inattentively passive or actively observant according to his different nature. Neither is aware of the other.

The series of Act II has depicted the possible modes of the relationship: first, together in the two extremes of static reconciliation and active repulsion; then, still together, on the ground in a middle state of unity without reconciliation and separation without rejection; and, finally, apart and alone. The series culminates in an idyllic picture of a separate existence that is free of conflict or temporary subjugation of one temperament to another. But the first three parts of the series have established too well the dynamics of attraction and repulsion to allow this relief to last. Like the moments which precede it, it is only for an instant. The effect of the series as a whole is to illustrate a kind of perpetual motion interrupted by ephemeral moments of stasis.

Smaller Mime Actions and Gestures

Distancing and concentration of the action through mime and tableau were a significant part of *Godot* even in the original version (cf. Lucky's dance, the Yoga 'tree', Estragon's and Vladimir's mimicking of Lucky's offstage fall, Vladimir's pose as a 'mannequin'). Not only in the *Wartestelle* but throughout the *Regiebuch*, Beckett noted these elements of mime and tableau mentioned or implied in the text and introduced new stage images in addition to those already there. For example, the name of the German Romantic painter, Kaspar David Friedrich is written beside the directions for the scene following the exit of the boy in A-6, indicating that the pictorial and symbolic quality of Friedrich's painting *Zwei Männer Betrachten den Mond* (Two Men Observing the Moon) is to be evoked:

> *Moon up.* 'At last' Vladimir contemplates the moon. E. stands with boot in each hand contemplates V. Tableau (F52, G34R). (See p. 120)*

These visual elements were not included under special headings as the more important *Wartestelle* were, but they are a part of the same concern to impart a pictorial quality to *Godot*.

The progression in the *Regiebuch* from larger to smaller visual aspects continues with the heading, 'Inspection hat/boot' on page 77 which follows *Wartestelle*. The heading identifies points

---

* Beckett identified this painting for Ruby Cohn who was attending rehearsals and told her he had seen it recently at the *Berliner Stättliche Museum*. (Interview 1982)

KASPAR DAVID FRIEDRICH'S *TWO MEN OBSERVING THE MOON*

at which Vladimir and Estragon make parallel gestures with hats and boots respectively. The section obviously represents only a preliminary stage of planning. Two of the four entries (a dropping of Vladimir's hat and Estragon's boot in A-4 and later 'by tree at end' in B-5) were questioned. Beckett was, however, certain about the parallel inspections of hat and boot in A-1 which he designated as 'correct'. In A-1 following two attempts to remove his boot — one unsuccessful and one successful — Estragon inspects his boot once. Vladimir inspects his hat three times.

In his successive, formalised inspections, Vladimir's gestures assume a pattern of increasing activity in keeping with his restless nature. His first examination has two parts, one look and one manual gesture: 'Look, shake.' His second has five parts, two looks and three manual gestures: 'Look, finger (i.e. running his finger round the inside band), tap, shake, look'. His third is in seven parts, two looks, four repeated manual gestures and a new one: 'Look, finger, tap, blow, tap, shake, look.' Directions for the opening scene (R 3) read: 'Play with removed boot (left) to mirror V's with hat.' Estragon also looks, feels with his finger, taps, but only once without the restless persistence of Vladimir. (He drops his boot to feel of his toes as Vladimir inspects his hat.) Thus at the very opening of the play, gesture is used to establish the complex relationship of similarity and difference between the two characters.

As in the case of the larger movements, Beckett's treatment of such smaller gestures as 'Inspection hat/boot' is a significant part of the controlling images of circle and cross. The circular gesture made by Vladimir as he runs his finger around the inside of his hat before his first 'Nothing to be done' is a smaller echo of the larger circular gesture with both hands made by Estragon with his 'Nothing to be done' which opens the play. Throughout the play similar circular gestures of hands and feet or small pivotal movements accompany references to temporal earthly existence.

As in the larger movements, clockwise motion is associated with life in the temporal world and counter-clockwise motion with attempts to escape from it. Estragon's 'gesture toward the universe' (already in the text) reproaches Vladimir for accepting the real world in rejection of his dream: 'This one is enough for you?'. This is a repeat of his opening gesture. When he rages at Vladimir for calling attention to the landscape ('Look at this muckheap'), Estragon turns 360 degrees clockwise.

Later, Estragon totters on one leg as he sticks out first one foot then the other one for Vladimir to put on his boot, after his line, 'We always find something don't we Didi to give us the impression we exist?' (F69, G44R). With each boot they pivot around Estragon's one leg in two 'half rounds' — first the left counter-clockwise then the right clockwise. The two 'half-rounds' with the boot are an important, more explicit illustration of the complementary half circles depicting the separation and interdependence of Vladimir and Estragon. In unmistakable, broad theatrical imagery they present clockwise and counter-clockwise semicircles and corresponding chords: after each of the 'half-rounds' Estragon tries out his boot by walking in short, straight lines. (See diagram p. 123)

Before Vladimir's line 'How time flies when one has fun!' (B-2, F46, G49R), Estragon and Vladimir waltz in a 'full turn' clockwise. (See diagram p. 123)

And after Vladimir's 'I knew it was the right place' (F71, G46) Vladimir and Estragon begin the 'hat number' which accelerates to a large rapid counter-clockwise circulation of three hats for two heads before the extra hat (another circle) is discarded into the darkness backstage.

The most specific association of circular movement with the earth in the *Regiebuch* comes in Act II B-4, (F86-87, G55R) when Pozzo, now blind, asks, 'What's it like?' (referring to the place they are in). Vladimir turns in a clockwise circle to inventory the surroundings, stopping after the first quadrant for the 'It's indescribable', after the second 'It's like nothing', and after the third, 'There's nothing. There's a tree'. (See diagram p. 123) Both the dialogue and action were cut in performance to tighten the action.

With this cut Beckett eliminated the only circular action by Vladimir alone thus associating circularity exclusively with Estragon, the more earthbound of the two. The coordination of these gestures with references to earthly existence makes more explicit what is implied in the larger patterns of movement. The curves and circuits of 'Inspection of place', the approaches to the tree, and the 'little turns' are all part of the endless circularity of life on earth.

Calling attention to the cruciform patterns of the diagrams are recurrent gestures of outstretched arms at lines associated

First L foot after hopper of R , V on E's L .
▬▬ Half round anti CW↺ . V ← a little to
observe E's ⇄ so on E's right for R foot
& 2ⁿᵈ half round CW↻ . E's 2ⁿᵈ ← on other
side giving position at *hör auf*

E̲,   E̲̅,   V̲

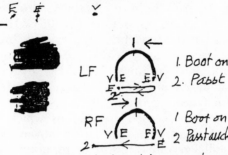

LF   1. Boot on
                      2. Passt

RF   1 Boot on
                      2 Passt auch

No return to hook him near stone

Jetzt setze ich E ← to stone + sit leaving ledge for V
on his L

"I might as well sit down"   2 Fits

                                           2 Fits too

(*Regiebuch* p. 36)

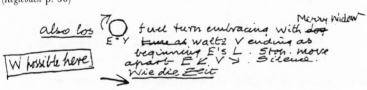

also los ⁷⁰ full turn embracing with ~~dog~~ Merry Widow
E∘Y ~~turn as~~ waltz V ending as
           beginning E's L . Stop. move
apart E K V ⅃ . Silence .
Wie die Zeit

W possible here →

"Here we go"   "How time flies"

(*Regiebuch* p. 41)

Man Kann es nicht beschreiben

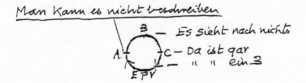

            B — Es sieht nach nichts
A   C — Da ist gar
             " " ein B
E P V

A "It is indescribable"
B "It looks like nothing"
C "There is nothing. There is tree"
(*Regiebuch* p. 47)

with suffering or punishment. One of the few visual aspects not mentioned or implied in the *Regiebuch* or the text, these were nevertheless an obvious part of both the performance in Berlin and in its subsequent American version. Near the outset, Estragon spreads his arms out to the sides for the lines, 'He wants to know if it hurts!' (F10, G7R). He does so again in Act II as he refers to 'Billions' of others, who are not saints but who have kept their appointment (F80, G51R). Again with palms upward to Heaven (after just previously brandishing his fists in that direction saying, 'God have pity on me!') he says, 'On me! On me! Pity! On me!' (F77, G51R). By the time Vladimir and Estragon re-enter the empty stage with widestretched arms for the final meeting forming the arms of the cross in B-2 (R40), the gesture has accrued associations which strengthen the less apparent pattern of their larger movements.

Parallel gestures are also an important means of establishing symmetry of the balanced dynamics of the conflict between Estragon and Vladimir. At several points they confront each other in little showdowns linked by echoing gestures. A note on page 36 for the scene where Vladimir explains to Estragon that his boots have been exchanged overnight illustrates the process:

> Vladimir's boots demonstration: *deine* (yours) . . . *seine* (his) with forefinger echoing (avenging) *Gogo leicht* (Gogo light) — *Didi schwere* (Didi heavy) E's eyes to and fro from boots to Vladimir to boots to V. uncomprehending.

At the tree A-2 (F17-18, G12R) Estragon had won a point when he aborted Vladimir's plan to hang themselves, now Vladimir wins his. Vladimir's discussion of the two thieves in A-1 (F11-13, G8R-9R), and Estragon's questioning of the day of their appointment with Godot A-2 (F14-15, G10 L-11 L,), comprise a similar pair. In the first Vladimir moves in on Estragon in stages using his finger to represent each number ('two thieves,' 'four Gospels,' 'one of them says . . .' etc.) as he forces an uninterested Estragon to consider the two thieves. In the second, Estragon moves in on Vladimir making similar staccato movements each time he mentions a day of the week ('. . . is it Saturday . . . or Sunday . . . or Friday . . . or Thursday?') as he attacks Vladimir's confidence that they have come to the right place on the right day. (The parallel also serves a thematic purpose by connecting the discussion of their appointment with the discussion of the two thieves.)

VERBAL MOTIFS

Doubts and Confusions

Having dealt with the more visual elements, the *Regiebuch* moves next to more abstract areas. The remaining topics in the second half of the *Regiebuch* arise from verbal repetitions and the larger themes of the play. The first of these topics to be taken up counterbalances the specific associations of the geometric configuration and gestures. Beckett devoted a large portion of the notebook to the uncertainties of the play which help to 'avoid definition.'

Although they do not appear sequentially, three of the headings are closely related accounts of the mental confusion that permeates the play. Under the heading 'Doubts, confusions' Beckett brought together various entries dealing with 'doubts, time, place identity' and 'confusion of persons.' (E.g. in A-2 Estragon 'casts doubt on [their] appointment'; there is no answer from Vladimir. In B-1 he 'casts doubt on yesterday'; in B-3 he 'denies they were there yesterday' while Vladimir asserting contrary, etc.) The final heading of the *Regiebuch* '*Erinnern*' — remembering — notes the places at which memory fails or characters are unwilling to remember. Estragon won't recall the central image of the Gospels (F12, G8R). Vladimir is unwilling to remember the facts of their past life (Estragon: 'Do you remember the day I threw myself into the Rhone . . .?' Vladimir: 'That's all dead and buried.').

The heading '*Was sagt ich noch*' — 'What was I saying' — ('written out earlier but also listed as the first item under '*Erinnern*'), is another catalogue of points of mental confusion. This question, already identical at each occurrence in the French and English text but not in the German, was regularised for the Schiller-Theater. It introduces instances in Act I where obvious realities of the present situation are momentarily forgotten even in the process of speaking about them. Each recurrence of the question is followed by a pause before the forgotten subject is supplied.

In A-1 (F12, G9L) Vladimir forgets that he was discussing the Gospels but finally remembers, 'Ah, yes, the two thieves.' Pozzo forgets in A-3 (F31, G21L) that he was explaining why Lucky never lays down his burden. And although Lucky is in full view, Pozzo must ask the question twice before Estragon and Vladimir remind him — Vladimir by mimicking Lucky and

Estragon by pointing to him and saying, 'Bags ... Why ... Always hold ... Never put down ... Why?' Again at A-4 (F37, G25, L), Pozzo forgets that he was describing the coming of darkness. The text is cut here to eliminate play with the whip and vapouriser and an exchange of courtesies between Pozzo and Estragon to make a clear, quick succession —:

> Pozzo: 'Shall I tell you?' — 'What was I saying?'
> Estragon: 'Let's go.'
> Pozzo: 'Ah yes! The night.'

And in B-2 (F65, G42 L), Vladimir forgets that he wanted to direct Estragon's attention to the change from yesterday, 'Ah, yes! The tree!'

The result is a verbal motif which works much like the *Wartestelle* of Act I to point out the essentials of the situation which may be lost sight of temporarily but never really forgotten: Vladimir and Estragon face an uncertain fate with an even chance ('or nearly') of salvation; they confront two possibilities for salvation — a burdensome wait for an indifferent master, or an end to waiting brought about by time; in the meanwhile, they exist in the present reality of the physical situation, signified by the tree.

Come Let's Go

Following 'Doubts and Confusion' Beckett turned to the verbal refrain 'Come, let's go', which leads to 'We are waiting for Godot', listing eight occurrences and noting which were 'models' and which variants. While this was a theme of major importance to be made prominent through exact repetition, the implications for performance were too obvious to require extended treatment.

Help

At the next heading, entitled 'Help', Beckett once again merely listed the times when the characters call for aid in their difficulties without commentary, and tabulated the responses (R 89).

        21 in all
        14 ignored
         4 answered
         1 attempt made
         1 not known
         1 on condition

The various cries of 'Help!' are by themselves another verbal motif. In his first notes in the white Suhrkamp edition he had numbered each occurrence of the word: 'H-1' 'H-2', etc., but unlike 'confusions' and the recurrent phrase, 'Come, let's go' which are developed almost exclusively through dialogue, this verbal motif was coordinated in the directions in the *Regiebuch* with a series of stage actions which give structure to the theme. On page three Beckett identified Estragon's first two calls for Vladimir to help him off with his boots as 'SOS-1' and SOS-2.' After the second he wrote, 'from outset no help.' These two appeals are part of a series, mentioned earlier under the heading 'E's feet', in which Estragon 'presents his foot four times in vain.' (R 65). The third occurs shortly after to make a triad at the beginning of the play. The fourth comes at the end of the play (F90, G58 L) when Estragon presents 'both [feet] with 'Help me!' after failure to stand.'

Between Estragon's vain gestures with one boot at the beginning and with two boots at the end of the play are four echoing scenes in which Estragon presents his leg and Vladimir does assist him: the two 'half-rounds' discussed above where Vladimir who at first will not help Estragon remove his painful boots now insists that he put them on, and the two scenes in which Vladimir inspects Estragon's wound received from Lucky (A-4, p. 16; B-4, p. 43). Estragon's staggering on one leg, one foot outstretched to Vladimir; the presentation of the wrong foot first each time; and Vladimir's gruff commands 'Show' 'The other, pig!' as he prepares to poke the wound, and 'The other, hog! . . . Higher!' as he puts on Estragon's boot, make the parallels between these two paired actions unmistakable. Ironically, Vladimir gives aid only when it is useless or when it leads to eventual discomfort.

On page 25, Beckett noted that whereas Pozzo and Lucky fall on their own in the 'stylised' two-part action described earlier — 'first knees then forward on face', Vladimir and Estragon fall 'backward into heap with help of helped hand', Vladimir drawn down by Pozzo and Estragon by Vladimir. The addition of a new line, 'Up!' for Estragon just before he is pulled down into the heap makes the contrast more evident. And when Estragon and Vladimir do rise, they get up separately, unassisted. The coordination of action and text makes clear the conditions that prevail — not only is mutual assistance usually denied or futile in the situation; but when it is attempted, it only leads to increased distress.

Sky

The next heading, 'Sky' (R93) lists nine references to the sky or the heavens. Numbers to the left indicate that at seven of the nine references, characters look up. (The two exceptions come in Lucky's speech at 'blast hell to heaven' and 'the air and the earth abode of stones.') These seven looks set up a stronger contrast than in the printed text between the passage of time in the two acts. Six of the looks come in Act I; they all express a sense of approaching night. The first two (Vladimir's 'It's still day' A-2 — see additions p. 153, and Pozzo's '. . . there is no denying it is still day' A-4, F29, G19R) confirm that the time for the appointment with Godot has not yet run out. The second two (Vladimir's cries, 'Will night never come?' A-4, F33, G22L; see list of changes) express anticipation for the end of the day's waiting. The next one (Pozzo's, 'Look! . . . Will you look at the sky, pig!' A-4, F37, G25L) calls attention to the sky to refute Vladimir's contention that time has stopped. The last look (after Vladimir's 'at last' A-6, F52, G34R) accompanies a rare moment of fulfilled expectation as Estragon and Vladimir observe the fall of night.

In the printed text, Act II contains two looks at the sky, both of which were cut from the Berlin production, one by Vladimir after Pozzo's question 'What time is it?' and one by Vladimir and Estragon after Pozzo's line, 'Is it evening?' By the time Beckett made this listing in the *Regiebuch* he had already cut the text to exclude these references as well as Vladimir's long speech about the passage of time: 'It is evening . . . night is drawing nigh . . . It is not for nothing I have lived through this long day and I can assure you it is very near the end of its repertory.' In Act II as performed in Berlin there is only one look at the sky: the seventh on Beckett's list in the *Regiebuch*. It occurs in B-4 at a point corresponding structurally to the one in A-4 at which Pozzo commands the others to look at the sky to affirm that time has not stopped. It contains no premonition that night will ever come. Estragon and Vladimir are lying on the ground before getting up. For no apparent reason Estragon points with 'raised index' to the sky and says, 'Look at that little cloud . . . there in the zenith' (B-4, F83-84, G54 L). He and Vladimir look, but this time the sky imparts no indication of passing time — or of anything else. Vladimir's only comment is, 'Well? What is so wonderful about that?' Estragon lets the matter drop, 'Let's pass on now to something else, do you mind.' From the evidence of the sky, time has stopped in Act II.

The looks at the sky also mark a progression in the attitude toward waiting. In the first two instances, waiting is still accompanied by positive expectations. The first comes as Vladimir asserts that sleep in Godot's loft is worth waiting for — perhaps 'not all night' as Estragon objects, but at least as long as it is day. The second comes as Pozzo presents waiting as an obligation with ambiguous outcome but incumbent so long as there is daylight. 'Suppose you go now while it is still day. What happens in that case?' The next two, Vladimir's cries 'Will night never come?', express a desire for waiting to end. In the final two there is a positive anticipation of an end to waiting and fulfillment of that anticipation. Pozzo commands them to look at the sky as he refutes Vladimir's fear that 'Time has stopped' by explaining that night is charging and will burst upon them. When night does fall, Vladimir experiences a rare moment of fulfilled expectation and exclaims 'At last!'. By the time they look at the little cloud in the zenith in the one instance in Act II, however, their looks register neither positive nor negative anticipation. If they still have any expectations, they have become less active in manifesting them.

Sleep

Under the next heading, 'Sleep', Beckett simply copied fourteen references to sleep without further comment. Estragon's sleeps on the stone are not included but a cross-reference to them precedes the rest of the list. A number of points are evident from these entries. At some time in the play all of the characters either sleep or ask whether their waking life has not been a kind of sleep. Estragon and Lucky actually do sleep while Pozzo and Vladimir only speculate on the subject. The theme culminates in B-5 (F90, G58L) with Vladimir's long soliloquy 'Was I sleeping while the others suffered?' which is balanced by Estragon's 'Was I long asleep?' the final reference in the play to sleep.

Only the opening line of Vladimir's monologue is quoted in the *Regiebuch*. In the section 'Sleep' in the green notebook Beckett wrote out a long portion of the beginning and ending of the passage. It is the only speech in either notebook singled out in this manner. The theme of sleep is adequately visualised by three tableaux — Estragon's sleep on the stone, the *'Wartestelle'* at 'Pan sleeps', and Lucky 'asleep on his feet' in A-3, but no formalised verbal or visual motif is introduced in the directions to connect or structure all the lines developing the important theme of life as a waking dream of sleepers and watchers. It is the one major theme to be brought together by a single passage. Not surprisingly in the light of Beckett's practice in his later plays, that passage is a soliloquy near the end of the play.

Lighting

The *Regiebuch* closes with a section on 'lighting'. (R 107). Written in ballpoint, it is obviously a record of decisions made during rehearsals after the exits of the boy were changed. There are three levels of light: 'half evening light' (A), 'full evening light' (B), and 'moonlight' (C). In Beckett's *Godot*, there was a cast of twilight even to the day. The three levels are varied in the same five-part pattern in each act:

> CURTAIN
> 1) Fade up to half-light between the curtain and the opening line.
> 2) Fade up to full light with the opening action.
> 3) Fade down to half-light at the exit of Pozzo and Lucky.
> 4) Fade down to 'moonlight' simultaneous with the boy's exit.
> 5) Fade out after a five second pause following the last line ('Let's go')
> CURTAIN

The balanced asymmetry so basic to the structure of the whole play is repeated by the coordination of action and dialogue with the changes in light. Half-light ends in Act I with Estragon's opening line, 'Nothing to be done.' In Act II it ends with 'tomb', the last word of Vladimir's opening song. In Act I Vladimir's approach to Estragon 'bring(s)' full light 'reached with V's halt.' In Act II it is Estragon's approach to Vladimir which 'bring(s)' full light also reached with Estragon's 'halt'. The parallel exits of Pozzo and Lucky bring half-light to each act. Vladimir's lines initiating the boy's identical exits and the simultaneous fades to moonlight contain similar words but in contrasting forms: an affirmative question, 'You did see us, didn't you?' in Act I and an implied negative question, 'You won't . . . tell me that you never saw me!' in Act II.

In the lighting, as throughout the action, there is an approach by stages. The play emerges out of darkness, to half-light, then to full light. Once the main action is begun, it is played in full light until the exit of Pozzo and Lucky when it returns to the half-light of the opening and it is concluded in moonlight. The curtain closes after a fade-down to darkness which parallels the opening fade up to half light.

AUDIAL ELEMENTS: THE MUSIC OF *GODOT*

As the organisation makes clear, the *Regiebuch* is primarily a blueprint for establishing the visual structure of the play, with secondary attention to the verbal structure. There are no sections dealing explicitly with sound patterns. In the additional stage directions there are only a few notes specifying how lines are to be delivered: e.g. a 'stage whisper' for the final words of Vladimir's dog song in Act II and the points of stress and 'shocks' in Lucky's speech.

The only auditory element treated systematically in the *Regiebuch* is the series of four 'tunes' in Act II. Beckett's original plan (R 38) was to have four repetitions of 'the dog tune', once with words, three times without them. Vladimir's mechanical delivery of the march rhythms of the round beginning the act would have established the 'tune' for the whole series. The lullaby, the 'nightmare march' immediately following it (as Vladimir and Estragon try to walk off the effect of the bad dream), and the 'reconciliation waltz' (when Vladimir and Estragon reunite in a circle after a brief separation), were all to have been sung in the same martial rhythm. The machine-like rhythm and tune for round, lullaby, march and waltz would thus have made another four part motif suggesting the unrelieved tedium and repetitions underlying even ostensibly different activities. This was the effect of the music in the 1964 Royal Court production. With Beckett's approval, Nicol Williamson as Vladimir sang the round to the rhythm of 'Carnival in Venice' and the 'Bye, Bye, Bye, Bye' of the lullaby in just two alternate high and low tones — 'like the siren of an ambulance.' (Interview Nicol Williamson, 1978).

Beckett crossed out this first plan and introduced instead four different tunes. The dog tune remained unchanged. For the lullaby he chose '*Schlafe Mein Prinzchen Schlaf ein.*' The walk following is to the wordless accompaniment of Chopin's 'Funeral March' and the 'reconciliation waltz' is to the hummed strains of 'The Merry Widow Waltz.' These four tunes make a typically balanced set of similarities and contrasts. The series opens with the verbal circle made by the words of the round, which has no definite end and only fizzles down to a stage

whisper after false starts and new beginnings. The series closes
with the physical circle of the wordless waltz. Between these two
come the paired lullaby associated with the beginning of life —
without words but so familiar that the tune suggests them —
and the following wordless funeral march associated with the
end of life. The first two songs with lyrics sung or implied
balance the second two without any lyrics. The sombre round
about the dog's grave and the funeral dirge alternate with the
soothing lullaby and the merry waltz. *Wartestelle* following the
lullaby and the waltz set up a further correspondence between
them while also breaking the series into two sections defined by
the long silence in the middle and at the end. Rather than the
effect of one underlying mechanical rhythm of the first plan, the
alternation of sombre marches, and happier melodies, give the
sounds of a life overshadowed by unhappiness and endless
monotony lightened by brief moments of solace and joy. The
concluding waltz, though different in spirit from the opening
march, still has a heavily stressed, unsubtle rhythm which
conveys in a more comical way some of the same sense of
automatic repetition.

The progression from Act I in which there is no music to Act
II with its 'tunes' still does not provide a musical resolution. The
distinction made in the *Regiebuch* between songs with words and
tunes without them is not incidental. Vladimir sings in the play
but the four pieces of music in the second act make it clear that
everything does not 'end in song' according to the French
proverb alluded to in *Endgame*. The series of 'tunes' begins with
the dog song with lyrics about an ending but in a form that is
endless, and it continues with a remnant of a lullaby. In the
original German text Vladimir sings only the empty syllables 'Ei
a po pi a' of the first line of the lullaby, but in the green notebook
Beckett wrote out the words of the first half-stanza of the lullaby.
Unsung lyrics are still implied. The series closes with two
progressively shorter bits of music, Chopin's funeral march and
the 'Merry Widow Waltz', which are not 'songs' at all. Far from a
musical resolution, the one quick turn of the waltz evokes a
sense of musical form left incomplete.

Not only the pattern of the music but the thematic relevance
of the implied lyrics of the lullaby seem to have occupied
Beckett's attention. Although he copied out the text of 'Eia
Popia' in the green notebook, the lullaby was changed in the red
Regiebuch to '*Schlafe mein Prinzchen*.' It was necessary to find a

lullaby familiar to the German audience and one with appropriate connotations. These connotations are largely absent in the original French where the 'do, do, do' of the text are merely musical syllables with no specific connection to any text. In English 'bye, bye, bye' echoes part of 'Rock-a-bye baby' which is further established by the melody. The words of that song,

> 'Rock a bye baby in the tree top . . .
> When the bough breaks the baby will fall
> Down will come baby, cradle and all'

relates directly to Estragon's dream of falling from a high place and thus to the theme of the fallen state as well as to the tree. Those connections were not inherent in lullabies most familiar to a German audience.

In a German context, Brahms' *Weigenlied*, '*Guten Abend. Gute Nacht*', (Lullaby and Good Night') would have been the most obvious selection. Its reference to a benevolent Christian God watching over the sleeper and its emphasis on waking in the morning would have made an appropriate, but perhaps too blatant, ironic commentary on the situation in the play. 'Eia Popia' of the original German translation, was familiar enough to be recalled and served a more specific function — connecting the lullaby thematically with the round. The dog of the round is given an endless existence in the eyes of those 'to come' by a burial and tombstone usually reserved for humans. The lyrics of the lullaby copied out by Beckett in the green notebook show a similar misattribution of human needs and customs to animals:

> Eia Popia
> What rustles in the straw.
> The goslings go barefoot
> for they have no shoes.

In light of Estragon's boots, it would be more appropriate to lament that men are not shoeless like geese rather than to lament that geese have no shoes.

The change from 'Eia Popia' to '*Schlafe mein Prinzchen, schlaf ein*' forfeits the contrast between men and animals. It introduces a greater note of concern for the sleeper.

> Sleep, my Princeling, go to sleep
> the lambs and small birds are at rest
> Garden and meadow are silent,

not even a Bee is still humming.
Luna with silver light
Peeps in through the window
Sleep in the silver light
Sleep, my princeling, go to sleep
go to sleep, go to sleep

All in the Palace's lain down
All is cradled in slumber
No mouse stirs about any more
Cellar and kitchen are empty
Only in the chambermaid's room
there sounds a yearning 'Ach!'
What kind of 'Ach' can it be?
　　Sleep, my Princeling, etc.

Who is more lucky than you?
Nothing but pleasure and rest.
Full up with toys and sugar
And wagons still on the go
All is prepared and ready
so that my Princeling won't cry.
And think what the future will bring
　　Sleep, etc.

(Authors' literal translations)

There is something precarious about his sleep and uncertain about the future. The palace is quiet, he is at rest, but all must be prepared to keep him from crying. And in the second verse there is after all the background sound of a yearning, '*Ach!*' (as in Estragon's repeated refrain '*Ach ja*' (Ah yes) that follows Vladimir's announcements that they are 'waiting for Godot'). The singer asks, 'What kind of an 'Ach' can that be?' The third verse concludes with the imperative question 'Think what the future will bring?' an assurance of a safe and happy awakening, but also with a note of ambiguity appropriate to the situation in the play. '*Schlafe mein Prinzchen*' thus provides much more direct commentary on sleep as a temporary respite from a world of activity, desire, and uncertainties. It also indicates an even more tender concern of Vladimir for Estragon than 'Eia Popia'.

If it received less prominent treatment in the *Regiebuch* than the visual elements and verbal motifs, the music was nevertheless an important and effective part of the shape of Beckett's *Godot*.

Beckett's *Regiebuch* for *Warten auf Godot* with its important changes in text and stage directions is a part of a 'definitive' version. Beckett has made disclaimers about the writing of *Godot* to suggest that it was 'unvisualised', but the *Regiebuch* makes many points that are only implicit in the original play definite and explicit. Though they were tightened in the translation for the Schiller-Theater, the verbal motifs were basic to *Godot* from the first. The coordination of hat and boot gesture and the parallel actions with outstretched leg made more definite in the *Regiebuch* were already discernible in the original directions. If not worked out so consistently, the approach by stages and comings together and goings apart were also obviously present in the repeated direction, 'step forward', separating Estragon's lines leading up to their 'embrace' and 'recoil' in A-2. Ten of the lines introducing possible *Wartestelle* were already followed in the original French text (though not always in the translation) by 'Silence' as opposed to 'Pause'. Early in his association with Alan Schneider, Beckett pointed out 'moments of stillness' which were to stop the action in a particular scene. The innovation of the *Regiebuch* is in the use of the *Wartestelle* to create a greater parallel between the opening and closing of the two acts and the greater clarity achieved by the reduction from fourteen *Wartestelle* to two structured sets of four.

The subliminal stage imagery of circle and cross were present in the original text in less defined form. Estragon's gesture towards the world on the line, 'This one is enough for you?' (A-2) is not specified, but the directions indicate 'gesture' at this point. The detailed directions for the hat routine mention no circle but if followed exactly result inevitably in one. Even in the original text, Pozzo fell three times in B-3, the 'staggering scene', giving that action a formalised pattern. And from the first, the horizontal and vertical components of Estragon's attempted escape were related and balanced by symmetry of voluntary and involuntary action: Estragon exits stage left on his own; then he resists Vladimir, pulling away to exit stage right. Vladimir stops him with the cry 'Imbecile!' when he tries to exit upstage centre but Estragon's own reluctance keeps him from following Vladimir's urging to exit downstage centre.

Even as he wrote *Godot* Beckett envisioned in some detail how it would appear in a final staging. In assisting and advising early productions, he was able to guide others towards that kind of performance. When he saw or heard of productions that departed widely from what the text stated or implied, he pronounced them wrong. In Berlin he at last chose to assume the dual roles of author and director in order to give *Godot* the fully visualised stage performance inherent in his text from the beginning.

WALTER ASMUS' REHEARSAL DIARY

Walter D. Asmus was Beckett's associate director for the Schiller *Warten auf Godot*, toured with the play, and directed a television adaptation of it. His rehearsal diary is an account of Beckett's work with the German company to achieve the carefully structured performance set forth in the *Regiebuch*.[2]

A Rehearsal Diary

Beckett is coming to Berlin to direct *Waiting for Godot*. He is no stranger to the Schiller-Theater: after *Endgame, Krapp's Last Tape* and *Happy Days*, this is his fourth visit as a director. He also took part in the rehearsals of *Godot* ten years ago, and met the actors Bollmann, Wigger and Herm then. He and Bollmann also worked together on *Endgame* in 1967.

Rehearsal conditions are ideal: from 28 December to 8 March, mornings only, mostly on stage. Everybody taking part in the production brings enormous sympathy and respect towards Beckett. But he is not only respected as an authority, and as a competent interpreter of his own script; more than that, the working relationship with him is characterised by caution, attention, concessions and openness. On this basis, everybody tries not to disturb, to strengthen the tacit mutual trust, and to do their job with the highest possible degree of understanding and appreciation for Beckett.

When misunderstandings do arise, through chance mishearings, everybody, even those taking part only indirectly, is willing to help and clear them up. This atmosphere of constant, concentrated alertness is a further result of the 'unauthoritarian' working relationship.

The rehearsals are carried out in a rather conventional way: after a relatively fast read-through of the script, the detailed work follows with increasing intensity. Content is not discussed, but situations are cleared up, and explanations about the characters are given.

Beckett constantly subjects his own script to critical control in the most amazing and sympathetic way. He is always open to suggestions and even asks for them. He is not at all interested in carrying out a rigid concept, but aims for the best possible interpretation of his script.

Should uncertainty occur, he is ready with a new suggestion the next day, always precise and well considered — even if it does not always work immediately. So it happens that before the second full rehearsal, there is a two-page cut to be discussed, because the presentation on stage remains unsatisfactory. The high degree of consciousness and self-control does not strike the actors as turning them into performing animals — indeed, they consciously accept it, intensify it, and build on it.

Friday, 27 December, 1974

Technical rehearsal. Matias, Beckett's designer, talks with the technical director about the set design, on the stage.

As the chief of the costume department comes up to talk to him, he stands up to explain details about the costumes from the designs. Vladimir is going to wear black and grey striped trousers which fit him, with a black jacket, which is too small for him; the jacket belonged originally to Estragon. Estragon, on the other hand, wears black trousers which fit him, with a striped jacket which is too big for him; it originally belonged to Vladimir. In this way, the differing physiques of the two actors, Bollmann and Wigger, become part of a whole visual concept. Similarly, Lucky's shoes are the same colour as Pozzo's hat, his checked waistcoat matches Pozzo's checked trousers, and his grey trousers match Pozzo's grey jacket.

About Estragon and Vladimir, Beckett says that Estragon is on the ground, he belongs to the stone. Vladimir is light, he is oriented towards the sky. He belongs to the tree. Is the rehearsal stage the same size as this one? It is very important because of the distance between stone and tree. This distance must be very nearly the same, and we are using a raked stage, too.

Are we going to start with the first act up to the Pozzo-Lucky scene tomorrow? I ask him. No, he would like to start off with Lucky's monologue.

Estragon and Vladimir are going to join us at noon. In the meantime, the rake has been built. The carpenters are still experimenting with the moon — the same moon as the one used ten years ago when *Godot* was last played at the Schiller-Theater, partly with Beckett's help. Wigger comes and greets Beckett warmly: 'I am looking forward to the work very much.' Other members of the company come to shake his hand and are obviously pleased to see him again.

Saturday, 28 December

10 a.m. on the rehearsal stage: the slope is there, the stone is marked by a wooden box, a blooming apple tree presents itself in Chekhovian fashion.

Almost abruptly, Beckett starts to talk about Lucky's monologue. It is not as difficult as it may seem, he says. It will be divided into three parts and the second part is going to be divided again into two sections. The first part is about the indifference of heaven, about divine apathy. This part ends with 'but not so fast . . .' The second part starts off with 'considering what is more', and is about man, who is shrinking — about man who is dwindling. Not only the dwindling is important here, but the shrinking too. These two points represent the two subsections of the second part. The theme of the third part is 'the earth abode of stones' and starts with 'considering what is more, much more grave.' Beckett is very concerned to be exact in his explanations and to repeat certain ideas, underlining them with short movements of his hand while we look for them and mark them in the text.

Herm would like to know how to deal with the end of the monologue. Beckett explains that the different elements of the first sections return at the end. He compares these with a cadenza in music: the threads and themes are gathered together. The theme of the monologue is the shrinking of man under an indifferent heaven on an impossible earth.

Herm starts to read. Beckett stops him, to make an alteration in the script. Instead of '*von der anthropopopometrischen Akakakakademie*' it should read '*von der akakakakademie der anthropopopometrie*' (as it stands in the English version). The alteration is purely for rhythmical reasons. Herm repeats the line several times. Beckett insists on an exact, rhythmical rendering and reads each syllable with him, underlining it with gestures.

Herm continues reading. Beckett interrupts again, reading the lines together with the actor: '. . . that man in short, that man in brief in spite of the strides of alimentation and defecation is seen to waste and pine . . .' He stresses the word *mensch* (man) making the 'sch' into a long, hissing sound. 'Dwindle' is the climax, he says.

In the next section 'the earth abode of stones' is most important. The earth is good only for stones. 'I looked up the meaning of Apathie, Athambie, Aphasie: indifference, imperturbability and muteness.' Herm explains. Beckett concurs. Yes, that is right. It concerns a God who turns himself in all directions at the same time. Lucky wants to say 'Quaquaquaquaversalis', but he can't bring it out, instead he only says, 'quaquaquaqua', Herm has looked up the names: 'Petermann was a cartographer.' It is all about stones, about the world of stones, says Beckett. 'Petermann exists,' Herm contends. Beckett hadn't thought of that, and the name Steinweg is not a specific reference either. 'Belcher was a navigator . . .' Beckett interrupts him, excited and with delight. Belcher, is the opposite of Fartov, English 'to fart'. And Belcher, 'to belch'. With one blow the mysticism about Beckett's use of names is destroyed.

Beckett again returns to the ideas he thinks most important. He scans 'to shrink and dwindle', making a prophetic and threatening gesture with his finger 'To shrink and dwindle . . .' will cause bewilderment for the public but at this point everything will be absolutely clear — for Lucky. Lucky's thinking isn't as good as it used to be: 'He even used to think prettily once . . .,' as Pozzo says. Herm could play it that way, watching Pozzo from time to time. And the two others, too. He is not talking simply to himself. He is not completely on his own.

'But he kind of refuses at first, he doesn't like the idea of thinking . . .' says Herm.

Beckett explains that Lucky would like to amuse Pozzo. Pozzo would like to get rid of him, but if he finds Lucky touching, he might keep him.

'He gives Estragon a long look at one point. What does he mean to say with this long look?' Herm asks. It's a kind of look you can't explain in a few words. There is a lot in that look. Lucky wants the bones of course. So does Estragon. Here is a confrontation, a meeting, of two very poor people. 'Something like solidarity, is that in it, too?' Herm wants to know. Yes, there are so many things in his head. Recognising his counterpart's situation, that is very important — but also some pride, that he is free to refuse the bones, as opposed to Estragon. But Lucky does not forget either. The kick in the shin later on is Lucky's revenge on Estragon for taking the bones.

Beckett continues his explanation of the play. It should be done very simply, without long passages. To give confusion a shape, he says, a shape through visual repetition of themes. Not only themes in the dialogue, but also visual themes of the body. At the beginning when Estragon is asleep sitting on the stone, that is the theme repeated throughout the play. There are fixed moments of stillness, where everything stands completely still and silence threatens to swallow everything up. Then the action starts again.

'But in spite of everything, it is at times quite a cheerful game,' Wigger points out. Yes, of course, but it must be done very exactly. The coming together and parting of Vladimir and Estragon is an example; they are, in fact, inseparable. 'Like a rubber band, they come together time after time,' Wigger says. Yes, Beckett agrees. The principle is: they have to come together step by step.

Beckett walks on the stage, his eyes fixed on the ground, and shows the movement as he speaks Estragon's lines; 'You had something to say to me? . . . You're angry? . . . Forgive me . . . Come, Didi. Give me your hand . . .' With each sentence Beckett makes a step towards the imaginary partner. Always a step then the line. Beckett calls this step-by-step approach a physical theme; it comes up five, six or seven times, and has got to be done very exactly. This is the element of ballet. Or for another example, Lucky falls twice; this mustn't de done realistically, but very cleanly. 'Does that mean that there is to be no naturalism whatsoever?' Wigger wants to know. Beckett demonstrates: he falls to his knees, stretches his arms above his head, and then out before him as he finally slides to the ground. 'But how can one prevent the loss of the human element, how can one prevent it from becoming sterile?' It is a game, everything is a game. When all four of them are lying on the ground, that cannot be handled naturalistically. That has got to be done artificially, with beauty, like ballet. Otherwise everything becomes only an imitation, an imitation of reality. Wigger asks, 'Should it take on a dryness?' Beckett stands up. It should become clear and transparent, not dry. It is a game in order to survive. Beckett continues to think out loud about the play. He is very concerned to find points of access and to convey them to the cast. 'Relaxation' is a word of Estragon's. It is his dream, to be able to keep still. Vladimir is more animated. 'Jupiter's son' is wrong: Atlas was not Jupiter's, but Japethos' son . . . 'And no one noticed this in all these years!' laughs Wigger.

Beckett does not like to speak generally about the play. He brings up the divisions. In the first act there are six parts, in the second there are five. They are identified as A1 to A6 and B1 to B5. Everybody makes the divisions in their scripts. The moments of stillness (which are not necessarily in accordance with the divisions of the script) are also fixed.

Right at the very beginning there is an alteration. Estragon is sitting on the stone. Vladimir is standing in the shadow near the tree; he is barely visible. This is the first moment of stillness. This is an important change, both characters are on stage right from the start and also at the beginning of the second act. The stage direction in the script still reads: 'Estragon, sitting on a low mound, is trying to take off his boot . . . Enter Vladimir.'

Bollmann and Wigger are sitting next to each other, reading the script from the beginning up to the entrance of Pozzo and Lucky. After that the blocking starts. Beckett is on stage and demonstrates each move exactly on cue while speaking the lines, which he knows by heart.

Bollmann and Wigger repeat the movements and make notes in their scripts. What Beckett described just now as an approach is made clear visually: Vladimir is constantly in motion, Estragon sticks to his stone. The reason for the divisions becomes clear: A2 starts when Estragon stands up and begins to move. With an almost frightening concentration and willpower, A1 and A2 are gone over with absolute precision until the scene with Pozzo and Lucky. The uncompromising attitude with which Beckett returned to the script time after time in the earlier discussion is now transformed into practice.

Tuesday, 14 January

The section from the entrance of Pozzo and Lucky is being worked out. There is a variation in the step-by-step approach. Just after he stops, Pozzo is to make four single forward steps toward Vladimir and Estragon and they are to pull back one step each time. Beckett indicates the cues in the dialogue for each step.

Pozzo's tone toward Lucky is sharp and loud, but he addresses Vladimir and Estragon amiably. Beckett makes it clear that Pozzo is not to be played as a superior figure (as he usually is). Instead, all four characters should be equal. Pozzo is, so to speak, a proletarian Pozzo. He plays the lord — magnanimous, frightening — but only because he is unsure of himself. And his monologue about the heavens is to be seen as a 'number' to hold the attention of Vladimir and Estragon. He doesn't want to lose their company.

Sections A3 and A4, from the entry of Pozzo until shortly after his 'number', are run through relatively swiftly.

Thursday, 6 February

B1 and B2, the first two sections of Act II, up to the second entrance of Pozzo and Lucky, are to be rehearsed. Beckett decides on a change in the text. The tree should be referred to as 'pale and stark' instead of 'black and stark', because like the stone it is the colour of bone.

They run through the first scene. In the second, Beckett insists on a pause for 'suspense'. After Vladimir has helped him remove both shoes, Estragon goes to the stone and again tries on both shoes for size. Vladimir looks at him. Then Estragon stands before the stone, looks toward the audience and Vladimir asks 'Well?' Only after a long pause does he turn to Vladimir and say 'It fits'.

After the lullaby on the stone, a new 'march' is introduced. Earlier the kitchen song ('A dog came in the kitchen . . .') was delivered in the rhythm of a march. Now Beckett suggests the funeral march from Chopin as the rhythmical basis for this action. Wigger and Bollmann do their 'walk' with this in mind — slowly and ceremoniously. Beckett laughs, but asks them to temper the over-exaggeration. Now that the march rhythm of the kitchen song has been established Beckett suggests that the dancing motion of Vladimir and Estragon when they come together be given a different underlying music. 'The Merry Widow' is tried: they hum it as they do their little waltz. As at other points it provides a moment of good humour between them.

Friday, 7 February

The conclusions of both acts, sections A6 and B5, are to be worked on. Beckett would like more tension in the entrance of the boy. Vladimir and Estragon should turn to him very slowly and more pauses are added. Estragon's approach to the boy is changed. He runs directly to him in short spurts and grabs his arm. Up to now Estragon had run in a circular motion around the boy. Bollmann remembers the parallel circles when Estragon goes up to Pozzo. Now he would like to change that approach, too, so it will correspond to this one. Beckett keeps the circular movement in the scene with Pozzo because Estragon is afraid of Pozzo.

It is important to Beckett that after the exit of Pozzo and Lucky everything would be slower, both the movements and the words. The movement of Vladimir and Estragon from the tree to the stone is rehearsed again with this thought in mind. The steps are counted; there are two sets of eight steps. When Estragon moves to his stone, Vladimir follows behind very slowly in the same rhythm and then sits down too.

At the end of Act II the entrance of the boy is also given a different accentuation by the alternation of passages spoken matter-of-factly and whispered. When Vladimir asks about Godot, the boy whispers and bows his head.

Beckett is still unsure whether slowing down the end of both acts is right. The resulting air of intimacy is obvious, but he wonders if the quiet passages can be heard well enough. He will balance that out later. He points out the 'moments of stillness' once more. The actors should try to make the frozen picture of waiting into a major motif of the play.

Beckett has made notes on several points in Act I which must be corrected. He would like Vladimir's speech about the Eiffel Tower to be more lyrical, as if he were speaking of a honeymoon, or a dream. Wigger makes the change, and continues. Beckett interrupts at Vladimir's 'What are you doing?' He would like this sentence, in which Vladimir reacts to Estragon's boot, to sound very astonished, as if Vladimir had never seen anything like it.

Following the runthrough, several other small corrections are made. As he says 'Forgive me', Estragon should be standing very close to Vladimir. Then after they embrace, Estragon should jump back (a parallel to 'Who farted?' in Act II).

Beckett goes to the stage and demonstrates again Estragon's gestures under the tree. At 'Let's hang ourselves immediately', Bollmann should point very precisely with his index finger at whatever he speaks of — at Gogo, at Didi, at the tree. In the action with the carrot, Vladimir should hold it out as if he were coaxing a donkey with it.

At another point Beckett points out a great danger. He wants more colour in the lines. He would like the lines spoken with feeling. He is afraid they will otherwise lapse into a mechanical way of speaking.

They do the passage 'Where are all these corpses from?' again, this time much slower. Beckett wants to retain the tempo but also to have more colour. It is still too mechanical to him.

In quick succession a number of passages are polished up. Beckett is very intense and his attitude infects the actors. They take his observations very precisely — every passage which they work on can become noticeably better. It becomes clear that the rehearsals have reached a stage at which minute observations give new animation to whole scenes. They have established a basis on which the detailed inner structure of the play can be worked on without obstruction.

There are difficulties at the death march by Chopin, when Estragon wakes from his dream and Vladimir leads him back and forth. Vladimir hasn't got the pacing right. Beckett directs the rhythm of the music. Finally he sings it for them. Wigger tries it, still doesn't get it right. He would like to listen to the music and then try it alone. In the end Vladimir will intone the music 'Bom-Bom-ba-Bom; -Bom-ba-Bom-ba-Bom-ba-Bom'.

The routine with the hats is rehearsed in detail. There is a long tableau after the first exchange then gradually the action accelerates to a rapid circular action. The entanglement after Lucky's speech is worked out precisely. Beckett points out to Radditz that Pozzo does not need to be so frail in Act II.

After the entrance of Pozzo the individual actions now become calmer. Pozzo's coat is made simpler. Beckett would like the distance between Pozzo's stool and Estragon's stone to be as great as possible. The stool is moved. Beckett remembers a moment in an earlier rehearsal when Estragon examined Lucky's baggage. He had made the suitcase swing back and forth. Beckett would like to retain that. Bollmann goes up to Lucky and sets the suitcase in motion. Herm also sets his whole body into the swinging motion. When Estragon sets the basket in the other hand swinging, only Lucky's arm swings, almost gracefully. Beckett laughs, satisfied.

He would like to cut the text from Pozzo's collapse, 'I can't bear it . . . any longer . . .' to 'He used to be so kind'. He has the impression that it is difficult for Pozzo to maintain the mood in the face of the dialogue of Estragon and Vladimir. The actors protest the cut: the passage is so 'good'. The passage remains.

Saturday, 15 February

A runthrough with interruptions is planned. The opening is three weeks away. Beckett begins at once with a major problem. He would like to go through the scene where everyone is on the ground again. Estragon and Vladimir should not get up to look at Pozzo. The scene should be quite calm.

The runthrough begins; Beckett interrupts the scene with Pozzo and Lucky. He brings up a suggestion I had made several days earlier. Pozzo's relationship to Lucky should be made clearer at 'So much the worse for me', shortly before Pozzo's monologue. And his intention to be a benefactor of Estragon and Vladimir should also be clearer. This leads to more pauses, more conscious accentuation. Beckett also divides Pozzo's 'Shall we have him dance or sing, or recite . . .' into individual sentences. Pozzo should deliver the lines as if he is waiting after each question for a reaction that never comes.

Both acts are run through without interruption. At the end of the rehearsal there is a short discussion of the runthrough. The 'staggering' and the complete motionless of the scene on the ground are unconvincing to Beckett. He decides to cut a few lines in these scenes.

Monday, 17 February

Beckett would like to begin after the fourth 'moment of stillness' in Act II. He has three slips of paper with him on which he has written cuts for the scene on the ground and the staggering which follows it. He would like to give these two crucial passages a more concentrated form by tightening up the text. He makes further cuts as he gives directions for the positioning of bodies. Then text and positioning are subjected to additional control as they are combined onstage.

Estragon and Vladimir prop themselves up on their right arms as they look behind them upstage (instead of simply lying there motionless and looking frontward as they did yesterday). The section is played again. Beckett would like it a bit more animated. The movements of Estragon and Vladimir as they get up are coordinated.

The staggering — up to now Wigger especially had moved about on his feet. Now all three stand quietly next to each other, only their bodies sway back and forth. They remain facing front without exchanging looks. Radditz asks that the swaying from left to right and from front to back be established exactly. The movements are counted.

Another problem with this section is the difference in the size of the three actors. Radditz is supposed to put his arms around the shoulders of the other two and hang between them. Bollmann tells Wigger, 'You'll have to bend a little my way'. 'I am as I am; I can't grow any,' Wigger replies. 'You've got three weeks before the opening,' Bollmann warns.

Beckett interrupts the following section at the place where

Estragon kicks Lucky and hurts his foot, and following that runs to his stone. The timing is changed. Beckett wants the same motion as in Act I when Lucky kicks Estragon who then runs to his stone. And there is a textual correspondence between the lines: 'My friend has hurt himself' and 'Show . . . He's bleeding'.

As Lucky gets up, Vladimir should comment on the action instead of watching silently: 'He's picking up his baggage' and 'Now he is all set'. Vladimir's astonishment thus becomes clearer without destroying the silent gestures of the whole situation. A further change seems called for by Beckett. Pozzo says somebody should see if Lucky is wounded as Estragon and Vladimir stare on. Vladimir: (to Estragon) 'You go' . . . Pozzo: 'Yes, yes. Let your friend go. He stinks so. What is he waiting for?' . . . Vladimir: (to Estragon) 'What are you waiting for?' . . . Estragon: 'I'm waiting for Godot.'

Bollman says, 'I'm waiting for Godot' in a mixture of naïveté and obstinacy which has too much of a comic effect. Beckett doesn't like it. Bollmann tries it in a more neutral manner with a shrug and a more matter-of-fact intonation. He wants to avoid a superficial comic effect at this point.

After a short pause there are further corrections. The reactions of Vladimir and Estragon during Lucky's monologue are rehearsed. They shouldn't overdo it. At the end of the rehearsal Beckett gives me his *Regiebuch* so that reproductions for the programme can be made.

The transition from joking to talking to concentrated rehearsal occurs naturally, almost without a break. The subjective, private attitudes of the actors, and the play as an objective work are coming together to create an atmosphere of 'relaxed tension'.

Bollmann, Wigger and Radditz are lying on the ground. Herm's position is marked by a rolled-out carpet. There is no need for him to lie there all the time. The scene begins. Pozzo creeps away; Estragon and Vladimir call to him. As they get up, there is an interruption. The structure here has been fixed for quite a while, but Beckett would like to tighten it once again. At first the getting up should be done in a normal way, but after that the movements should be slowed down. Once again Bollmann and Wigger go over their mutually agreed gestures. They come halfway up with a slight jerk and support themselves with their outstretched hands (they are lying next to each other). As they begin to get to their feet, they turn away from each other toward the back slowing the tempo as they rise until it is almost slow motion and then they turn face to face. After a short pause, Estragon makes a slow, graceful gesture with both arms and says 'Child's play'. Vladimir accentuates his line, 'Simple question of will-power', by flexing his arm in the familiar gesture of strength. Beckett calls this process 'ballet-like'. By this kind of formal precision the meaning is both cancelled and evident at the same time.

Tuesday, 18 February

The actors are on stage. It is the usual relaxed starting ritual. While they are still chatting, Beckett walks up and down the stage, his eyes fixed on the ground, glancing at the actors from time to time. He is concentrating entirely on the coming scene. As decided the previous day, the rehearsal begins at Estragon's line 'Sweet mother earth', where they are lying on the ground in the second act. The actors take up their positions of their own accord.

Beckett smiles a little unsure. Bollmann and Wigger spank Herm on the backside with mock seriousness. Beckett laughs in a way that recalls the pleasure he always shows at a similar situation in the play.

> ESTRAGON: And suppose, we gave him a good beating, the two of us?
> VLADIMIR: You mean, if we fell on him in his sleep?
> ESTRAGON: Yes.
> VLADIMIR: That seems a good idea all right.

Bollmann and Wigger are carrying out privately an action they perform in the context of the play, going through a whole range of emotions — joyful, childish, naive and sadistic — with an infectious comic anticipation.

The getting up is repeated, and then Vladimir's and Estragon's 'staggering' is tidied up. Beckett has got some doubts about the turn after Pozzo's question 'What is it like?' and would like to cut it. He is very much concerned with tightening the action at this point. They try it without the 360 degree turn: Beckett asks what the cast thinks. Herm wants to keep the turn: 'It is good to have some motion at this point.' I agree too: 'I find that Estragon's line "Some diversion" comes out much more strongly after the movement.' The turn is retained for the time being.

Starting with 'Sweet mother earth', the scene is being played continuously until the next exit of Pozzo and Lucky. When Estragon and Vladimir — both lying on the ground — shout 'Pozzo', Beckett makes a small alteration. Instead of facing Pozzo, Estragon should say his 'We might try him with other names' directly to Vladimir. A small intimate moment of conspiracy is created at this point, which is reminiscent of similar moments throughout the play.

After a short break for cigarettes, there is a run-through of the whole section from the entrance of Pozzo and Lucky until the end of the play. Beckett is sitting in the auditorium at his desk with his cigarillo, watching anxiously the 'conspiracy scene' between Estragon and Vladimir shortly after the start. He makes a remark from time to time, but without interrupting the action; 'Glance towards Pozzo' 'Both on tip toes' — reminding them of things previously agreed upon.

The end of the play. Estragon's trousers fall down according to directions. There is loud laughter from the auditorium. Beckett laughs too. Bollmann's undershirt has been altered. It now reaches to his calves. It is made of pink material, which has been added to, but not yet sewn on properly. Bollmann stands there looking like an unhappy old woman.

Beckett is very pleased with Wigger's monologue shortly before the entrance of the boy. Wigger looks very relaxed, very intense, listening inwardly, making only very brief glances around him. The key to this point of the action is silence. After the break all scenes starting from Pozzo's entrance to the end of the play are rehearsed again. Beckett sits. Short corrections are made: The 'walk' of Estragon and Vladimir should be played through without stopping, the tiger should 'rush' more in Vladimir's description. After 'Who farted?' jump back further. The pulling up of trousers only needs to be indicated. Bollmann tries. He holds his trousers at his belly with his right hand, his pink shirt hanging out on the side. He makes a deplorable but touching picture.[2]

AN AMERICAN BECKETT *GODOT*: LEPERCQ SPACE, BROOKLYN ACADEMY OF MUSIC, 1978.[3]

Correctly billed as 'Samuel Beckett's Production' of *Waiting for Godot*, this production was directed by Walter D. Asmus, based on the Schiller performance of 1975. It was, as Asmus defined it,

> An attempt to transfer the basic spirit and intention of
> Beckett's production to an English version as faithfully as
> possible, keeping in mind the fact that the play would be
> different with different actors and on a different stage.
>
> (Interview, 1978)

In preparation for this production, Asmus travelled to Paris for discussions with Beckett. They went over a check list of points about text and production, made textual changes, and discussed the possibility of adapting topical references to more local allusions for an American audience. During their discussions Beckett told Asmus jokingly that *Waiting for Godot* was 'badly translated'.

In the text for the Schiller-Theater production of *Warten auf Godot* Beckett had made changes to tighten the action, strengthen themes, clarify patterns previously established, further delineate characterisation, and generally to bring about a textual ordering of the 'mess', even as he had sought to accomplish this from a visual point of view. The English text for Brooklyn duplicated these changes.

Some of the attention to text was also to improve troublesome spots in the English translation and restore lines of the French original which he had left out. For example, Estragon's formalised response, 'Ah, yes,' to Vladimir's 'We are waiting for Godot' is emended from 'Ah!' at six points in the play. This motif is strengthened by further emendations from other exclamations: 'Good idea,' 'Fancy that,' 'True,' and in one instance it replaces a groan of recognition. Thus Beckett brought the English translation of this important motif into alignment with the corresponding French '*C'est vrai*' and the German '*Ach ja*' already in existence, providing a better English equivalent for a phrase he had previously found 'impossible to translate adequately'.

One change in the text was to make topical allusions in the French more accessible to American audiences. Asmus mentioned the difficulty he was having with the 'Macon — Cacon' section in Act II due to the unfamiliarity of the Macon wine region to Americans. He finally decided, with Beckett's approval, to change 'Macon' to 'Napa' and 'Cacon' to 'Crappa', retaining the scatological reference. (For a complete list of emendations of the English text see p. 153.)

Asmus's production choices in Brooklyn reflected Beckett's own in Berlin. Beckett had, for example, chosen the larger stage of the Schiller-Theater rather than that of the smaller *Werkstatt* so there would be a greater sense of isolation of the characters and their setting. The stage of the Lepercq Space of the Brooklyn Academy of Music was much smaller than the large stage of the theatre in Berlin. Asmus compensated by having the designer Carole Lee Carroll create the largest possible stage area available in the small Lepercq workspace using only a minimal offstage area for exits and entrances. She used the total thirty-foot height of the Lepercq stage space to make up in vertical expanse what was not available horizontally.

In casting, Asmus retained the by now well-established physical contrast between the two main characters. Sam Waterston as Vladimir was tall and thin, Austin Pendleton as Estragon was shorter and somewhat frail. As Vladimir, Waterston assumed the bowed back, slightly off-balance gait and stiff slightly twisted hands that were part of Stefan Wigger's posture in Berlin. Michael Egan as Pozzo was corpulent and wore his own short black beard. Milo O'Shea who played Lucky was of medium build but still noticeably less bulky than Pozzo. At the Schiller the juvenile actor who would normally have played the boy had been replaced by a younger actor nine years old because he appeared too adolescent and knowing. In Brooklyn, the boy was played by R.J. Murray, Jr., also nine years old, round-faced and almost cherubic — a confident actor but still evidently shy and ignorant.

The set was extremely simple, following the spirit of Matias' design for the Schiller-Theater exactly. There was a clearly perceptible but unobtrusive slope to all sides covered in a mottled textured grey groundcloth to create a plateau. The raked stage thus presented a grey mound with two focal points: Estragon's small rectangular grey stone as far downstage right as possible and Vladimir's spare thin tree upstage left. In spite of Beckett's note at the end of the *Regiebuch*, '(Tree) was not right . . . two branches only, two leaves, third couple,' the tree in Brooklyn still had three branches, one branch curved downward to stage right and two nearly symmetrical branches curved downward to stage left, as in the Berlin production. The backdrop was even more neutral grey than in Berlin where Beckett had been unable to get the background devoid of all variation of colour and texture which he had wanted. There were two three-foot wide black velour-covered wings to mark and mask exits and entrances as there had been on the Schiller stage.

As in Berlin, the effect of the lighting was of unrelieved coldness (achieved by using blue lamps and gels); the characters cast no shadows, due to carefully focused upstage area lighting. As Beckett had specified in his Berlin *Regiebuch*, the right and left sides of the stage were in shadow, so that the plateau was surrounded by darkness and the tableaux accentuated. The cold, pale moon was presented with the same geometrical precision as at the Schiller. A lighted, round box behind the cyclorama made a perfect circle of uniform colour and intensity. The box was fixed to a sixteen-foot bar which pivoted so that the moon made the same graceful arc as it had in Berlin.

The stage properties were, in Asmus's words, 'as simple as possible'. Lucky carried a rectangular brown suitcase, aged but not dilapidated, and an ordinary picnic basket with handles. His whip was a regular leather thong, about eight feet long. He ate real chicken, which he reduced to the bones thrown to Estragon, and drank red wine from an ordinary wine bottle. Some properties did create special visual effects: Pozzo's folding canvas camp stool was extremely small for his considerable bulk. The carrot which Vladimir gives to Estragon was ridiculously small and dangled like a pendulum from a nearly invisible top. And the thick rope which connects Lucky and Pozzo was grey rather than brown hemp, with a very thickly braided heavy noose for Lucky's neck.

Costuming followed exactly the criss-cross ill-matching of trousers and jackets as at the Schiller, but in light and darker shades of grey. Make-up was light and muted with just a suggestion of age for Vladimir and Estragon. The underlying paleness visible in Berlin was not as obvious in the Brooklyn production.

The aesthetic distance and Brechtian alienation techniques of the Schiller performance were preserved in the Brooklyn production. The movement and gestures were highly formalised, the action disparate from the line. The production re-created the patterns of circles and crosses in the blocking and retained the smaller gestures which helped to establish them. Other action was noticeably located at points almost geometrically determined. Major speeches and exchanges took place at artificial coordinates: Vladimir's tree upstage left; Estragon's stone as far downstage right as possible; Pozzo's stool opposite at downstage left; Lucky's position midstage; and The Boy's position upstage centre. The area upstage right was noticeably vacant — the scene of action only when an arrival or exit occurred or was anticipated.

Key thematic lines, particularly Vladimir's, were delivered directly to the audience from set points downstage centre, midstage and occasionally from Estragon's stone and Vladimir's position downstage left: eg. The first 'We're waiting for Godot.' (F14, G10L); Vladimir's 'One [of the thieves] is supposed to have been saved.' (F12, G9L); and his 'It's the way of doing it . . . if you want to go on living.' (F60, G38R). This stylised delivery is parodied near the end of Act I when Vladimir diverts his attention from the boy and turns towards the audience to echo in a bored tone Hamlet's 'Words, words.' (F50, G33R).

The dialogue was deliberately 'understated', usually avoiding the inflections of a performance striving for realism, 'but not flat and unvaried'. At certain points there was an extremely wide range of artificial vocal dynamics. Vladimir begins the dog tune in a high falsetto, then starts again in a lower key; he whispers the last words of the round and finally repeats them silently. Estragon mimes his question to Pozzo about Lucky's disposition: 'You – want – to – get – rid – of – him?' Estragon and Vladimir mouth their 'Adieu' to Pozzo and Lucky and wave their hats with broad gesturing. Estragon shouts 'vehemently' 'No, no, no laces, no laces!' (F69, G44R).

Exaggerated delivery highlighted selected parts of the text. In Act II Vladimir's line 'We nearly hanged ourselves from it' is changed to produce a series of staccato monosyllables: 'Yes, that's right-all-but-hanged-ourselves-from-it.' Certain words are emphasised by being separated into syllables and drawn out: 'Ap — palled,' 'Ti — ed,' 'Caawm' and 'Save — your', (for 'Saviour.') Estragon and Vladimir break into a sing-song falsetto for the lines 'I am happy,' 'So am I,' 'We are happy.' They face front and deliver the section about 'All the dead voices', in a style reminiscent of operatic recitative. Pozzo's Latin quotation *Memoria praeteritorum bonorum . . .* is chanted almost as if it were a fragment from the Mass. This intonation is an echo of the earlier antiphonal question and response, when Vladimir and Estragon run to opposite sides of the stage completing the transcept of the cross, 'Do you see anything co – ming?' 'You must have had a vis – ion.' 'No need to sh – out.' (F74-75, G48L).

Direct comic interplay with the audience which had been somewhat held down in Berlin was given wider range in Brooklyn. A distinct pause separates Estragon's answer: 'Not –

enough' following Vladimir's observation 'This is becoming really insignificant.' (F68, G44L). After Estragon's 'Charming spot', he turns, stops, looks directly at the audience and says, 'Inspiring prospects', and finally, 'Let's go.' (F13-14, G10L). Estragon's flight upstage away from the audience is met by Vladimir's 'Imbecile! There's no way out there!' And when Vladimir pushes Estragon toward the audience he retreats in dismay with Vladimir's assent, 'You won't? Well I can understand that.' (F74, G47R). Estragon points at the audience on the line, 'There is no lack of void', and again as he refers to '. . . that bog.' (F15, G10R).

This was an American production for American audiences, with American actors more accustomed to a naturalistic style of acting than the performers at the Schiller, but in its uncluttered simplicity and formalisation this production did achieve the goal of 'transferring the basic spirit and intention' of Beckett's direction. The production, however, met with an unenthusiastic reception from American critics and audiences.

TEXTUAL CHANGES

In the following list of textual changes made in the 1975 Schiller-Theater production, the left marginal listing of pages refers to the Faber and Grove texts; 'PS' indicates emendations also made in the original *Godot* prompt script; 'RC,' changes also made in The Royal Court 1964 production; and 'T,' revisions made in English which bring the text into alignment with the French text in the Suhrkamp trilingual edition.

Page	Cuts	From beginning phrase	To beginning phrase
F13;G9R	PS T	E: 'I thought you said hell'	E: 'Well what of it?'
F14;G10R		V: 'Why?'	V: (Angrily.) 'Nothing is certain when you're about.'
F17;G12L	PS	V: 'Hmm'	V: 'It'd give us an erection.'
F20;G14L	PS	E: 'I'll never forget this carrot'	E: 'Ah yes, now I remember.'
F22;G15R	PS T	P: 'Pozzo!'	P: (Silence.) 'Does that name mean nothing to you?'

F24;G16R PS	P: 'Yes,'	P: 'six hours, that's right, six hours on end, and never a soul in sight.'
F25;G17R	E: 'I see nothing.'	E: 'Oh I say!'
F26;G18L	P: (*He strikes a match and begins to light his pipe*)	(*Estragon sees the chicken bones on the ground and stares at them greedily.*)
F26;G18L RC	(*As Lucky does not move Pozzo throws the match angrily away and jerks the rope.*)	P: 'Basket!'
F26;G18L	(*Pozzo strikes another match and lights his pipe*)	P: 'Ah! That's better.'
F27;G18R	P: (*He puffs at his pipe*)	V: (exploding) 'It's a scandal!'
F28;G19R	P: (*He knocks out his pipe against his whip, gets up*)	P: 'I must be getting on'
F28;G19L	P: 'I'm not in the habit of smoking two pipes one on top of the other . . .'	P: . . . 'it makes (*hand to heart*) my heart go pit-a-pat.'
F28;G19R	P: *He fills his pipe.*)	V: (*vehemently*) 'Let's go!'
F28;G19R RC	P: (*having lit his pipe*) 'The second is never so sweet . . .'	V: I'm going.
F29;G19R	P: 'He can no longer endure my presence.'	P: (to Vladimir) 'Think twice before you do anything rash.'
F29;G19R RC	P: (*he takes the pipe out of his mouth . . .*)	P: '. . . to your appoint-ment with this . . . Godet . . . Godot . . . Godin . . .'
F30;G20R	P: (*. . . puts back the vapouriser in his pocket . . .*)	P: (*. . . sprays his throat again . . .*)
F32-33;G22L	E: (*On one leg*). 'I'll never walk again.'	P: 'He's stopped crying.'
F33;G22L	V: 'Try and walk.'	P: 'Guess who taught me all these beautiful things.'
F33;G22R	V: (*looking at the sky*). 'Will night never come?'	P: 'But for him all my thoughts, all my feelings, would have been of common things.'
F34;G23L	V: 'What?'	V: 'I don't know.'
F37;G24R RC	P: 'A little attention, if you please.'	(*Vladimir and Estragon continue their fiddling, Lucky is half asleep.*)
F37;G24R RC	P: (*Pozzo cracks his whip feebly.*)	P: 'What was I saying?'

F37;G25L RC	E: 'But take the weight off your feet, I implore you, you'll catch your death.'	P: (*who hasn't listened*). 'Ah yes! The night.'
F37;G25L RC	P: 'But be a little more attentive . . .'	P: (*He looks at the sky.*)
F38;G25R	E: 'Oh tray bong, tray tray tray bong.'	P: (*reverently*). 'Bless you gentlemen . . .'
F40;G26R	*Silence*. (after V: 'Then let him dance')	P: 'Dance, misery!'
F40;G27L RC	E: 'The Scapegoat's Agony.'	P: 'The Net . . .'
F40;G27L RC	V: (*squirming like an aesthete*) . . .	E: 'Nothing happens, nobody comes, nobody goes, it's awful!'
F47;G31R	P: 'On!' (2nd 'on!' after crack of whip.)	E: 'On!'
F47;G31R	P: 'Adieu' (*after Pozzo throws stool to Lucky.*)	V: 'Stool!' (*change from* (*waving*) 'Adieu!; Adieu!')
F48;G31R	P: 'Faster! On! Adieu! . . .'	E: 'On!' V: 'On!' (additions)
F53;G35L T	E: 'Wait!' (after V: 'I'm cold')	E: (*He moves away from V.*)

Act II

F65;G42L T	V: (*He takes off his hat, concentrates.*)	V: 'What was I saying, we could go on from there.'
F66;G43L	V: 'And . . .' (after E: 'Alas')	V: '. . . Pozzo? And Lucky?'
F77;G49R T	V: 'Gogo!'	P: (*clutching on to Lucky who staggers*). 'What is it? Who is it?'
F79;G50R T	P: 'Help!' (after 'But there's one thing I'm afraid of.')	E: 'What?'
F79;G51L PS	P: 'Help!' (after V: 'No, the best would be to take advantage of Pozzo's calling for help–')	V: 'In anticipation of some tangible return.'
F80;G51R T	P: 'Help!'	V: 'Or for night to fall.'
F81;G52L	V: '. . . . They'll kill me!'	P: 'Where am I?'
F82;G53L	V: 'Were you asleep?'	V: 'It's this bastard Pozzo at it again.'
F83;G53R	V: 'Perhaps I could crawl to him'	V: 'Perhaps I could call to him' (changed from 'Or I could call to him.')
F83;G53R	V: 'He moved.'	E: 'We might try him with other names.'

155

F83;G53R	T	V: 'I'm afraid he's dying'	E: 'It'd be amusing.'
F85;G54R	PS	P: '—but are you friends?'	E: (*irritably*) 'Expand! Expand!' (F86;G55R)
F86;G55R	T	P: 'Quite wonderful!'	P: 'I woke up one fine day as blind as Fortune'
F86;G55R		E: 'I'm going'	P: 'Where's my menial?' (F87;G56L)
F87;G56L		'What happened exactly?'	P: 'Go and see is he hurt.'
F90;G58L		E: 'Didi!' (after 'Ow!')	V: 'I don't know what to think any more.'

Additions
Act I

Page	Additions	Phrase Before	Phrase After
F15;G10R	V: 'that stone . . .'	V: 'that tree . . .'	(*turning towards auditorium*) 'that bog . . .'
F19;G13R	E: 'Let's go. V: Where? (*Pause*). Perhaps we'll sleep tonight in his loft. Snug and dry, our bellies full, in the hay. That's worth waiting for. No? E: Not all night V: It's still day.' (*Pause*)	T *Silence*	E: (Violently) 'I'm hungry!'
F22;G15L	P: 'Faster!'	T P: (*off*) 'On!'	(*crack of whip . . .*)
F37;G25L	P: 'At this time of year'	P: It is pale and luminous like any sky at this hour of the day.	(*Pause.*)
F40;G27L	V: 'He is tired.'	T E: 'With a little practice'	P: 'He used to dance the farandole . . .'
F45;G30L	V: 'Come on!'	T PS E: 'What does he take us for?'	P: 'Don't let him go!'
F46;G30R	P: 'Perhaps I dropped it.'	T P: 'Twas my grampa gave it to me!'	P: (*He searches on the ground, V & E likewise.*)
F46;G31L	P: '. . . on the Steinway.'	P: 'I must have left it at the manor . . .'	*Silence.*

F48;G31R	E: 'On!' V: 'On!' P: 'Adieu!' E & V: 'Adieu!' P: 'Adieu!' E & V: 'Adieu!' (ad lib)	*Long Silence.*	V: 'That passed the time.'

Act II

F60;G38R	V: 'But enough about that. There you are back and there I am happy.'	T V: 'But it's the way of doing it that counts, the way of doing it, if you want to go on living.'	E: 'I wasn't doing anything.'
F61;G39	V: (*He considers*) 'Yes, that's right-all-but-hanged-ourselves-from it.'	T V: 'We all but hanged ourselves from it.'	V: 'But you wouldn't. Do you not remember?'
F67;G43R	V: 'There.'	E: 'Because they were hurting me!'	V: (triumph-antly, point to the boots). 'There they are!'
F73;G47L	E: 'I'm going.'	V: 'Dance, hog!' (*He writhes.*)	E: (*Exit E. left precipitately.*)
F73;G47R	E: 'To the foot of the rise.'	T V: '. . . . I thought you were gone forever.'	E: 'They're coming!'
F73;G47R	V: 'Come!'	T V: 'Let's go and meet him!'	V: (*He drags E. towards the wings.*)
F74;G47R	E: 'To the foot of the rise. V: No doubt, we're on a plateau. Served up on a plateau. E: They're coming there too!' (entire exchange changed from E: 'They're coming there too!')	T V: 'Where were you?'	V: 'We're surrounded!'
F79;G51L	P: 'Help!'	V: 'all mankind is us whether we like it or not . . .'	V: 'Let us make the most of it . . .'

F82;G52R	E: 'Up!'	T E: (*He stretches out his hand which V. makes haste to seize.*)	V: 'Pull!'
F82;G53L	E: 'What?'	T E: (*With a start.*)	E: 'What is it?'
F83;G53R	P: Lucky!'	V: (*Vladimir, propped on his elbow*)	V: (*observes his retreat.*)
F83;G53R	P: 'Lucky!'	(*Pozzo collapses*)	V: 'He's down!'
F83;G53R	E: 'Let's see.'	T E: (*He reflects.*)	E: 'Abel! Abel!'
F84;G54R	E: 'He's doing it on purpose!'	E: (*They help Pozzo to his feet, let him go. He falls.*)	V: 'We must hold him.'
F84;G54R	V: 'Blind!'	*Silence*	E: 'Perhaps he can see into the future.'
F84;G54R	V: 'Blind!'	E: 'Perhaps he can see into the future'	V: 'Since when?'
F86;G55R	P: 'Quite wonderful.'	T V: '*Memoria praeteritorum bonorum* — that must be unpleasant.'	V: 'And it came on you all of a sudden?'
F93;G60L	V: 'Let's go.'	T V: 'I don't know. A willow.'	*Vladimir draws Estragon towards the tree. (Change from Estragon draws Vladimir towards the tree.)*

Altered Lines
Act I

Page	Former Text	Present Text with Change
F18;G12L	E: 'Good idea'	E: 'Ah yes'
F21;G14R	E: 'Fancy that'	E: 'Ah yes'
F30;G20R	T P: 'Is everybody listening? Is everybody ready?' (*He looks at them all in turn, jerks the rope.*) 'Hog!' (*Lucky raises his head*)	P: 'Is everybody listening?' (*He looks at them all in turn, jerks the rope.*) 'Hog!' (*Lucky raises his head*) 'Is everybody ready?'
F31;G21L	P: '. . . Atlas, son of Jupiter!'	P: 'Atlas, son of Japetos!'
F33;G22L	V: 'Try and walk.'	V: 'Will night never come?'

F36;G24R T P: 'No doubt you are right.' (*He sits down.*) 'Done it again!' (Pause.) 'Thank you dear fellow.'

P: 'No doubt you are right. Thank you dear fellow.' (*He sits down.*) 'Done it again!' (Pause.)

F38;G25R P: (*to Estragon*) 'And you, Sir?' E: 'Oh Tray bong, tray tray tray bong.'

P: (*To E.*) 'And you, Sir?' (*Thumb up gesture*) E: (*Thumb up gesture.*)

F45;G30L T V: 'But will he be able to walk?' P: 'Walk or crawl!' (*He kicks Lucky.*)

V: 'But will he be able to orientate himself?' P: 'I'll orientate him' (*He kicks Lucky*)

F47;G31R (. . . . *Exit Lucky.*) Pozzo: 'On! On!'

(Exit Lucky.) E: 'Faster!' V: 'Faster!'

F47;G31R V: E: (*waving*) 'Adieu! Adieu!'

V: 'Stool!' E: 'Stool!'

F60;G39L T V: 'Wait for Godot.' (*Estragon groans. Silence.*)

V: 'Wait for Godot' E: 'Ah Yes.'

F61;G39L T V: 'We nearly hanged ourselves from it.'

V: 'We all but hanged ourselves from it.'

F61;G39L V: 'All the same, you can't tell me that this' (*gesture*) 'bears any resemblance to . . .' (*he hesitates*) 'to the Macon country for example . . .' E: 'The Macon country! Who's talking to you about the Macon country?' V: 'But you were there yourself . . . in the Macon country.' E: 'No, I was never in the Macon country! I've puked my puke of a life away here, I tell you! Here! In the Cacon country!'

V: 'All the same you can't tell me that this' (*gesture*) 'bears any resemblance to . . .' (*he hesitates*) 'to the Napa Valley for example.' E: 'The Napa Valley! Who's talking to you about the Napa Valley?' V: 'But you were there yourself in the Napa Valley.' E: 'No, I was never in the Napa Valley! I've puked my puke of a life away here, I tell you! Here! in the Crappa Valley!'

F63;G41L T V: 'Say something!' E: 'I'm trying'

V: 'Say something.' E: 'I'm seeking.'

F63;G41L T V: 'Wait for Godot.' E: 'Ah!'

V: 'Wait for Godot' E: 'Ah yes!'

F62-63;G41T V: 'Help me!' E: 'I'm trying'

V: 'Help me!' E: 'I'm seeking.'

F66;G42R V: 'But yesterday evening it was all black and bare. And now it's covered with leaves.'

V: 'But yesterday evening it was all pale and stark as a skeleton. And now it's covered with leaves.'

F68;G44L T V: 'We're waiting for Godot'
E: 'Ah!' (*Pause. Despairing*) 'What'll we do, what'll we do!'

V: 'We're Waiting for Godot.'
E: 'Ah! yes.' (*Pause. Despairing*) 'What'll we do. What'll we do!'

F71;G45R T V: 'We're waiting for Godot'
E: 'Ah!'

V: 'We're waiting for Godot.'
E: 'Ah! yes.'

F73;G47L V: 'Tell me to dance.'
E: 'I'm going'

V: 'Tell me to dance'
E: 'That's enough of that.'

F74;G47L T V: 'Where were you?'
E: 'They're coming there too!'

V: 'Where were you?'
E: 'To the foot of the rise'

F78;G50L E V: 'We're waiting for Godot.'
E: 'Ah!'

V: 'We're waiting for Godot.'
E: 'Ah yes.'

F78;G50R T V: 'And that we should subordinate our good offices to certain conditions?'
E: 'What?'

V: 'And that we should subordinate our good offices to certain conditions?'
E: 'Yes.'

F80;G51R T V: '. . . We are waiting for Godot to come —'
E: 'Ah!'

V: '. . . We are waiting for Godot to come —'
E: 'Ah! Yes.'

F83;G53R V: (*Vladimir, propped on his elbow, observes his retreat.*) He's off! (*Pozzo collapses.*) He's down!

(*Vladimir, propped on his elbow*), 1) P: 'Lucky!' 2) V: (*observes his retreat.*) He's off! (*Pozzo collapses.*) 3) P: 'Lucky!' 4) V: 'He's down!'

Act II

F83;G53R V: 'Or I could call to him.'
E: 'Yes, call to him.'

V: 'Perhaps I could call to him'
E: 'Yes, call to him.'

F84;G54L T V: 'We're waiting for Godot.'
E: 'Ah!' (*Despairing*) 'What'll we do, what'll we do!'

V: 'We're waiting for Godot.'
E: 'Ah! Yes.' (*Despairing*) 'What'll we do, what'll we do!'

F86;G55R T V: '*Memoria praeteritorum bonorum* — that must be unpleasant.'
E: 'We wouldn't know.'

V: '. . . *Memoria praeteritorum bonorum* — that must be unpleasant.'
P: 'Quite wonderful'

F88-89; G57L T (*Lucky gets up, gathers up his burdens.*) V: 'Where do you go from here.' P: 'On.' (*Lucky, laden down takes his place before Pozzo.*)

(*Lucky gets up, gathers up his burdens.*) V: 'He's getting up.' P: 'He'd better!' V: 'He's picking up his bags. Now he's all set.'

'Whip!' (*Lucky puts everything down, looks for whip, finds it, puts it into Pozzo's hand, takes up everything again.*) 'Rope!' (*Lucky puts everything down, puts end of rope into Pozzo's hand, takes up everything again.*)

P: 'Whip!'
V: 'Where do you go from here?'
P: 'None of my [sic] business.'
V: 'How changed you are!'
P: 'Whip'
  'Rope.'
V: 'What is there in the bag?'

F90;G57R T V: '. . . I wonder is he really blind.'
E: 'Blind? Who?'
V: 'Pozzo.'
E: 'Blind?'
V: 'He told us he was blind.'
E: 'Well, what about it?'

V: 'I wonder is he really blind.'
E: 'Who?'
V: 'Would one truly blind say he had no sense of time?'
E: 'Who?'
V: 'Pozzo'
E: 'He is blind?'
V: 'So he said'
E: 'Well, what about it?'

F92;G59L V: (*softly*) 'Has he a beard, Mr. Godot?'
Boy: 'Yes Sir.'
V: 'Fair or . . . (*he hesitates*) . . . or black?'
Boy: 'I think it's white, Sir'

V: (*softly*) 'Has he a beard, Mr. Godot?'
Boy: 'Yes Sir.'
V: 'Fair or . . . (*he hesitates*) . . . or black . . . or red?'
Boy: 'I think it's white, Sir.'

F97;G60L T V: 'Pull on your trousers.'
E: (*realising his trousers are down.*) 'True.'

V: 'Pull on your trousers.'
E: (*realising his trousers are down.*) 'Ah, yes.'

CHAPTER FOUR
Endgame

GENERAL STATEMENTS

For you, if you really want it, but only if you really want it because it really has meaning, the others are only every day.
(Note to Roger Blin sent with typescript of *Fin de partie* quoted in Deirdre Bair, *Samuel Beckett*, p. 479, Bair's translation)

I suppose the one I dislike the least is *Endgame*.
(To Professor Tom Bishop of New York University 1978)

You must realise that Hamm and Clov are Didi and Gogo at a later date, at the end of their lives . . . Actually they are Suzanne and me.
(To Roger Blin and Jean Martin at rehearsals of the original production quoted in Bair, *Samuel Beckett* p. 483)

Hamm as stated and Clov as stated, *nec tecum nec sine te*, in such a place, and in such a world, that's all I can manage, more than I could.
(Letter to Alan Schneider, December 29, 1957 in *Village Voice Reader* p. 185)

In *Godot*, the audience wonders if Godot will ever come, in *Endgame*, it wonders if Clov will ever leave.
(To Alec Reid in *All I Can Manage More Than I Could*, p. 71)

It will never be the way I hear it. It's a cantata for two voices.
(To Georges Pelorson about a *Théâtre de la Huchette* performance of *Fin de partie* which he had attended. Interview 1977)

ORIGINS

Acte sans paroles I

According to Deryk Mendel *Fin de partie* was begun as a companion piece to *Acte sans paroles I*.

> I wanted some pantomimes for my cabaret act so I wrote to Ionesco, Adamov, Audiberti, and Beckett, asking them to write 'libretti' for me. Beckett was the only one who wrote anything. He sent me *Acte sans paroles I*. But it wasn't quite right for a cabaret, it really belonged on a regular stage. It was theatre, but on the other hand, it wouldn't fill a whole evening. It was too short. So he said, OK I'll write something to go along with it. That was *Endgame*. (Interview Deryk Mendel 1976)

The first performance of *Fin de partie* at the Royal Court Theatre in London (April 3, 1957) and the first Paris performance (April 27, 1957) were both parts of double bills of *Fin de partie* and *Acte sans paroles I*. Deryk Mendel directed and 'danced' in both performances of the mime. The mime has consistently been published with *Endgame*: in the French *Fin de partie, suivi de Acte sans paroles,* Paris Editions de Minuit, 1957; and *Endgame* followed by *Act Without Words,* New York, Grove Press, 1958 (Evergreen Book E-96) and Faber and Faber, 1958.

The final lines in the early version of *Endgame* (which Beckett called *Avant fin de partie*), 'Bom . . . That poor old woman who asked for a drop of water,' suggests the connection between the appeals of Mother Pegg for pity in *Endgame* and the water withheld in *Act Without Words I*. The unspecified 'familiar gesture' of the man in the mime in the English text is more specific in the French where 'he folds and unfolds his handkerchief' — a direct connection with Hamm.

Mime du Rêveur

Much of *Fin de partie* was implied in another earlier mime play. In the period just after writing *Godot*, Beckett wrote an unfinished four page typescript of a work entitled *Mime du Rêveur*.* In it a single character performs a mime in response to a second mime depicting his dreams. In its protagonist, A, we see the beginnings of the stylised Hamm making an almost

---

* This fragment is contained in a photocopy at Baker Library, Dartmouth College. The dating is based upon the informed conjecture of Lawrence Harvey.

symbolic response to the confines of his consciousness. He is an old man not yet immobilised like Hamm but tottering and dependent upon his rocking chair in which he passes the greater part of his existence, in dream-tormented sleep. He inhabits a skull-like interior with two circular curtained windows fixed high on the wall. Like Clov in the opening mime of *Fin de partie*, he climbs a stool to make a serial inspection of the two windows and the world outside them. Like Hamm, he exhibits a preoccupation with his proper place on the stage as defined by cardinal points and axies of the set. And he moves his chair in a circuit from corner to corner and to the centre presenting a different profile at each spot. And like Hamm who requests Clov to wheel him on a 'little tour' to inspect the perimeter of their shelter and its hollow bricks, he feels his own way along the wall of his abode in another circuit. He does not staunch the dripping of a heart in his head as Hamm does, but he shields his ears with his hands from the sound of the wind which accompanies his memories — an action which replaces cancelled directions for the use of surgical cotton to stuff his ears. His main activity, however, is to inject himself with a soporific painkiller — a kind of relief Hamm longs for but which is no longer available to him. In depicting A's attempt to escape the pain of existence in his closed interior world, *Mime du Rêveur* was the first step toward Hamm and *Fin de partie*.

Avant Fin de partie

Equally evident as the stylised universal Hamm in the protagonist A of *Mime du Rêveur* are the seeds of Krapp — a man concerned with realistic individualised memories and painful self-appraisal. (See p. 243 below). Just as he had questioned theatrical methods in *Eleuthéria* before undertaking *Godot*, in the fragment *Avant Fin de partie** Beckett weighed the alternatives of universal and individualised characterisation before beginning the drafts of *Fin de partie* itself. The fragment depicts a master, X, and his factotum, F. As his algebraic designation X as opposed to Beckett's usual A for unnamed characters implies, the protagonist is still an undetermined quantity. X questions in his opening monologue the veracity of his own presentation and what it means to be a *'simple particular'* — whether he is a representative of all humanity like

* At Reading University. The title was given at the time of presentation.

'billions' (or perhaps only 'thousands' or 'hundreds') or is a unique individual 'the last of his species'. This was also the question Beckett faced in determining how he would develop the protagonist taken over from *Mime du Rêveur*.

At this stage the issue was never really in doubt. X alludes to a life that is more like Krapp's than the one depicted in the fragment. His life is one of '*Misère! Vieillesse! Solitude! Souvenirs! (un temps) Constipation!*' (Misery! Old Age! Solitude! Memories! *Pause* Constipation) But it is only an allusion. He is at most a Krapp *manqué*. Despite his pointed denial, 'I and those who live with me signify nothing'; the working fiction in this fragment is clearly that X is the abstracted embodiment of any half of numerous human relationships of which F is the other half — a master, lover, parent, or child — and not the real son of a real mother. (It is their function as generalised representations rather than unique individuals which accounts for the seemingly arbitrary assignment of a variety of names to F, and F's search for a proper appellation for X as they assume the different roles of their half of the relationship.)

Still distrustful of old dramatic methods, Beckett again resorted in *Avant fin de partie* to an abortive dramaticule like *Human Wishes* to parody any attempt at realistic individual presentation. Shortly before the conclusion of the fragment is another burlesque of dramatic exposition. Having just raised the question of how much of what his servant says is lies and how much truth, X begins arbitrarily to establish the facts of his individual existence. He commands F to describe the place. There follows a blatantly artificial identification of locus of the action narrowing down from the region to the interior in which they find themselves. This is followed by an equally artificial location of the events first in history and then in the more immediate time down to the hour. The importance of all this factual background is treated ironically. '*Tout s'explique,*' says X. '*D'une blancheur de craie*' ('White as chalk' the equivalent of 'Clear as a bell') replies F.

A following scene between X and his mother in which they discuss their relationship ostensibly gives evidence of the family context so central to conventional characterisation. But this realistic background is unreal. The role of the mother is only enacted by F in a ludicrous disguise, and her account of events is exactly contrary to the salient points of X's account of his family. Moreover, she is herself a kind of Pirandellian abstraction of a conventional stage role like those seen in *Eleuthéria*. She is an infirm remnant of the past, miraculously restored to activity after years of ill-health and hiding in a corner. The only realism connected with the scene is her son's long naturalistic account of her before she enters. The scene reveals almost nothing about the protagonist. In the end the whole process is dismissed as outmoded and unsuitable. In a passage echoing the Spectator's description of *Eleuthéria* as an ill-played chess match, X complains of their performance. '*Il joue de plus en plus mal. Moi aussi . . . Nous sommes trop vieux, le jeu est trop vieux, nous n'en pouvons plus, de jouer toujours les mêmes vieilleries.*' ('He plays worse and worse. So do I . . . We are too old, the play is too old, we can't do it any more, play the same old things.') The assumptions of their little drama are that the circumstances detailed all appear true and that events are leading to some new outcome: '*que cette nuit — (Il s'interrompt. Un temps)*'. ('That this night . . . (*He breaks off. Pause.*)) Implied is the assumption of conventional drama that there is something extraordinary transpiring which will lead to a dramatic conclusion. But X knows his existence to be different. '*Non, non, cette nuit sera comme les autres nuits, à peine plus noire, et demain, demain sera guère plus interminable qu'aujourd'hui.*' ('No, no, this night will be like all the other nights, hardly more black, and tomorrow will be little more interminable than today.')

In place of the tired old game they have been playing, X proposes a new order for the day. They should concern themselves with 'the affair of Bom'. The allusion to the Russian clown Bom and her unanswered plea for water — suggests an alternative to the kind of drama just parodied. That alternative would be at once more comic and more tragic and more universal.

Geulincx

The *Ethica* of Arnold Geulincx, which Beckett indicated as one of the origins of *Godot*, is also evident as an early influence on *Endgame*. A cancelled passage in the preliminary two-act version defines the relationship between master and servant in terms of obligations, closely parallel and in the same order as those defining man's relation to God in the *Ethica*. The Master lists the servant's four obligations:

1. 'When I call you, you come immediately'
2. 'When I don't call you, you don't come'

3. 'When I tell you to remain, you remain'
4. 'When I tell you to go away, you go'

And he goes on to define his own reciprocal responsibility, 'I keep you alive. It is necessary to believe that you are alive and that it is I who arranges it.' (Authors' translation, TS at Ohio State University)

Also central to that version are eating and procreation which are linked, as they are in Geulincx's third obligation, as the two basic acts emblematic of man's duty to perpetuate human existence. And the curse against progenitors, proscribed in the seventh obligation, is, of course, a major element of *Endgame*.

COMPOSITION

Composition of *Fin de partie* was to   Beckett's recollection begun in 1954. Two preliminary versions preceded the final text for publication.* As he worked on the play he wrote to Alan Schneider describing his progress in terms suggesting Hamm's dog.

> Dec. 27, 1955
> Dear Alan:
> If I don't get away now and try to work I'll explode or implode. So I have retreated to my hole in the Marne mud and am struggling with a play.
> Yours, Sam

> January 11, 1956
> P.S. I am writing an even worse affair and have got down the gist of the first act (of two).

> April 12, 1956
> Afraid no plays to show you. I did finish another, but don't like it. It has turned out a three-legged giraffe, to mention only the architectonics, and leaves me in doubt whether to take a leg off or add one on.

> June 21, 1956
> . . . Have at last written another, one act, longish hour and a quarter I fancy. Rather difficult and elliptic, mostly depending on the power of the text to claw, more inhuman than 'Godot'. My feeling, strong, at the moment, is to leave it in French for a year at least . . .-I'm in a ditch somewhere near the last stretch and would like to crawl up out of it.
> (*Village Voice Reader*, p. 183).

---

* Ruby Cohn, Stanley Gontarski, John Fletcher and others have dealt at length with the composition of *Endgame*. The observations on composition offered here are only for the implications involving productions.

PRODUCTIONS

Beckett has assisted other directors in four productions of *Endgame*: the French premiere of *Fin de partie* in London (1957), the Paris-London productions in English (1964), the German *Endspiel* in Berlin (1967), and The Royal Court London 'Beckett Season' production in 1976.

Fin de partie is dedicated to Roger Blin. Blin directed and played Hamm for the original production in French which opened April 3, 1957 at the Royal Court Theatre in London and then moved on April 22 to the Studio des Champs-Elysées in Paris. Beckett attended rehearsals and made suggestions, but the direction remained under Blin's control. He also helped with the final rehearsals of the 1958 Royal Court production directed by George Devine who also played Hamm opposite Jack MacGowran's Clov.

The first *Endgame* strongly marked by Beckett's direction was the 'English Theatre in Paris' production which was rehearsed in London, and opened at the Studio du Théâtre des Champs-Elysées, Paris, February 20, 1964 and ran later at the Aldwych Theatre, London. Michael Blake was assigned to the production and listed as director in the programme. According to Jack MacGowran, however, Beckett himself asked MacGowran to play Clov, approved of his suggestion that Patrick Magee play Hamm and in fact directed the play. According to Patrick Magee, Beckett directed the whole production for six weeks in London. 'All of the direction came from Sam. We worked very, very deliberately and very finely on the show for six solid weeks before we went to Paris.'[1]

In 1976 Donald McWhinnie directed *Endgame* as part of the Royal Court Theatre's '70th Birthday Beckett Season'. Patrick Magee again played Hamm. Beckett attended the final stages of rehearsals and made production notes and suggestions.

The following accounts by Roger Blin, Jean Martin, Clancy Sigal, Jack MacGowran, Patrick Magee, and Donald McWhinnie show Beckett's growing involvement with the practical demands of his text.

The original *Fin de partie*: Roger Blin and Jean Martin

Roger Blin:
Fin de partie is a tragic play, but Beckett denies that there is a drama there; he believes that the public is alerted from the first to the fact that nothing takes place. Beckett attended all

ORIGINAL *FIN DE PARTIE* — ROYAL COURT THEATRE 1957

the rehearsals. Had definite ideas about his text. The form was very important to him and we took great pains with it: for example, he asked that a certain phrase which occurs throughout the text be spoken in exactly the same way each time with the same tone, like a note of music played in an invariable way by the same instrument.

I saw in *Fin de partie* the theme of the death of kings. Perhaps unduly but nevertheless deliberately, I slanted Hamm toward King Lear. From set designer Jacques Noel I asked an armchair evoking a Gothic cathedral, a bathrobe of crimson velvet with strips of fur, and a scepter like a gaff for Hamm. Whatever was regal in the text, imperious in the character, was taken as Shakespearian. Beckett was not opposed to it.[2]

When the production moved to Paris, however, the regal aspects of the set and costumes were played down at Beckett's suggestion. A worn coat replaced the velvet robe and the throne-like chair was changed to a simple wooden one on wheels.

Jean Martin:
Sam showed me how to walk,* and every single movement of Clov's was made exactly precise by Sam. Even the way I had to say, 'I'll leave you.' Sam even asked me to count time to get the number and timing of the steps right. He did one thing that seemed too unnatural to me. He made me draw out Clov's first word *'fini'* like the English 'finished'. I remember perfectly well when he opened the window, Hamm asks, 'How is the sky?' and Sam said, 'like the most disgusting thing in the world.' Because it was grey for Sam at that moment. It was like death, dust. And it was not day, it was not night. It was just grey.

The set was oval. It was like the top of a tower, with grey walls, grey stone. They were like real stones, painted stones . . . a tower and just the two windows on each side and the small kitchen on the right with the small narrow door. With yellow light from the kitchen. And a wonderful throne in the centre. Exactly in the centre. This is a joke: 'A little bit on the left, a little bit on the right, am I in the centre? Yes you are.' But of course he isn't . . . Sam measured the stage to make sure . . . And the height of the windows too. They have to be too high. Clov has to climb up the ladder to get to them . . . And the dimensions of the kitchen are important. It's not only mathematics but to indicate the impossibility of escape. When you have been in front of a small wall for 20 or 30 years you get to know the measurement of that wall exactly. It's big enough to exist in

---

* The stooped posture of Clov adopted by Martin in this first production has been a feature of all Clovs directed by Beckett.

JEAN MARTIN AS CLOV — STUDIO DES CHAMPS ELYSÉES 1957

but too small to really live in. You can only wait. You can't leave; you can't stay.

One of the most important things to Sam is the last monologue of Clov, when he says, 'When I fall I'll weep for happiness.' Sam said, 'Please, please don't cry. To die is a most happy thing. So don't be laughing, but never cry. Never cry.' (Interview, 1976)

Beckett was pleased with this production as his letters to Alan Schneider indicate:

April 30, 1957
P.S. I quite agree that my work is for the small theatre. The Royal Court is not big, but *Fin de partie* gains unquestionably in the greater smallness of the Studio.

August 12, 1959
The creation in French at the Royal Court was rather grim, like playing to mahogany, or rather teak. In the little Studio des Champs-Elysées the hooks went in . . . It would be fine if you get over to see it. You know by experience what little help I am with my own work and I have little or no advice for you. But simply to see the production here, for which I am very grateful, while not altogether agreeing, might be of some use to you. (*Village Voice Reader* p. 185)

English Theatre in Paris — The 1964 *Endgame*: Jack MacGowran to Richard Toscan

T. Did you discuss *Endgame* in some detail with Beckett?
M. Oh yes. Actually, the best *Endgame* we ever played was directed by Beckett in Paris in 1964. I got Patrick Magee to play Hamm, and I played Clov, and we got two very good character players to play the dustbin people. Beckett came over and spent six weeks directing it . . . Beckett is a marvellous director of his own work, but he's a strict disciplinarian. The play ran for nine weeks in Paris, then for two seasons at the Aldwych Theatre in London and was still playing to packed houses when we closed it.
T. What was Beckett's interpretation of the play as he approached it from the point of view of a director?
M. Interdependency — that man must depend upon his fellow man in some way no matter how awful; a love-hate relationship between Hamm and Clov which exists right through the play.
T. So he put the major emphasis on their relationship, rather than the 'something' that's taking its course outside?
M. Yes. Harold Pinter came to see it one night. He dashed around afterwards — he's an honest man, Pinter, and a very good playwright influenced by Beckett's work. He said to

me and Pat Magee, 'You know, it's not what you were saying to each other, it's what was happening in between that gave me tickles up my spine.' So, you see, the relationship was working. This is what Sam made sure would happen — that the relationship he wanted between Hamm and Clov was taking place. Clov takes an insane delight in saying, 'There's no more pain-killer', and when he wheels Hamm to the centre, he *doesn't* wheel him to the centre. Clov is constantly *not* doing what Hamm wants him to do. Hamm knows he's not in the centre; he has a sixth sense for knowing. He places a terrible curse on Clov when he says, 'One day you'll be blind like me . . . except that you won't have anyone with you.' This hurts Clov, this worries him a lot. So they hurt each other mentally. They're mentally both very damaged people anyway.

T. Did Beckett ever talk about what it was that has decimated the population and left only Hamm and Clov?

M. No, never. It's some vision — there is a visionary in Beckett. The seeds of *Endgame* were in fact in Lucky's speech — 'In the great deeps, the great cold on sea, on land and in the air' — referring to the return of the world to its former state of a ball of fire, or the glacial age which will get rid of all the population and perhaps, by sheer luck, two people will remain. Lucky also says, 'In the year of their Lord six hundred and something . . .' Beckett can't remember the actual date, but he read it somewhere, and it was nearest the glacial age the earth ever got in mankind's time. I have part of the original manuscript of this scene; it's much longer than the English translation and Clov talks at great length about what he's seeing outside. But Beckett wanted to leave a doubt about the existence of human life and he cut that sequence out, so as to make Clov less sure of going. Hamm says, 'I don't need you anymore.' Clov doesn't like the fact that he's not needed — he must be needed. That is why he never leaves.

T. There is the suggestion in *Endgame* that the flea might be the first chain in the development of a new race of humans.

M. That's right, and it's so awful that they want to kill it quickly before it starts, because the same thing will happen again.

T. In Hamm's story, he refers to the baby who was brought to him by the man who came crawling . . .

M. I played it as if Clov was the person who was brought there by the man, so that the story is not really fiction at all. It's a retelling of those early years, which Clov may or may not remember because he has been there so long.

T. What was Beckett's attitude toward Hamm's parents who were in the dustbins?

M. I think he feels that's the way most of us, in later life, treat

174

our own parents — we put them into homes and we give them the minimum kind of treatment to keep them alive for as long as we can. The human race generally does that to an aging parent and this was his conception of how stark it could be — putting them into dustbins and giving them a biscuit or a biscuit and a half a day, anything to keep them going just for a while.

T. I gather that Beckett would dismiss the critical approach to *Endgame* that says it takes place in the mind of one man and the parents in the dustbins symbolise subconscious repression.

M. He would reject that idea completely. People may think that because the play makes it possible to think that way. But I know for a fact that that's not Beckett's idea of what's happening.

T. When you work with Beckett, does he treat the plays that he has written first in French and then translated into English as equivalent plays, that is, does he make references back to the French text as being different from the English version?

M. Yes, he does. There was a point in *Endgame* which worried me. When Clov realises that he's had a little victory over Hamm, he starts humming and Hamm, if you recall, says 'Don't sing,' and Clov says, 'One hasn't the right to sing anymore.' Hamm says, 'No,' and Clov says, 'Then how can it end?' I said to Beckett, 'I'm really not quite sure what that means'. He said, 'When I wrote it in French, there is a French proverb which is well known, "Everything ends with a song", and I could not translate that proverb which is particularly French into English unless I did it that way.' You see, it was more readily understood in French, Clov intimating that this is the end of their relationship.[3]*

---

*The song which Clov sings in the French text was never included in Beckett's English translation and it was cut from the production text of his Schiller *Endspiel*. According to Beckett it is an 'old French ditty'. The words are ironically appropriate:

Joli oiseau, quitte ta cage,
Vol vers ma bien aimée,
Niche-toi dans son corsage,
Dis lui combien je suis emerdé.

Pretty bird, leave your cage,
Fly to my well-beloved,
Nestle to his breast,
Tell him how I am entrapped. (*Emerdé*, bogged down in excrement)

To John Fletcher, Beckett supplied the words of another verse:

I will be sixteen years old like the new flowers
Like the bird when Summer comes
I feel my young wings opening.

(Authors' literal translations)

The 1964 Aldwych and 1976 Royal Court *Endgame*

Donald McWhinnie:

Sam leaves me alone to get on with it. When I have something to offer he looks at it. This time he came after about two weeks of rehearsals. He seemed delighted. I've worked with him long enough so that he could point out anything he didn't like. If he doesn't say anything, it's okay. Those eyes don't miss anything. He makes written notes in the dark. I asked him if he could see in the dark. He said, 'I've been writing in the dark all my life.'

He's very free about stage business, about areas of dialogue, about whether Hamm is mad, for example. But about certain areas of the text, and about the importance of rhythm, he is rigid. In this performance he paid special attention to Clov's first and last soliloquy. He said, 'It's fine, but —' And then he hesitated as if he didn't want to disturb anybody. 'It's fine, but —' And I said, 'Sam, you say.' And he said, 'Well, I'll read it to you. But don't try to copy me, I can't do it.' (He can of course.) There's a kind of musical guide to the structure of his speech that is more important than the interpretation of his speech, whether Hamm is angry or not. He wants to get it as exact as the human instrument can get it. He also worked with Stephen Rea to get Clov's walk right. 'It's never been done satisfactorily,' he said. They tried one stiff leg. Then Sam said, 'What about a slight limp?' Stephen tried two stiff legs, and Sam said, 'No, one leg is better.' Stephen spent a long time walking and just feeling about physically. Finally Sam said, 'That's it.' Clov is also bent over with a curved back . . . to indicate the pressures of the world. If a speech was not quite right, we would ask him, 'Is there a word to describe it, Sam?' Then he would take off his spectacles, think with his head bowed down perhaps a full minute, mull the line over a bit to himself, then offer it to the actor by repeating it over and over again. Then maybe he would offer just one single adjective. If he can't find the word, he won't choose the easier words, he will search for the exact one. He'll never offer any substitute. The set was done without his prior knowledge. Sam had asked me at the Aldwych production, 'Couldn't we get a greyer light?' I said, 'Sam, if there is too much colour it's not in the light . . . next time we'll do it with a grey set.' That's the reason for the grey set in this production. He specifically wanted to have the curtains make noise. He asked for that in connection with the Aldwych production too. Originally in this production the curtains had been on wires. He changed them so they would make that clacking noise. Beckett was very explicit about the fact that there are supposed to be four sounds of objects in the opening prologue to the play: the first curtain, the second curtain, the first dustbin, the second dustbin. He especially liked the way Nagg's voice was done in this production. When he heard Leslie Sarony do the part of Nagg, he said, 'Oh, he's an old music hall actor is he? I've never heard the tailor's speech better given.' (Interview, 1976)

Patrick Magee:

Sam makes everything clear and simple. There's a line from *Endgame* which says, 'And the sun?' Clov says, 'Sunk,' I think is the line. Hamm says, 'But it should be sinking. Look again.' I said to Sam, 'What in the name of God does that line mean, Sam?': He said, 'You see, Hamm is the kind of man who likes things coming to an end but doesn't want them to end just yet.' Another example is a line in the play where he says, 'It must be very calm. I'm asking you, is it very calm?' Clov says 'Yes', And the next line is 'It's because there are no more navigators.' I said to Donald, 'What does that mean?' Donald said, 'I don't know, let's ask Sam.' Sam said, 'Well you see, it's not worth the waves' while being angry because there are no more navigators to drown.' Now it's simple. But I couldn't work it out and McWhinnie couldn't work it out. That's what I mean by making things clear and simple rather than complicated. Somebody told me to say 'There we are,' meaning 'There we all are under the great empyrean.' But when you ask Sam 'What does "There we are" mean?' he says, 'You've been saying it all your life.' People think he complicates matters. On the contrary, he simplifies matters. He's very precise.

He doesn't want as much blood as used to be because the idea is the blood is dripping in his head. 'Ever since the fontanelles.' Something dripping in my head 'ever since the fontanelles'. There's the blood and the handkerchief is 'Old stancher' because he can't find an English equivalent for the French. Stanch means to stop; the handkerchief is the stancher. In the end he says, 'Old stancher . . . you . . . remain.' That stops the bleeding. That stanches the bleeding in his head.

This 1976 Royal Court is the first time in any English production of *Endgame* that they have both laughed at 'bread' and 'brat'.* Sam said at the very final dress rehearsal, 'I've got an idea. If you don't think it'll work don't do it. So it'll go like this. "It wouldn't be the bread, ha-ha-ha-ha-," the two of them laugh, "or the brat," they laugh a little louder. The next line is, "The whole thing is comical, I grant you that. Let's have a good guffaw, the two of us together."' That's the first time it's ever been done. Ever. In

---

* Although this was the first English production to have this feature, it had been a part of the 1967 Schiller-Theater production of *Endspiel*.

this production. It's not in the text. He just said it at the dress rehearsal, 'Wonder if this would be a good idea.' One of the things that seemed most important to him were Hamm's white eyes. Hamm's glasses are white, and his eyes are too. The white glasses came about by accident at rehearsals for the Royal Shakespeare Company's 1964 production. There weren't any tinted glasses available so we stuck white paper on a pair of ordinary spectacles. Sam decided to keep that. In this production he said to me, 'Pat, there is something quite mysterious about the fact that Hamm's eyes have gone all white, can you do that?' I did the line, 'It seems they've gone all white' like this (in a whisper). 'That's right,' he said. I told him, 'I can't do that in the theatre, Sam.' He agreed, but said that was the effect he wanted. 'I know you can't do that on stage, but you know what I mean.' I asked him, 'What's the significance?' He didn't want to answer, so I stopped. But all through his work there is white, white, white. †

I play less of the magisterial word-man and more of a kind of testy patriarch rather than a king. The French did not like our production. Roger Blin and Jean Martin played it as if it were a king and a servant. That's one way of doing it of course. There are many ways of doing it. They didn't like it because Jackie and I played it like King Lear and The Fool on a bad day in Dublin . . . That's not my quote. This time I think what we're playing is a testy old grandfather and his rebellious grandson or son. The whole paternal theme is much more strongly stressed.

Some critics say I over-played Hamm. But that's the way Sam wrote it: 'Me to play' 'Our revels now are ended'. Hamm's assurance is a front. He's a jelly underneath all that. 'Hypomania' was a good word Sam used to me about it. He swings from heights to depths in a flash. (Interview 1976)

Clancy Sigal: *Rehearsal Diary*, Aldwych Theatre 1964.[4]

Samuel Beckett was recently in London supervising a new production, in English, of his one-act play, *Endgame*. The rehearsals were put on daily, in various locations, according to a strict plan worked out between the author and his young producer, Michael Blake. The work atmosphere was always quiet, curiously formal, even delicate, often intense.*

† In *Echo's Bones* through *Murphy, Endgame, The Unnamable, How It Is,* and *A Piece of Monologue* for instance, white is associated with the memorable residue of an absent past. It is thus appropriate that Hamm, who has a heart dripping in his head, should also have eyes that have 'gone white'.

* In this production Patrick Magee played Hamm, Jack MacGowran: Clov, Sydney Bromley: Nagg, and Nancy Cole: Nell (later replaced by Elvi Hale). The set and costumes were designed by Ralph Koltai.

Endgame

First Day

Blake, the producer, is fond of using words like ambiguity and paradox. MacGowran and Magee, the Irish campaigners, are politely sceptical. 'Death', explains Blake, 'has no finality'. 'Yeah', scowls Magee, 'but how do you play it?'

Second Day

Beckett has arrived.

The actors are more hesitant, much less sure of themselves in his presence.

They are working, downstairs, in the small well of a cabaret room, circumscribed on one side by the hammering of unseen carpenters, on the other by tables and chairs stacked up to the high ceiling. Beckett positions himself in front of the actors, a few feet away. The producer, Blake, his eyes bright and loving on the action, hunches over elaborate graphs, marks and notes at a nearby table.

As the players run through their lines Beckett pours over the text as though hearing it for the first time. He glares sharply, neutrally, at the action, infrequently prompting. 'A little more pause there.' A grainy, almost silent voice, a courteous Irish lilt and lisp, with a repressed, lean bark. Leanness is the chief, the central characteristic of this man.

On Clov's dead-pan observation, muttered at the height of a violent quarrel with his master Hamm, 'Things are livening up', Sydney Bromley and Nancy Cole bend over with soft, public laughter. Beckett looks over his spectacles, surprised: what are they laughing at?

All morning, Beckett stands leaning lightly against the wooden barrier at the back of the cabaret, hands in pockets, fascinated as Hamm and Clov wrench out their splendid racking arguments. ('If I could kill him I would', Clov tells the audience.) He flowers, tightly smiles, under the anguished raillery. Clearly, he admires the actors.

Magee discovers it increasingly difficult to play the lines. When he runs head-on into another, he troubles, 'That's another one, Sam,' the question implicit. Everyone laughs quietly, this time including the author. The joke is to remain unburst throughout all the rehearsals: none of the actors is quite sure what the play is about, Beckett affects complete ignorance of the larger implications. 'I only know what's on the page', he says with a friendly gesture 'Do it your way'. Later

Beckett advises: 'You should be horrified by Hamm, and also sorry for him ... Hamm is not assured. Feverish. His assurance is always put on. He is afraid.' Once more, Magee and MacGowran take on the text, busying themselves with the first movements of the play. Beckett leans forward. He is crucially interested in the problem of the actual stage space in which the players manipulate themselves.

In the afternoon, Beckett is critically attentive of Nagg and Nell, with whom he is never quite happy. He tells Sydney and Nancy to delete the emotion from their faces. 'Murmur,' he tells them. 'No smile at all, completely impassive.'

Third Day

A gloomy, slow morning.

MacGowran's Clov is lack-lustre today. Nobody is much good. Yet, for some unapparent reason, the author is beginning to swing with his play. He smiles with rather grim satisfaction over Hamm and Clov. He consults the printed page. His interventions are almost always not on the side of subtlety but of simplicity. 'No. Make it rational. Like a German professor.' He gets an idea. 'Use a German accent.' Everyone laughs; it seems a good idea. Trouble is, Magee can't do a German accent. 'It's all right,' he says easily, 'I know a feller can teach me one.'

Magee steadily corkscrews into the role, is gradually less blindly emphatic, gently and firmly Beckett guides them to concrete, exact and simple actions.

Beckett mouths the words, again and again, of the opening exchange between Hamm and Clov, his eyes with a kind of piercing stillness on the actors. Later, Clov: 'Do you believe in a life to come?' Hamm: 'Mine was always that.' Beckett nods sharply, the point has been driven in.

'Speciality. Use speci-a-lity,' urges Beckett.

'But Sam,' protests Magee, 'I spent years learning not to use speci-a-lity.'

Everyone laughs, Beckett sweetly, calmly.

Fourth Day

Beckett alone with MacGowran and Magee. Working out the 'business' of Clov placing the ladder under the two windows at the start of the play. This is obviously central to Beckett, that the audience immediately be told something is wrong on the day the play opens.

As Beckett directs numerous changes of detail, something emerges: his closest attention and affection are reserved for Clov, the creative intelligence, the strung-up 'eyes' of Hamm. Toward Hamm, the blind crippled will, he displays a cruel, respectful distance.

Beckett never quite knows where to put his hands. He directs with awkward, jabbing, chopping motions.

In the afternoon Magee asks, with extreme diffidence: 'Sam — Hamm, what does he look like?' 'Like you.' 'Well,' grins the actor, 'that's a blessing.' A moment later, as he tends to do when he fears he may have given too sharp, or conceivably flip, reply, Beckett adds something. 'A bit of a monster. Yes, the remains of a monster.'

The actors are afraid to read their lines normally, with the usual associations. This is exactly what the author wants them to do. He continues to emphasise the clarity and normality of the responses of Clov and Hamm. 'More interest, more interest, Jackie.' 'You're terribly worried, Pat. Something's happening, but you don't know what it is.'

In a good run-through Beckett sits entranced with satisfaction. At Clov's fiendish line, 'I see . . . a multitude . . . in transports . . . of joy' (after which he pats his telescope, with which he has been viewing the audience — 'That's what I call a magnifier'), Beckett suddenly rasps irritably: 'It's a rotten line. Bad translation.* No time to do it now.' *Endgame*, originally written in French, was translated by the author.

At the end of the day, Beckett says: 'Don't look for symbols in my plays'. Magee lights a cigarette and grins, *sotto voce*: 'He means don't *play* it like symbols'.

Over lunch today Magee, asked why there were so many wisecracks and naughty capers at the rehearsals, said: 'They're alarmed. Very alarmed. Like me. Oh, yes, now it's O.K., we're in the cocoon. But, man, in that theatre . . . You can't do tricks in this play. No, not in this one. It won't stand rubbishy acting, the tricks.'

Fifth Day

Beckett's face is utterly transformed watching the play

---

* The original lines read:
'Je vois . . . une foule en délire. (un temps) Ça, alors, pour une longue-vue c'est une longue-vue. (*Fin de partie Editions de Minuit* p. 45) The problem is how to render in English all the references and connotations *longue-vue*: an optical instrument, long-distance lens, a long term perspective, far-sightedness.

unfold. It screws up, particularly during the Hamm-Clov exchanges, in an unselfconscious, lamenting, mask-like grin. When Nancy and Sydney mis-line each other they go on, almost like Nell and Nagg; when Magee or MacGowran do it they touch each other in apology or fellow feeling.

Beckett, in the afternoon, is asked if he ever sees anything new in his work, this play. 'Yes. Mistakes . . . The more I go on the more I think things are untranslatable.'

Sixth Day

This afternoon, MacGowran is burrowed into himself; he is fully engaged, has taken to Beckett's habit of following the lines with his lips when offstage. During a break he finally notices someone, sighs Hamm's ironic line: 'A prolonged creative effort'. He looks very tired, very Clov. Later, in a group around the visitor, he muses another line of Hamm's, scratching his head in wonderment. 'Did your seeds come up? Now where would Clov plant seeds? Where? It's screamingly funny when you think about it.' This may not be the moment he first reckons the play to be extremely, brutally funny, but it looks like the moment.

The visitor asks Beckett if, just conceivably, Hamm believes Clov's seeds might sprout, thus implying some hope for the future. Beckett is instantly on guard. 'I don't know what's in Hamm's head', he politely replies, moving off aloofly, not unkindly, even a little regretfully. He doesn't like questions like that.

Seventh Day

It is learned that the toque, the skull cap which is part of Hamm's costume, will be lent by Sean O'Casey. The programme is to read: 'Hat by Sean O'Casey'.

The room is cold, quiet. Beckett, in overcoat, idly strolls about, in apparent reverie, but is alert when Magee launches Hamm's long, halting chronicle narrative of how he refused aid to a dying survivor and his son, who might have been Clov. An expression of repressed glee passes over Beckett's face. 'Oh, I see', says Magee after Beckett briefly explains a point. 'I was thinking something different.' Beckett is genuinely interested. 'What were you thinking?' he asks. Magee shakes his head, grinning. 'Oh no, I won't tell you what I was thinking. Too, too.'

Eighth Day

A distracting, unfocused day. Beckett looks out of a window, remarks he once lived for two years in Chelsea's World's End. He didn't like it. He doesn't like London, or much fancy England. He is not willing to pursue the matter except: 'The rules. The silly rules . . .' A few moments later he says: 'They always know you're an Irishman. The porter in the hotel. His tone changes. The taxi-man says, "Another sixpence, Pat." They call you Pat.'

As Sydney expels his speech of paternal spite against Hamm ('Yes, I hope I'll live till then, to hear you calling me like when you were a tiny boy, and were frightened in the dark, and I was your only hope'), Beckett urges more venom: 'It's a *malediction*'. Sydney does not believe in the play but is hauling stoutly. He says: 'I resist learning the lines. Yes, I think so.'

Beckett develops a different facial expression as the rehearsals go on. He looks older. He cocks his head, and especially in Hamm's big speeches now, silently enquires his way; Hamm now gently obsesses him; he is listening for something, seeking something.

Slowly Beckett's face, hitherto frozen, comes alive, mobile, plastic, the chin up, the lips pressed together, the mouth drawn back in a tightly concentrated grin. He walks forward slowly and smiles intently on MacGowran and Magee shouting hatred on each other. Suddenly Sydney, on cue, comes up from behind his couch ashcan. Beckett goes over to a wall seat. He sits, head in hand, rubs his eyes tiredly. He glances up balefully as the ice breaks under Sydney, stares down discouraged.

Ninth Day

A much more rousing run-through today. In Clov's reaction to a portion of Hamm's long 'chronicle', MacGowran spontaneously decides to laugh at everything Hamm brings up instead of only one word.

Off to one side, Sydney and Nancy discuss *Endgame*. Both agree the play is simple. The difficulty is reading the lines simply.

Tenth Day

When Beckett returns he resumes, stern and consummately attentive to Hamm's opening speech from the wheel-chair. This is the speech, Hamm's slow and lordly exposition of his sufferings before the day's anxiety sets in, that 'opens up' Beckett.

The few visitors come and go. A nice gentleman from a literary agency drops in, takes a seat, watches the rehearsal a few moments and falls asleep sitting up.

At the end of the day, as the light dies behind Sloane Square, the venom re-emerges and the play abruptly comes alive with a shattering rendering of Hamm's 'Old stancher' speech by Magee, the final stoical act of Hamm meeting his death; Beckett having ridden it out to the last echo, turns away; that is over.

Eleventh Day

A slow start. Beckett alone with his two chief actors. He wants Hamm to loosen up a bit. 'Let's get as many laughs as we can out of this horrible mess', meaning the play. He drives hard on plausibility, and Hamm and Clov being possessed of a markedly human relationship; he sees them as two distinct human beings, which the actors do not, quite yet. Beckett always knows exactly how he wants lines read.

Magee and MacGowran work out a quick movement with the wheelchair seven times before it is right. Magee begins to speak, whipping up Hamm's brief exclamation of anxiety over his geographic position ('Put me right in the centre!') to a terrible, bowel-shaking crescendo. Then, like the adept he is, he immediately turns to a totally different voice: 'Sam, something bothers me', about a line he once had right but now has forgotten how to say. (Hamm is worried that Clov may have seen something move beyond the window.) Beckett says: 'Anxiety, Pat. There should be nothing out there. There be nothing out there . . . I'm explaining it badly. He wants Clov to see what he's going out into, but if there is something out there alive, it is not as he supposed, and that would be terrible.' At the end of this short exposition Magee looks up at Beckett. Both men shy off. They have edged into the taboo; explicit meaning. There is a sudden cessation, an embarrassment.

Last Day

Upstairs Magee and MacGowran are closeted alone, while on a lower floor, under a stairwell, Beckett and his producer are working with Nagg and Nell. Nancy has taken on a cracked, old-woman's voice. Why? She had it much righter before.

Now is the last afternoon . . . There is the last run-through
with all present. Magee is slouched, waiting in the wheelchair,
his beard half-grown, his eyes concealed behind pasted-up
spectacles. It starts. (Clov: 'Finished, it's finished, nearly
finished . . .') Beckett's face takes on that fantastic drawn grin,
his features stretched tight and working along with the staccato recriminations between MacGowran and Magee. The
timing is good, intensities and voice levels locked high. Now it
is Hamm-Magee who commands. The play takes its course.
MacGowran's burst of hoarse, put-on laughter breaks up Beckett who laughs louder than I have ever heard him. The thing
has taken flight.

BECKETT'S *ENDGAME*: SCHILLER-THEATER 1967

In 1967 after assisting others there for ten years Beckett directed *Endspiel* for the *Schiller-Theater Werkstatt* in Berlin. His name
appeared for the first time in a programme as director of his
own work. Ernst Schroeder played Hamm; Horst Bollman was
Clov; Gudrun Genest, Nell; and Werner Stock, Nagg. The set
and costumes were designed by Matias. Beckett's production
assistant was Michael Haerdter.

Director's Notebook

Beckett prepared and brought with him to Berlin a Director's
Notebook. Compared to the far more elaborate Notebooks
which he made later for *Godot* and *Krapp*, Beckett's first
Notebook is a sparse document. It is written in English with
line references to the text in German. It comprises only 43
pages organized with recto pages providing the main running
account of the action while facing verso pages are reserved for
listing the relevant text to which the main account is keyed.
Because of this system of coordination, nearly half the pages
are blank or contain only a few words. It consists almost
exclusively of detailed stage directions for the action at each of
the lines of text. For the larger patterns of action like Hamm's
two 'little turns' and Clov's 'thinking walk' there are diagrams.
At a few places like the opening, the prayer scene, and Nagg's
curse special tableau or mime effects significantly expanding
the stage directions of the text are designated. Verbal motifs
are only implied by numbers beside the line listings to indi-

cate the recurrences of a phrase and very rare comments in the main account. (E.g. ' "Why this farce?" same quality as "Let's stop playing." ') The only subject treated separately and exhaustively are Clov's entrances and exits and 'walks' which are merely listed in order of occurrence on the last two pages.*

While Beckett did bring the Notebook to rehearsals, he did not enter changes made at rehearsals in it. His working document for the production was rather his annotated copy of the Suhrkamp trilingual edition of *Endspiel*. This Production Text therefore provides in most instances a fuller indication of Beckett's first direction than his Notebook.

The most instructive item in the Notebook was not transferred to the Production Script. It is Beckett's division of the play into sixteen sections on the opening pages. (See p. 187) The length, number of actors, and variety of material in the various sections suggest that the breakdown reflects Beckett's own concept of the structure of his play rather than merely a practical plan for scheduling rehearsals.

The divisions and Beckett's final bracketing of them indicate a structure based upon a carefully balanced set of theatrical beginnings and endings and a cumulative set of

---

* The following extracts are indicative of the material in the notebook.

> Opening. Tableau. Clov bowed head. Then Clov's eyes to Hamm, to bins (if nec. slight move forward) to see window (if nec. slight move back) to earth window. Then a moment with bowed head. Then hurriedly off.
>
> Prayer Scene
>
> Hamm's hands clasped for 1st '*Last uns*' ('Let us pray')
> Unclasped on '*Es ist ein Ratte*' ('There's a Rat')
> Reclasped on '*erledigen*' ('finish') for 2nd '*Lass uns*' ('Let us pray')
> Clov's hands clasped on *meinetwegen*' ('Off we go, literally 'for my part')
> Nagg's hands clasped on '*Seid ihr bereit*' ('Are you right?')
> Hamm's unclasped on '*Na?*' ('Well?')
> Clov's unclasped on '*Denkste*' ('What a hope!')
> Nagg's unclasped on '*Keine Spur*' ('Nothing')

(The effect of this action is a kind of ballet of the hands coordinated with the text to indicate interrupted and unanswered prayer.)

> Clov during Nagg's curse
>
> One long look toward kitchen from '*Wen riefst Du*' ('Whom did you call?') to '*schlaffen zu können*' ('sleep in peace')
> One long look at Nagg from '*Ich hoffe*' ('I hope') to '*Hoffnung war*' ('only hope')
> After second '*Nell*' and exit Nagg, looks at Hamm.

(This is an important preparation for the end of the play. Clov's looks relate Nagg's curse to himself and his later refusal to respond to Hamm's call fulfilling both Nagg's and Hamm's own prophecy of the moment they will find themselves alone, their call unanswered.)

1. Opening 1st Inspection-Unveiling
2. 'Finished' to 'We're getting on'
3. Nagg-Nell scene from 'What is it my pet' to 'Silence'
4. 'You could see down to the bottom' to 'Don't stand there' (1st little turn)
5. 'If I could kill him' to 'Don't stand there' (2nd Inspection)
6. 'Why this farce' to 'we'd be bitched' (flea)
7. 'What about that pee?' to 'imploring me.' (Hamm's prophecy. Dog)
8. 'I'll leave you.' to 'Silence!' (Mother Pegg-Boathook-mad painter-alarm clock)
9. Hamm's story 'Where was I?' to 'Where would I look for them?'
10. 'Let us pray to God' to 'only hope' (prayer-Nagg's curse)
11. 'Our revels now are ended'... 'Not to my knowledge.'
12. 'Bring me under the window' to 'Don't stay there.' (second turn)
13. 'Father!' to 'if I don't kill that rat... that's right' (Rug-Clov's refusal to touch Hamm)
14. Hamm's self prophetic monologue 'Me to play' to 'get it over'
15. 'What? Neither gone nor dead?' to 'We are obloged to each other' [in the altered German text: '*entlassen Einander*,' 'let each other go'] (Rat escaped-no more painkiller 3rd inspection-mutual dismissal)
16. Hamm's last monologue ('One thing more.' to 'You remain')

(Beckett's sections of *Endspiel* from opening page of his Director's Notebook, Schiller-Theater 1967; English text for German lines supplied by Authors) prayers, prophecies, and curses organising the action leading to Hamm's final isolation as his calls to Clov remain unanswered. In the centre and then interspersed as a counter theme or sub-plot indicating the possibility of a new beginning is Hamm's story of the boy and his father.

Sections One through Three are the conventional beginning of a play — exposition of character. Clov first, then Hamm and Clov, and then Nagg and Nell. (As Beckett's brackets suggest, these are balanced by three sections of ending in Sections Fourteen through Sixteen.)

Having depicted character in conventional exposition scenes, the play moves in the next five sections to a systematic treatment of the other elements of conventional drama. Sections Four and Five define the current situation: that inside the shelter with the 'first little turn' in Section Four and that outside in the '2nd inspection' of Section Five.

With character and situation defined, the play progresses to the statement of the major themes. Sections Six and Seven present the questions to be resolved in this play about the possibility of endings and the likelihood of unexpected new beginnings. In the flea and the dog there is physical representation of beginning and ending. The action with the flea of Section Six, presents an ending mingled with thoughts of a beginning. The attempt to put an end to the flea finishes in the suggestion that the flea might yet be the ultimate source of renewed life on earth. Section Seven presents in Hamm's dog the beginning of an object associated with the end. The dog is still unfinished and in the process of being created by Clov; but it is obviously Hamm's last resort, intended for the time when all human company has gone. The discussion is dominated by what 'goes on in the end'. And the section contains the first of the prophecies of the end. The implicit allusion to the parasitical relationship of fleas and dogs underscores the connection between frustration of the desire to end by undesired new beginnings.

Section Eight concludes the expository portion of the play with a summary recapitulation. It is based upon the scene referring to Mother Pegg, Hamm's attempt to move himself about with the boathook, the account of the mad painter who recoiled from what he saw outside, and the Alarm which will signal that Clov has departed and will not answer Hamm's call. In a world where there is real need expressed in appeals for aid, self-help is not sufficient, retreat into a corner at the prospect of a world in ashes is equally insufficient, and those who might respond to appeals will ultimately be absent.

The total exposition complete, the beginning part of the play over, the action proper begins. The play concentrates next on plot in Hamm's 'Story'. This first instalment of his story stands apart in the middle dividing the play between its comic first half essentially concentrated upon exposition, and its more tragic last half essentially concentrated upon concluding action. The narrative element begun here, although a sub-plot of the possibility of Hamm's harboring another child, is continued later and then concluded at the end of the play. In this first presentation the story may still be seen as part of a comic beginning and there is still laughter, albeit sardonic, at the mention of the child. In the final section the laughter will be replaced by concentration on the tragic fate of 'hunger, cold, and death to crown it all' which awaits the child.*

The next four sections corresponding to the five sections of broader exposition of the comic first half of the play are action leading to a recognisably more tragic conclusion. In a mirror of the pattern of the first half, the last half opens with a summary like the recapitulation with which the first half closed. Section Ten presents in the prayer and Nagg's curse the plight of the protagonist Hamm and the fate which awaits him. His pleas whether to Divinity or to humanity will be unanswered.

Section Eleven, opening with the line from *The Tempest* 'Our Revels now are ended,' clearly announces the change from a comic to a tragic mode and the approach of the end. Clov's 'dream of order' and his unsuccessful attempt to pick up and dispose properly of all the stage properties, Hamm's 'news' that his story is progressing, and the death of Nell are all signs of the end.

Section Twelve, the 'second turn' presents the former world in a new state of quiescence. There is no light from the earth window and the sea is calm. This is met by Hamm with an attitude of tragic acceptance.

Section Thirteen, Clov's inability to provide a rug to keep

---

* In the unfinished two act version the structure of a comic first half and tragic second half is stated directly. A hand-written note heading the typescript reads: 'Act I. *Hilare*. Act II *Mortellement triste*' In that version Act II begins with the line '*Finie la rigolade*' a translation of the line from *The Tempest* 'Our revels now are ended.'

Hamm warm and his unloving refusal to touch Hamm are
foreshadowing and preparation for Clov's ultimate refusal to
respond to Hamm's call with which the play culminates.

The final three sections corresponding to the opening three
are a concentrated theatrical conclusion focused upon
Hamm's 'last soliloquy' in sections Fourteen and Sixteen but
interrupted by further action with Clov in Section Fifteen. As
in the earlier sections developing the themes of the play, there
is no absolute finality.

After Hamm's self prophecy of his final isolation in Section
Fourteen, the fulfilment is delayed by Section Fifteen in which
new beginnings and completions alternate in a regular
pattern. The rat has escaped so that the possibility of life
continuing to evolve is maintained. The time for Hamm's
painkiller has finally arrived, but his supply has come to an
end. Clov's '3rd inspection' reveals the young boy who might
reestablish a relationship like the one with Clov which seems
now to be ending. And finally Hamm and Clov engage in their
'mutual dismissal', verbally at least ending their relationship.

The play concludes in Section Sixteen with Hamm's last
monologue in which his prophecy for Clov, Nagg's curse on
him, and his own prophecy are all explicitly or implicitly
fulfilled.

The Production Script

In a copy of the 1956 Suhrkamp trilingual edition, including
Elmar Tophoven's German translation of *Fin de partie*, now at
Washington University, Beckett made textual alterations,
deletions, additions and drawings in preparation for the
Schiller-Theater *Endspiel*. Beckett's text, heavily annotated in a
random mixture of English, German, and occasionally
French, is referred to here as the Schiller production text. The
textual changes which Beckett made when he directed the play
in Berlin reveal a fascinating attempt to exploit the possibilities
of German for his dramatic ends and to specify the stage
action and dynamics which he as author had left up to
directors.

Decor

A number of the changes in the Schiller production text
establish the physical aspects of the production. Beckett's
drawing on the fly-leaf depicts a three-sided set with wings at
an angle a little greater than 90 degrees rather than the oval set

of the first productions. (The actual set as designed by Matias for the Schiller production was three-sided.)* Beckett also indicates the 'places' of the characters on the set. Significantly, Clov's place is now between Hamm and the door rather than close beside Hamm's chair. In 1980 when he directed the San Quentin Drama Workshop production at Riverside Studios, he again diagrammed the set on the opening page of his production text, designated Clov's place as 'A', and incorporated stage directions so that Clov more consistently begins from or is stopped at his place at 'A':

XSW   EWX

H   A   K→

NN

Reference to the red faces of Clov and Hamm is deleted (p. 13); Hamm's glasses are designated 'milky white' rather than black. (But in performance the glasses were still dark) The dog is no longer a Spitz but a poodle. (See photo p. 219 below) (According to Elmar Tophoven, this change was in honour of Schopenhauer, who fancied poodles.) † And Clov's pants are fitted with an 'elastic waist' instead of buttons to speed up the comic stage business when he shakes powder in his pants to kill the flea (p. 59).

---

* Beckett stated that this 'represented an alternative, not a change'. (Authors' interview 1981). The choice of an angular set was probably to achieve the effect of a 'fourth wall' closing off the world of Hamm and Clov from the audience. (See p. 225 below).

† Schopenhauer's comments on the comedy and tragedy of life are much like Beckett's own 'Nothing is funnier than unhappiness', which he called the most important line in the play:

> Life viewed as a whole is really a tragedy; but gone through in detail it has the character of a comedy. For the doings and worries of the day, the restless mockeries of the moment, the desires and fears of the week, the mishaps of every hour, are all brought about by chance that is always bent on some mischievous trick; they are nothing but scenes from a comedy. The never-fulfilled wishes, the frustrated efforts, the hopes mercilessly blighted by fate, the unfortunate mistakes of the whole life, with increasing suffering and death at the end, always give us a tragedy. Thus, as if fate wishes to add mockery to the misery of our existence, our life must contain all the woes of tragedy, and yet we cannot even assert the dignity of tragic characters, but, in the broad detail of life, are inevitably the foolish characters of a comedy.
>
> (*The World as Will and Representation*, trans. E.F. Payne (New York: Dover Publications, 1966), 1:322.

The association of the dog with the play itself, which like the play in *Eleuthéria* must *tenir debut* (stand up), and with Schopenhauer's view of life as both comedy and tragedy reflects the tragi-comic structure.

SKETCH BY MATIAS FOR *ENDSPIEL* — SCHILLER-THEATER 1967

Textual Changes

Other changes alter the connotations of words or phrases in the original German translation.* The 'large wound' in Hamm's breast (p. 55) becomes a 'small wound'. Throughout the text, Hamm's *'Pillen'* ('Pills') are specified as *'Beruhigungsmittel'* ('Calmative'). Nagg's account of the tailor is referred to consistently as a *'Witz'* ('Joke')† rather than a *'Geschichte'* ('Story'). The phrase *'Was es ist'* ('What it is') is changed to *'Wie es ist'* ('How it is'), p. 61, so that it echoes the title of Beckett's novel. In her description of Lake Como, Nell uses the word *'weiss'* ('white') instead of *'hell'* ('bright') and *'rein'* ('clean') instead of *'klar'* ('clear'), p. 39. One series changes connotations of sudden malfunction to those of extended decline. Instead of saying that the world outside is *'kaputt'* ('broken'', 'out of order') Clov says that it is *'aus'* ('expended' 'extinguished'), p. 53, and later Hamm's *'es ist zerbrochen. Wir sind zerbrochen'* ('It is broken, we are broken'), p. 83, is also changed to read *'Es ist aus. Mit uns ist es aus.'* ('It is over. With us it is over.') And finally the important line which divides the play into parts, *'Das Spass ist zu Ende'* ('The fun is over') is changed to *'Die Fest ist jetzt zu ende,'* from Friedrich Schlegel's translation of the line from *The Tempest:* 'Our revels now are ended.'

Some words are replaced with others whose literal meanings carry fewer overtones of an ordered, predictable world. *'Natürlich'* ('naturally'), p. 69, is changed to *'Selbstverständlich'* ('obviously'). *'Es ist in ordnung'* ('It's in order'), p. 91, becomes *'es ist normal'* ('That's normal') and *'warscheinlich'* ('probably'), p. 99, is replaced by *'vermutlich'* ('presumably').

Two cuts intensified the sense of the shelter as a closed off world. Nell no longer refers to Clov's fetching sand for the bins from the shore (p. 33) Clov's confinement is unrelieved by exits even in performance of his duties. And there is no longer a sense of spectators external to the action on stage. Clov's interplay with the audience, I see a multitude in transports of joy! (p. 51) is marked through. (See p. 225 below for Beckett's comments.)

Two other cuts removed allusions likely to be missed by a

---

* All lines are the authors' literal translations and reflect the connotations of the German rather than the corresponding words of Beckett's English translation.

† The joke told by Nagg is even more prominent in early versions of *Fin de partie* than in the final one-act form. The idea that life is a bad joke perpetrated by God is made even more explicit in *Happy Days*.

German audience.He deleted the exchange about Clov's song (See p. 175 above) and a passage describing the boy sighted by Clov (pp. 125-127) containing a subtle reference identifying him with Dante's Belacqua seated by a stone viewing paradise.

Beckett made only two additions to the text. Clov drops the picture before replacing it on the wall with the alarm clock thereby giving it more prominence. (See p. 237 below for comments in rehearsal) And at the mention of the man who wanted bread for his brat (p. 97) Hamm and Clov are to laugh on 'bread' and 'brat' in a stylized coordinated manner like that of Winnie and Willie at God's poor joke in *Happy Days*.

Verbal Motifs

Often the changes serve to create or reinforce verbal echoes or correspondences in the play. Clov's response to Hamm's question whether he had 'got' the flea in his pants, '*Es sieht so aus*' ('It looks like it') is altered to '*Es scheint so*' ('It appears so'), p. 59, to echo exactly his response to Hamm's remark that it is 'an evening like any other' (p. 29). Hamm's question to Clov '*Fühlst du dich nicht wohl?*' ('Don't you feel well?') becomes '*Ist dir nicht wohl?*' ('Are you not well?'), the same wording as Nagg's question to Nell (p. 35). When Hamm, in his final speech, recalls the father's desire to keep his child with him, the phrase '*ob er seinen Kleinen mitbringen dürfe*' ('if he might bring his little one with him'), p. 135, is changed to '*Ob er seinen Kleinen bei sich behalten dürfe*' ('keep his little one with him') so that he repeats the same words he had used when he told the incident in his 'story' (p. 99). When Hamm says to Nagg, '*Es gibt keine Pralinen mehr*' ('There are no more candies'*), p. 91, Beckett adds '*Du wirst nie wieder eine Praline Bekommen*' ('You will never get another candy'). Clov's later lines to Hamm, '*Es gibt keine Beruhigungsmittel mehr. Du wirst nie wieder Beruhigungsmittel bekommen*' ('There is no more pain killer. You will never get any more pain killer'), p. 105 thus becomes a clear echo of Hamm's sadistic promise to his father.

Stage Action: Clov's Exits

The majority of the changes accommodate the details of stage action to the themes of the play. One of the major motifs of the

---

* in Faber text: sugar plum.

play — Clov's constant attempt to reach his doorway — is greatly strengthened by Beckett's new directions. Clov's 'place' is no longer 'beside the chair' but at a point slightly stage left, between Hamm and the door. In the production script Clov's first movement in response to Hamm's command *also lauf* ('go then'), p. 21, is toward the door, not toward the rear wall. And in this version Clov no longer returns to his place beside Hamm each time after bringing Nagg's biscuit (p. 25), taking Nell's pulse (p. 43), and looking to see if Nell is still alive (p. 107). Instead, he starts from the bins toward the door after each of these actions and is involuntarily halted at his 'spot' by a question or command from Hamm.

The movement from the bins to the door is given even greater emphasis in new directions for the scene in which Clov is told to ask Nagg to listen to Hamm's story (p. 179). Three times in this scene Clov moves toward the door (the first time on tiptoe) only to be called back by new commands from Hamm. When he finally reaches the door the action is much less conclusive than in the original version. In both the French original and the first German translation (but not in the English translation) Clov opens the door and exits slamming it. A large marginal note in the production text (p. 81) reads 'No door'; Clov may have achieved his temporary exit but it lacks the finality of a door opening and closing.

Throughout the production text, Beckett changed Clov's recurring line *'Ich gehe jetzt'* ('I'm going now') to *'Ich verlasse dich'* ('I'm leaving you'), pp. 21, 31, twice on p. 65, 67, 69, 79, 95, 109, 129. In the last eight occurrences this change in the verbal motif is accompanied by added directions for Clov to move toward the door after this line, but to be stopped each time by Hamm's next speech. The use of the prefixes *'ver'* and *'ent'* with the root verb *'lassen'* in German allowed Beckett to create a verbal link between Clov's attempts to exit and the climactic scene in which Hamm tells Clov that he is releasing him. In that scene Hamm's line *'Ich brauche dich nicht mehr'* ('I don't need you any more'), p. 133 is changed to *'Ich entlasse dich'* ('I'm letting you go'). Clov responds, *'moment mal bitte. Ich entlasse dich'* ('Just a minute please. I'm letting you go') and Hamm counters with *'Wir entlassen einander'* ('We are letting each other go'). Thus the verbal motif begun and developed in Clov's earlier instances of *'Verlassen'* culminates in the thrice repeated *'Entlassen'* of the later scene.

In both the original and the production text Clov does have a final exit following this exchange and then returns again dressed for a journey (p. 137). In the original, Clov remains poised to make what will surely be his final exit, but remains motionless as Hamm delivers his last speech. In the production text Clov, though silent and unperceived by Hamm, is still responsive to him. He 'flinches aside' when Hamm whistles and again when Hamm calls his name. The tension between Clov's desire to go and his response to Hamm's summons is thus maintained up to the very end of the play.

Stage Action: Circuits and Counter Circuits

At five places Beckett has amplified stage directions with diagrams specifying large patterns of clockwise and counterclockwise movement. (See p. 197) Like the circles in his directions for *Godot*, the clockwise circuits are associated with activity and earthly involvements while the counterclockwise circuits are associated with extrication. In both notebooks Beckett referred to these circuits as 'little turns'. In these diagrams Clov's movements are angular, broken by sharp turns, mostly 45 or 90 degrees, while the movement of Hamm's chair follows unbroken curved lines, but Clov and Hamm both move in patterns that suggest circles or semi-circles.

The first diagram, on page 10, shows Clov's movement in the opening pantomime. The first part — from the opening curtain to his departure from the ashbins — is a closed circuit. Clov starts from a position near the door of his kitchen, crosses the whole stage, goes upstage right to the sea window, opens the curtain and looks. Then he moves clockwise stage left to the earth window where he repeats the same action. He continues to move clockwise downstage right to the ashbins, thus completing his circuit in the process. The second part of Clov's pantomime — his movement from the ashbins to the place of his monologue — comprises a clockwise semi-circle. From the ashbins, he moves upstage left to Hamm's chair and then downstage left to a point on a line with his kitchen door and equidistant from it and Hamm. Here, he pauses to deliver his first long monologue beginning with 'Finished'. After his monologue he moves directly in a straight line stage left to the door of his kitchen. The large circle, the semi-circle, and the

Endgame

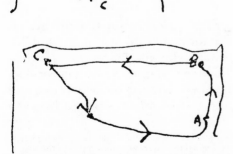

(Finished)

Am I exactly, etc.
We will
We must

A My legs
B Having an idea
C AH!

A Dog
B Glass to "last dust"
C Boathook
D Sprinkler

A Do you remember, etc.
B There! Already, etc.
C Is it light? etc.

DIAGRAMS OF PP. 10, 45, 77, 93, 101 OF BECKETT'S *ENDSPIEL* PRODUCTION TEXT (Corresponding English lines supplied by Authors)

197

straight line exit to the door set up patterns which will be echoed or mirrored later in the play by both Hamm and Clov.

The second of the large circuits in the play is Hamm's 'turn round the world' (p. 45). A diagram at the bottom of the page indicates a complete clockwise circle, beginning and ending at the initial position of Hamm's chair slightly off-centre, with stops for dialogue at extreme upstage right and extreme upstage left. This 'turn' will be mirrored later when Clov wheels Hamm to the window in a large counter-clockwise circle of the set.

Two smaller movements by Clov intervene between Hamm's first 'little turn' and his second. When Hamm tells Clov to 'Have an idea', the stage directions in the text call only for Clov to pace to and fro, with his hands behind his back and eyes fixed on the ground. The third diagram, at the bottom of page 77, gives a more detailed indication of Clov's movement and the points at which it is interrupted by dialogue.* Clov does not merely move back and forth but makes a kind of figure eight pattern composed of a large clockwise circuit followed by a smaller counter-clockwise one. Beginning from his place by Hamm's chair, Clov moves downstage left towards his door, then turns clockwise to a point (A) a little off-centre left where he delivers the line 'The pains in my legs. It's unbelievable.' Then he moves upstage in a perpendicular line slightly past Hamm. He then turns counter-clockwise 45 degrees to a point (B) where he pauses to answer Hamm's question, 'What are you doing?' with the line *'Ich plane'* ('Having an idea') after which he turns again 45 degrees counter-clockwise to a point (C) halfway between the door and Hamm. To say 'Ah!' announcing that he has found a solution.

This pattern shows Clov's persistent inclination to leave his place beside Hamm and move toward the door and his constant turning back toward Hamm. The two connecting circuits, one counter to the other, suggest that whatever plan he may devise there is no single irreversible action that will achieve completion. In the end he remains poised between Hamm and the door.

* In his production text for the simplified and streamlined 1980 San Quentin Drama Workshop production, Beckett heightened the contrasting movement of the two circuits by changing the stage directions so that in the first he 'pulls' Hamm's chair but in the second 'pushes' as in the published directions.

Later in the play Clov makes another series of movements which illustrate even more clearly an unsuccessful attempt to reach finality. Beckett diagrammed this action at the bottom of page 93. Just after Hamm announces the final section of the play with his line, 'Our revels now are ended', Clov begins a ritual attempt to create order by picking up the props that have been scattered about the stage. As in the second part of his opening pantomime, Clov moves in a semi-circle towards more disorder. From his place by Hamm's chair, he moves upstage left to retrieve the dog, (A), then directly downstage to pick up the glass (B), pausing midway in the action to deliver the speech, 'I love order. It's my dream. A world in which all would be silent and still and each thing in its last place under the last dust.' Then he moves downstage right to pick up the boathook (C). He completes his semi-circle by moving stage right to the 'sprinkler' (D), but he does not pick up this last prop. Interrupted by Hamm's 'Drop it!' he lets the items he has collected fall to the floor. Clov's incomplete circuit, his failure to pick up the can of flea powder (earlier associated with an end to procreation) and the re-scattering of the objects make up a clear physical action that shows his attempt to create order, to provide a proper ending, has failed.

The last of the large patterns to appear in the play is Hamm's 'second turn' about the stage as Clov wheels him under the windows. The scene is an obvious parallel to his earlier 'turn round the world', with single stops upstage right and upstage left and the same concluding comment by Hamm, 'Don't stand there!' The scene also parallels the first part of Clov's opening pantomime where he circles the stage and looks out both windows. The movement sketched out in Beckett's diagram at the bottom of p. 101 is counter-clockwise. It is thus opposite to that of both Hamm's earlier circuit and Clov's opening one, presenting a pattern which would seem to cancel out the earlier actions. As with almost everything else in the play, there is an attempt to reach a conclusion by undoing what has been done, but the process of countermotion and cancellation brings no finality. At the end of this movement Hamm and Clov are as they were — it is as if they had never moved at all.*

---

* The metaphor of the game of chess is relevant to these patterns of action. The movements are like those in the game which Murphy plays with Mr. Endon. In that game dominated by the circular action of the knights, Murphy systematically attempts to cancel out moves in one direction by countermoves in the opposite direction.

Several of Beckett's changes in the production text make a much clearer parallel and contrast between the scene in which Clov looks out from the earth window and the one in which he looks out of the sea window. Hamm's command for the beginning of the earth window scene (p. 115) is changed from '*Schau nach der Erde*' (roughly, 'Look upon the earth') to *Schau dir die Erde an.* ('Look at the earth'), a more exact echo of '*Schau dir den Ozean an.*' (p. 53) with which the sea window scene begins. Beckett strengthened the contrast between the scenes by eliminating from the sea window scene nine stage directions for Clov to look through the telescope in response to Hamm's questions about what is outside. In the production text after a brief look at the sea (as opposed to the 'long' look stricken out) Clov remains on the ladder, telescope in hand, but instead of looking through the telescope each time to verify his answers to Hamm's questions, he faces Hamm, answering him without further observation. This is in direct contrast with Clov's action in the window scene. There his attention is focused on the outside (which he observes without the aid of the telescope) and Hamm's statements about his own condition come as interruptions of Clov's intent observation. As in the sea window scene, there is a nine part pattern. Four times Clov alternates his look from the scene outside to Hamm inside and back again. After these eight paired movements, Clov in a final movement casts his eyes to heaven and throws up his hands with clenched fists in exasperation. By eliminating Clov's nine looks from the first scene, Beckett makes him in this scene as laconic and removed from the outside as Hamm is in the second. The contrasting action shows that although Hamm and Clov both have an interest in life inside and outside their shelter, their common interests seem never to coincide in time and place. When Hamm wants to find out about the sea, Clov fixes his attention on Hamm. When Clov wants to look at the earth, Hamm's attention is on himself inside.

Beckett also changed the final window scene in which Clov sights the boy (p. 125-127). The passage in which Hamm questions Clov about what he has sighted — the lines from '*Ein blatt*' ('a leaf') through '*er is vielleicht tod*' ('He's dead perhaps') — are cut. Clov no longer dismounts the ladder twice, to get the telescope and to adjust the ladder for a better view. He no longer runs to the door in an attempt to go to meet the boy or returns to the ladder. In the production script his action is simpler and more sharply defined. He mounts the ladder with the telescope in hand, looks out twice, announces almost immediately that he has sighted the boy. He dismounts at once, throws away the telescope and, in an action added in a marginal note, knocks over the ladder. This quicker, simpler, more dramatic action comes just before Hamm's climactic '*Es ist aus mit uns. Clov, ich entlasse dich.*' ('It's over for us. Clov, I'm letting you go.'). It is as if seeing the boy, throwing away the telescope, and knocking over the ladder are three quick, successive actions leading to a conclusion.

Emotional Dynamics

As Beckett remarked to Ernst Schroeder during rehearsals for the Schiller production, *Endgame* is like fire and ashes. The antagonism between characters flares up and subsides and flares again. Several of the most interesting changes and additions in the Schiller production script are stage directions and added marginal indications of the way passages are to be delivered to heighten this effect.

Nagg's look at Nell when he tells her to return to her ashbin (p. 33) is deleted so that his later turn of the head, indicated by a new stage direction (p. 93), comes as a more singular movement introducing his curse on Hamm. The curse, one of the major climactic points of the play, is emphasised by the marginal notation 'Violent' beside it, and the addition of the direction 'Long' for the pause that precedes it.

Most of the changes which affect the dynamics of the play concern the action and dialogue between Hamm and Clov. The conflict between them is given visual form early in the play when an addition to the directions has Clov 'moving in' on Hamm as he says to him, '*Du solltest nicht so zu mir sprechen*' ('You shouldn't speak to me like that'), p. 27. This movement of Clov's is repeated four times according to new directions in the text. It occurs when Hamm tells of the engraver who alone was spared to see the world in ashes from the window of an asylum (p. 73). It is present when Clov tells Hamm that Nagg does not want to hear his story (p. 81) and when Hamm commands Clov to enquire about his story (p. 95). And it occurs again when Clov descends the ladder after observing the earth through the window (p. 121).

At five places Beckett has marked exchanges between

Hamm and Clov with a vertical line in the text, and has added indications of intensity in the margin. When Clov refuses to get an oil can for the casters of Hamm's chair and complains about Hamm's questioning of his reference to 'Yesterday' (p. 73) Beckett has written 'Violent' in the margin. The marginal notation, 'Violent', occurs again when Hamm and Clov argue about why the alarm clock might not work (p. 79). When Clov is interrupted by Hamm as he tries to look outside (p. 119) the exchange is 'fast and violent', but it modulates to 'soft venom' a few lines later as Clov recalls how Hamm refused oil to Mother Pegg. The passage in which Hamm relates his 'story' to Clov is designated '*sehr gespielt*' ('very theatrical') like 'a great writer with his disciple' (p. 95-97). Hamm's speech near the end in which he pleads for Clov to hit him with a boathook, hammer or axe instead of the dog (p. 123) is to be delivered in short bursts with the intensity of physical 'blows'.

Additional directions for Clov to turn towards Hamm or away from him almost systematically indicate the points at which conflict flares and subsides. In the production script Clov, who has had his back to Hamm during the line, 'Do this, do that,' turns to Hamm to say, 'I never refuse. Why?' (p. 69). At the end of the violent exchange about the oil can (p. 73) Clov turns away as the antagonism diminishes. In the scene where Clov 'has an idea' (p. 77), two unemphatic '*Jas*' and the former stage directions, '*nicht sehr überzeugt*' ('not very convinced') and '*überzeugt*' ('more convinced'), are replaced by one emphatic 'Ah!'. Clov has his back to Hamm as the idea comes to him but turns to Hamm to announce his plan to set the alarm which will signal his departure.

Aware of the visual metaphor of a fire springing up from ashes, Beckett inserted a direction for Clov to turn to Hamm at the mention of the word 'Ashes' (p. 73). This attentive posture is in contrast to Clov's 'fixed gaze' and 'toneless' delivery when he says later, '*Die Erde erloschen ist, obgleich ich sie nie glühen sah.*' ('The earth is extinguished though I never saw it lit.'), p. 133. A change in this line from '*brennen*' ('burning') to '*glühen*' ('glowing') also helps to strengthen the metaphor of a fire not constantly ablaze but which glows to life out of the ashes, from time to time.

End and Beginning

Other changes bring the end of the play into closer parallel with the beginning. The opening speech in both versions is a monologue by Clov. In the original version Clov's final long speech (p. 133) is nearly a monologue, but it is interrupted twice by Hamm — once when he orders Clov to 'articulate' and once when he declares, 'Enough'. Clov ignores both intrusions. In the production text, Hamm's two interventions are omitted. Clov's first and last long speeches are uninterrupted monologues delivered as if Hamm did not exist. The parallel between them is made even clearer by additional stage directions. Both of Clov's monologues are punctuated almost exactly midway by the identical 'slight move to door immediately checked'. At the end of the play as at the beginning, Clov moves towards the door as he begins to speak of himself in the first person. His movement is, however, checked by something internal as it is at other points by Hamm's external commands.

Hamm's dialogue and action at the beginning and end are also made to coincide more exactly. His line 'Clov! (Pause) *Nein, ich bin allein*' in the opening (p. 15) is changed to 'Clov! (Pause) *Nein?* (Pause) *Gut*.' And his '*Vater*! (Pause) *Vater*! (Pause) *Gut*' in the last scene is changed to '*Vater*! (Pause) *Nein?* (Pause) *Gut*.' (p. 137). At both the opening and closing Hamm calls out to someone, questions 'No?' when he does not get a response, and then says 'Good' as if resigned to the situation of total isolation.

Hamm's action with the handkerchief is changed in the production text to give greater emphasis to the prop as a drape at the beginning and end of the play. In the production text Hamm no longer takes out his handkerchief to wipe his face near the middle of the play (pp. 67, 69), and during his final soliloquy he wipes his glasses on the dog (p. 135) instead of on the handkerchief. After the beginning, the handkerchief is no longer a cleaning rag but is exclusively a curtain for Hamm's face, first in his mock ending (p. 109) and then in his final action (p. 137).

This Schiller production text contains many changes never incorporated into any published text. But a significant number of changes introduced for the Schiller-Theater production appear in the 1976 Suhrkamp edition. That text therefore represents Beckett's most thorough and most recent published emendation of this play.

Michael Haerdter: A Rehearsal Diary

The actors have gathered together in the court of the Schiller-Theater. Werner Stock is playing Nagg; he played the part in the first German production of *Endgame*. Gundrun Genest is Nell, Horst Bellmann is Clov, and Ernst Schroeder is to play Hamm.

Beckett has come in almost unnoticed. He pulls his text out of a thin black portfolio. He's been working it over in Paris, he says, along with Tophoven his translator, and has brought along a better German version. All replies which refer to the public have been removed ('a multitude in transports of joy!' etc.): the action is to be entirely concentrated on the dwellers of the lair. There is surprise when Beckett explains this by means of a principle of naturalistic theatre — 'the play is to be acted as though there were a fourth wall where the footlights are. I don't want to talk about my play, it has to be taken purely dramatically to take shape on the stage. There's nothing in it about philosophy,' he says emphatically, and adds '— maybe about poetry.' Then he ends with a surprising conclusion which prevents any objections — 'Here the only interest of the play is as dramatic material.'

Saturday, 19 August
Matias, the stage designer, a friend of Beckett's from Paris, presents his model: the classical 'bunker' or 'shelter' in its simplest shape. An even mouse-grey upon a darker ground for the walls, mixed here and there with yellow. Two narrow, high-set little windows in the side walls, with dirty-grey bunches of curtain to close them. Left, the 'sea window', right, the 'earth window'. Black traces of dried dirt from dust and rain beneath both windows. Right front a low doorless opening: the entrance in Clov's kingdom, the kitchen. Two dyed corks mark the ash-bins. The props — cloth dog, alarm clock, biscuit, telescope etc. — are examined and discussion ensues regarding the final shapes, colours, sizes and quality. 'Keep it simple, everything simple,' Beckett says.

When the work starts, Beckett seems transformed. His awkward shyness around people has given way to intense concentration. He stands on stage by the footlights, cigarette-butt glowing in his left hand, observing through thick eyeglasses Clov's pantomime which opens *Endgame*.

'What kind of laugh should it be?' asks Bollmann. 'You

laugh as soon as you see something definite.' Beckett's directions are brisk and explicit. 'In your moving you must give the impression that you were trying to walk but can't.'

Clov suffers from a sickness — endemic in Beckett's world — which keeps him from sitting and bothers him while walking. Beckett acts out the entrance. Upper body bent, arms hanging loose, he trots out onto the stage as if his legs couldn't keep up with his head and his will. He stops next to Hamm's chair with eyes averted and fixed on the ground — his stance demonstrating resignation, yet resistance to his fate, Hamm.

'There must be maximum aggression between them from the first exchange of words onward. Their war is the nucleus of the play.'

Monday, 21 August
Individual rehearsal with Ernst Schroeder in the evening. Beckett's chair is set on the small stage, directly at the footlights.

Hamm's first long monologue, the story of the beggar and his son, who is perhaps identical with Clov. Schroeder has prepared it. Enthroned in fullness of power upon the wheeled chair, he presents a study of a crippled but powerful tyrant. Hamm's brimless cap is pulled far down on the forehead. The opaque glasses are not yet there. Danger and contempt glitter out of his little eyes. His thin lips, drawn downward at the corners, make the mouth of a beast of prey. Out of it all comes a frightening mask of pride and threat and, with the power of voice and movement added, a picture of evil vitality, which Schroeder lightens by mixing instants of self-satisfied or mocking sneers.

Beckett's nervous finger-tapping announces some objection. 'I'd like to make a few suggestions,' he says modestly but with a determination allowing for no opposition. Hamm's monologue, it appears, involves a voice problem and a physical problem. Beckett lectures softly and penetratingly: three or four voices have to be connected with distinct attitudes. First Hamm carries on a monologue, second, he speaks to the beggar he is imagining lying at his feet, third, he lends the latter his own voice, and he uses the fourth to recite the epic, linking text of his own story. Each voice corresponds to a distinct attitude.

Beckett drags his chair over next to Hamm's throne. Using

brisk gestures and an exaggerated tone of voice, he assigns each sentence its exact position in a theoretical system of co-ordinates. He throws out his hand pointing to the floor — 'there's the man!' Finger-pointing, body leaning to left front; straightens body and looks up right, then returns to position of rest, etc. 'Bread!' says Hamm first an aside to the right, only in the next instant to scream 'I've got no bread!' to the beggar. Schroeder rehearses it — first in his own voice, then in the beggar's voice, finally in the narrator's voice. Overall the soliloquy should be given an extreme, but completely internal sort of tension. Schroeder nods, reflectively.

After rehearsal Beckett suggests a system for future work. Therefore he has divided his play into sections. He recites the cue-words by heart; the result is sixteen surveyable units of varying length: connections of subject and atmosphere.

1. Clov's mime-show and first soliloquy.
2. Hamm's wakening, first soliloquy, first dialogue with Clov.
3. Dialogue, Nagg and Nell.
4. The dialogue between Hamm and Clov including the 'little turn-right round the world!' and ending with Clov's ah-me, 'If I could kill him . . .'
5. Clov's 'comedy' with ladder and telescope.
6. Hamm's interrogation of Clov, rising to the burlesque flea scene.
7. Dialogue between Hamm and Clov, ending with the ironic mirror image of the dog episode.
8. Clov's rebellion, leading into Hamm's story of the madman and trailing off into the alarm clock scene.
9. Hamm's story of the beggar.
10. The prayer, ending with Nagg's curse.
11. Hamm's and Clov's play within a play: Hamm's chronicle.
12. The second turn with the chair.
13. Dialogue between Hamm and Clov, leading into:
14. Hamm's rôle.
15. Emancipation of Clov, ending with his monologue and exit.
16. Hamm's final monologue.

Tuesday, 22 August

Nagg and Nell are not very large parts, 'but difficult, difficult,' Beckett prophesises during the reading rehearsal. Nagg and Nell's dialogue, Beckett explains, has to be spoken quickly, 'without colour'. A few pauses are to be used to divide the flow of words.

'Please hold back completely.' Beckett pronounces a couple of lines from memory, almost tonelessly, but articulating clearly. He lets colour into a few words or phrases: indignant emphasis of repeated remarks ('Our hearing'; 'And it's sand'); giggling together, abruptly broken off (the tandem accident); note of reproach ('Can you not be a little accurate, Nagg?') etc. And of course Nagg's play within a play, his joke about the trousers must have expression.

They stop, and decide to keep going rather than repeat. Beckett is obviously shy of anything that might look like tutelage. He is keeping a courteous distance. But his reserve, and the sureness of his directions and suggestions lend him a natural authority. This is what establishes the ambiance of the rehearsal: intense objectivity, earnest and at times rather precarious tension. Beckett knows how to keep anyone from raising questions about his play. Everyone respects his reserve.

Clov's business with the ladder and telescope and his paces are carefully established. The ladder has to be taken offstage after the entrance scene, as Clov will have to bring it in again. It had been forgotten. Bollmann is supposed to test the telescope before putting it to his eye, by striking it softly on the palm of his hand. There he points it toward 'Zero . . . Zero . . . and Zero' — clearly in three different directions.

They run through again, the scene goes quite briskly, allegro. The dialogue's rapid exchange generates some fun for the first time. 'You're not looking outside any more here; Clov already knows there's nothing there.' Beckett's directions resemble hammer blows.

I ask Beckett after the rehearsal, are you satisfied? He answers a hesitant 'Yes'. Bollmann isn't really the type for Clov. He's solidly built, comfortably stout and endowed with the calm appeal of a melancholy Schweik. Well, how do you picture Clov? 'Thin, skinny, nervous.' Beckett quickly tags on, 'The outer appearance isn't important, it's a matter of the inner shape'. He uses '*intériorité*'. Bollmann'll be able to manage that. No exteriorising, no theatricality. Inner tension. 'Pathos is the death of the play.'

Wednesday, 23 August

Endgame has been laid out in bold strokes. Now the laborious work on details has begun. Beckett is a demanding director. Example: he breaks in with 'You forgot a "yes".' He has a full

command of the German script down to word order, inter-
jections and commas. 'Go and get two bicycle-wheels,' orders
Hamm. Beckett reacts immediately — 'There's a period after
"wheels".' As work goes on, Beckett continually proposes slight
changes in the script. He follows a set principle: his echo
principle. 'The play is full of echoes; they all answer each other.'
Thus for instance he has Hamm call 'Clov' a second time, in his
first monologue, thereby setting up a correspondence, in
addition to the immediate echo effect, with the double 'Nell —
Nell,' 'Father — Father'. Clov must now say 'You told me to get
out to hell' instead of 'You told me to go to hell' at the beginning
of the play, since by saying it toward the end he evokes the fate of
Mother Pegg who has begged Hamm in vain for oil. Beckett
wants Clov's repeated lines 'I'm going now' to be replaced
throughout by 'I'm leaving you'. Hamm's repeated lines 'Open
it then' turn into 'Then open it', corresponding to his 'Then
walk' and 'Then go'. Each 'ever' gets turned into a 'never'. Along
with these and other echoes, two ironic allusions have a similar
reflective effect: 'My kingdom for a nightman' (Shakespeare's
Richard III); 'The poor dead' (following Baudelaire, '*Les pauvres
morts, les pauvres morts, ils ont des grandes douleurs*'); Beckett had
introduced a third one when he made the English translation:
'Our revels now are ended' (Prospero, *The Tempest*, 4th act) was to
be Hamm's reply to Nagg's curse. We search out the translation
by Schlegel: '*Das Fest ist jetzt zu Ende.*'

Beckett even wants 'echoes' built into the acting. Clov's
position in the first scene — looking toward Hamm standing
before the kitchen opening — is to correspond exactly with the
last scene. Beckett would like a stereotyped 'stance' for Clov's
repeated position of servitude, on the right of Hamm's chair. He
demonstrates a slightly angled-off position from which Clov can
turn toward Hamm as quickly as toward his kitchen. The chair is
set off-centre a half metre to the left, so that Clov can have more
space for his numerous passages between Hamm and the door.

Details. Beckett constantly breaks into the flow. Clov's laugh is
to be only a hint, not from the diaphragm, between tongue and
teeth. The objects of the shelter are brought into the action
through Clov's 'looking' at them, carefully, in a controlled way.
'You check to see whether anything has changed, and ascertain
that nothing has.' Beckett establishes this order: Hamm,
ashbins, sea window, earth window. Schroeder's motions in
polishing his glasses and folding the handkerchief are too

exaggerated for Beckett — 'Please, don't move your arms, only the hands.'

There's no breathing spell in the step-by-step rehearsal, correcting, changing, repeating. Beckett is feverishly involved. When he watches the action, he drums his knee with his fingers. He sits on the edge of his chair, ready to leap up.

In the prayer scene, he is concerned with the symmetry of the three pairs of praying hands and the attitudes of the heads. Hamm, Clov and Nagg come to the end of their prayers one by one. Beckett suggests an exact timing. Nagg's monologue follows. 'It's a curse,' he explains, so say it 'strongly, but not loudly.' He kneels on the floor in front of Stock and intones a couple of sentences in a soft, pressing tone. 'Speak with internal intensity and increase the tension by steps.' He gives the cue words. Clov, standing next to the chair, must look at Nagg first during this exchange, then register Hamm's reaction with malicious attention.

The 11th section (the play within a play of Hamm and Clov) brings a liberating change of atmosphere from tense drama to relaxed cheerfulness. The comedy of this scene is already infectious. Even Beckett grins.

Thursday, 24 August

Schroeder apologises for his 'dilettantism'. The script, he says, is hard to learn. Beckett nods and smiles understandingly. Beckett is more communicative than on the previous days. 'I want to get rid of everything external', he explains his approach. The very red face of Hamm and Clov and the very white face of Nagg and Nell called for in the printed text is to give way to a simple make-up. *'C'était trop recherché'* — occasionally, rarely, he speaks French. The lines are to be spoken very simply, colourlessly. It sounds almost like an excuse when he adds, 'psychologically, morally nothing must be done in the play; one can experience it only in the acting'. Perhaps he is bothered by the unspoken question about the meaning of *Endgame* which is on the tip of everyone's tongue.

Nagg and Nell are in the ashbins for the first time today. Beckett's interest in Nagg and Nell is evident. With Hamm he keeps a respectful though critical distance; he seems connected to Clov by a kind of complicity. For the inhabitants of the ashbins however, he seems to possess something that is like sympathy, even tenderness. Their dialogue, he says, is so difficult because all that they have left as an acting medium is voice and glance. They must not look at each other. Turning their heads toward each other, which was tried in rehearsal yesterday ('A little kiss' — 'Try'), Beckett now deletes. All that remains is a bare hint of an inclination of their bodies, while their eyes remain fixed straight forward. Beckett here gives up realism ('Can you see me?' — 'Poorly') in favour of a total effect of stillness. Nagg's and Nell's 'entries' are rehearsed: first the hands appear, grasping the edges of the ashbins, then their heads push up the lids and as soon as their shoulders are visible they must cease movement.

Beckett enjoys the macabre epiphany. He has them speak almost without voice and colour. He hunts for the proper German word and, satisfied, says 'ein-tö-nig' in a monotone. Once the right tone is found, he says, then it will be possible to 'send the voice out' more strongly. Miss Genest is almost whispering. 'More tempo on the whole', puts in Beckett. She arrives perfectly upon the note of rigidity of old age, in which life is the burning out of a distant memory. Stock gives more intensity to this dying fire. He leads the conversation and here and there allows himself to appear a little more enthusiastic and amused. 'But *piano, piano,*' Beckett warns — 'Colouration is only for their memories.' He has in mind those few remembrances which the perishing couple link with their vanished past.

'Nothing is funnier than unhappiness,' Nell says in a weak voice. Beckett suddenly breaks in — 'That for me is the most important sentence in the play.' He says it with unexpected emphasis, overcoming his usual shyness.

Friday, 25 August

Endgame sets forth a whole catalogue of objects which are no longer available: nature, bicycles, coffins, tranquilisers, and so on. Beckett wants a kind of 'alienation' in all the phrases which convey this. So that it can be recognised each time. 'There is no more pap.' He suggests the rhythmical intonation of the English production: 'there — is — no — more — pap.' This has to be worked out at rehearsal.

Run through again from the start. Bollmann's tragic laugh is superb, almost a sob. He has practised the bent-over stance and the shuffle of a semi-cripple. 'All movements as small as possible,' repeats Beckett, and reminds Clov of the identical positions into which he must return. Schroeder is dissatisfied with himself. He is not yet at home with Hamm's fear — the fear of the 'other Hell' beyond the grey walls, his fear of Clov, who (as

Beckett explains) makes Hamm try to be friendly to him, but then always causes him to find refuge in a tyrannical attitude. 'It's got to be a lot more distracted.'

Beckett has requested the sections to be held separate from each other and the 'changes of atmosphere' in the play to be made clear. 'Take the following very lightly,' he directs for the transition to the fifth section. Clov's business with ladder and telescope. 'Please, more tempo, tok-tok-tok.' He has Clov place only a few accents into the swift rhythm of the dialogue. Especially Clov's '*Aus!*' He takes out the hand motions and limits the tone. Along with the glance toward Hamm, and nearly whispered as it is, the word, prepared for by a tense pause, gets the colour of sinister comedy and 'inner intensity'. The episode of the ruined lighthouse is to produce a moment of dramatic tension shortly thereafter.

Much effort is spent upon Clov's business with the ashbins (end of the eighth section). The back-and-forth of little shuffling steps, the volume of the muttering with Nagg — in brief, the action is to dovetail exactly with the responses.

Beckett's directing follows a guiding principle which one would have believed alien to the dramatic stage: a decided split between action and speech. As though he were delivering a course in mechanics, he lectures — 'Never let your changes of position and voice come together. First comes (a) the altered bodily stance; after it, following a slight pause, comes (b) the corresponding utterance.'

Saturday, 26 August

Individual rehearsal with Miss Genest and Werner Stock. It is incredible how many subtle nuances of diction and action Beckett can work out of a few minutes of dialogue exchanged by two unmoving heads in monotone. Here instead of small hammerstrokes of rectification one must rather speak of a watch-maker's technique: the precise adjustment of a miniature movement. Examples: the appearance of the hands, at a set distance apart and their symmetrical placement on the rims of the ashbins. (See p. 212) There they rest unmoving save for when they have a task in the action, like Nagg's right hand in the biscuit episode; Nell's left arm before her 'exit' in the scene with Clov. The biscuit, too, is only to come in sight of the audience when it 'acts'. So Nagg's shirt must be given a pocket to hold the biscuit.

NAGG AND NELL — BECKETT'S *ENDSPIEL*, SCHILLER-THEATER, 1967

Beckett finds an echo of motion to express her feeling. Nell, instead of crying, turns her head a little away from Nagg, whose own head, after a 'little pause' (*'Pauschen'*, a word Beckett loves), repeats the gesture, before he asks, 'Are you crying again?' Clov: 'He's crying.' 'Then he's living' (Hamm's commentary on Nagg) is the line he likes best in *Endgame*, Stock says. Discussion breaks out: 'Weeping takes place three times in the play,' explains Beckett — 'To each his own tears.' Is that by accident, someone asks, for the sake of asking. Beckett, apodictically — 'No, there are no accidents in *Endgame*, it is all built upon analogies and repetitions.' His explanations always sound like final lines. It is hard to keep the discussion going. Miss Genest tries to do so, rather timidly, with a leading question — Nell, doesn't she die after all? Beckett supplies a pause and then entrenches himself smilingly behind an ironic disclaimer of special knowledge — 'So it seems, but no one knows.'

Nagg's joke about the trousers. Beckett explains the analogy — 'Nagg, like Hamm in his narration, works with three voices which he must distinguish clearly.' Where narrator, first-person voice and beggar alternate with Hamm, with Nagg narrator varies with customer and tailor. This correspondence, the 'echo', is to be made clear to the audience. As in Hamm's case, a focused look must make the exchange between 'rôles' clear. The customer stands, the tailor kneels . . . Gesture, please, toward the world and the pants.' Hand and glance suggest the objects to left and right of the ashbins.

Monday, 28 August
Endgame must move today into a plain cubic room, our new rehearsal stage. Beckett asks the actors to agree to afternoon rehearsals on the stage as often as possible; he seems to set great account by this. 'The play can only be learnt in the acting. It's impossible to talk about it off-stage.'

The question arises about the rug which surrounds Hamm's lamed legs. 'Perhaps we don't need it', Beckett considers. Schroeder's opinion is different. In order to feel the cripple's immobility and hold only his upper body free to move, he wants to keep his legs bound together. Should Nagg and Nell appear with their teeth painted out? 'No, that's not necessary, for Nell anyway.'

Attention turns to Hamm's 'rôle', the opening monologue. Schroeder has been working on it over the weekend. Beckett wants to drop Hamm's introductory business with the hand-kerchief; the grey rag, free of the blood-spots of the printed version, is to be used only twice, at beginning and end of the play. Someone risks the question, does it represent the curtain? and draws a curt '*Ja*' from Beckett.

Beckett once more requests 'interior tension'. His delivery of certain phrases is done with a voice compressed into an excited whisper vibrating with contempt and spite — 'the place was crawling with them'. Schroeder's sketch of Hamm brings out the actorish quality of the 'rôle'. 'Me to play', — consciously he sets the play in relief against the play, makes visible the double foundation in his grimace of whining self-pity, with cross, quarrelsome tone of voice.

Beckett walks up to Schroeder and puts his hand lightly on his shoulder — 'Aren't you tired?' This thoughtful gesture lasts a few seconds. Then he turns quickly away. 'We have to retrench everything even further, it's got to become absolutely simple, just a few small, precise motions.'

Tuesday, 29 August

Evening rehearsal on stage. A joyless, slightly irritable atmosphere. The actors are working off the book; the promptress hasn't a moment's rest.

'There — is — no — more — pap.' Beckett isn't satisfied with it. It doesn't work with the alienation. An attempt is made to speak the sentence 'normally'. Even this seems to displease Beckett; he wants it 'more cutting' on repetition. Schroeder has an objection from the practical theatre man's point of view. All important phrases ought to be spoken as lightly as possible in order to get them across to the audience. Beckett stares sullenly in front of himself. He insists — 'it has to be stressed.'

Beckett's ear is like a seismograph for stresses and tempos. 'Faster here please', he spurs, and marks the rhythm with a 'tok tok tok' tapping. One significant example: the dialogue of Hamm and Clov after their tour 'round the world' (Section 4). Hamm has allowed himself to be shoved back into his spot. 'Is that my place?' he enquires fearfully, 'Am I right in the centre?' (an especially ironic commentary on this positioning is that Hamm isn't at all in the centre). 'Here it oughtn't to be played logically', Beckett interrupts. Clov's small indignant shoving against the chair only pretending to correct its position, must correspond to the quick pace of the interchanges, just as 'unrealistically'. And against it two small precise pauses are inlaid. 'Pure acting', Beckett calls this; it has to be carefully rehearsed.

Beckett gives *Endgame* the character of repetitiousness; this gradually reveals itself as one of the formal principles of his directing. Nothing changes in the shelter. All changes are immobilised as reminiscences: ('Do you remember — . . . when we crashed on our tandem and lost our shanks', asks Nagg) or stamped with the seal of appearance: (Hamm, showing interest in Nell: 'Go and see is she dead'; Clov: 'Looks like it'), or else transposed into a vague future: (Hamm to Clov: 'One day you'll be blind, like me'). Time stands still on stage. Beckett's characters have only one desire, to escape the oppressive presence of time. But then boredom and weariness always gain the upper hand again, and point the tedious way to the 'end' before their eyes. Hamm, gloomily: 'Then it's a day like any other day.' Clov: 'As long as it lasts. (Pause) All life long, the same inanities.' They are acting out a game, playing repeated 'rôles' for all eternity.

In some scenes Beckett has this musically-arranged set routine interrupted by apparent spontaneity. In these Beckett gives the acting a logical foundation. Thus, for instance, he requests Bollmann, before his 'Have you bled?' to cast a glance at Hamm — 'You see something in his face, that's why you're asking.' Hamm's anxious question, 'Do you hear? Hollow bricks!' is to be answered by Clov by his bending toward the wall. At the finish of the flea story (end of 6th section) Clov, peering at the annoying parasite, looks into his trousers one more time: this provides him with the association for the question to Hamm, 'What about that pee?'. The blind Hamm must feel the light upon his face, Clov perceive the objects on the other side of the windows, Nagg take the hard biscuit in his mouth, before — after a proper interval — they express their reactions to their doing so.

Wednesday, 30 August

Beckett seems to attribute the greatest significance to the manifold 'echoes'. The quality of Clov's laughter, for example, is important to him, its resigned, reserved bitterness wherever it recurs. Bollmann's muffled chest tone adds persuasively the element of helplessness. For the resignation itself, Beckett finds a gesture echo: he has Clov straighten up, raise his arms pityingly, and remain so for a moment, before sinking back into his obsequious attitude and turning his head away again. 'We have to have time to perceive this picture over again.' Beckett also sets up the few transient instants of reconciliation in the standing war between Hamm and Clov as a recurring picture (Clov: 'Have you bled?' — Hamm: 'Less.' — Clov: 'Why this farce, day after day?' — Hamm: 'Routine. One never knows.' etc.) Clov's right hand on Hamm's right shoulder, Hamm's left hand on Clov's left hand, which is resting on the chair arm: an impression of a closed circle of arms which Beckett each time has 'held' for an instant; then Clov is to turn abruptly away. This is still another 'echo' gesture. A phonetic separation of echoes arises in the knocking scene. Hamm must knock twice on the 'hollow wall' with a clearly scanned sequence of three short strokes of his knuckles. As he does so he echoes 'Do you hear? — Do you hear?' 'Please separate them clearly from each other,' requests

Beckett — 'Knock, question, knock, question.' Nagg's double knocking on Nell's ashbin produces the melodic echo to this scene — 'His second "Nell!" is almost a small cry for help.' Beckett has them give to these scenes an eerie coloration (*Unheimlichkeit*). He asks Schroeder for a 'more mysterious' diction — 'hollow bricks'.

The burlesque action with the alarm. Hamm and Clov follow the ringing as devotedly as the andante in a symphony (Clov: 'The end is terrific!' — Hamm: 'I prefer the middle.'). Beckett's tense features smooth out into a satisfied smile; apparently the symmetry of the two heads surrounding the alarm clock pleases his sense of order. He has them point up the comic grotesqueness: Bollmann lays his head over on his left hand and shuts his eyes as though asleep. 'Fit to wake the dead', he comments on the ringing, as soon as it runs down. 'Three dial-faces of the end!' says Schroeder, and Bollmann adds 'One of them is off'. During the action, with the two heads close together, the wings of the armchair get in the way. 'Take them off', is Beckett's brusque decision.

Thursday, 31 August

Rehearsal on the main stage, morning.

'Hold back' is Beckett's *ceterum censeo*. Clov's first soliloquy is to be held back to the 'limits of audibility'. The four repetitions of 'Finished' with which the play begins thus cast a shadow upon the words right from the start. 'As small as possible' and 'closer to Hamm', he tells Bollmann. As for Clov's recurring 'Yes', with which he answers Hamm — 'Just the suspicion of a "yes", please.' Even Clov's sigh, in response to Hamm's 'All right, be off', must be made 'smaller': In order for Schroeder to hear it, Bollmann must approach closer to him a dozen interchanges earlier, threatening: 'You shouldn't speak to me like that'. What is especially striking is how Beckett groups his two protagonists into a tightly coupled pair whenever the action allows. Over and over he has them freeze for seconds at a time into a tableau which is to achieve its effect through repetition. 'Why don't you kill me?' asks Hamm head averted leaning back in his armchair. 'I don't know the combination of the larder', answers Clov turning his bent head to the left. 'A pause', directs Beckett. The two adversaries carry on their 'war' in a duel, man to man.

For the last few days Schroeder has had his personal props —

REHEARSAL OF CLOCK SCENE — BECKETT'S *ENDSPIEL*, SCHILLER-
THEATER, 1967

skull cap, handkerchief, whistle — augmented by dark glasses. The round lenses don't cover his eyes, bigger ones will have to be obtained. Beckett wants Hamm's blindness played realistically: unsure turning of the head in the direction of his interlocutors, searching and feeling-out with the hands after an object, the gaff for instance or the 'dog'.

The action with the dog. The prop department has provided a half life-sized cloth poodle. Black unspotted velvet, sparkling glass eyes, shining locks between the ears. 'He's too pretty', Beckett thinks. It has to be credible that Clov's amateur hands have made the dog. The text calls for a Spitz; that has to be changed. It's a sort of poodle. Then Beckett asks Bollmann to find a name for it — 'It's an indefinable promenade mixture'. One hind leg is immediately amputated so that it can tumble down; now the dog's a cripple, like Clov. Beckett stresses the relationship by having Clov cower down over right near the armchair and like the poodle he's holding, look dog-like at Hamm.

The prayer action is musically arranged: parallelism of postures, hands together upon 'let's go', closing of the eyes and successive re-opening of them at the ostentatious lowering of the hands. Beckett — 'All of it faster, please'. They go over it a few times.

Beckett's happy with the rehearsal, he says. He has his shy smile back on, masklike and adds, apologising as he does so — 'It isn't yet to where I want it. We have to hold it all down even more.'

Friday, 1 September
Main stage, morning.

'I would like as much laughter as possible in this play', explains Beckett. 'It is a playful piece.' He means the laughter of his characters, not the audience's amusement. It ought to sound plausible when Hamm says to Clov: 'Ah great fun we had, the two of us, great fun'.

Hamm, the cripple, is the moving element in the play, Clov his game-cock. Clov is his means of keeping the dying world still in motion and holding off the end which he fears. Bollmann wants to know whether Clov should react with a routine gesture or reluctantly to Hamm's order to make another turn around. 'Reluctantly', says Beckett without hesitation — 'Clov has only one wish, to get back into his kitchen — that must be always

HAMM'S POODLE — BECKETT'S *ENDSPIEL*, SCHILLER-THEATER, 1967

evident, just like Hamm's constant effort to stop him. This tension is an essential motif of the play.'

If one takes account of the strictness of his conception, Beckett's vivid dramatic imagination is striking; in any case, the director yields nothing here to the author. However, Beckett concedes only where the play's artistic structure is underlined instead of undermined by 'pure acting'. For instance, in Bollmann's first dialogue with Hamm — at his resigned cry 'all life long the same questions, the same answers' — Beckett has him cover his temples with his hands in a pathetic gesture of despair, then immediately admonishing — 'that's too much'. But Bollmann can play the telescope scene. He's to try out the glass 'mathematically', less nervously, striking once upon his lefthand palm. 'Play the scene like a merchant offering his goods', he suggests. The development is to be 'realistic': a questioning of the 'client' Hamm, 'What's all that?' — a motion of patience — 'Just a sec' — a viewing of the 'goods' beyond the window and offering of the 'goods', 'All gone!'. He has this moment taken up as an 'echo' in the second telescope scene. Here in addition Beckett suggests a business-like rubbing of Clov's hands at the lines — 'Any particular section you fancy? Or merely the whole thing?' In the burlesque episode of the first scene (Hamm: 'So is it night already?' — Clov: 'It's grey.') Bollmann slowly rises up behind the armchair like the Devil in the puppet-theatre. 'Grey', he whispers over the left corner of the chair into Hamm's ear, as he listens while bending to the right. Hamm's head whirls around shocked while Clov repeats his game: 'Light black. From pole to pole.' Bollmann whispers with the Mephistophelean mimicry of the classical seducer.

Over again from the top. Beckett seems to be thinking about the audience only when he warns the actors not to make them accomplices of their acting. Clearly he regards his play as a 'closed system', to be perfected for its own sake. The directing, or so it seems, is (like the writing) an end in itself for him and not designed to win the approval of the stalls. Several times a small controversy arises between the director and his actors over this point.

'The atmosphere was good at the start', Beckett interrupts, for example, when the bicycle episode comes on too 'strong' for him. Schroeder says no; the atmosphere's set now, and Hamm and Clov have to show they're still alive — 'or else they'll go to sleep down there!' Beckett, unwillingly, gives in.

Rehearsal stage. Hamm's armchair has acquired a wide foot-rest and large rollers set in their own suspension. The effect is quite massive; but above all it's now too mobile, it reacts to every motion, every push. The little, squeaky casters will have to go back on. The foot-rest, too, ought to be simpler in Beckett's opinion. As a whole, the black-brown piece is functional and has a puritanical simplicity.

Beckett introduces a new term into his verbal directing. Hamm's part contains some passages that Schroeder must speak in a 'life-voice'. What does it mean? Bringing the words out, stressing them — a lyrical tone, as here for instance: 'But beyond the hills? Eh? Perhaps it's still green? Eh? Flora! Pomona! Ceres!' An expression of hope? asks Schroeder. 'Not hope,' specifies Beckett, 'but the possibility of another situation than the present one.'

Hamm's story. Beckett explains once more his principle of strict articulation and clear structuring. First the change of posture, then of voice, in between the ordering pauses. Action and word never allowed to fall together. And again the request for 'really simple action'. 'Hamm is fenced in, crippled; it is an effort for him to bend forward, to reach out his arm.' How is the fourfold 'weather report' to be built in? (Hamm's information about atmospheric conditions, with the enigmatic degree indications 0-50-100-0). Beckett suggests speaking it as a 'filler'. Hamm meanwhile could be 'inventing' his story thinking about how to continue it.

Of course even this playing with numbers is not an accident; what does it mean? Hamm's story occupies nearly the centre of *Endgame*. A standing increase, if not of tension (the development of the story-line for it is lacking) at least of the expectation of a development, is obvious until this moment (0-50-100). The culminating point is reached in the 'story'. With the return to 'zero' the play's future progress is foretold: in Nagg's cursing of Hamm, following almost directly on the 'story', the plunge into despair fulfils itself. Despair is the basis, the dark foundation of the play. Hamm sets the zero point: 'Our revels now are ended.' What comes afterward — the second half of *Endgame* — is a mere passing of time, a pure delaying of the end. Clov picks the theme up again in his 'dream' of order: 'A world in which all would be silent and still and each thing kept in its final place, under final dust.' The variations mark off the zero level upon which one 'keeps going'. There is still another aspect present: the degree numbers of the 'weather report' seem at the same time to describe an interior graph of tension within the 'story' itself, which corresponds completely to the play's formal refinement, to its structure.

Schroeder today is quiet, restrained; Beckett even has to encourage him now and then — 'More wrath, please, in the order to Clov — "So open it"' — etc. However 'interiority' is what he desires for Hamm's recollection of the madman who painted pictures in the institution. 'At "Look! There! All that rising corn!" — gesture with left hand in the direction of the earth window and — life voice please — "And there! Look! The sails of the herring fleet!" — gesture with right hand toward the sea window.' Beckett spreads out both his arms at 'All that loveliness!'. He wants this phrase spoken 'large'. Schroeder tries it; Beckett nods in agreement, satisfied. 'Clov's interest is awakened at the word "ashes"', Beckett says to Bollmann. From Clov's normally averted stance next to the armchair, he is to turn his head slowly toward Hamm; 'here he feels himself appealed to'. Does the madman returning 'to his corner' because he has seen 'only ashes' outside, refer to Clov who describes nature as a waste and prefers to stare at the wall in his kitchen? Beckett's directing leaves no doubt about it. Bollmann is supposed to approach close to Hamm and enquire with inquisitorial strictness: 'A madman? When was that?'.*

Monday, 4 September
Rehearsal stage. *Endgame* has been in rehearsal for two weeks, four hours per day. It is now fully orchestrated; in some passages the instruments even make music. What is still missing is the consonance. Beckett turns the directing more strongly toward this aspect. His verbal directing, based on coloration and accentuation of single words and phrases, increasingly becomes 'musical' direction, bringing the melody to a scene or an entire 'section'.

An interruption in the second section: Clov's walk to the door and back to the armchair on Hamm's leash. Beckett has Bollmann, at 'Then move!' tiptoe a few steps away and call 'Here' faintly, as though from a distance. He tiptoes back upon Hamm's order — 'Where are you?' is the anxious question and Clov's clear answer repeats: 'Here'. 'We have to find a tune for this', is Beckett's assignment.

---

* The main allusion is to William Blake and Plate 5 of his *Book of Job* which featured the line "I only am escaped alone to tell . . .", reporting the death of Job's family and friends.

Musical terms are turning up more often now. By 'legato' Beckett designates the swift, soaring type of speech that is as difficult for the German tongue as it is easy for the French or English. This is supposed to free the 'pure acting' from a false burden of meaning. Also 'andante', 'piano', 'scherzo' are recurring directions. They indicate Beckett's purpose: a subdued and swift pace overall.

For the echo phrase, 'There is no more pap' etc., a new tone has to be found — 'Try to speak it lightly'. It seems that this whole scene of the second section is in danger if spoken too heavily, too slowly. 'Everything light, loose and quick, please'; Beckett drums rhythmically with his fingers like a bird pecking.

A break. Beckett confirms what his critic Hugh Kenner has observed: Hamm and Clov confront each other as king and knight of an imaginary chess match. And the inhabitants of the ashbins? 'Well, one can't carry the comparison too far.' Beckett's good mood today encourages further questions. Bollmann wants to know why Clov is treated like a dog by Hamm, whereas he calls him 'son' as soon as he is alone? 'The love-hate relationship, the typical relationship of marriage partners', explains Beckett. 'You know the Latin proverb: *Nec tecum, nec sine te*. It's like that here.' Does the law of attraction and repulsion apply as well to the relationship of Hamm and Nagg? 'Not really', is Beckett's hesitating answer — 'sons easily free themselves from their fathers. But that is a large subject.' He removes himself so obviously from the discussion by a step or two backward that Schroeder, amused, reassures him that no one will bring up the matter any more.

Tuesday, 5 September
Evening rehearsal on the main stage.

Beckett still isn't pleased with the blocking of Clov's action at the ashbins. He experiments further. Bollmann is to try to lift up the lids in front, at the outer rim. Then he can do it without the handles. Besides, Bollmann's head is already bent forward for the look into the bins anyway; the action becomes 'more harmonious'. Bollmann tries it; he too feels better doing it this way. For his little scene with Miss Genest, Beckett wishes still sharper articulation and distinct action. Nell's left arm is to hold back the lid so that Clov can easily feel her pulse in full view. Beckett stands at the pit in front of the bins and surveys the scene like a technician watching over his machine — 'Simpler motions, please everything as economical as possible'.

Repeat from the beginning. Beckett comes up with still another nuance for Clov's mime: he's to lift a corner of the handkerchief covering Hamm's face and then laugh bitterly.

Small corrections and specifications. In the rapid routine pace of the first telescope scene Hamm's reply 'And the sun?' must be stressed. Gulls, horizon, waves — he already knows there are no more of them. 'With the sun, he's not certain; he hopes that it is still there . . . Please give it with a "life voice".' Beckett wants Clov's 'Light black. From pole to pole' *not* delivered as a 'joke'. 'That has always bothered me', Beckett says. Schroeder lends a special voice to 'rational being'. He is to underline this alienation with a gesture. 'A Frenchman would lay his finger on his nose.' Schroeder comes up with a characteristic finger-tapping on his forehead. 'That's good.'

The scene with the dog. ('Your dogs are here.') Can Clov, with his leg affliction, really go down on his knee? Beckett — 'His difficulty in walking must not be stiffness.' He refers to the captain in Hamsun 'who also is unable to sit but otherwise is quite mobile'. It's a matter of dramatics, he says, not of logic.

An advance into fresh terrain. The last scenes of the play are scarcely blocked out, and need a lot of work. Beckett again acts it out. He sees a problem in Clov's little comic turn with the ladder (Section 15); Bollmann can, he says, speak his echo-phrase 'I say to myself —' 'privately' on the way between the windows, or else 'stressed', while standing on the first step of the ladder. Bollmann prefers the latter, stronger echo effect. Beckett has doubts — 'Isn't that too much symmetry?' Clov can keep a lookout at the window like a sailor, Beckett suggests. Bollmann strikes a comic general's pose, puts his right arm behind his back, shades his eyes with his left hand so as to leave his face and expression visible.

Hamm's last monologue. Beckett has one 'No!' and one 'Clov!' inserted in order to strengthen the melodic symmetry here as well. Who is this 'No' addressed to, then, Schroeder asks. The answer sounds like an oracle — 'Hamm says the No against the nothingness.' The preparation is again a matter of precisely organising the numerous layers and phrases. Mightn't Clov after all do him the final mercy of covering him up once again with the linen sheet, suggests Schroeder; the handkerchief will also be a clear allusion of the situation at the start. Beckett counters with the disarming logic peculiar to him — 'Between the beginning

and the end lies a small distinction which is that between
"beginning" and "end".'

Wednesday, 6 September

Mainstage, morning. Work on the last two sections of the play.
'Musical' directing. The first exchanges 'light and quick'. At the
enquiry about the 'rat', slow down and stress, above all the
repeated 'pain killer'. There should be an overall holding back
— 'never get loud; soft, but intense'. And 'economical gestures'
for Clov. Two moments of 'cheerfulness' for Clov's echo-phrase,
'then it passes off and I'm as lucid as before', following upon the
first echo-phrase, 'sometimes I wonder if I'm in my right mind'.
Then comes an emotional climax where Clov's rage turns into
action and he deals Hamm a hefty blow over his head with the
dog: 'There's your dog for you.' The next interchanges, after a
pause, are to follow blow after blow. Schroeder laments with
exaggerated pathos: 'If you have to hit me, hit me with the axe.
Or with the gaff, yes, hit me with the gaff. Not with the dog. With
the gaff. Or with the axe.' Beckett breaks in — 'Say it in
monotone and rhythmically, please. The words are blows, dry
blows. One hammerstroke is like the next one.' The word 'dog'
is to fall 'softly', as softly as the object it represents — 'Five strong
blows, then, and one soft one. Small pauses between them, please.
It's passionate, but controlled.' Schroeder rehearses it passion-
ately. 'Is *this* okay?' Beckett — 'Better.' Schroeder — 'That's not
sufficient. Is this in the right direction?' Beckett — 'Yes it is.'

Interiorising, simplifying, is again the leitmotiv. Clov is to
have no 'exterior action of rage' after the blow with the dog,
rather he remains motionless with eyes fixed on Hamm. Beckett
would now like to undo the repeated 'closed circle' of Hamm's
and Clov's arms; Bollmann is to make only the gesture of
approach without actually touching Schroeder's shoulder. 'I
think the touching's not possible.' In Clov's action at the bins
(11th section — 'Look and see is she dead') Beckett wants 'the
contact with the house' to be avoided; Bollmann is not, as
previously, to stare out over the footlights into the far distance,
but instead to look parallel to the lights along the imaginary
fourth wall. 'Looks like it': the possibility of a change (Nell's
death) being at least indicated here, a 'new feeling' is arising in
Clov, 'a confusion, a lack of understanding', which then recurs in
Clov's last monologue as a strong melody. The echo must be

acted out, a tone found for it: here is where the ending is prepared.

Clov's monologue, 'of the five dispensers of life's con-solations', as Beckett calls it. According to him, both of Clov's monologues are 'frightfully difficult; because one must work with so few means'. Beckett acts it out; he is in full command of the script, his identification with Clov seems complete here. With weak, dangling arms and head raised, he has sunk down into himself as if he practised it daily. He speaks simply, but with a precise, rather pointed articulation: the 'dispensers of con-solation' — love, friendship, etc. — receive a breath of colour. Beckett gives brief explanations where their sense is not immediately clear: ' "... look at all that beauty. That order!" Nature is meant here. "All becomes clear. And simple!" That is science.' 'And the art of caring for the mortally wounded?' Bollman wants to know. 'That is mercy.' 'Why must Clov learn to suffer better, why must he be there better?' Bollmann asks. 'The notion,' Beckett answers, 'is that when one has given the tyrant his full account of suffering, he lets his victim go. Only when one has given life its full share can one leave it.' The 'words that remain'? Reality, life is what remains. 'They have nothing to say' — Beckett wants Clov to bring this line out strongly, and he adds — 'Then the happiness starts (with Clov's line): "I open the door of the cell and go ..." The end must have a mysterious climate.' Beckett conducts — 'as quiet as possible'. Bollman is taking notes.

After rehearsal. The actors have taken their leave. Beckett is satisfied with the work. The contours are gradually becoming visible. There are 'still many false notes' and 'still no rhythm'. It's now a case of realising the 'analogies', recurring speech, motion, gestures. 'The main job will come along in the last week.' The German habit of having two '*Hauptproben*' (final rehearsals without interventions) and one '*Generalprobe*' (dress rehearsal) is new to Beckett. He wants regular rehearsals up to the first night, he responds nervously. *Applausordnung*? No, no curtain calls! He's extremely alarmed, his tone is suddenly tough — 'That's repugnant to me'. The lights are only to come up a couple of times after the blackout, while Hamm and Clov must remain unmoving in their final positions; Nagg and Nell must not show themselves any more — 'No entries, no bows'. Can he expect to gain any understanding for this on the part of the actors? He himself certainly won't be in the theatre on opening night, neither in the house nor backstage. Why not? Beckett mutters something about his 'appearance' after the première of *Godot* ten years ago in the Schlosspark-Theater, this sly calculation to provoke applause. '*C'est abominable.*' He loads the words with all the disgust possible. It is obvious that he will not be reasoned with on this point.

Thursday, 7 September

Continuing work with Hamm's next-to-last monologue, his 'rôle' (14th section). Like Clov's business with the ashbins, it is supposed to prepare for an 'echo effect'. Beckett explains — 'This is the anticipation, in Hamm's imagination, of what happens after the end of the play.' So the action here must also be an anticipation of the last scene of the play: the stiff sitting posture, the arms resting on the chair. For Beckett the division and rhythm of the action are of cardinal significance. The commencement is 'calm reflection' with restful position in the armchair: 'You weep and weep . . .'. The intensification, a threefold intensification of universal reproach, first starts with 'Use your head!' This phrase is to be spoken 'still pleadingly', the next stage 'sternly': 'Get out of here and love one another.' In the third, Hamm is to be 'raging': 'Out of my sight and back to your petting parties!' Fruitless attempt by Hamm to get himself up ('perhaps I could throw myself out on the floor'). Hamm is bent over now, posture and voice expressing the emotion which his vision of the end imposes on him ('It will be the end . . .' etc.) Only afterward does he sink back into his armchair: 'Moment upon moment . . .': 'That is pure meditation', explains Beckett — 'very quietly, please.'

Schroeder's acting has great simplicity now. His Hamm seems greater, more deeply threatening, during this rehearsal. 'Please, no pathos on "father" and "son"', Beckett breaks in. ' "Son" can have an ironic touch instead. What is meant here is that which has served me as a son.' Schroeder agrees — 'Right, it oughtn't to go off into sentimentality.' The monologue, he says, is like 'heat lightning'; he makes a flickering movement with his hand. 'It isn't delirious enough yet.' This may be a way, Beckett specifies, to find the 'climate'. 'But then reduce, reduce.'

There are more obvious questions asked and Beckett now provides willing answers. What's going on with the 'grains of millet'? 'Those are the sophist Zeno's grains, a logical jest.' Beckett turns academic and with evident pleasure enumerates the antinomies of the Eliatic: Achilles unable to overtake the tortoise, the arrow hanging in the air . . . And what's the meaning of Clov's 'impossible heap'? Beckett explains: 'What is a heap? It can't possibly exist, since one grain isn't a heap, and two aren't either: one no-heap plus one no-heap can't produce any heap, and so on, on . . . Ergo: the grain must be the heap.' (Zeno's proposition, which involves the noise of falling grain, is thus modified here.) Beckett grins archly. Now he's named only a formula and hasn't given away too much.

Friday, 8 September

Hamm's closing monologue, 'Me to play'. Beckett delivers explanations about the part — 'He's the king in this chess match lost-from-the-start. He knows from the beginning that he is only making meaningless moves; for instance, that he won't get anywhere with the boat gaff. Now at the last he's making a couple of meaningless moves still, as only a poor player does, a good one would have given up long ago; he's only trying to postpone the unavoidable end. Each of his motions is one of the final useless moves to delay the end. He's a poor player.' 'And a poor loser', supplies Schroeder.

Work on details. Beckett again orders the course 'musically' and in precise sequences of speech and action. 'Raise hat . . . And put on again.' 'Wipe. And put on again.': Hamm's talking like two persons here: first he gives himself the order, then he carries it out. 'Peace to our . . . arses': theatrically. 'A bit of poetry': take it lightly. 'You prayed . . . you cried for night': very theatrically! 'Nicely put, that': dry, self-satisfied. Again Beckett asks for a threefold intensification in the three questions beginning with 'You want'. They're to carry the curve of tension on to 'Oh, I put him before his responsibilities!' Again Beckett desires clarity of relations: where the 'son' is meant ('He doesn't realise . . .') Hamm's glance is to place him to his right; where the son's father is addressed ('But you! You ought to know . . .') the position of his head and the finger-pointing echoes the prostration of the petitioner at front left, at Hamm's feet. Here a pause interrupts this last continuation of Hamm's story with the bitter, sarcastic renunciation of life upon 'earth . . . nowadays'. Hamm, who had bent forward, now leans backward in his armchair again: 'that's enough'. With this he is already grasping his signal-whistle in his left hand. Hesitation — decision: 'Yes, truly!' blowing the whistle. Beckett orchestrates Hamm's separation from his objects: the dog is to be tossed to the right and just afterward the whistle to the left. This allows a logical transition to the next step. Hamm, blind as a mole, sniffs in the direction of the kitchen, from which Clov (he smells, as we know) had already reappeared in travel clothes at the start of the monologue. Then he calls him, twice. Clov is shaken by these commands, stronger even the second time: he has to hold onto himself in order not to give in to the reflex to obey. Then comes Hamm's last 'good'. His cadence is to correspond to Clov's 'I'm leaving you': just as quiet, just as definitive. Hamm's last phrase — 'very soft, interiorised'. Only at 'old stancher!' does Hamm 'slowly' unfold, with two 'simple' movements, the handkerchief and spread it plainly over his face. His hands slowly come to rest upon the chair arms. Schroeder sketches a death-agony by slightly closing his hands over the ends of the chair arms, then loosening his grasp. Beckett warns — 'Not too much!'

Saturday, 9 September

Mainstage, morning. The second half of the play being rehearsed, in stages. Beckett is watchful to see that the action remains clear. Speeches and moves again never intersect. Clov must always have reached his goals, the armchair or the threshold, upon his beaten path between Hamm and the kitchen, before Hamm directs his speech to Clov or he begins speaking himself. Beckett is afraid that too much pantomime from Hamm and Clov during Nagg's curse may distract from the speech; therefore he has the action held all the way back.

'Musical' directing. In the praying scene Beckett directs attention to an 'instrumental effect' which he wants to have realised clearly and rhythmically. Hamm, Clov and Nagg, after the prayer, let their hand drop upon chair arms, thighs and ashbin rims respectively thus producing a three-note chord. A few seconds later each of these three notes is answered by the echoes of the dialogue: 'What a hope!' 'Sweet damn all!' 'Nothing doing!'

During the second round with the wheelchair (12th section) Beckett, with a rhythmical 'tok-tok-tok', asks Bollmann for an accelerated pace, and warns — 'You oughtn't even to walk slowly, it's dangerous for the play.'

In the final scene the question once more arises of Hamm's death. Does he cover himself with the handkerchief in order to die? Beckett — 'No, only in order to be more silent.' Afterward he has the whole play 'run through' from the beginning without interruption for the first time since the start of rehearsals. The playing time is determined: 85 minutes.

I walk with Beckett after the rehearsal. A thousand questions run through my mind; which to choose so as not to spoil the chance? Why did you choose *Endgame* for your first independent directing? 'It's my favourite of my plays . . .' After a bit he adds — 'I saw photographs of the first Berlin production; everything is wrong in it. The ashbins are separated, you can see Hamm's feet, they're touching the ground . . .' So you wanted to give Berlin the authentic version? 'No, I don't claim my interpretation is the only correct one. It's possible to do the play quite differently, different music, movements, different rhythm, the kitchen can be differently located and so on . . .' — What does the theatre mean to you? 'Theatre for me is mainly a recreation from working on the novel. One has a given space to deal with, and people in that space. That is relaxing.' — The directing too? Beckett laughs — 'No, not so much, that's hard work.' Every afternoon, he says, he works on his director's book. Do you have anything new you're working on, a novel or anything for the stage? 'No, absolutely nothing. But I'm trying to come back to prose writing.'

A couple of days ago I had asked Beckett about the relationship between 'inside' and 'outside', between the shelter and the wasteland beyond the small windows, so important in dialogue and action of *Endgame*. His reaction was a strong hands-off — 'I'd rather not talk about it!' Now, unprompted, he begins to talk about his work, and what he says is an answer to my question, in a way. He speaks in French. I can tell that he is making me a gift, and yet can detect, in the flow of his speech, the resistance that must be overcome. — 'Can one call what we make "novels"? It's something different; we don't write novels any longer. I don't like to talk about it, but it's a work of imagination, *c'est un travail d'imagination*.' And the preoccupation with onself, with one's own past? — 'No, hardly that, pure force of imagination . . . Naturally memory plays a part, but it's a matter of imagination; of the attempt to escape from the tangle.' The tangle of life? — 'Of things! There are so many things; the eye is as incapable of comprehending them as the mind of grasping them . . . So a person creates his own world, *un univers à part*, to withdraw when one gets tired.' In order to rest? — 'Yes, in order to get away from the chaos into a simpler world . . .' That's Clov's dream! — 'Yes,

Clov too has this need for order . . . I have progressively simplified situations and persons, *toujours plus simples.*' We occupy ourselves silently for a while with knife and fork. Then Beckett spins his thread out farther — 'The crisis started with the end of the seventeenth century, after Galileo. The eighteenth century has been called the century of reason, *le siècle de la raison.* I've never understood that: they're all mad, *ils sont tous fous, ils déraisonnent*! They give reason a responsibility which it simply can't bear, it's too weak. The Encyclopedists wanted to know everything . . . But that direct relation between the self and — as the Italians say — *lo scibile*, the knowable, was already broken.' Beckett, chewing thoughtfully, stares at his plate. 'Leonardo da Vinci still had everything in his head, still knew everything. But now!' He looks up with a smile that plays between bitterness and resignation — 'Now it's no longer possible to know everything, the tie between the self and things no longer exists . . . one must make a world of one's own in order to satisfy one's need to know, to understand, one's need for order.' Beckett's speech is now quite easy, his emotional involvement has given way to an almost cheerful consideration. 'There, for me, lies the value of the theatre. One turns out a small world with its own laws, conducts the action as if upon a chessboard . . . Yes, even the game of chess is still too complex.'

Monday, 11 September
Rehearsal stage. Start of the 'run-through rehearsals'. After the first run-through Beckett has a table set up on stage again and requests a second reading rehearsal; he wants to get the rhythm down theoretically one more time. The answer 'less' occurs twice in the play: to Clov's question 'Have you bled?' and to Hamm's question 'Have you had your visions?'. Beckett suggests two possible intonations — 'euphoric or downcast', and prompts — 'You choose, both are correct, but they must be identical.' 'Louder' and 'softer', 'quicker' and 'slower', 'stronger' and 'more mysterious', are frequently recurring directions, are pointers as well to the antithetic structure of *Endgame*. A relative *fortissimo* is to be added at one point in the muffled process: Hamm's outburst 'What happened! Use your head, can't you! What has happened?' (Section 15). That is the play's fatal question.

It is often a matter of nuances. 'That old doctor, he's dead, naturally?' states Hamm, with an enquiring tone. Clov in answer: 'You ask me that?' Beckett wants 'you' accented here. Why? 'Clov holds Hamm responsible for everything connected with death.' There are reductions: no threatening with the finger by Clov at his 'you shouldn't talk to me that way'; only *one* testing blow with the telescope in his hand, etc. And corrections: Beckett holds that the repeated 'closed circle' of Hamm's and Clov's arms is impossible even in open form — 'it looks as though they were touching each other. Clov must never touch Hamm!' During an earlier rehearsal Beckett had changed the recurring word 'world' into 'earth'. He gave the name of the naked planet preference over the term for the inhabited *orbis terrarum*. Now he has it changed back into 'world', since it is more correct and stylistically better. His resigned comment — 'We can't get rid of the world — in the play.' He says it with a smile.

Wednesday, 13 September

Main stage, morning. The costume department has sent a washed-out green heavy dressing-gown for Schroeder to try out. 'I'll sweat in it', he says. Beckett wants an additional cut in the Nagg-Nell dialogue: the remark that 'he' (Clov?) brings the sand for the ashbins from the shore. With this cut vanishes the last allusion to Clov's ever having left the shelter, ever being able to leave it. One more request to Schroeder regarding the folding and unfolding of the handkerchief; it is now to be folded and unfolded to the rhythm of four slowly spoken phrases each time, so as to bring out the parallels of the beginning and end of the play.

During the run-through Beckett scribbles his critique on a large envelope. 'Silence,' after Hamm's knocking on the wall, 'so that the fear can build up.' Schroeder has spoken his order to Clov: 'Look at the earth' (Section 14) in a 'small' voice. That's much better this way, Beckett thinks. The next line, 'Since it's calling to you', is moreover to come out choked, unclear; Clov's query 'Is your throat sore?' thus seems logical. Beckett operates again and again with the number three, this Pythagorean symbol of totality. He asks Bollman for a more bent posture in the alarm-clock action, so that the 'three heads' can appear in line next to each other. When Clov checks whether Nagg and Nell are dead, he has Schroeder hold his cap in his uplifted hand and put it back on after the action at the ashbins as a third 'lid', a third note in the same chord.

A discussion about the humour in *Endgame*. Beckett would

like to get as much comedy as possible into the play; but he
defines the limits of the possible more narrowly than his actors.
Thus he decisively resists Bollmann's idea of connecting, for
comic purposes, his line about the many 'terrible things' to the
'pictures' painted by the madman, and not to Hamm's story.
And he reacts with scepticism to the notion of playing up the
comic parts and inserting 'pauses for effect' here and there.
Contrary to this Beckett now suggests to him, in his action with
the ladder (Section 15), to speak the first of his echo phrases
('Sometimes I wonder if I'm in my right mind.') 'cheerfully', the
second ('then it passes, and I'm as lucid as before') 'sadly',
instead of, as previously, the other way around — 'That would be
more comic. Clov would be pleased if he didn't have any more
mind.'

Beckett thankfully accepts a suggestion of Schroeder's: Could
Clov in the go-between scene ('Ask my father if he wants to listen
to my story' — Section 8) retreat from the ashbin a few steps with
each of his three reports, so that Hamm can call him back with a
fresh direction? — 'Yes, that's more comic.' It is also more comic
if Clov reacts with 'astonishment' to Hamm's line 'He'll get a
sugar plum'; his line of thought is more or less 'What a day! All
this generosity in him, it can't be real!' In the 'negotiation' with
Nagg he has Bollmann stick his head almost all the way into the
ashbin; that too is more comic.

Thursday, 14 September
Main stage, morning. Run-through rehearsal. In the Nagg-
Nell dialogue Beckett sits in front of the ashbins again like a
conductor and indicates intonations. Nell's 'so white. So clean.'
is to be held longer. Thus Nagg must delay his joke.

Hamm's closing monologue. Beckett wants to have it 'simpler
still'. He asks Schroeder to take his time (this will also help
Bollmann who has only a few lines' time to put on his 'travel
habit') — 'Very cold and quiet, but with inner tension'. The
polishing of the eyeglasses is reworked: with one hand in the fur
of the dog in Hamm's lap, instead of with the handkerchief.
From this point onward, tone and movement are to be gradually
reduced. 'He still allows himself a bit of luxury, poetry . . .'
Rhythmic unfolding of the handkerchief at the end and no
closing of the hands. There is identity of mood and intonation
between the last and the first monologue — 'The voice comes
out of the silence and returns into silence.'

Friday, 15 September

Main stage, evening. We have an audience for the first time. Under the critical glance and amused participation of Madame Beckett, new values emerge in the play, old ones are displaced. It is all more colourful than before, the pace quicker. Mezzoforte changes to forte, unexpected fortissimi manifest themselves. The contrast with the softer passages thus becomes more dramatic than in any earlier rehearsal. A long general pause after Nagg's curse now halves *Endgame* in an impressive manner. 'Our revels now are ended': Schroeder places the quotation carefully and definitively in a restrained, 'white' voice against silence. The action hastens onward to new high points. The last pain-killer episode is acted to the hilt. Hamm's 'Ah, at last!' is the outcry of a man dying of thirst in front of the well. His 'Give it to me!' rings out quick and hard. Clov this time allows himself a moment before striking back decisively, with sadistic enjoyment, 'There's no more pain-killer.'

The former balance of *Endgame* is disturbed. But the 'public' has had the effect of a catalyst, the play's elements have for the first time been reduced to a unity, however precarious it might be.

'*C'est formidable*' calls out Madame Beckett with straightforward emphasis. Beckett's dry comment runs — '*Il y a encore du travail.*'

Saturday, 16 September

Run-through with interruptions. How, asks Bollmann, am I to turn around when Hamm has stopped me? — 'Very quietly, very simply. Take your time, it doesn't need to be quick. Above all it's a problem of time.' The shuffling of the slippers and their flopping against the feet gives Clov's nervous, stiff-legged, musically regular gait, his physical abnormality, a remarkable acoustic effect. The shuffling of the second section ('Then move!' — 'Where are you?') becomes now too obtrusive. Beckett requests a change — 'That's a gag; that won't do.' Clov is to shuffle his constant way to the door and back again. He is to place his hands on the window sill in the same way he does on the back of the chair; this placement further parallels the position of Nagg's hands on the rim of the ashbin. In the joke with the trousers Beckett wants a reductive correction: no gesture of resignation as previously ('I never told it worse'), no movement of the hand, only of the head, once for 'world' and once for 'trousers'. Stock suggests that he disappear into the ashbin not after Hamm's 'Silence!' but only with his 'Will this never finish?'; joyful agreement by Beckett — 'Finish — lid, that's good.' While doing it Stock goes slowly to his knees, then pulls his head in quickly, so that the lid snaps shut loudly.

Repeat with accompanying critique in detail of glances, gestures, movements and intonations. With his first 'What's happening?' (2nd section), Hamm is to cross his arms fearfully on his chest, so that the same phrase will be instantly recognised at its repetition (6th section) by the identical gesture and intonation. 'God be with the days!' (Clov means the times before birth): 'Please don't throw it away! Speak the phrase with more nostalgic flavour.' Beckett says this emphatically, and adds — 'Hamm too had his "golden age", that old Greek, then!'

In the last tableau Bollmann has entered with heavy high-laced boots. He wears a grey-green worn-out coat and carries casually over his left arm an old trenchcoat. In his left hand he holds a big black umbrella, in his right an antique travelling bag. Beckett observes him thoughtfully for a moment, head inclined. Then he asks him for the things and re-arranges them: the bag on the left, the umbrella over it, the coat on the right; the clumsy, unconvincing gear of someone who's never 'gotten away' and seems totally incapable of doing so anyway. It's a lot more comic and effective this way.

Individual rehearsal with Bollmann and Schroeder 'only for the movements', for all entrances and exits. 'I have it all analysed, it'll go quickly.' Beckett holds his director's book shut in his hand, he has the arithmetic in his head. Clov has 16 entrances and 16 exits, Hamm stops him 26 times. How is this divided up? Clov comes at Hamm's whistle five times (four times as far as his place next to the armchair; once he stays in the doorway). The other eleven entrances divide into four with an object and the echo-phrase 'I'm back again with . . .' and some other 'object entrances' without this phrase. The props are to be carried in plain view in the raised hand, preferably the left (the one toward the audience). Could Bollmann stop, 'call out' each object, then walk onward? That is Beckett's separation of action and word. No, it's better with no halt. Bollmann practises Clov's rapid, shuffling gait, looking for the proper rhythm. He makes a turn around, whistling 'toot-toots' like a boy. He seems to be enjoying it. Something mechanical comes into his walk, the stamping of a damaged but still powerful machine. Beckett watches him with satisfaction. How many steps does he need to get from the door to the armchair? Nine, counts Bollmann. Beckett prefers eight. 'The rhythm is better', agrees Schroeder. The total depends upon the off-stage position and the foot chosen for the first step. 'It's almost like a dance,' says Beckett, 'equal number of paces, rhythm kept equal.' Bollmann is working like a horse. 'Isn't it getting too hard?' Beckett asks him, concerned for him. He shakes his head. 'It is all part of my profession.' All of Clov's movements are subjected to the 'system'. When he goes up to Hamm ('Have you bled?' etc.) or leaves him and is stopped ('I'll go and get the catheter,' etc.) he is to take four steps, sometimes eight, less often two ('A madman? When was that?'), Clov's parody of a peripatetic in the thinker-episode ('What are you doing?' — 'Having an idea.') is likewise altered by Beckett into an ordered zigzag course of 6 + 4 + 6 + 4 short steps. 'A thought-ballet', comments Schroeder enthusiastically. This rhythm, he feels, makes their 'war' all the more threatening. Beckett nods and says, 'Yes, this whispering tread on the earth.'

As we leave the rehearsal, Beckett is in good spirits. 'It's much, much better this way', he remarks of his *Endgame* arithmetic. 'It was dirty before, now it's clear.' Even if no one observes it, it will still register on the unconscious. He compares it to the effect of those recurring images inserted into films for propaganda purposes which penetrate the subconscious by constant repetition. I ask Beckett about the connections of these not merely rational, whole, but also even numbers. '*Oui, c'est pythagoréen,*' he says quickly. *Ratio* conquers the irrational! My sentiment is repaid by a mocking smile; yet he reinforces it with a sardonic stress '*L'affreux irrationnel*'.

Tuesday, 19 September

The stage set is now in place for the first time. A dark grey carpeting covers the boards. Matias, the stage designer, is once again present. He notes what he wants changed. He doesn't like the small lights in the ashbins at all, their ghostly footlight effect. Beckett desires a symmetrical position of the opened lids, a breaking device must be added. The curtains, curtain rods and the picture still have to be sprayed with grey paint, as well as the two sheets for the ashbins and Hamm. They are to look dirty, used. Beckett is still not pleased with the armchair.

Although it's regained its little, noisy rollers, their solid suspension is too heavy for him, too 'theatre-like'. Can't it simply be placed under the chair-legs?

Afternoon. Lighting rehearsal. There will be only one lighting set-up, no change of light. The general direction is: cold light. Beckett modifies the first 'cue' — gradual reduction to a dull interior. He has the lights focused on the door, the ashbins and the armchair. The darkness spills over the dark grey surfaces into the scene. This neutral illumination creates a simple effect. Will it be light enough all over? They check, two stage hands occupy extreme stage positions. Beckett wants still more 'coldness'. Light-blue gels are added. Lights have meanwhile been set up behind each window. The left one, behind the 'sea window', has to be brought in a little stronger than the one on the right, which casts a weak gleam on the 'earth window'.

Thursday, 21 September

Rehearsal in costume, make-up, lighting. Beckett requests a last regular rehearsal with interruptions. In Clov's 'small round of respect' Bollmann is now to take the picture off the wall and drop it, before hanging the alarm on the hook. The symbolic *memento mori* (rather: *memento finire*) thus gains more importance. The business of the curtain calls has to be set straight. The actors agree: no change in the final tableau. Beckett seems surprised and relieved. 'It would have hurt me,' he says gratefully, 'to break up the picture at the end.' It must be allowed to sink into the audience. It can hold for five seconds or longer until the blackout. That has to be rehearsed.

Friday, 22 September

First '*Hauptprobe*'. Technical corrections are still necessary. The ashbins have now been dented and sprayed so as to look old and dirty. Fingerprints have been painted on the rims but they don't coincide with the placement of the hands. Bollmann is wearing a hat today after all, a straw hat sprayed grey. It's too grey, Beckett says, the original yellow ought to show through slightly. On the other hand, Clov's travelling bag hasn't enough of patina, the painters will have to do it over again. Beckett dispenses with these questions quickly, they seem to bore him.

Once again Beckett instructs his actors to mute the dialogue, to hold down, to act as if in front of a fourth wall. He gives them another image to suggest the climate: *Endgame* is like a burnt-out hearth from which flames break out from time to time, to sink back again into the ashes.

Saturday, 23 September
Second '*Hauptprobe*'.
A small incident: when the dog strikes Hamm's skull (Bollmann hits it against the chair behind Schroeder's head), the cloth bursts and a rain of coloured pieces of foam rubber pours over the floor. Beckett is delighted — 'Can we keep that in?'[5]

ONE HAMMER, THREE NAILS, Ernst Schroeder:
Experiences of an Actor with Dramatist Samuel Beckett as Director

This play is like 'fire and ashes', said Beckett as the auditorium was darkening for the general rehearsal; it occurred to him over his 'breakfast beer'. Hamm and Clov, he says, are both focused on quiet and inner contemplation, but one of them is always disturbing the other; the other is always the peacebreaker, and fire suddenly flares out of the ashes of quietness. (*Embers*, I remembered, is the title of a play by Beckett.) 'You can do what you want now, the script belongs to you, the structure's set.' I *couldn't* do what I wanted — outside the fact that that wasn't what I had in mind — all I could do was what was musically correct . . .

Speculative requests for interpretation had been put down at the first rehearsal when Beckett, in response to our questions, set out the phonetics of the names of the parts. Anyone who had read Esslin or Adorno had it brought back vividly: Hamm is an abbreviation of the German word *Hammer*, Clov is French *clou*, a nail, and therefore not to be pronounced Clav; Nagg short for German *Nagel* (nail), Nell comes from English *nail*. So it's a play for a hammer and three nails? 'If you like!' A play, after all, not confined entirely to the stage and *not* one of those not to be discussed off stage. It first arises in space, and Beckett insisted that for the actors this space ought to have a fourth wall, facing the audience. To fit the specialised space we must find the exact timing for the play's progress. On the little stage, the pauses can be smaller, the movements are bound to be so anyway, and gestures must be held down, as small as possible; large gestures would make the area even smaller. Recognition of the space time relationships on stage which I have worked out by years of practice with students were obvious to Beckett. Thus in the workshop of the Schiller-Theater originated surely the shortest presentation of all productions of *Endgame*.

The author-director had not spent hours discussing it with us, no play-doctoring; he hadn't rehearsed up and down, paid hommage to sad clowns and their fashionable melancholy, instead, from the first day forward, he had established the basic gestures of the characters and given the precise tempos, the pauses and their respective durations. The sole general pause — of crucial point for interpretation-mongers! — he set after Nagg's curse: 'Yes, I hope I live till then, to hear you calling me like when you were a tiny boy and were frightened, in the dark, and I was your only hope!'

The marvellous musicality of this script became evident. Supervised by Beckett with utter accuracy in three languages, examined and improved for the German version even to details of punctuation: when such scripts are produced for the musically attuned ear, their sense structure becomes apparent automatically. Their musical and intellectual expression converge.

Now, one mustn't imagine that those orchestrating 'tactics' are exercised without irony, and irony that casts a glaring light on the play's landscape. Some examples of this: Beckett, the fanatic for pauses, tells the actor representing Clov to answer Hamm's question 'Did you ever have an instant of happiness?' immediately with 'Not to my knowledge', since Clov knows this without stopping to think. Or when Beckett in three phrases manages to keep Hamm's end from sentimentality by means of sarcasm: 'Peace to our . . . to our arses.'; 'A few more squirms like that and I'll call.'; 'A little poetry.' Hamm isn't a poor loser, Beckett told me. Like the king in a chess game, who at the end can only make a few meaningless moves, he plays them out in an almost ironically withdrawn way, conscious of their meaninglessness to the close. 'No? Good.' Hamm escapes sentimentality and behaves almost heroically.

Of course I occasionally tried to entice a comment out of the taciturn man as to the psychology of the part. I finally told him that the actor in a rehearsal is studying not only the part, he's also studying himself under the magnifying-glass of the part. And finally, that this magnifying-glass, in this case, was especially obscured by the filter of the author. Beckett, smiling, agreed this was so. We were working on Hamm's last monologue: 'You weep, and weep, for nothing, so as not to laugh, and little by little . . . you begin to grieve. All those I might have helped. Helped! Saved. Saved! The place was crawling with them!' Irony in the word 'help', requests Beckett; for what is a grain of wheat worth against starvation in the world? I ask Beckett whether the mighty Hamm does not after all have a bad conscience. He looks at me, a crafty countenance, a bit amazed and just a little unhappy, and says softly 'Do you think so?' I don't know any author or any director who would have answered that way. At that moment 'Hamm' began to draw breath as a human being. He was no longer a rôle; Hamm was an acquaintance of Beckett's and mine.[6]

CHAPTER FIVE

Krapp's Last Tape

ORIGINS AND COMPOSITION

Mime du Rêveur

Krapp's Last Tape is the fulfilment of Beckett's long time interest in integrating mime and dialogue. The principle of separating action and speech, so evident in his direction of *Godot* and in the opening and closing mimes and monologues of *Endgame*, is fundamental both to the inception of *Krapp* and to the significant alterations Beckett has made in the productions of *Krapp* in which he has been involved. And in the unpublished work *Mime du Rêveur* A, written ca. 1954,[1] Beckett had worked on a play which focused on a single character, portrayed in the present through an extended pantomime which is seen in counterpoint to sounds of wind and sighs and a second mimed dream of the dreamer and a now-absent lover.

Like Krapp, A is occupied by the mundane particulars of his physical existence. He digs in his pockets for the numerous objects that keep his daily life going. Wears a cap and mittens against the cold. Scratches himself. Must hold objects close to his eyes to compensate for failing vision and bad light. And like Krapp his main action apart from seeking relief through injections is the juxtaposed contemplation of a memory and contemplation of himself. He first examines in great detail a small photograph in an aged frame, presumably of a departed loved one from the distant past. (Beckett told Marcel Mihalovici that Krapp's tapes were comparable to a photograph album)[2]. Cancelled lines had called for A to cast his eyes upward to heaven as he reflects before each new stage of examination of the photograph — a gesture of fear or guilt like Krapp's looks over his shoulder for 'old Nick' in the darkness before switching on the tapes of his 'farewell to love'. After injecting himself with painkiller, falling asleep briefly, and striking an item from his small notebook, A then regards himself up close in a small looking-glass. A's two acts of contemplation are linked by his striking two matches in each case to provide the light for inspection. In both cases contemplation brings pain as the matches burn his fingers. But as with Krapp, who learns from slipping on the first banana peel not to throw the second underfoot, A blows out the second match lit to view the photograph before it can burn him. Contemplation of self proves even more painful than memory of love for both A and Krapp, and both remain fixed in lifeless reverie at the end of the process. Caught in that state, A lets the second match burn his fingers before putting the looking glass back in his pocket.

In this earliest seed of *Krapp* we see Beckett's first tentative use of mime to depict personal psychology rather than a general condition of existence. It was an important step not only toward *Krapp*, but also toward *Not I, Footfalls*, and the cinematic works *Film* and *Eh Joe*.

Magee Monologue

The introduction of the technical device of a tape recorder as an active stage presence allowed Beckett to present on stage the memories which evoke the mimed reaction and to integrate monologue and mime while still maintaining nearly absolute separation between voice and physical action. Beckett has never explained what led him to think of the recorder, but in part the origin of *Krapp*, like that of *Eh Joe* later, lay in the wish to use a particular technical medium as a vehicle for a particular actor.

In 1958 while working with director Donald McWhinnie and actor Pat Magee on the BBC radio production of *All that Fall*, Beckett had been involved with professional tape recording and had been captivated by Magee's voice, which he had first heard in France in a reading from *Molloy* on the BBC. After returning to France, he began in February to write a play for Magee's voice under the working title *Magee Monologue*. In March he wrote to McWhinnie asking for operating instructions for a tape recorder so that he could incorporate the recorder realistically in his play.

The holograph drafts under the heading *Magee Monologue*, on MS pages 11 through 25, in Beckett's 'Été 56' notebook are dated 20-2-58. In his usual fashion Beckett wrote a first draft (three and one half pages) on the recto leaves. Then, beginning on the recto pages after the end of this first draft, a second draft of nine pages finished on two verso pages at the front of the notebook. He completed the basis for the published text by writing four typescript revisions heavily emended in pen.[2]. In these early stages of composition and in the English original *Krapp* was not yet the complete play that it was to become in later versions. In revising his text for publication, Beckett concentrated on the thematic elements of the monologue, providing only more general stage directions than those he would ultimately establish. Only in successive productions would Beckett evolve the detailed stage directions for the mime action in response to the monologue which is in essence the plot of the play.

Beckett's first draft presents Krapp (still designated as A) finding and 'separating' 'box three' of his tapes from the others, removing spool five and turning from the ledger to box to spool as he finds the passage he wants to hear. His one reference from the ledger in this first version is simply the word 'Passim', which he repeats: *'finally, softly,* Passim!' indicating a life reduced to pedantic notation of frequently recurring elements.

The passage which Krapp selects is the review of his 30th year which he made on his 31st birthday. It is not yet so clear that the year under review was the one in which Krapp made the crucial decisions that have shaped his later life. But even in this earliest presentation, Krapp sees his life as a series of turning points or moments of decision. He describes himself 'at the peak of my powers,' prays 'with fervour' to be 'given the strength in the coming years' to make changes in his life. This birthday he feels is an especially crucial day. 'Oh I know, I know,' he says, 'I have had these crises before but at no time so acutely as this afternoon.' And this draft breaks off with the line '— a moment in the life of all pioneers' — a more hopeful early version of his 'farewell to love'. The moment he is about to hear reviewed is the one when those who set out for new territory must part from the loved ones they leave behind.

Already in the first draft there were the basic elements of the Manichean ethics which Beckett later identified explicitly in his director's notebook for the 1969 Berlin production. The setting emphasises the separation and contrast of light and dark fundamental to Manicheanism: 'Table and immediately adjacent zone in a circle of strong light rest of stage in shadow.' Krapp finds his table unsteady and moves it to the front of the stage 'out of the zone of light': 'sits down in shadow', 'The light moves and comes to rest on him in his new position'.

When he goes backstage 'into shadow' for a drink he makes a noticeable re-entry to the 'zone of light' 'in a kind of shuffling dance' 'from an unexpected angle'.

The dichotomy of spirit and flesh associated in Manicheanism with light and dark is basic to the structure of the one short taped fragment in this draft. Krapp's assessment of his physical strength 'sound in wind and limb', except for my 'old trouble' [bowel condition], is juxtaposed with his assessment of his intellectual strength and his prayer to 'All-merciful Providence'. (A note in TSI, 'wind rhymes with mind', points out the duality).

The germs of the more specific Manichean organisation and images which Beckett was to develop later were also present in this first draft. After appealing to Providence Krapp prays, 'may the star that stood above my bassinet continue to burn in my breast and on my labours.' In spite of 'resolutions and aspirations' he remains in violation of the three 'seals' or principal prohibitions of the Manicheans as described in the 11th edition of the *Encyclopedia Britannica* which Beckett used as his source. In his dedication to his 'labours' (later referred to as 'the shadow of the *magnum opus*') Krapp violates the *signaculum manus* (seal of the hands) forbidding to the elect the dedication to a profession. By aspiring to a 'fuller sex life' he violates the *signaculum sinus* (seal of the breast) against all sexual desire. And most obviously, as his resolution to drink less and exits to drink show, Krapp is in violation of the *signaculum oris* (seal of the mouth) which forbids drinking wine.

In the second draft and the four typescripts Beckett devoted much of his attention to expanding and refining the Manichean elements inherent in the first draft, laying down a much more systematic structure for the play than is at first evident. The only reference from the ledger, the one word 'Passim', was broadened to include the references to the three major turning points of the past year which Krapp will listen to later on tape: his mother's death, his 'vision' on the night of the 'memorable equinox,' and his 'farewell to love' in the lake scene. In the more developed presentations on the tape, Beckett makes clear that these three moments are all incidents from Krapp's life in which light and dark, spirit and sensuality, are mingled. But as portrayed in the ledger, they outline a progression of the three 'moments' central to Manichean belief: 1. the past when spirit and matter were separate and matter exclusively contained in a world of feminine darkness: 'mother at rest at last', 'the black ball', 'the dark nurse'; 2. the present when light and dark are mingled but the process of redemptive separation is in progress, 'memorable equinox'; and 3. the future when the separation of light and dark is completed, 'farewell to love', (cf. *Encyclopedia Britannica*, Vol XVII, 11th edition, p. 573).

New dialogue in the second draft describes Krapp in the winehouse (dark) 'sitting before the fire' (light) 'separating the grain from the chaff' — an act described by Beckett in his Berlin director's notebook as the Manichean 'separation of light from darkness' (See p. 260). The inescapability of light and dark, illustrated in the first version of the 'monologue' when the light follows Krapp as he attempts to move his table out of it, is given more plausible and evident presentation in TS1, this time in words, as Krapp refers to his new light and the darkness about him.

Krapp's 'aspirations and resolutions' at age 27, which comprised nearly all of the tape of the first draft, are still present in the second draft but now, as in the final text, only in the form of a summary reported by the 39-year-old Krapp as he reviews them in preparation for his summary of the current year. References to his resolution 'to drink less', desire to lead 'a fuller sex life', and concern for 'his life's work' present his violation of the three Manichean seals in a more condensed and easily perceptible form.

The fullest and most obvious expansion of the Manichean materials is in the taped account of the three incidents referred to in the ledger. In these, Beckett, drawing partly on his own imagery and partly on traditional Manichean 'emblems' as presented in the *Encyclopedia Britannica*, shows that in spite of his intentions to effect a separation, Krapp's actions nevertheless consistently involve a mingling of light and dark. The 'black ball' which he gave to the dog at the time of his mother's death (described in the final version as 'a small, old, black, hard, solid rubber ball') is in the second draft of the monologue 'an old tennis ball, all black and sodden but not punctured'. The ball, originally white, is now black. It is unpunctured—still containing undefiled air—one of the five Manichean 'elements of light'. It has become sullied with impure water (an element of darkness).

In presenting the 'memorable equinox' and 'boat scene' Beckett also systematically interspersed the five Manichean 'emblems' of light: zephyr, wind, light, quickening fire, clear water with the emblems of dark: mist, heat, sirocco, darkness, vapour, in the form given in the *Encyclopedia Britannica*.

Krapp sums up his experience on the night of the memorable equinox as a 'strange association' of 'storm and night' with the 'light of understanding and peace' which he will remember until his 'dying day'. Later, in TS3 this passage is changed to 'unshatterable association until my dissolution' — a formulation suggesting more directly physical mingling and ultimate separation. The description of the physical scene* begins with Beckett's own image of mingling: 'Great granite rocks' (dark stone with embedded shiny crystalline flecks). It continues with a specifically Manichean 'emblem': the 'foam' flying up in the light of the 'beacon' is Beckett's representation of 'vapour' (cf. Director's Notebook, p. 47). The 'anemometer spinning like a propeller' is itself an ambiguous combination of the properties of the 'quickening wind' of light and the 'destructive wind' of darkness. Beckett also changed the phrase describing the period before this turning point; 'Creatively a year of disappointment' of the second draft became in TS1 'Spiritually a year of profound gloom'.

The greatest incorporation of explicit Manichean emblems comes in the boat scene as Krapp bids 'farewell to love'. The opening fragment on the tape is highlighted by isolation and repetition as Krapp at first winds the tape too far into the passage and must return to the beginning. It is a concentrated presentation of his breech of the three seals: my 'face [*signaculum oris*] in her breasts [*signaculum sinus* . . .] my hand on her [*signaculum manus*].' As Beckett later noted in his Berlin notebook, the 'bit of a breeze' (changed in the Faber proofs to 'light breeze') and 'the water nice and lively' represent the light emblems of 'mild zephyr, cooling wind' and 'clear water', while the 'Hot sun' ('Sun blazing down' in the final texts) represents the dark emblem of 'heat'. The addition of a reference to 'the glare' in TS1 counterbalances this by presenting the sun as 'bright light'.

The Manichean elements culminate in Krapp's new recording as he interrupts his thoughts of the year just past to

---

* The Dun Laoghaire jetty where this autobiographical experience actually occurred is itself a bifurcated scene with light on one hand and dark on the other. (See opposite).

JETTY AT DUN LAOGHAIRE — SITE OF 'MEMORABLE EQUINOX'

recall once again the girl in the boat: 'The eyes she had [. . .] Everything there, everything . . . all the light and dark of the [*hesitates*] ages.' This passage, Krapp's most enduring memory, had been prepared for by including references to the eyes of the other women from Krapp's past. At the mention of Bianca, Beckett added in TS3 the sentence 'not much about her apart from a tribute to her eyes. Very warm.' The detailed description of the dark nurse with 'eyes like moonstone' was an addition on the verso of the second draft. In TS4 'chrysolite' replaced 'moonstone'. By creating an allusion to Shakespeare's Desdemona as a world of 'perfect chrysolite', Beckett prepares for the later equation of the eyes of the lake girl with the world and strengthens the themes of betrayal and the exchange of love for other values.*

In the boat scene on the tape, Krapp bends over the girl to get her eyes 'in shadow' — a correct Manichean response to keep more light from becoming entrapped in a feminine body. But his request to her when she opens her eyes, 'Let me in' would, if granted, cancel this positive action by having Krapp himself enter that dark feminine body through those eyes. In revising the final reference to her eyes, the negative implications of Krapp's request are made more apparent. In an addition to the second draft of *Magee Monologue* Beckett included the pejorative 'bleeding' ('every bleeding thing') reflecting a Manichean rejection of blood as a dark and sensual substance. This phrase was replaced in TS2 with 'Everything there, Everything on earth'. IN TS1 he added the phrase 'vice and crystal' in apposition to 'everything'. That was replaced in TS2 by 'hunger and famine'. His final formulation (found only in the printed text), 'everything on this old muck-ball', associates her eyes explicitly with the Manichean image of the physical world as a 'bolus' of dark excrement left after spirit and light are liberated from it (cf. *Encyclopedia Britannica*, 11th ed. p. 574).

Krapp's original characterisation of his present life as 'reverie and constipation' is further indication of a process of excremental purgation that is blocked as Krapp remains haunted by his recollections of the women in his life. This is given stronger expression in TS4 when it is restated as 'sour cud [the rumination of past experience] and the iron stool'.

---

* *Othello*, Act V, sc. II Nay, had she been true / If heaven would make me such another world / of one entire and perfect chrysolite / I'd not have sold her for it.

The choice in TS2 of the name Crapp with its excremental reference is an elaboration of this concept.*

Krapp's decision to abandon recording for the evening as presented in the second draft, 'Finish this *vomit* tomorrow,' continues the metaphor of evacuation as a means of separation. But Beckett softened 'vomit' to 'drivel' in TS4 so that in the published text the single image of the 'muckball' is uncomplicated by tangential association.

Manichean structure and imagery are also prevalent in details of Krapp's new recording in the present. In the summary of his 68th year, he appears again to have been turning from dark to light. In a passage from the first draft later deleted, Krapp scorns progeny like a good Manichean ascetic, referring to 'the brats and skivies'. His thoughts of happiness with Effie † 'up there on the cold sea' is as Beckett points out in the Berlin notebook 'a turning to the north' considered by Manicheans to be 'the seat of light'. But ultimately he does not make 'the last effort'; he has decided in the night to reject 'all that old misery'. Instead, he decides to 'leave it at that'. He returns to darkness and forbidden drink. He will 'Empty the bottle', go to bed and 'Lie propped up in the dark and wander'. These mental wanderings would lead him to 'be again'. Even his final rejection of his past years, 'I wouldn't want them back. No I wouldn't have them back. Not with the fire in me now,' is unsuccessful. In the second draft of *Magee Monologue* the first of these sentences originally read, 'I wouldn't have them back.' Beckett changed 'have' to 'want' creating contrast between the first formulation and the repetition. Krapp is not free to choose. He may not *want* his past years with all their dark associations but he does *have* them in his dreams.

Krapp's enslavement to his memories leaves him suffering the ultimate punishment of those who fail to observe the precepts of Manicheanism. Because Krapp has not successfully rejected darkness, it still burns within him as it had from infancy. In the deleted reference to the star that burned above his bassinet in North Great George Street, fire seems a benign

* The name Krapp is also associated with bourgeois family life. Like the later Krapp, the protagonist of *Eleuthéria*, Victor Krap, has severed his connections with the family Krap and rejected marriage with Mademoiselle Piouk. Beckett has on several occasions said that he might have written a play in which Krapp was equally dissatisfied by life with Mrs. Krapp — formerly the girl in the boat.

† The heroine of Theodore Fontane's novel, but also, according to Patrick Magee, a real-life acquaintance of Beckett.

enough element of light, but in the progression of the play and of Krapp's life it becomes more evidently ambiguous and finally clearly a source of tormenting heat. At 27 Krapp sat before the fire 'with closed eyes' unknowingly shutting out light while absorbing heat. The insight revealed '10 or 12 years later' at the memorable equinox was described first as the 'wonder that made it possible' then altered in TS1 to the 'fire which set it alight'. Krapp may well believe that he was inspired by the 'quickening fire' of light, but as the addition of the words 'warm or cold' in TS4 to describe his memory of the occurrence suggests, it may have been the 'destructive fire'. Thirty years later the 69-year-old Krapp sits 'shuddering in the park, *drowned* in dreams and *burning* to be gone' (italics added). And he has '*scalded* the eyes out of [himself] reading Effie again' (italics added). The changes from 'wishing' to 'burning' in connection with drowning and from 'burn' to 'scald' are instances of the forbidden mixture of fire and water which produces the negative mingled element 'vapour' thus removing the ambiguous possibility that the fire is not destructive. Krapp's final utterance referring to 'the fire in me now' which precludes his return to a happier state confirms Mani's prediction of the fate of the unfaithful: 'They also that adore the fire, the burning, by this they recognise that their end shall be in fire,' (*Encyclopedia Britannica*, p. 575).

Many of Beckett's revisions of the four typescripts added incidental details of light and dark to create images of the mingled duality that pervades Krapp's life. Old Mrs. Williams becomes first 'Mrs. Beamish' (TS1) and finally Mrs. McGlome (TS4). 'Alba in Trafalgar Street' becomes Bianca in *Kedar* St. (italics added) an anagram for dark. The dark nurse acquires a white starched uniform (TS2). The dog to which he gives the black ball changes from 'a wire-haired fox-terrier' (TS4) to 'a little white dog' (Faber Text). Krapp's magnum opus becomes a 'shadow' (TS1). The hymn introduced is of the dying light of evening (TS2).

In TS2 Beckett made a major addition, The Banana Walk, which he wrote out in longhand on the verso of page one. It is a further elaboration in action of the Manichean dualism inherent in Krapp's whole existence. Krapp oscillates back and forth within the zone of light eating and meditating but finally exits into darkness to pursue his sensual appetite. He performs an act of separation as he peels the bananas, but the act is incomplete and the remains which he has failed to get rid of nearly cause his downfall. His handling and eating of the two bananas as he avidly consumes one and throws the uneaten portion of the other on the floor illustrates his mixture of appentency and rejection.

The act of eating the bananas is itself ostensibly a compliance with the all-encompassing Manichean commandment to liberate light from imprisoning darkness. While forbidden to consume wine and meat because they embody darkness, the elect were enjoined to eat ritual meals of fruit in order to incorporate in a pure body the light stored up in them. But, in discarding the uneaten portion, and thereby allowing it to remain in the impure physical world, Krapp commits sacrilege. In the final Faber text Krapp stuffs the uneaten portion into his vest pocket rather than throw it away. The remnant of what he sought to reject keeps a reminder before the audience of Krapp's failure in his pursuit of asceticism. In a triad of gestures concluding the mime, Krapp in quick succession wipes his mouth, wipes his hand on the front of his vest (i.e., his breast), and then rubs his hands and claps them together, illustrating by gesture the three *signaculum* of *oris, sinus,* and *manus*, which he violates.

Presentation of the result of Krapp's Manichean asceticism — his loneliness — was begun in the second draft but only completed as Beckett revised the typescripts. In the first draft version of Krapp's decision to lead 'a fuller sex life' Beckett struck out his original phrase, 'with some partners' — emphasising a desire for companionship — and added in the margin 'more engrossing' and '*Inter*course!' — emphasising the physical mingling of the sex act itself. In TS2 Beckett changed 'more engrossing' to 'less engrossing' in keeping with the greater emphasis on Krapp's rejection of old lovers begun in the second draft.

While condensing Krapp's resolutions and aspirations to a reported account in the second draft, Beckett surrounded them with new references to partners and other women now gone from Krapp's life: Old Mrs. Williams, Alba, 'the girl in a shabby green coat on a railway platform', the dark nurse who rejected his approaches, and his dead mother. Later revisions systematically associate these women with death, creating a greater sense of their absence. When Old Mrs. Williams doesn't sing, Krapp says in the second draft, 'I hope nothing has happened to her.' Beckett deleted this in TS2 leaving only, 'Not tonight.' No longer in doubt, her absence becomes absolute as the night 30 years ago and the present night, when she is certainly dead, are joined. Immediately following his reference to Alba, Beckett added in TS2 the sentence 'These old P.M.'s [post mortems] are gruesome' to describe his annual ritual of listening to tapes from the past. The 'dark nurse' is associated with death by the addition in TS3 of the phrase 'most funereal thing' describing her black pram. And also in TS3, Fanny, Krapp's last 'partner', though undoubtedly still alive, is nevertheless characterised in imagery of both a skeleton and a spirit — 'a bony old ghost of a whore'.

Notably, the lake girl and the girl in the shabby green coat are exceptions to the pattern. While both are remembered at moments of separation, there is only a hint of their death contained in a pun. Unlike the others whom Krapp has mentally laid to rest, these two are still present as irreducible memories. They are 'what *remains*'* of 'all that old misery' (italics added).

Other typescript alterations make Krapp's state of solitude even more complete. At TS1 Beckett deleted the phrase, 'The coming year will decide . . .' following the first occurrence of the conclusion of the tape he has chosen to review, 'Past midnight never knew such silence.' He replaced it with, 'Here I end . . .' so that the lonely silence which surrounds Krapp seems a final state rather than one that might be altered in the future. And at TS3 to the first and third repetitions of this fragment, he added 'the earth might be uninhabited', making the solitude absolute. To TS3 Beckett added to the list in the register the reference to his 'father's last illness'. At TS4 he removed the reference to sitting among the 'brats and skivies' in the park from Krapp's recording of his present year. In the final text Krapp is alone in the park. 'Not a soul,' he says, echoing the same phrase near the beginning of the tape describing the scene in the winehouse 30 years earlier.

The focus on Krapp himself as a bereaved lone survivor was one of Beckett's main concerns in revising the typescripts. In them he expanded the simple references in the second draft to Krapp's mother's 'long widowhood' into a major action. In

* Patrick Magee was asked to stress the word so that the overtones of a corpse would be apparent.

TS2 he changed 'widowhood' to the more salient Latinate 'viduity' and has Krapp repeat the word questioningly. Krapp then 'goes back stage into darkness, comes back with the Concise Oxford, lays it on the table, sits down, looks up viduity, reads, nods'. A marginal note in pen reads 'Or Johnson's dictionary and quote example'. In TS3 the quotation is still only a suggestion in the stage direction, 'quote dictionary if possible'. The emphasis on the word 'viduity' is, however, strengthened by additions: Krapp 'starts' and 'switches off' when he hears the word, winds back to repeat it twice after moments of hesitation. The dictionary he consults is no longer the Concise Oxford but is 'enormous', and Krapp's lips move silently in the syllables of 'viduity' as he returns with it.

In a marginal handwritten addition in TS4 Beckett did incorporate the definition. However, Dr. Johnson's one word definition of viduity, 'widowhood', obviously did not provide the example Beckett desired so he turned to the Oxford English Dictionary. The definition he finally provided is a composite, drawing upon the Oxford and expanded with additions of his own. In making his compilation, Beckett shifted the emphasis from his mother's widowhood to Krapp himself in a state of bereavement. The Oxford English Dictionary entry for 'viduity', is a 'state of being or remaining a widow'. The time during which a woman is 'a widow' defined a female state and it gave no examples. Beckett turned to the entry for 'widowhood' and chose for his example the citation from Bulwer Lytton's play *Lucretia* (II, xvii). 'Lucretia's deep weeds of widowhood'. The citation integrated the theme of dead mates with the imagery of light and dark. By eliminating the name 'Lucretia' Beckett removed the association of the term with the female only but sacrificed another mingling of light and dark.

The second definition of 'widowhood' in the Oxford English Dictionary noted that the term could also apply to males and gave the phrase, 'also of animals, especially of birds', thus pointing in the direction of the entry 'widowbird'. This entry provided the image of a male in the dark colours of mourning. The entry as the Latin name of the species 'Vidua' and the vernacular 'weaver bird', which Beckett included, points out that the name comes from the 'dark plumage of the males'. Krapp reads that phrase then 'looks up with relish' and repeats 'Vidua bird'.

The phrase 'the state of being or remaining' in the Oxford's definition of 'viduity', which Beckett has Krapp repeat in puzzlement, was fortuitous. It foreshadows Krapp's condition at the end of the play caught between the alternative to 'Be again' by returning if only in memory to 'his best years when there was a chance of happiness' or to remain in his present state.

Because of his inability to effect a total separation of conflicting dichotomies in his life, Krapp lives in a constant state of alternation between extremes. Two changes in the initial description of himself very near the beginning of the tape of his 39th year help to establish the pattern of Krapp's existence. Krapp's self appraisal in the *Magee Monologue*, 'sound in wind and limb,' focused on his physical being. That was changed in TS2 to 'sound as a whistle', underscoring the auditory aspects of the play. In TS3 Beckett added a hesitation before 'whistle' calling attention to the metaphor. In TS4 he emended this to 'sound as a *(hesitates)* bell', retaining the auditory focus while linking the opening of the tape with the closing '. . . stop and listen to the bells . . . And so on . . . Be again, be again'. This change at the very beginning of the tape introduced an image announcing Krapp's many oscillations in the play. His identification with a metaphorical bell at the beginning and his rejection of the memories associated with a real bell in the final taped passage with which the play ends constitute one of the oscillations which the metaphor points out. Beckett had already begun to strengthen the suggestion of oscillation in the metaphors Krapp uses to describe himself initially in TS3 where he had changed the opening phrase '. . . at the *(hesitates)* peak of my powers' first to '. . . at the apogee of my powers', and then to '. . . at the *(hesitates)* crest of my powers'. In TS4 he arrived at the formulation '. . . at the *(hesitates)* crest of the wave' giving an image of undulation implying a continuous rise and fall.

PRODUCTIONS

Patrick Magee: the Original *Krapp*

The premiere of *Krapp* — in 1958 at the Royal Court Theatre — was directed by Donald McWhinnie with Patrick Magee in the title role. Beckett attended rehearsal but did not take as active a role as he did in later productions. Because Magee's

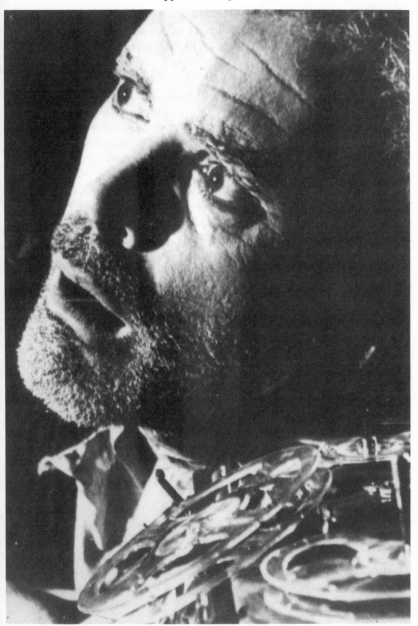

PATRICK MAGEE AS KRAPP — ROYAL COURT THEATRE 1958

voice and stage presence were models for Krapp, the actor did not need detailed instructions to be accommodated to the role. And Beckett's respect for McWhinnie as director kept him from interposing himself between actor and director or taking over the responsibility for details of performance. He made no full-scale plan for this production and according to Magee gave only very general suggestions at rehearsals. When McWhinnie directed Magee as Krapp for BBC Television on October 25, 1972, Beckett sent notes but again refrained from imposing his version on the production. Some changes made in Berlin — like the introduction of tin boxes rather than cardboard for additional sound — were included, but the explicit directions for new action and gesture were not. Nor did he send or mention the brief television script, written for the *Westdeutsche Rundfunk*, reflecting changes made for the 1969 Schiller production. (See p. 287 below)

However by 1975 when Magee was directing Max Wall in the role of Krapp, Beckett considered the changes which had evolved in later productions important enough to write to him saying that the changes he had made with Held in Berlin seemed well suited to Wall's style and that he hoped they could go over them together. As it turned out Beckett did not work with Magee to make his production reflect in detail Beckett's in Berlin. The fact that he mentioned the changes but made no attempt to impose them on Magee's direction suggests that he maintained his image of Magee as the original Krapp (as he later confirmed to Jean Martin) but also thought that the innovations arrived at with Held formed an integral part of his play.

Jean Martin: Théâtre Récamier 1960 and 1970

When Jean Martin who had played Lucky in the original *Godot*, and Clov in the original *Fin de partie*, and asssisted Roger Blin in directing *Krapp* with Beckett's help 10 years earlier at the same theatre played Krapp at Jean-Louis Barrault's *Théâtre Récamier* in 1970, Beckett took over much of the directing. His annotated script (Lilly Library, Indiana University) and Martin's recollections of the 1960 and 1970 productions, show Beckett moving from the first toward the fuller version of the play he was to develop in Berlin.

Martin's account of the work on the *Théâtre Récamier* productions indicates that the main elements in the Berlin version of *Krapp* were in Beckett's mind very early. The first *Récamier* production included the closet, revised actions for the opening, and a coordination of gestures that were to become part of his most complete version.

> Sam absolutely wanted the play to be performed without sentimentality .... All our work consisted in making Krapp an old man who remembers his past, but without detachment, only a little disgust. This play is to a certain extent very autobiographical, which explains the refusal of Sam to make it sentimental while he was keeping its dimension which one might call almost tragic ... I remember particularly the mother's death, with the episode of the little dog and the ball. Sam insisted I play the scene without adding any sentimentality. The difficulty was to avoid being cold and neutral because Sam did not want that either. And I had to be sure not to fall into emotional remembrance; it was rather some sort of *disgust.*
>
> Another difficulty came from the fact that the play had been written in English and then translated into French, but it had been originally thought out with words and breathing in English which brings up a different direction in French. And Sam was very insistent that we find in French the sort of rhythm that is found in English.
>
> Since the first production of the play Sam has always indicated that at some very precise moments Krapp would turn slightly to look back in the dark. That has always been done and always been carefully staged just like the three trips to go and get the tapes, the register, and the tape player.
>
> There are details like the bananas to which Sam has always wanted us to give great attention. And he wanted Krapp to bend more and more toward the tape recorder as the play went on, in order to end up completely lying over it, and almost to give the impression that Krapp acts with the tape recorder as he had been acting with a woman in the boat.
>
> I don't believe that there have been any great changes since Sam worked with the play the first time. Simply a greater precision and attention to representing the play in a more clinical way with never *any sentimentality.* A lot of emotion but always subdued. I know that Sam has always said that on the morning after the play Krapp was surely *dead.* He has always insisted on the fact that Krapp is debris. Some sort of an old man with hardly any age at all and just before his end.
>
> (Jean Martin, Letter to authors 1977)

The marginal notes in the script and a one-page list of changes indicate gestures which emphasise the Manichean seals of hands, and mouth and breast. The theme of women and the *signaculum sinus* is to be established by the repeated gesture of crossing his breast as he puts his hand to his throat at each mention of them. And although the notes do not specify how and where, Krapp is clearly to 'dream'.

BECKETT'S *KRAPP: SCHILLER-THEATER WERKSTATT 1969*

Beckett's direction of Das letzte Band at the Schiller-Theater *Werkstatt* in 1969 with Martin Held as Krapp approached ballet in its meticulous use of gesture and movement to portray the themes of the play. At one point Beckett even cautioned himself 'avoid excess of stylisation'. For this production he made the textual changes and additions of stage actions which complete the original Faber edition. This version had its origins in the 71 leaved Director's Notebook (designated parenthetically DN) which Beckett prepared before arriving in Berlin, but also owes much to details developed during rehearsals.[4] Beckett's notebook reflects the process: pages 1-81, (written in French while he was still in Paris or Ussy) contain his preliminary plan for the presentation he envisioned — often with questions and alternatives. Pages 83-91 under the heading '*Endgültig — Werkstatt 5/10/69*' (Final — *Werkstatt*) are a detailed summary in English and German of the action worked out in rehearsals. The 1970 published text of the Suhrkamp *Regiebuch der Berliner Inszenierung* (designated parenthetically as RB), based on Held's annotated acting script and authorised by Beckett, contains a usually more complete and infrequently different version than the notebook of the changes made for this production. It also has 113 photographs showing Held's posture and gestures. It is by far the most definitive published text of *Krapp*. These three versions are seldom in conflict but often do complement each other. The following account draws upon all of them.

The version of *Das letzte Band* finally presented was a better integrated and more powerful play than the one implied in either the English original or the preliminary outline made before rehearsals. The development of this version, through the stages of the director's notebook into the published text of the *Regiebuch*, is one of the best examples of Beckett as director using practical experience of rehearsals to make changes as author.

Set and Costume

Beckett's preliminary plan reflects the importance of the Manichean ethics and imagery so carefully incorporated in composition. These are outlined under the heading 'Mani':

> Ascetic ethics, particularly abstinence from sexual enjoyment. Sexual desire, marriage, forbidden ... (*signaculum sinus*) ... Worshipper turned towards sun or moon or north (seat of light) ... DN p. 45)

The cause of Krapp's failure in his attempt to adhere to the principles of Manicheanism is specified:

> ... [Krapp] decrees physical (ethical) incompatibility of light (spiritual) and dark (sensual) only when he intuits possibility of their reconciliation intellectually as rational-irrational. He turns from fact of anti-mind alien to mind to thought of anti-mind constituent of mind. He is thus ethically correct (*signaculum sinus*) through intellectual transgression, the duty of reason being not to join but to separate (deliverance of imprisoned light). For this sin he is punished as shown by the aeons. [. . .] note that if the giving of the black ball to the white dog represents the sacrifice of sense to spirit the form here too is that of a mingling. (DN p. 47)

On the first page of this section Beckett lists 27 points in the play at which the contrast of light and dark is stressed. On the verso page he indicates the 18 instances in which there is 'Explicit integration of light and dark' (DN p. 42, 43). (See p. 260)

Specifications for set and stage properties stress these mingled dichotomies. Under the heading 'Cagibi' (cubby hole), Beckett introduced a major addition to the set design. Instead of disappearing into undefined darkness, Krapp now goes into a closet for tapes, ledger, recorder, dictionary, microphone, and drinks. At the rise of the curtain, the cagibi's interior is 'lit with white light masked from the rest of the stage by an opaque curtain'. On the first of Krapp's exits, which Beckett calls 'voyages', to get the ledger; Krapp pulls this curtain halfway open as he enters and leaves it in this position for the remainder of the play (DN p. 5).

Two other mingled images of light and dark were also incorporated in the set. The tape recorder was equipped with a 'magic eye', a small 'control lamp' on the front which continued to burn at the end of the play after the lights on the stage and in the 'Cagibi' fade out. And a small metal disc designed and constructed by Matias met the specifications of

MANI

1. Eclairage scène et cagibi.
2. Cheveux, visage, pantalon, gilet, chemise, chaussures — gris ex noir, gris ex blanc.

~~████████████████████~~
~~████████████████████~~
~~████████████████████~~

3. 56. "Der schwarze Ball."
4. " "Das dunkle Dienstmädchen"
5. " "Denkwürdiges Aquinoktium"
6. 59 "Das neue Licht ... Bei all der Dunkelheit ..."
7. 60 "Heute Nacht jedoch nicht"
8. " "Bianca in der Kedar St."
9. 61 "Schatten des Opus"
10. 62 "Der Tag ist auf der Neige ..."
11. " "Schwarzes Gefieder"
12. 63 "Junge dunkelhaarige Schönheit etc."
13. " "weissen Hund"
14. 64 "schwarzen Ball"
15. " "Nacht im März ... als mir plötzlich alles klar wurde. Die Erleuchtung."
16. " "Im Licht des Leuchtturms ... mir endlich klar, dass das Dunkle ..."
17. 65 "Verbindung von Sturm u. Nacht mit dem Licht ... u. dem Feuer..."
18. " "Nach Mitternacht"
19. 65-66. "Sonne ·· Schatten" (yeux)
20. 67 "Der ganze alte Dreckball, altes Licht u. dunkel"
21. 68 "Vesper ... Kurze Hosen (Morgen)"
22. " "Der Tag ist auf der Neige ..."
23. " "manchmal nachts gefragt ..."
24. 69 "Leg dich ins Dunkel ..."
25. " "Sonne ·· Schatten" (yeux)
26. 70 "Nach Mitternacht."
27. Voyant blanc du magnétophon dans l'obscurité.

Explicit integration light dark :
1. 2. 5. 6. 8. 10. 12. 13/14. 15. 16. 17. 19.
20. 21. 22. 25. 27.

MANICHEAN EMBLEMS P. 43 DIRECTOR'S NOTEBOOK — *DAS LETZTE BAND*
SCHILLER-THEATER, 1969

another emblem Beckett set down in his notebook: 'High on wall to *cour** of Cagibi, a small convex glass or polished metal gives meaningless gleam throughout' (DN p. 95).

At '*Accessoires Costume*' Beckett sets up the contrast of light and dark by describing the ledger as 'large, black and worn', while the dictionary is to be covered in 'bright, light coloured leather'. Krapp's 'turnip' watch has a silver chain. The address and notes on both sides of the white envelope are to be written in black ink and the envelope itself is to be large enough so that the white can protrude from the pocket of Krapp's black vest. The lamp is to have a 'white shade, rather low' (DN pp. 71, 73). (Beckett later noted 'Extinguished finally Berlin because cold light unobtainable from this source.') The table is to be of 'light oak'. The costume into which Krapp has 'perhaps just changed' corresponds to the principles Beckett laid down at item 2 under 'Mani': 'Hair, face, pants, vest, shirt, shoes — grey ex black, grey ex white.' (DN p. 43). The notes on p. 72 specify:

> Vest and pants dirty black, dirty white shirt without collar black buttons on the sleeves [in production no buttons were visible because Held wore his sleeves rolled up nearly to his elbow], dirty white shoes [. . .] the pants too long [in production they covered the tops of the shoes but without exaggerated effect].

LISTENING AND NON-LISTENING

While the visual imagery of the play is based on the Manichean dichotomy of light and dark, the action and structure are based on the contrast of listening and non-listening. Even before hearing and seeing Held in the role of Krapp, Beckett read the text for himself and timed it. On page 77 he notes that there are 'approximately' [!] 17 minutes and 15 seconds of non-listening in the 35 minute play. And, 'the piece is therefore composed of two fairly equal parts of listening and non-listening'. The six '*Sections Travail*' (working sections) with 18 subdivisions laid out on pages 58 and 59 show the regularity of Krapp's alternation between non-listening in odd-numbered sections and listening in the even-numbered ones. To the left in a note on the order of rehearsals, Beckett

* The *cour* (court) refers to the court-yard on one side of the theatre as opposed to 'jardin' ('garden') on the other side. It is used by Beckett to refer to stage right.

identified sections I, III 10 and 11, V and VI 17 as 'non-listening'.

			Working sections
Minutes	Approx		
			1. Table, bananas, voyages 1, 2, 3, back at table
	6	I	2. Boxes, tape, recorder
			3. Ledger
12			
			4. Tape 39: Winehouse — den
	6	II	5. Significance of 'Grain'
			6. Miss McGlone
			7. The stupid bastard . . . girl on a railway platform
16			
			8. Voyage 4, Drink 1
	4	III	9. Tape 39: canal, viduity
			10. Voyage 5 Dictionary
			11. Consult
11			
			12. Tape 39 canal
	7	IV	13. Equinox Lake 1 end and midnight
			14. Lake 2 complete and midnight abridged
19			
			15. Voyage 6 Drink 2 change of tapes
	9	V	Voyage 7 (microphone) (?)
			16. Tape 69
12			
		VI	17. Replacing tapes
3	3		19. Lake 3 second part and midnight and end
35			

That is

Love	I	To the beginning of listening
When I	II	To the first interruption of listening (voyage drink)
Viduabird	III	Voyage and resumption of listening up to second interruption
Never knew	IV	Resumption of listening up to the third interruption of listening (voyage drink)
Lay down across her	V	Voyage change of tapes and recording until its interruption
want them back	VI	Change of tapes, resumption of listening and end

Four interruptions, 3 listening, 1 recording

(Authors' translation of Beckett's SECTIONS TRAVAIL. The words in the lower left designate the cues in the dialogue for the interruptions of listening.)

In practice Beckett elected to rehearse the non-listening sections first so the tape could be accommodated to the visual responses it engendered, but in the plan in the notebook Beckett dealt first with the sections of listening.

Under the heading 'Cuts' are the equations 'listening = immobility, non-listening = agitation' (DN p. 77). This alternating pattern of stillness and motion is to be stressed throughout by sudden change:

> [Cut] everything which hinders abrupt shift from immobility to movement or slows down the latter. (DN p. 13)

Conversely, an earlier note stresses that Krapp is to assume an attitude of complete stillness each time before listening. 'Principle: always reassume listening position before turning on recorder' (DN p. 33).

In the section '*Avant l'Écoute*' ('Before Listening'), he paid special attention to the introductory portion of the play before Krapp begins to listen to the tapes. He established clearly Krapp's naturalistic motivation making explicit that it is his birthday and he is awaiting the hour of his birth to begin part of his yearly ritual with the tapes.

Opening Mime Prologue

While still reflecting this motivation, both the Notebook and the Suhrkamp *Regiebuch* provide expanded stage directions for Krapp's actions before his listening begins, creating an expanding three-part visual prologue structured around Manichean principles and emphasising Krapp's characteristic alternation between contraries. The original pantomime of the 'banana walk' was simplified and stylised. Two essentially new sections of pantomime were provided by the description of Krapp's movements while seated at his table before the 'banana walk' and his three 'voyages' to the cubby hole for 'ledger, tapes, and recorder', after it.

In order to simplify the opening prologue, Beckett dispensed with the keys with which Krapp unlocked the drawers and decided on one lateral drawer instead of the two opening towards the audience as originally called for in the Faber text. He dispensed with the examination of the envelope in this scene; it protrudes from Krapp's pocket not to be taken out until Krapp records. Avoiding the possibility that the mime would be seen merely as characterisation of Krapp as clownish, he eliminated two comic elements from the description of Krapp — his too-short trousers and his 'purple nose' (probably intended originally as another Manichean image of the darkness of wine and blood).*

In the greatly expanded version of Krapp's actions at the now 'bare' table which open the play in Suhrkamp *Regiebuch*, the visible parts of his body alternate from one state to another in a carefully orchestrated series of stylised movements of hands, eyes, head and torso. In its larger pattern, this opening section with Krapp at his table shows him after a moment of

---

* In no production with which Beckett has been associated has Krapp been played with a purple nose.

stillness actually moving silently up and down and from side to side in the present — a parallel and contrast with the end of the play when he is motionless, in the same attitude as at the rise of the curtain, as his taped voice describes the movement 'up and down and from side to side' in the past. He is first seen with both hands on the table, in what Beckett described in his notebook as 'Attitude 1' 'hands groping'. He then takes both hands from the table to cross his arms, 'the right hand over the left arm and the left over the right arm'. After correcting his seat, he lays both hands on the table again. At the rise of the curtain his eyes are open, staring in front of him. After a moment he closes them, and then only after crossing his arms, he opens them again to look at his watch.

In Krapp's horizontal movement there is a disjunction of head and body which presents visually the dichotomy of spirit and flesh. The play opens with his body faced forward, but his head slightly to the left. Head and body are next coordinated momentarily when he sinks his head further down upon his body. This coordination is interrupted when he turns his body somewhat left while his head remains in its original position staring forward as before. Finally, after a while he looks to the left side of the table again, bringing head and body into accord.

Krapp's vertical movements present a pattern of sinking and rising like his later transitions into and out of a dream state, and from initial assurance in the tone of voice to dejection and back again. He begins with head and body up, lowers his head while his body remains erect, lowers his head still further until it rests on his body. From this lowest position he begins to rise. He brings his head up a little to look at his watch, he then raises his head to return to the 'opening position', and concludes the first section of the prologue by standing up 'laboriously' with the aid of his hands leaning on the table.

The second section of the prologue, the banana walk, was modified to make more clearly contrasting pairs of actions reflecting Krapp's choice between the light and dark side of his nature. Two parallel 'peels' near the centre of the circle of light around Krapp's table are matched by two 'broods' at the periphery of light and a final exit into the darkness. (See Beckett's even clearer diagram for the 1973 Royal Court production overleaf.)

264

BECKETT'S PRODUCTION SCRIPT FOR *KRAPP* — ROYAL COURT, 1973

In the plan made before rehearsals, Beckett struggled to establish parallel actions with the two bananas while still eliminating actions to make a simpler more evident pattern. He rejected having Krapp return to his seat between the two bananas in order to provide a clear caesura in the two-part action (DN p. 13), and he rejected a plan for two looks at the watch — one in each half of the banana walk (DN 61).

The paired actions as set out in the *Regiebuch* do establish more clearly than the Faber text the contrast between the first banana and the second and between light and dark. Krapp extracts the first banana from the drawer with his left hand while facing the audience. He reaches in for the second with his right hand — 'his back toward the public'. As in the original version he lets the peel of the first drop, later slips on it. Having learned from that experience he throws the peel of the second upstage into darkness rather than pushing it into 'the pit' as in the Faber text. Krapp finishes eating the first banana entirely and then wipes his fingers on the front of his vest, signalling completion, rather than waiting until he is finished with both bananas. As in the original, he does not eat all the second banana but also discards the uneaten half into the dark, instead of pocketing it, as he rushes out to his 'cubby hole'. (In the rehearsal notes script for the 1970 production in Paris, Beckett pointed out the desired contrast between appetency and rejection which is underscored by the detailed stage directions for Held in Berlin: 'simplify and accelerate bananas — the first with avidity, 2nd pocketed in state of peeledness'.)

Krapp's acceptance of the first banana and ultimate rejection of the second, portray physical choices between light and dark like the ethical choices between spirit and sensuality which occur later in the play. By eating the banana, Krapp would appear to be obeying the fundamental Manichean injunction to separate light from dark both physically and ethically. While forbidden to ingest the dark substances of meat and wine, the faithful are encouraged to eat plants which have stored up the light of the sun, thereby restoring to purity a portion of light entrapped in the darkness of the earth. With both bananas, however, Krapp fails to make a separation.

Krapp's *failure* to separate light from dark is also more evident in the *Regiebuch*. (The bananas themselves are designated in the Notebook as *'petite'* and *'verte'* — the repository of only a small amount of light and of some unripened darkness.) Instead of the general stage directions 'pacing to and fro in the light not more than four or five paces either way', there are detailed entrances and exits into and out of the zone of light. He consumes the first half of the banana while pacing into the darkness. He counterbalances this by consuming the second half only after re-entering the zone of light. The net result is no change in the balance of light and dark. In the case of the second banana, Krapp remains in the 'circle of light' to eat the first half but he undoes that action by throwing the second half into the darkness behind him. This rejection into darkness of what he should have retained in light is the obverse of his mistake with the first banana where by dropping the peel in front of his table, he retains in the sphere of light what he should have rejected into the dark.

The final triad of actions of the Faber text suggesting the three bodily seals of the Manicheans was also changed. The wiping of the mouth and hands on the front waist-coat at the end of the mime was deleted, but two new images suggesting breaking of the *'signaculum sinus'* and *'signaculum oris'* are provided in the first and second sections of the prologue. In section one of the mime, as he tries to remember about the lake girl, Krapp lifts his hands from the table, puts his arms about his body the right on the left upper arm, the left on the right, shudders (RB. p.10). It is, however, only a momentary sealing off of his breast, his arms open out — for the watch business which follows immediately — breaking the seal. The action of the opening of section two, as Krapp turns his attention to the bananas, is to be played 'with mouth slightly open' — a breach of the *'signaculum oris'*. In the 1970 Paris production with Jean Martin, Beckett also introduced similar gestures. He called attention to the *'signaculum sinus'* by having Krapp partially cover his breast each time he thinks of the women from his past — *'pour les femmes — main à sa gorge'* [for the women — hand to his throat]. And he called attention to the *'signaculum oris'* by stipulating that during the opening prologue Krapp be unable to keep his mouth closed — *'bouche ouverte — il la ferme — elle se rouvre aussitôt'* [mouth open — he closes it — it re-opens immediately]. (Beckett's unpaged directing script at Lilly Library, Indiana University.)

The two part action with the bananas themselves is interrupted by three 'halts'. Three times Krapp stops his pacing in the present to pause at the edge of the circle of light, deep in thought about the past, as he tries to remember 'about the lake girl — what year, how old . . .'. These three moments of stillness contrast with the activity of the rest of this section, but consonant with the mingling and alternation in the main body of the play, the moments of stillness focused on thought exhibit a progression out of thought into greater activity. Beckett listed these halts in his Notebook (p. 82) and recorded the progression of intensified action in the series. At the first 'vain brood', Krapp 'tries again' [to remember] but simply 'gives up, moves on'. At the second he 'tries again, gives up, goes for banana 2'. At the third halt, he 'tries again, succeeds, makes for cagibi'. (See diagram p. 264 above)

As described in the *Regiebuch*, these halts continue the prominent use of hands, eyes and head of the first part of the prologue when Krapp is seated at the table. The hands which command so much attention during the banana business are inactive in these pauses and attention is focused on the eyes and head. At the first 'vain brood' Krapp 'stares before him, closes his eyes, sinks his head, broods'. At the second he merely 'broods', but does not close his eyes or sink his head. Finally at the third, when he succeeds, he does 'turn his head backwards towards the door [of the cubby hole]'.

The new final section of the introductory mime — Krapp's

three 'voyages' to his cubby hole 'for ledger, tapes and recorder' — are a further breach of the *'signaculum manus'* begun in the 'banana walk', with detailed directions for switching the bananas from right to left hands. Beckett's specification in the Notebook of the dark coloured ledger, the shiny metal boxes tied with 'dark ribbon', and 'heavy tape recorder with white cord to be dragged in to plug at end of [black] cable lying on floor coming from dark of *cour* front' (DN p. 84), make clear that the items Krapp brings back to his circle of light from the unlighted area backstage have darkness imprisoned within them.

Sounds were added to call attention to the objects. Beckett notes that there should be 'as much noise as poss. with the objects throughout' (DN p. 85). In the *Regiebuch*, specific sounds are indicated in the directions. As he reaches for the bananas, Krapp is to shut the drawer each time with a loud slam — the initial sound is identified as 'fast, first explosion' (DN p. 83). (This sound, completing a triad, is repeated when Krapp takes out the 'virgin reels from drawer and place[s] on machine banging drawer shut' (DN p. 91).

As Krapp returns to his table with 'ledger, tapes and recorder', he deposits the ledger and boxes on the table with 'a noticeable slam', and puts the recorder down to the accompanying 'sounds of effort' and 'a cough'. Krapp himself is to make sounds when he handles objects (i.e., he 'grunts unintelligibly' as he consults his watch and 'murmurs' before taking out each banana).

In his unsuccessful attempt to adhere to 'ascetic' ethics, Krapp is vulnerable to the major objection raised against the Manicheans by St. Augustine in *De Moribus Manicheanorum* that they were not concerned with people but with things.

The tendency to establish an emotional relationship with objects which Beckett pointed out under the heading 'General' is basic to Krapp's character. And while his special 'rapport' with the tape recorder described in the notebook is not yet established in the prologue, the 'voyages' prepare for the significance of objects and the portrayal of Krapp as a man who has substituted a relationship with things for one with people.

The three voyages also prepare for and lead into the body of the play. In the 'banana walk' Krapp had three halts just before leaving the table area. In this section he makes three departures, oscillating between the 'zone of light' about his table and the darkness surrounding the 'cubby hole'. Later in the play he will make three more voyages for the dictionary, a drink, and the microphone.

In his notebook, Beckett gives the reason for the order of the objects (ledger, boxes, recorder) brought in. It retained 'the explanatory element' until the appearance of the tape recorder. It registered Krapp's fatigue as the objects increase in weight. And it allowed his *'circulation'* to continue without the interruption of the plugging in of the tape recorder. By eliminating the first drink present in the original script, Beckett removed another action which would have interrupted Krapp's rapid *'circulation'* and maintained suspense by taking out the immediate motivation for Krapp's hasty departure backstage.

The actions of this section as described in the *Regiebuch* present Krapp as a character in evident but unclearly motivated movement — another visualisation of his journeying between alternatives. He makes unexplained disappearances into the *cagibi*, followed 'immediately' by sudden re-appearances; he labours to maintain the same pace while carrying increasingly heavy objects. He makes three rapid unbroken circuits between cubby hole and table, accompanied by the shuffling sound of his slippers. The series thus provides a crescendo of effort and expectation which finally directs the focus of attention to the tape recorder, and serves as a bridge between the opening mime and the central action of listening.

Listening Actions

Although the principle of separation between periods of immobility and activity provides the fundamental larger structure of the play, that principle was not absolute in the original version and particularly not in Beckett's Berlin production. Even within the sections of listening, Krapp breaks out of immobility to respond to key words of the tape. His reactions identify the themes contained in the text and present in a continued pantomime the major action of Krapp in the present which forms the central plot of the play. The choices Beckett made in giving structure to this plot and in finding exact gestures to express it were as much acts of playwriting as directing. No other aspect occupied him more in arriving at the new version of *Krapp* finally seen on stage in Berlin.

That version evolved in four stages. In the longest section of the Notebook, *'Jeux Écoute'* (Listening Actions) pp. 21-33, Beckett first made a list of 24 key words after which Krapp responds. In this first listing, Beckett made suggestions and speculations for the gestures that were the core of the plot. Then on the following page he made a second list headed *Aliter* apparently of those items from the first which he wished finally to retain. Though it is much more detailed, the contents of Beckett's first list differ little from his second. All but two of the items first listed were retained in the second, and the more condensed form of the actions in the second list reflects the essence of the fuller notes first made by Beckett. Both of the responses not included in the second list, *Aliter*, of actions did ultimately find expression in the production.

In the *Aliter* list Beckett laid out plans of a version of *Krapp* which set the directions of the final one. The actions retained in the second list present Krapp in alternation between increasingly hostile and 'feverishly' active responses to himself, and increasingly tender and stiller reactions to the women in his memory, in a clear but not overly systematised pattern. (The following discussion is keyed to the *Aliter* list and the 'How Often Seized by Dream' page of the Notebook which amplifies it. See pp. 271 and 273 below)

Both lines of action lead to greater and greater identification with the recorder until it becomes first Krapp himself and then the lake girl. As Beckett explains in the notebook section 'General',

> [Krapp has the] tendency of the solitary to have an emotional rapport with objects — here in particular with the recorder. Smiles, looks, reproaches, caresses, raps, apostrophes, (Du . . .) etc. and actions throughout. *Always slight.* (DN 79)
>
> recorder companion of his solitude agent of masturbation
>
> Tendency to become what he handles and the object of an animisation corresponding negatively and positively. Anger and tenderness of Krapp toward object itself is begun by the words 'the stupid bastard' or the lake girl. (DN p. 67)

Krapp's response to self is one of growing estrangement and irritation reaching a climax of feverish anger and then winding down to quietude. In responses to himself Krapp progresses forward in time as he becomes estranged and hostile. As the taped voice mentions his name for the first and only time in the play, 'back to me . . . Krapp', he merely registers surprise with a look (1A). Next he participates in the 39-year-old Krapp's direct questioning of the past, lowering his head (2A) in anticipation of the delayed third 'No!' which follows. 'Shall I sing [. . .] No!', 'Did I sing [. . .] No . . Did I ever sing [. . .]

Aliter

	1	Sound as a bell	Knocks off ledger etc.
	1A	*Krapp*	looks at recorder
	2	*Try and imagine*	closes eyes, head raised a little until *I strain*
	2A	*ever sing?*	movement head V. IX 2A, p. 21
	3	*Her eyes* (Bianca) (see IX 2B p. 22 Principle: always assumes listening position *before* switching recorder on.)	head, dream, cut off on *to me*, dream turn on and resume listening at *a help*
with tape	4	*Resolutions*	
alone	5	*To drink less*	Laughs, raises head
with tape	6	*yelp*	
	7	*Misery*	reentry [replonger] to listening
	8	*Railway platform*	head, dream
	9	*When I*	cut, dream, exit
	10	*Viduity*	Looks at recorder etc., exits
	11	*What eyes* (Nurse) (see 3 above)	head, dream, cut off on *as* dream, turn back on and reassume listening at *the blind*
	12	*Spiritually a year—*	begins to get annoyed at the recorder. Look
	13	*namely*	
	14	*most*	fever, more rapid
	15	*fire*	
	16	*from side to side*	head, dream
	17	*Here I end*	dream
	18	*from side to side*	switch off and quickly backward head dream or already on 'we lay there etc.' which he has already heard and
	good		therefore he switches off earlier in view (the opposite) of 20
	19	*Never knew*	switch off, dream, exit
	20	*We lay there*	lowers head a little [légèrement]
	21	*from side to side*	raises head and presents face until the end

(Authors' translation from German and French of pages 32-33 of Director's Notebook.)

No!' Then he raises his head to join the 39-year-old Krapp as he laughs scornfully at the mention of the 'Resolutions' of an even younger Krapp (4). His head remains raised as he laughs alone (5) at the specific resolution to 'drink less' and then laughs again (6) with the 39-year-old Krapp at his earlier 'yelp to Providence'.

He is perplexed as the voice mentions 'Viduity' implying his present condition and 'looks at the machine as if it had behaved improperly', (DN p. 24, authors' translation from the German) before switching off and exiting for the dictionary (10). His reaction to himself reaches its climax at the second replay of the night of the 'memorable equinox' when he believed himself to be making the basic choice between the light and the dark side of his nature which still determines his present life. At the word 'Spiritually' he becomes impatient with the voice and 'begins to grow angry at the machine' fixing it with a look (12). His anger becomes a 'fever' as he winds the tape rapidly forward manually without cutting the sound three times in an ever faster 'crescendo of ejaculation'. These reactions occur first at the introduction of the belief, 'namely' (13) then at the assertion that the dark he struggled to keep under was the 'best' (14), and finally at the reference to the 'fire' (15) that set him alight. (This climax of sound Beckett pointed out in his first enumeration of listening actions was part of a regular sound pattern (*'plan sonore'*) in which manipulation of the recorder accompanied by Krapp's own vocal noises of sighs, anger, and impatience, were to be contrasted with the 'silence of the listening' making an auditory 'couple' duplicating of the contrast between im- mobility and agitation (DN p. 27).

His crescendo of ejaculation past, Krapp's anger subsides in the two final reactions to himself. At 'Here I end' during the description of midnight concluding the tape 30 years earlier, he winds the tape rapidly once in the same manner as before but this time backwards and without accompanying sound (17). Then at 'never knew' he stops the recorder, assumes briefly for the first time the dream attitude in response to a reference to himself, and exits for the microphone (18), his listening apparently over. As tape and listening both seem to have come to an end, the silence and solitude of midnight in the past and midnight in the present become one — Krapp's progression from past to present is complete.

In contrast to his response to himself, Krapp's response to the women in his life progresses toward union with them as he moves backward in memory from more recent to more distant past. In this progression he is plunged deeper and deeper into dream. On the final pages of the notebook in an amalgam of English and German, Beckett noted the points at which Krapp is 'seized by dream' and explained the nature of the process:

How often seized by dream?

1.	Opening	
2.	Before end of Banana 1	__ effort to remember
3.	At end of Banana 1	what, when, what yr.
4.	At beginning of Banana 2	what age
5.	Black ball	Brief do. [ditto]
6.	Dark nurse	
7.	Memorable equinox	
8.	Love	
9.	Bianca . . . her eyes	Long
10.	Girl in a shabby green raincoat	Long
11.	Dark-haired beauty, eyes like chrysolite	Long
12.	From side to side	Long
13.	We lay there head down across her	Long
14.	What eyes she had	Long before and after switch off
15.	Between *enough for you* and *lie down across her*	Long
16.	From *gooseberries* or a few words later in Attitude 1 till end	

Roused by *Das Weibliche** dream seizes hold of him, that he can't move, releases him more or less later. Hold once broken by Hain.

Aliter Opens and engulfs him.
cf drowned in dreams
Empty dream
Dream — Nothing
A life consumed by dream (nothing)
From the sensual dreams himself into the spiritual, from the spiritual into the spiritual

Dreameaten man

(From pages 95 and unpaginated 97 DN)

---

* Authors' translations of Beckett's German. *Das Weibliche* is a somewhat ironic echo of '*Das ewig Weibliche das zeiht uns hinein*' 'Eternal Feminine which draws us on' (to salvation) of Goethe's *Faust*. There are other Faustian overtones closer to Marlowe's presentation in Krapp's looks over his shoulder at 'Hain' or 'Old Nick' as he gives in to his attraction to women even as midnight approaches. For a discussion of 'Hain' see p. 281 below.

As set out in the *Aliter* list, Krapp's reaction toward women begins with a general voluntary memory: 'Try to imagine them' ['those things worth having']. Krapp closes his eyes (2) as he did in the Faber original but does not stop the tape. There follows a series of involuntary dreams, not in the original series, evoked by mention of eyes. At 'a tribute to her eyes' (3), referring to Bianca, Krapp raises his head to assume for the first time the dream 'attitude' he will reassume at references to other women, then stops the tape and remains in that attitude.

Bianca is at first the remembered subject of a eulogy, part of a '*post mortem*'; his tribute to her is in the past, his excitement, the subject of an unenthusiastic commentary in a later state.

At mention of the girl on the railroad platform (8), Krapp is again seized by dream and again raises his head in the dream attitude. This woman is not yet departed like Bianca, but we see the moment of departure. At the moment of parting there is notably no attraction to the eyes; Krapp's only comment 'No.'

The next eyes to rouse Krapp to dreams are those of the dark nurse (11). The scene is one of incipient attraction (although one-sided) as opposed to the finality of the passage about Bianca and separation from the girl on the platform. In contrast to Bianca where the tapes reaction 12 years later came as an afterthought to the 'tribute to her eyes', the exclamatory phrase which evokes this reaction, ('the eyes she had!') still contains its own enthusiasm. To emphasise the connection and contrast, Krapp repeats the same pattern of actions as at the passage on Bianca. The conclusion in the final version, centred on three replays of the 'Lake Scene' and the recording, involved major changes from both the published version and Beckett's *Aliter* plan.

The Original Conclusion

The version of the conclusion of the play as set out in the Faber text is based on a series of three contrasting listenings to the end of the tape which emphasise Krapp's solitude. In that version Krapp hears the lake passage through the first time without specific visual response, the transition to midnight marked only by a pause. Hearing the voice announce the end, he switches off. Only his rewinding to replay the passage just heard indicates attraction to the lake girl and her eyes.

At the second replay of the end of the tape there is still no reaction to the lake scene but the growing hold of that scene on him is indicated by the fact that he switches off to wind back a little earlier on 'Never knew' instead of 'Here I end'. And he gives a brief 'brood' before exiting.

On the third playback of the end of the tape, Krapp's growing attraction to the lake scene and the hold of dream upon him is clearly indicated by the gesture of 'staring front'. And he does for the first time respond specifically to the lake scene, in the pause that follows 'from side to side'. At the end of this repetition his 'lips move' but there is 'no sound'. While this gesture contributes to the growing atmosphere of silence, it is not a direct representation of listening, dreaming, or Krapp's engagement with the recorder or the lake girl. An echo of Krapp's earlier action, '[. . .] lips move in the syllables of "viduity" No sound', it shifts the focus of attention away from Krapp's relationship to the girl and the machine to Krapp as a survivor. After this response there is an indication of a new relationship to the tape. In contrast to the two previous playbacks of this portion of the tape, Krapp does not switch off when he becomes aware that the tape is coming to an end but, apparently no longer involved with the tape at all, he remains motionless as the tape runs on in silence.

The *Aliter* List Conclusion

Krapp's last four reactions to women (16, 18, 20, and 21) come in response to the girl in three playbacks of the lake scene. His new gesture of lowering his head to dream at the line 'We Lay There' (20) is both the climax of his seizure by dream and the climax of listening. The introduction of gestures with thematic associations allowed Beckett to give *Krapp* a more structured conclusion than the original. Krapp's final four reactions to the lake girl are interspersed with his final two reactions to himself (17 and 19) to form part of a structured conclusion of six actions, three pairs, which recapitulates the alternation between self and women, activity and dream, past and present, in a perfectly symmetrical pattern. It also isolates phrases summarizing the action and Krapp's final state, and it presents in two new final contrasting gestures Krapp's immersion in dream.

Actions 16-19 constitute a balanced unit of two pairs. These reactions to himself and women occur in quick succession. The pattern of alternations is made clear by the repetition of reaction to the phrase 'from side to side' followed each time by reaction to a phrase which in German ends in *'ich'* ('I'). The repeated phrase 'from side to side' states verbally the concept of alternatives presented structurally. The two intervening phrases announce the end and summarise Krapp's life just reviewed. With *'beende ich'*, ('Here I end') (17) Krapp's present and past are united. The voice on the tape merely announces the end of a tape, but it is also 'past midnight' in the present and the state of solitude described next has become Krapp's permanent condition. With *'nie erlebte ich'* (19) ('Never knew') Krapp's failure to comprehend his ethical choices or experience lasting love find succinct expression. The irony of situation and phrase underscores Krapp's poignancy. The silence and solitude 'never known' 30 years in the past have become Krapp's best known experience. This state is all the more vivid because it appears in the context of the memory of a moment of intimacy.

Krapp's actions in this series also display in quick succession his increasing engulfment in dream. At the first 'side by side' (16) he raises his head and dreams; at 'here I end' (17) he stops the tape then winds it backwards in retreat, achieving momentary release from the hold of dream. At the second occurrence of 'side by side' (18) he is seized again and dreams exactly as at the first occurrence. Finally at 'Never knew' (19) he stops the tape and dreams again. The dreaming heretofore evoked by thoughts of women finally consumes him at thoughts of himself which are unmediated by a response to the tape. At this point, Krapp seems to have ended his listening and thereby broken the hold of the dream, and the series seems to be complete momentarily as he switches off and exits for the microphone.

The hold of dream, however, is not broken as it appears to be and in the final pair of contrasting actions (20, 21) during the third replay of the lake scene, Krapp is again drawn back to listening and is even more consumed by dream. On the climactic line 'We lay there' (20) he 'lowers his head slightly'. On the final 'side to side' he raises his head but not to escape. As the play closes, he remains until the end caught head up 'presenting his face', a variation of the posture previously associated with dreams.

The *Regiebuch* Conclusion

The greater thematic unity of the first Notebook version became even more pronounced in the version worked out in rehearsals and published as the *Regiebuch*. The actions and phrases of 1-15 leading up to the three playbacks of the

'Farewell to Love' were unaltered. But in the final version Beckett changed the key phrases, structure, and gestures of actions 16-21 to create a new conclusion,* and he made additions to actions 1-15 which integrated that conclusion with the rest of the play.

In the final version Beckett kept the progression of the three occurrences of the lake scene as the basis of the structure, but he made a major change by moving the reactions formerly in the third playback to the second. The climax of Krapp's listening no longer comes in the structurally anti-climactic position *following* recording, but *before* recording. The phrases at which Krapp responds were also changed to give greater emphasis to the thematic elements. 'My hand on her' replaced 'from side to side' as the recurrent structural element and also replaced 'We lay there' as the climax of listening. It is now unmistakable that it is *'das Weibliche'* that 'rouses' Krapp to dream each time in the lake scene. His seizure by dream is also given new emphasis. Occurring within the lake passage rather than at the end of it, Krapp's response at 'My hand on her' now presents him held for a moment of dreaming within the context of the memory that evokes the dreams.

Not only do the themes of *das Weibliche* and seizure by dream now reach a climax in the second playback, but simultaneously

---

* *Regiebuch* Conclusion

Lake passage I	
[16] My hand on her	Krapp lowers head slowly toward recorder
[17] from side to side	raises up, switches off, hesitates motionless
[18] Here I end	turns off, stares motionless, pause
[19] My hand on her	
Lake passage II	Lowers head closer and closer to recorder during the following passage [from the opening of Lake passage II] finally lays his face on the table and listens completely motionless [. . .] At 'my hand on her' Krapp has his head completely on the table.
[20] Never knew	Switches off, raises up, wipes dream away shudders exits for microphone —

Recording	
[21] Lake scene III	'Attitude 1' throughout

(Authors' list, translation, and numbering of new stage directions in *Regiebuch* text.)

his rapport with the tape recorder also reaches its ultimate point. The effect contemplated in making the preliminary plan, but not incorporated so effectively is achieved in this new version. A general note preceding the first itemization of listening actions had read:

> During listening left hand on the switch of the recorder, right hand well in view on the table with the possibility of slight action where needed (eg. the beginning of impatience) [. . .] during listening to the boat [scene] left hand should become (How?) 'My hand on her' (DN p. 20)

The concentration and change of emphasis achieved by placing the response in the second playback of the lake scene and making 'My hand on her' the central phrase were further strengthened by a new structure and new gestures. An inversion of the previous pattern, the *Regiebuch* version presents at Lake Scene I the pair of contrasting gestures presented in the earlier version at Lake Scene III. They are, however, not culminating gestures but incomplete adumbrations of the broad gestures to come in the second and third occurrence of the lake scene.

While adumbrating the later actions, the phrases and gestures of this first pair define the nature of the phrases which dominate Krapp's existence. Krapp is first drawn toward intimacy with the lake girl on listening to the tape bowing his head toward the recorder on the first 'My hand on her' in Lake Scene I. Then 'roused to dream', he rises out of listening to begin the oscillation from 'sensual to spiritual' implied by 'side to side'. Following this introductory pair of actions, Krapp's next three responses recapitulate his alternation throughout the play between self and women, enthralment and disengagement, listening and dream. In response to himself at 'Here I end', Krapp briefly hesitates motionless as if about to begin to dream but is not yet completely drawn into dream. As his second replay of the lake passage begins, he begins his final 'plunge', slowly lowering his head down throughout the passage. He completes his descent to the deepest point of listening, 'drowning'. At 'never knew' he emerges from listening and the dream of women in a threefold action. First he switches off, then raises up, wipes the dream from his eyes, and then shudders.

These changes in Lake Scenes I and II affect the structure of the whole play. As played in Berlin, *Krapp* acquired a more balanced set of three culminations, progressing first from: 'Memorable Equinox', then to the 'Farewell to Love' in Lake Scenes I and II, and finally to a conclusion of stillness in Lake Scene III and closing midnight passage. Like the response to the 'Memorable Equinox', Krapp's response at Lake Scenes I and II now is contained in one clearly defined unit represented by the ledger entry 'Farewell to Love', and extends over that unit in a recognisable pattern of rising action, climax and conclusion.

The removal of the two active responses from the Lake Scene III distinguish the conclusion from the previous occurrences of that scene. It too becomes a distinct unit with the response protracted over the whole passage. Krapp is seen motionless throughout in the attitude first seen at the rise of the curtain. It is an attitude not associated with his previous reactions to women, and one which indicates a new relationship with the recorder — his head is up out of the 'listening position', his hands are no longer on the machine but on the table. It represents clearly the third and final stage of his transition from agitation, to enthralment in the dream of *das Weibliche*, to empty dream.

In the new version the play subsides into the final overwhelming quietude which Beckett had announced as the guiding principle of the production when he told Held at an early rehearsal: 'We have determined upon stillness'. (*'Wir haben uns auf die Stille gesetzt'*)[5] In a new action introducing Lake Scene III, Krapp stands and listens actively a moment to make sure that he has the passage he wants (RB 119). When he does sit, he passes quickly to more passive stages. Unmarked in this version by interruption or gesture, the pauses in the tape formerly filled with action are now points of stillness making a recognisable progression. Even though he does not respond, Krapp still hears as the tape passes 'my hand on her' and concludes the lake passage at 'side to side'. At that point Krapp passes from listening to pure dream; after 'side to side' he 'no longer hears anything' (DN p. 86). The change in tone at 'Here I end' and 'Never knew' pass unnoticed. There is no response as there had been in the earlier replays to previously unheard material that follows. Finally, as the tape ends and the machine runs on in silence, Krapp dreams on of 'nothing' devoid even of memories — the 'dreameaten man' described in the notebook.

Beckett integrated and balanced nearly every other part of the play with the new conclusion. New gestures at the earlier references to women point ahead to the climax of the theme in the lake scene. Before raising his head to dream following the phrases already indicated in the *Aliter* list of listening actions, Krapp in the *Regiebuch* version lowers his head toward the recorder at each of the passages recalling women: after the sentence about living in Kedar Street with Bianca, after 'all the old misery', associated with the girl on the 'Railway platform', and after mention of the 'dark-haired beauty'.

To establish greater balance and a stronger sense of progression toward climax, Beckett added actions in the other major ledger entries like those he had made in the 'Farewell to Love' section. New actions in the 'Mother at Rest' passage begin the build up to the climax of agitation in the 'Memorable Equinox' passage. At 'there I sat' [on the bench by the wier] of the 'Mother at Rest' entry, Beckett restored an action from the first list of 'listening actions' omitted in the second. In the final version, Krapp 'switches off and dreams' following this reference to himself, establishing in this passage the same pattern of alternating reactions to self and *das Weibliche* found in the other ledger entries.

The 'Memorable Equinox' passage was given a clearer structure of mounting agitation; Krapp slaps the table once on 'wonder', and stamps his feet twice on 'finally', and shakes his head on 'clear' and again at 'best'. The garbled noise of the 'fast winds forward' was also timed to create a clear auditory crescendo. There are two seconds of noise at 'namely', four at 'best', and six at 'fire'.

Beckett introduced gestures which were not responses to the tape which signal the beginning of each of Krapp's two sessions of listening. Krapp gives two looks over his left shoulder into the dark corner where he previously threw the banana and the skins; the first signals the start of Krapp's active listening after consulting the ledger and finding the right 'spool'. The second signals his return to listening after recording. Beckett told Martin Held that Krapp looks over his shoulder because he feels 'Old Nick' behind him. In the notebook the gesture is called 'Hain'. Beckett referred James Knowlson for explanation to Mattheus Claudius' poem 'Death and the Maiden', the theme of which Schubert used in his final quintet.* In that poem, Death says to the maiden 'I am a friend. I do not come to punish. Be of good courage. I am not wild. You should sleep softly in my arms.' (Mattheus Claudius, *Sämtliche Werke*, Munich 1968, p. 87). The figure of death as both a protector friend and a threatening presence in *Krapp*, however, is much closer to the description of 'Hain' presented in the dedication to Claudius' collected works where the author explains the opening engraving of death and then goes on to dedicate his work to him.

> The first engraving (see page 282) is Friend Hain. I dedicate my book to him. He stands before the door as patron saint and household god of this book . . . There are those, called strong spirits, who have never let themselves be touched by the *Hain* and mock him and his thin legs behind his back. I am not a strong spirit; to tell the truth each time I look at you a cold shudder runs down my spine. And yet I'd like to think you are good when one knows you well enough; and it is as if I had a kind of homesickness and desire for you . . . to come release me from my humiliating bonds and lay me to rest in better times in a surer place . . . Here is my hand dear Hain! and when you come don't be too hard on me and on my friends.
> (Authors' translation)

Krapp's looks into the darkness register his sense of mortality, his accountability for the choices he has made, and his desire for release from the memories which captivate him.

Non-listening Actions

Recording

The same care for structure and detail attended the non-listening action that counterpoints the action of the mime plot. In addition to reworking the opening prologue as discussed earlier, Beckett made additions to the session of recording which bring it into closer parallel with the session of listening. Krapp's recording also opens with a new mime prologue echoing with subtle differences the one which preceded his listening. Krapp removes the virgin reels from the same drawer from which he had taken the bananas before listening. As in the first prologue, this is attended with a slam

---

* Schubert set the song (D. 531), but the string quintet (D 810) with all the overtones of Schubert's own death in December 1828 is far better known.

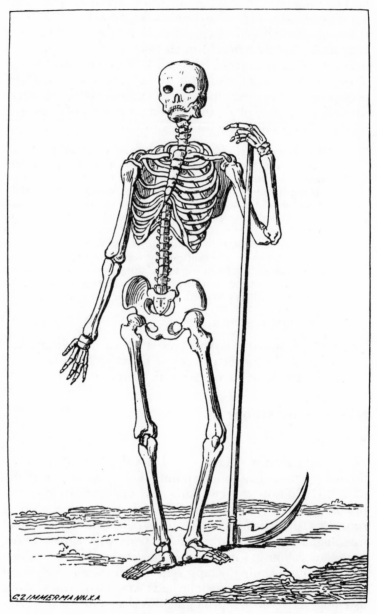

Freund Hain

FREUND HAIN FROM MATTHEUS CLAUDIUS' *SÄMTLICHE WERKE*

noticeably punctuating an otherwise silent section. This slam completes the triad begun with the bananas.

In preparation for his recording, Krapp reads from the envelope as he had read from the ledger in preparation for listening — but this time he reads silently, preserving the quality of pantomime. He then lays the envelope aside on the dictionary associated with 'viduity' — this action creates a distinction between recording and listening by contrasting with the action a few seconds earlier laying the tapes he has just heard on the ledger associated with 'Love'. Before starting to record he wipes his eyes as he had done at the opening of the play.

There is no extended equivalent of the banana walk, but that action and its Manichean overtones are recalled within the recording passage when Krapp crumples the envelope into a white ball and flips it with his thumb into the darkness where he had thrown the rejected portions of the banana.

New actions also relate the recording session to the session of listening which precedes it and prepare for Krapp's return to listening. Although Krapp has ostensibly completed the listening part of his annual ritual, this version makes clear that women remain in his consciousness ready to draw him back to listening and dream. Near the beginning of the recording session Krapp after the climactic cry 'yes!' affirming that there was 'everything there' in the eyes of the lake girl, 'puts his hand to his forehead'. He repeats this gesture near the end after 'all that old misery'. And three times at the other phrases alluding to the memories of women evoked by the tape — 'Everything', 'sour cud', 'Lie down across her' — he casts looks at the recorder.

Alternation between memories of self and women in recording as in listening is stressed first by 'a mistrustful' reaction to 'Could I?' [have been happy with Effie] followed immediately by a shake of the head at 'and she?' (RB p. 98) A 'scornful laugh' after 'Let all that go. Jesus!' and preceding the line 'Keep his mind off his homework' establishes a parallel with the scornful laughter while listening to the description of the resolution of Krapp as a young whelp. And in a disparagement of his 'magnum opus' like the 'scornful reaction' when his works are mentioned on the tape, Krapp points to the audience after 'trade price' and 'lending libraries' and then becomes 'resigned' for 'beyond the seas'.

One of the few textual alterations contributed another parallel. Beckett added 'The Voice' preceding 'God' (RB p. 92) so that the recording like the tape contains this scornful phrase very near the beginning.

Alterations of the smaller non-listening actions which interrupt the tape also tightened the structure of the play. In dealing with Krapp's drinks, Beckett organised them into a clearer pattern associated more closely with specific phrases indicating Krapp's mounting consternation at encountering his past. The first drink of the original text between the banana walk and placing the spools on the recorder was omitted. This preserved the uninterrupted action of the opening mime prologue. But it also delayed Krapp's resort to alcohol until it was a reaction to the tapes themselves. Although the number of drinks in this version is reduced from three to two, they are still part of a three part series. At the point in the play where Krapp had originally taken his first drink, he now only thinks of one. After 'I find' [these old post mortems] (RB p. 54) he switches off, looks at the table then at the door of his closet, starts to get up, sits down again and resumes listening. After 'when I look' [back over the year just past] (RB p. 60) Krapp does exit for one drink indicated by the sound of a bottle against glass and a short spurt of a siphon. And while going to get the microphone to begin the review of his 69th year, the sounds of the first drink are repeated twice, but in half the time of the first drink.

The notebook also contains one set of actions not recorded in the *Regiebuch* or the completed *Werkstatt* summary. In the preliminary plan, (DN p. 27) strangely as part of the first list of listening actions, Beckett had worked out in detail a set of parallel actions for the way Krapp was to handle and close the ledger and the dictionary which would establish a thematic connection between them. In an echo of the 'gag' with 'Banana 2' (not repeating his mistake of dropping the peel), both books were to be placed on the table upside down and the dictionary then quickly turned around. The ledger was to be closed from left to right on the word 'widowbird'. These actions would thus underscore the connection between Krapp's rejection of lovers and his present state as a lonely survivor.

The Tape

Although the visual actions in the present which constitute the plot occupied a greater part of Beckett's attention, he did not neglect the auditory portion of the play. He made minor changes in the text of the tape. The line 'better than a kick in the crutch' was changed to 'better than between thumb and forefinger'. More than an adjustment of tone, this change introduced a specific reference to masturbation pointing to the underlying sexual imagery, rhythm, and structure indicated in the notebook by references to the recorder as an 'agent of masturbation', the description of the 'old fashioned phallic microphone', and the rapid manual manipulation of the tapes forward as a 'crescendo of ejaculation'.

Like the visual action of the play, the tape also presents patterned oscillation. On pages 53-57 as part of the preliminary plan, Beckett set up the principles and made a list of the changes in the tone of the tape:

Vocal principal is one of slipping from major mode (initial tone) of assurance to minor which [is] an exception to the artifice. Providence separates and distinguishes the second.

'Rupture' more or less of this initial tone [is] brought about by the themes (often associated)
1) Solitude
2) Light-dark
3) Women

Not always the case — notably in 7 (*end of the jetty*): major, fever mounting

1.39 today	assurance
2.My new light — Krapp	slight fall
3.The wheat — try and imagine	resumes assurance
4.Extraordinary silence — Did I ever sing?	fall
5.Have just — quite enthusiastic	resumes assurance
6.Her eyes — Ah well	girl tone
7.these old P.M.'s — yelp to Providence	resumes assurance
8.What remains . . . No?	girl tone
9.When I — her virtue	resumes assurance
10.Her face Ah well	girl tone
11.There I sat	resumes assurance
12.Moments Ah well	fall
13.Spirituality — and the fire	resumes assurance
14.my face — uninhabited	max. fall. girl tone
15.Here I end	little rise
16.Never knew	girl tone going towards its max.
17.gooseberries	do.
18.Here I end them back	little rise

(Authors' translation from the French)

Although it includes verbal responses to light and dark not found in the list of 'Listening actions', the list of vocal changes is closely related to the list of reactions. Nine of Krapp's 14 modulations from major to minor occur at points which also evoke gestures from him. Krapp's alternating pattern: 'assurance', 'fall', 'resumes assurance', parallels his alternation between growing rejection of self and growing rapprochement with the women of his past. The taped voice of Krapp is most assured when he indulges in self-rejection and falls from assurance when he acknowledges his attraction to women. Only when he expresses superiority or is scornful of women (5 and 9) does he speak of them in an assured voice.

Two other salient aural modulations were not indicated in either Notebook or the text of the *Regiebuch*, but were marked features of the Berlin production and noted in the critical commentary and notes which follow the text in the *Regiebuch*. When Krapp 'revels' in the word 'Spool' he sings the word in a high thin voice with pitch falling an octave each time. But he begins each repetition at a little higher pitch than the previous one. The melody for the hymn 'Now the Day is Over' is neither of the two familiar tunes found in the Anglican Hymnal, but the lesser known Irish chorale, which Beckett wrote out for Held during rehearsals:

(RB p. 116)

Even visually there is an evident difference between the unvarying quality of the first hymnal tune with the same note repeated seven consecutive times and the undulating arpeggios of the chorale.

The detailed mime actions, changes in text, and modulations of voice which grew out of Beckett's direction of Martin Held are more than just Beckett's way of performing his play. They are so fundamental to the presentation of the character of Krapp that without them Krapp as understood by the author is only partially discernible in the text. And more importantly, they constitute the plot of the play which is only generally outlined in other published versions.

SUGGESTIONS FOR A T.V. *KRAPP*

The 'Suggestions for a T.V. *Krapp*'[6] which Beckett provided for the *Westdeutsche Rundfunk* video recording of Held's performance are a further elaboration of the effects of the Schiller production. As Clas Zilliacus has pointed out, Beckett used the camera to elucidate what he had already created on stage.

SUGGESTIONS FOR T.V. *KRAPP*

Two Cameras A and B. Cut from one to other as required.

A mere eye (except during Krapp's recording pp. [17—19] when its function changes slightly, see below), frontal, covering general situation and exits to "darkness" backstage and back to table. It is free to vary its images, i.e. to move forward and back and to left and right of general axis, provided no element of the total situation be at any moment lost in the process.

B investigates, from all angles and often from above, detail of table situation, hands, face, machine, ledger, boxes and tapes. This camera listens and its activity is affected by words spoken. It can thus be used, not only as "savage eye," but as a means to distinguish in this recorded past those moments which matter little or nothing to Krapp from those which matter much or extremely. It arrives at this by a corresponding reduction or cessation of activity expressive of Krapp's changing levels of attention. It would freeze completely for example:

1. pp. 12—13 from "living on and off" to "Incomparable".
2. p. 13 from "A girl in a shabby..." to end of *Pause*.
3. pp. 14—15 from "One dark young beauty" to "Ah well...;."
4. pp. 16—17 from "my face in her breasts" to "Here I end—"

it resumes then investigation of hands and machine and freezes again from "upper lake" to "Past midnight. Never knew—"

5. pp. 19—20 from "gooseberries" to "side to side."

Stills on 4 and 5 further pointed by conjuction with close up of face, whereas for 1, 2 and 3 camera simply freezes on whatever happens to be under examination when stop made.

Opening:

Long shot with A. Hold. Krapp at table, tiny island of light in midst of shadow. Move in till Krapp's first sign of life (sigh, watch) halts camera at a distance convenient for general image. Hold till return to table with tape-recorder and here [in Berlin the recorder was carried on stage by Krapp, after ledger and reels]

1st cut to B

1st cut back to A (p. 13 on *"goes backstage"*)

2nd cut to B (p. 14 on "back on the year")

2nd cut to A (p. 14 on *"goes backstage"*)

3rd cut to B (p. 14 on "bench by the weir")

3rd cut to A (p. 17 on *"goes backstage"*)

Krapp's recording:

When Krapp resumes seat at table with virgin reel, A may close in, losing general image, to full front shot of table and Krapp alone, far more general and extraneous than any of B's. From here, during Krapp's recording, its eye moves slowly over field with sudden stops at what it hears:

1. p. 18 from "The eyes" to "homework! Jesus!"
2. p. 18 from "...*Effie* again" to "Pah!"
3. p. 19 from "...stop and listen" to "Lie down across her"

The text to which Beckett's suggestions are most profitably applied is that of his own Berlin *Regiebuch*, meticulously edited and illustrated by some one hundred stills by Volker Canaris. In this book, the author's original stage directions are expanded and/or altered to reflect the progress of the Berlin performance; they also faithfully reflect what the WDR cameras saw. The hierarchy of Krapp's "levels of intentness, or listening values" finds obvious parallels in the *Regiebuch*: the cameras are made to reinforce particles or segments of action which have already been emphasized in performance. Thus with camera B — the "listening" camera — we notice that the five specific points at which Beckett calls for a freeze all rekindle erotic memories. For all of these, according to the *Regiebuch*, Krapp leans closer to the recorder. The last two, which are playbacks of the punt scene, are further accentuated by close-up of Krapp's face in conjunction with freeze. The first (and only undisrupted) punt-scene playback is described in the *Regiebuch* as follows: "Neigt den Kopf näher zum Gerät, legt schliesslich das Gesicht auf die Tischplatte und lauscht vollkommen regungslos." In this manner the scene is singled out, even more pointedly than in performance, as the vertex of the play; or rather, as the high point of the evening for Krapp. Camera A, too, whose function of mere eye is modified during Krapp's recording, stops on predominantly erotic motifs. These include strictly vicarious love: camera A stops on Krapp's tender thoughts of the heroine of Fontane's *Effi Briest*.

The ruling principle of Beckett's camera script is elucidative. In being transferred to television, the play as made for the stage is to be clarified. This is effected by switching from one camera to the other, by varying image and distance, and by exploiting a gamut that ranges from fierce motion to sudden immobility. By these means, the syntax of the play is brought out, and a system of italicization is superimposed on the events as staged. Beckett's television suggestions are most obliging towards the viewing public.

BECKETT'S OTHER *KRAPPS*

La dernière bande: Petit Théâtre d'Orsay 1975

Beckett had worked earlier with Pierre Chabert as both actor and director in the 1966 Paris production of Robert Pinget's *L'Hypothèse* (See p. 312). For this production of *Krapp* Beckett discussed the structural principles of the play at greater length than usual. Chabert's description of their work together is in some ways an even fuller indication than the Schiller notebook of the intricate coordination of all the elements of the play.

Krapp's Last Tape: a Ritual of Listening and Recording

The action is a repetition of Krapp's annual birthday ritual, with the single exception that this time it is the *last* tape. When well into the middle of his recording, Krapp perceives that he has nothing further to say, he tears off the spool, and plays again the end of the earlier tape, his 'farewell to love' which happened during one idyllic afternoon on the water. The *last* tape is not only the tape of his 69th year, but also that of his 39th year, when he renounced love to consecrate himself to his work (which is not described, but has to do with writing). But Beckett said to me, laughing, 'I thought of writing a play on the opposite situation with Mrs. Krapp, the girl in the punt, nagging away behind him, in which case his failure and his solitude would be exactly the same,' which only goes to show how little importance should be given to the plot seen in isolation.

Working with the Text and the Voice

The writing and the composition of the text are organised around a network of repetitions, echoes, alternances, oppositions and transpositions. This musical analogy can be analytically described on three levels: that of text alone considered like a score; that of the alternations between the two voices; that of the relationship between the recorded voice and the movement, thus bringing together all the factors which create the final 'score' and the staging of it. We can also isolate a fourth level, consisting of the visual score.

The Two Voices

The play is constructed around the confrontation and the alternation between the two voices, musically distinct, of the young and the old Krapp. As the body of the play is made up by listening to the live voice A, followed by the recorded one B, the author took great care to introduce the formula: b-A(b)-A-B-a-B. [Small letters indicate brief passages, and large letters indicate extensive passages.]

The live voice of Krapp makes itself heard right at the beginning through the reading of a ledger of themes contained on the spools he has recorded. In an abbreviated and elliptical form, the entries, 'mother . . . at rest at last' . . . 'memorable equinox', 'farewell to love', correspond to the three themes or stories on the spools. This reading is therefore like a musical announcement of the themes that Krapp and the listener will hear later. The voice of old Krapp is briefly re-introduced, at half-voice by the reading of the definition of the word 'viduity' in the dictionary (return of the reading voice and recapitulation of the book). Then when the three stories have partly been told in snatches, we hear the voice of the Old Krapp again before the new recording is made in order to give an opportunity for a third reprise after the recording (in the same way there are three successive jumps in the story of the equinox).

My first task with Beckett consisted of finding the right musical difference between the two voices. The difficulty consisted of finding the voice of the old man, without falling into the trap that one traditionally has in the theatre of imitating the voice of an old man. In fact, Krapp is not an old man, but rather someone who has grown old conserving a certain robustness at all times; the stage directions give him a cracked voice, an indication more psychological than physical, but always difficult to produce. After several tries, the author suggested a simple solution: a voice lightly cracked, technically obtained by placing the voice down in the throat, accompanying it with a laborious articulation, accentuated (a labial voice in the throat with articulation), and distinguished from the strong musical resonant voice of the young Krapp. But if the resonance changes as well as the retarded delivery of the phrasing, the intonations remain the same, most noticeably on certain specific expressions. One of the most troubling aspects of the staging lies in this rapport between two voices, different and yet similar.

The Work on the Text

Once the right sonority has been found for the voice, the next thing is to decipher the text as written: a score with all its variations, its particular nuances, made up of recapitulation, of echoing reprises, of broken rhythms, etc. It goes without saying that I cannot here relate in detail all the infinite work that we did on the intonation, the inflection, the accentuation, the silences and the pauses, the prolonging of syllable, etc. It was an endless labour which had to be reproduced at every performance. It was an infinite and rigorous task to avoid either the tyranny of the meaning or the gratuitousness of the musical scheme.

The Interruptions of the Recitation or Exclamations

The play is principally based on interchange and opposition between Krapp's recitation and his exclamations (or interrogations) which break the continuity of speech. This duality in the writing is the manifestation of the duality of Krapp's attitude. Krapp records: he puts down the principal event of his life in his annual journal. He does it with the desire to be precise, objective and detached. He throws in his remarks, strikes a balance, sometimes in the dryest possible way, simply enumerating, cataloguing ('Last illness of father. Flagging pursuit of happiness. Unattainable laxation'). He organises a detailed account of his life like a witness, more outside than inside the event, but is still capable of feeling (the death of his mother for example, in which he literally takes part at a distance). Then suddenly Krapp comes out of his reserve, his spectator's voice, and becoming involved literally shouts.

These lyrical outbursts, these sallies outside the continuity and apparent objectivity of the recitation, always show two of Krapp's opposite impulses: (1) his disgust, his self-contempt, his execration of his voice, and (2) his admiration and enthusiasm for a woman, her breasts, her eyes.

The two attitudes of the protagonist take substance in the diction by the opposition between a normal tone and these brusque forays. The normal tone goes with memory, distance, the look into the past. The voice is contained, concentrated, monotonous, unchanging. The exclamations and questions interrupt this 'normal' tone.

Exclaiming the Words

Beckett employs various means of putting words into relief, making them emerge from a phrase. In the same way as the young Krapp dreams and exclaims about women's eyes, the dream and the exclamation of the old Krapp have for their object the word itself. From the beginning, Krapp exclaims on the word *spool*, three times in a row each time drawing out the vowel at increasing length. The progression in exclaiming the word is well indicated by the way in which the author wrote the word in the text. *Bobine* (spool) first time, *bobiiine* (spoooool) the second two times and *bobiine* in the recording. Beckett every time varies the way in which the word is given which is always drawn out with a happy smile, a smile that has already been created by his manner of drawing out the vowel 'I'. It is with such a tiny detail . . . that Beckett manages to suggest the extreme solitude and the madness of Krapp — his decline in his relationship to his words — with careful understatement and economy of style. By playing on the word he reveals his regression without even mentioning the other symptoms.

The Interrogation and the Remembrance

In addition to the specific part played by exclamation, there is also the role played by interrogation, which is linked to memory, to the difficulty of bringing back the past. The interrogative form itself creates a resurgence of the things that belong to memory, to the past and to forgetting, and always with the same economy of means:

> (*He peers at ledger, reads entry at foot of page*) Mother at rest at last ... Hm ... The black ball ... (*he raises his head, stares blankly front. Puzzled*) Black ball? ... (...) Memorable ... what? (*He peers closer*) Equinox, memorable equinox ... Memorable equinox?

The Action, the Body, the Space, the Listening

The fundamental problem of the staging and of the performer's actions in dramatising the act of listening is how to make theatrically possible a play based on listening. Beckett has frequently insisted on the tension present in the act of listening. On the one hand this tension is a function of the physical relationship between the character — the face and body of the actor — and his voice, a physical relationship which can be established thanks to the material presence of the tape recorder. On the other hand, the tension is increased by the physical shortcomings of the character. Krapp is deaf and this deafness, pathetic in itself, is dramatic in the specific sense that it increases the tension of his listening by changing the effort into a struggle to catch the voice, hear it, and not lose the thread of the discourse. It is a law of Beckett's theatre (the dramatisation of physical effort) that we find at several levels in *Krapp's Last Tape*: the effort to hear, to see, to get started, to bring back memory. The tension instead of lying in a clash between personalities, as in conventional drama, takes place inside the body of the character himself.

The confrontation in Krapp lies in the relationship between a voice and a body (stretching his body to hear) and is externalised in his listening posture. The first task of the actor consists of finding this posture. We were helped by luck, the tape recorder that we chose had a handle. The character therefore can be seen with his hand clasping the recorder, bent or twisted over the machine, his ear almost glued to it, which puts into visual terms the physical confrontation and the attempt to give body to the voice. It was important to catch this posture as perfectly as possible to effect the desired image. Becoming one with the tape recorder became the principle visual image of the play. The body is bent, but the face looks up as if emerging from a common mass, allowing a perfect visibility to the public. The tension of listening is emphasised even more by total immobility, itself engendered by the intrinsic difficulty. The immobility contains a dramatic force in itself, by the expectation which is created and by the knowledge that it can be broken.

The Mask and the Expressions of the Face

The total immobility of the body and the tension of listening transform the character's face into a mask with a frozen expression that is unique, brought about by a tightening of the facial muscles. The eyebrows are raised, wrinkling the forehead, the cheeks are sucked in giving a drawn cavernous look, the mouth remains open. The mask is slightly grimacing, sad, hallucinated, rather grotesque.

The Reactions to Listening

By this I refer to specific reactions (outside of the expressions of face and mask) which bring into play movement and gesture, which can involve the head or the whole body. We can distinguish two types of reactions, the dreams and the emotional relationship with the machine, these constituting two new poles of opposition.

Dreams

The dreams, which take place during the breaks in listening, always consist of the physical prolonging of exclamations in the text. The memory of a woman evokes Krapp's *look*, sends him into a reverie, separates him from his listening and from the machine: his body unbends, unfolds, moves away from his listening posture, the trunk and the face slowly lift, a relaxation is produced in hand movement and facial expression. The reverie is similar to that of a reader of a book, the face is uplifted, the reverie follows, the look is lost, it detaches itself from the book. Here, the look controls the body, makes it breathe, lifts it, as if the character was following a vision seen from afar.

The Emotional Relationship with the Machine

Krapp is an old bachelor, who has emotional and physical relationships with objects and words. Beckett asks the actor to make the objects human and among these the recorder occupies a privileged place.

I should say a word about this recorder-object. At no time is it a symbol (of memory for example) but simply a machine possessing a faculty of replaying a recorded voice, becoming in this way the generator of the principal events of the play.

It is the generator of events insofar as it needs handling or manipulation having a physical relationship with the actor as he plugs in the cord, adjusts the spool, switches it on and off, etc. In this handling, the actor must have a naive contact with it, childish and unaffected, which brings it out of its purely machine-like function, especially as it is really a box of magic, a Pandora's Box. The emotional relationship between Krapp and his taped voice is manifested in the look, the touching, the physical posture: moving from and returning to the machine. The changing expressions are important; they are reproachful, interrogative, defiant, excited in those passages such as the grandiloquent recalling of the equinox, that are insupportable for the old Krapp. At other times they are expressions of complicity, love, good humour, as when Krapp laughs with his recorded voice.

As for the touching, apart from operating the recorder, Krapp changes and interrupts his normal listening posture in the middle of the story of the trip on the boat. The recorder becomes the girl and there is an image of tenderness between Krapp and the machine. His head sinks unconsciously, followed by the body and the right arm, coming to rejoin the machine. Finally his face turns and touches the surface of the machine. Beckett insisted on discretion in these reactions to the listening. This must be very delicately, barely observable and subtly played with great control.

The Dual Space

The space itself is divided between Krapp's table, as a combination of space and time together, and a little alcove placed backstage right which is hidden at the beginning by a curtain. These two places confront each other, obliquely by the positions they occupy on the stage.

They also represent opposite aspects of Krapp's existence. The table with its tape recorder is a place of dreams, of memory, of writing, (it is a writer's table). The alcove is an everyday space: that is where Krapp keeps his things, where he goes to get the recorder and the various objects necessary for the action, that is where he goes to drink. As Krapp leaves his table to disappear into the alcove, important breaks are created in the action that open up the space, breaks made of silence and pure pantomime. He disappears and the spectator is left looking at a void and the silence of stage space looking at the familiar objects, the table and a light, dramatic and pathetic in its own right. These trips to the alcove emphasise the physical relationship the character has with his table. It appears like a haven, a refuge from which he extricates himself with difficulty, while hanging on to it for safety and only leaving it at the last moment.

The Body

The body reacts to external stimuli and expresses mood and a sense of failure. Because it is winter, Krapp shivers with the cold. He is wrapped in a long dressing-gown, wears a cap and mittens presenting a pathetic portrait. The body in rags is both full of infirmity and vulnerable. His costume helps to isolate Krapp from the world and to physicalise his relationship to space and to objects.

The Silence and the Noises. The Music of Body and Things

Much importance is given to all sounds, all the noises provoked by the presence of a body in a space. First of all there are the noises of the body itself: Krapp's breath, panting slightly, accompanies his voice; his shivers, the sounds of mastication, his sighs of satisfaction or coughing when he drinks; the sounds of Krapp moving on the stage; the sound of objects kicked when walking, tins and spools he sweeps off the table in a moment of fury ('Krapp is walking on his life', Beckett said).

The objects are chosen because of the noises they can supply: metal tins, clashing together on the table, the clattering as they fall, the cacophony of sound on the floor, the ledger and heavy dictionary crashing on the table.

We can also hear the turning of pages as Krapp consults his ledger, the clink of the glass against the bottle while he is drinking and the noise of liquid being poured out, the whirring of the turning spool during the silences, the sound of garbled voices on the recorder when the character winds the spool forward. A precise musical and rhythmic quality is conferred on objects so much that the sounds can underline or punctuate the silences. Everything is organised in terms of repetition. Beckett never introduces a physical action, a movement, a gesture, a touching of objects without a subsequent repetition. Between Krapp's physical actions and movements, everything is repeated twice, creating a network of multiple repetitions and echoes. For example: there are two bananas, two drinks, two sighs, two looks backstage into the darkness behind him, etc. Beckett also introduces small variations into his repetitions: a variation in the size of the bananas, one small, one large, the first eaten, the second partially thrown away.

BECKETT'S SECOND BERLIN *KRAPP*: SAN QUENTIN DRAMA WORKSHOP, 1977

At the request of Rick Cluchey, the former convict who had staged *Godot* in San Quentin in 1961, Beckett agreed to direct him in an English version of *Krapp* at the *Academie der Künste* in Berlin in September, 1977 as part of the '*Berliner Festwochen*'. Most features of the 1969 Held production reappear in Cluchey's performance, but as Cluchey and Michael Haerdter point out, this production also had new features.

Michael Haerdter: Production Account

Beckett is willing to come to Berlin. More than that: the production will be a gift to his friend, Rick Cluchey, and the San Quentin Drama Workshop. A blessing considering the small budget that is available for this project. One of Beckett's requests was that Michael Haerdter would assist him with the work in Berlin. On 16 June, Rick Cluchey and Michael Haerdter made a trip to Stuttgart for a discussion of all the questions concerning the Berlin production. Organizational and practical questions are talked about. In spite of the excessive use of their studio theatre during the forthcoming *Festwochen* and the exhibition of the Council of Europe, the *Akademie der Künste* was willing to let their member Beckett use the stage for sufficient rehearsals and approximately 10 performances. But Beckett is not familiar with the stage. With the aid of sketches he is shown the size, equipment and technical possibilities. Krapp's table and den are drawn in.

Excerpts from two letters

In two letters Beckett specifies his working plan concerning the den. On 17 July, 1977, he writes to Rick Cluchey: 'I've been thinking about the den, how to dramatise to the utmost light and curtain.'

And on 16 August he writes to Richard Riddell:

> Here's briefly my thoughts on the 'den' (closet, Krapp has only one room).
> Opening: 1.80mm x 1m maximum.
> Light in den at curtain-up but invisible till K's first visit to fetch ledger ... Curtain only half drawn, blocked on rod halfway across. At each visit to and return from den the curtain set in motion. Material of curtain such that this motion takes as long as possible to settle. Ideally curtain will faintly be stirring throughout play, helped perhaps by ventilator fan. I realise this makes shadow effect difficult if not impossible. If one excludes the other, my preference is for curtain effect.
> If wall maintained for some degree of shadow, then a plain white surface.
> Opening a simple breach in black flats. No realistic wall, invisible in any case if general lighting correct.

The first reading rehearsal takes place in a conference room of the *Süddeutscher Rundfunk*. Rick Cluchey reads the text; Beckett gives notes about the situation in the play, the acting and makes a few explanations about the play itself. He has worked out a concept for the direction which simplifies his Krapp even further than in his earlier productions with a clearer concentration on the essence of an ageing writer's conflict with principle, symbolising Krapp's decision 'to turn away from the life of the body toward the life of the mind'. Beckett has written a plan for the directing in his small, clear handwriting, like copperplate, laying down in essential details the concept and the light-dark principle.

Who is Krapp?

Beckett doesn't analyse his plays, he doesn't discuss their philosophy; nevertheless, during the rehearsal period Beckett makes a series of remarks which form at the end a sort of X-ray-picture, helping to an understanding of the stage character.

Krapp is a 69-year-old writer, unsuccessful, still vigorous, 'in no way senile'. But 'there is something frozen about him' and he is confined within himself, 'filled up to his teeth with bitterness'. A man caught in loneliness who has spoken monologues to himself his entire life: 'this is what marks the character of his voice'. He is full of a dangerous, concentrated violence 'like a tiger in a cage'. He senses very strongly his confinement, 'he is trapped in himself'. In a letter, dated 17 July, Beckett writes to Rick: '. . . make the thing your own in terms of incarceration, for example. Incarceration in self. He escapes from the trap of the other only to be trapped in self.' For 45 years he suffers from his 'old weakness', constipation.

Since the age of 24 he has recorded notes of the year gone by, always on his birthday. It is his habit to celebrate this 'awful occasion' in a pub, alone, thinking about the recent past and taking notes. It is his habit as well, after getting back to his den, 'like a badger in his hole', in his old rags, to listen to a tape of one of the years passed before recording a new tape.

This time he wants to listen to the old tape where he recorded a love affair, the story with the girl in the boat. He tries to remember his corresponding age but he doesn't succeed with this right away. The only way is to find the right box and spool in his ledger, because there he enters the recorded events with keywords under the respective year. Finally he remembers: the tape he is looking for was recorded on his 39th birthday.

'It is his critical age.' In this year of 'profound gloom and indigence' he had a vision 'at the end of the jetty, in the howling wind'. Under its influence he made a decision of grave consequence: 'a farewell to love' and to turn away from 'the life of the body, the sexual life' and to turn towards 'the life of the mind, an intellectual life'. They are not compatible for Krapp. This is the 'Manichean' essence of the play which Beckett speaks of allusively. 'Krapp is an absolute being, he chooses either black or white.' His decision is against the light and for the darkness which for him is filled with his own fire, 'the fire in me'; a decision which for him is against social life and for the solitude in his — finally unsuccessful — struggle for his 'opus magnum'. The 'opus magnum' is an 'explanation of the dark side of humanity'. At the age of 39 Krapp has the vision that 'in the darkness, the dark side of the mind, truth is to be found'. If up to this point he was convinced that 'the dark cannot be formulated, that this darkness is impossible to describe, a material which cannot be communicated', he realises now is 'his chance as a writer in the research of this darkness'.

Thirty years later the old Krapp recognises that he was wrong. He is an 'arch dreamer', now he knows that he became 'the victim of his dreams' — 'they were his ruin'. He says to himself 'what a terrible mistake I made to take that for a vision.' But even though his decision failed him, 'he hasn't yet given up completely'. The old Krapp is more honest than the young one, though. The fire filling the young one was 'the fire of vision, the magnum opus'. The 69-year-old Krapp feels a fire burning in him too, 'but it is a different one, the old Krapp is 'burning to be gone'. Maybe because he knows 'whichever decision he might have taken, he would have failed'.

During a rehearsal break, Beckett depicts with a smile the image of an old Krapp who had made the opposite decision: surrounded by an aged wife and many, many children . . . 'good God!'

The Production of the Tape

17 July, Beckett writes a note to Rick saying among other things: 'The big problem is the tape. We should start recording Tuesday the 30th, or Wednesday the 31st, at the latest.'

Rick had made a first recording in the spring which he played for Beckett in Stuttgart. For Beckett there was too much colour in it, too much modulation. 'I hear a more balanced voice, sort of a soft fragility, not proclaiming.' Based on Beckett's working plan, a simple rehearsal tape is recorded for the preparatory work.

RIAS (one of Berlin's broadcasting stations) offered one of their new recording studios for the final cut of the tape under Beckett's direction. On 30 August and 1 September the tape was to be produced for the forthcoming rehearsals.

Beckett is giving some general explanations. He is more concerned with the tone quality of the voice than the brilliance of the recording. The musical quality of the tape is important to him. Therefore, line by line he explains intonations, pauses, tempi, voice level and voice volume.

As for the musical quality of the recording and its usefulness for the stage, the length of the pauses is of extreme importance. They are not only a reflection of Krapp's moods and his 'self-interrupting character', they also serve to give the actor on stage the necessary room for reactions and changes of position. Already here Beckett points out that the actor's gestures, changes of position and movements are never to coincide with the spoken word on the tape. Here the exact timing of the play will have to be established during rehearsal.

Later on, one result of this was that, for example, after the first words of the recording — 'Thirty-nine today' — an extension of a pause by two seconds became necessary to cover the drop of the ledger and Krapp's action. Correspondingly throughout the entire play, pauses were extended or shortened to link action and voice in such a way that optimal rhythmical quality was achieved.

The 39-year-old Krapp begins the tape with a 'firm statement' — 'Thirty-nine today.' 'Awful' means here, in the old sense of the word, as much as 'awesome', therefore it should be spoken with emphasis.

'Not a soul': this statement has to carry weight, the words are to be accentuated yet linked together. Later, in the repetition, ('hardly a soul', 'not a soul') they have to be recognised by the echo effect. On the whole, the text should be spoken lightly, flowingly and brought to a definite undertone so that light colouration, subtle accents and subdued voice changes are contrasted clearly.

For example, some colour and warmth for 'Good to be back in my den, in my old rags'. But not too much . . . 'Darkness' has to come out but not be overemphasised. The following phrases are delivered lightly, here the pace is important. No colour up to 'then back here to . . . me': here the feeling should be conveyed that Krapp is trying to escape from himself. A good pause before 'Krapp', which ought to be emphasised contemptuously.

Also in the following passage ['the grain, now what I wonder do I mean by that?'] Beckett sees the danger of overemphasis. Krapp is filled with himself but he should speak these phrases quite simply. 'What' gets some colour, 'my' is emphasised [in 'when all *my* dust has settled'].

New start with 'Extraordinary silence this evening'. Krapp loves the word extraordinary. Something is not right with this silence, Beckett explains, 'here is the beginning of the dark tone'. 'Old Miss McGlone' ought to 'glow', Beckett says. 'A woman's tone goes through the entire play, returning always, a lyrical tone.' There are eight women in the play, five young ones, three old ones. 'Krapp feels tenderness and frustration for the feminine beings.' 'Girl' is the key word in this passage, therefore it has to be emphasised.

The following three questions ['Shall I sing? . . . Did I sing? . . . ever sing?'] with the thrice returning 'No' have to stand in contrast to that with maximum interiority, no colouration at all. The phrases have to become increasingly pale, the thrice repeated 'No' completely grey (the last one almost inaudible) the pauses between question and answer each time a bit longer.

The first section is taped. It is not an immediate success. There are technical difficulties — a side noise has to be eliminated. And Rick has trouble controlling his temperament so as to hit the tone which Beckett desires. Because he has a tendency to add colour to the phrases, modulate them, Beckett's demand causes him to do the opposite, namely to speak them too monotonously and too slowly.

Beckett: the danger lies in too much slowness, the text has to be spoken very simply, smoothly, a few essential pauses and accents ought to interrupt and accentuate clearly the flow of words. Here Krapp's character is reflected, a notorious self-interrupter. 'His whole life has been interruption. Throughout, Krapp's tone is a 'tone of security being constantly threatened by insecurity'. This tone of the 'precarious security' is very hard to get, Beckett admits. And he adds to Rick 'don't worry, we're going to make it.'

The first day didn't bring a satisfying result. Rick had found the tone but the rhythm wasn't quite yet according to Beckett's wishes. On 31 August the recording studio was not at our disposal. We took this time to hold an intensive working meeting in Beckett's Studio at the *Akademie*.

A few returning phrases and sounds, echoing each other, play an important role for Beckett because they give the play its rhythmic structure. 'Ah well' returns four times, an expression of regret and resignation is the bridge each time from Krapp's fantasy world, the women in his life, back to himself. 'That you have to find, Rick.' It forms a further element of interruption in the play. Rick ought to bring out the musical quality, accentuate it, but then again not spend too much time with it. 'I nearly called the play "Ah well", it is very important in the play', Beckett explains. It indeed throws a strong light on Krapp's character.

Krapp's simultaneous laughter in the tape passage starting with 'Just been listening' also sheds sudden light on his change of character. On the tape the 39-year-old is mocking Krapp 12 years younger while the old man expresses with bitter laughter what he thinks about both of them. Here Beckett wants rhythm and clarity. The laughter from the tape and live-laughter should overlap each other exactly and after 'yelp to Providence' they should fill the pauses precisely and not cut into the following taped voice. Small detail: Rick ought to hold the live-laughter a bit longer than the tape-laughter. Beckett: 'The laughter ought to be very articulated, simple, quick, not too much colour. Almost a stage-laughter, not a natural laughter.'

The change of mood and the new tone in the passage beginning with 'Spiritually a year of profound gloom' are particularly important to Beckett. Clearly balanced intensification of the tone, 'an increase of tempo and voice volume'. 'What I suddenly saw then . . .'– here Krapp is taken by the excitement, the intellectual fever of his vision. Beckett: 'Everything here is in the rhythm and the lack of colour.' The pauses, or more precisely the interruptions, play an important role in this scene — they clarify Krapp's increasing impatience. Beckett has here the 'gabbling sound' inserted through a fast winding of the tape, increased in duration and volume. The lyrical tone filled with tenderness and devotion for the girl in the boat ('my face in her breasts') has to stand in sharp contrast to the previous scene. Here also flowing speech and generally little colour. Small pause before 'hopeless' where a little colour may be added. 'Let me in': each word spoken individually, slowly, rhythmically.

'The earth might be uninhabited' — Beckett: 'This is the most serious sentence of the play.' Nevertheless: no emphasis, no colour, then it will come out clearly. The last paragraph is spoken in one tone as well, diminishing gradually into the silence of the final position.

Small pause after 'Not with the fire in me now' — a moment for the 'diabolic temptation.' Yes, I would like to live these years again! Then Krapp gives himself the answer, quietly, without colour rhythically: 'No! I wouldn't want them back.' Beckett's comment is There should be a touch of certainty in this phrase, yet we feel already the weakness of Krapp.

On 1 September, the tape is successfully recorded at the RIAS-Recording Studio.

Simplifications and clarifications

Already in his working plan for the Berlin production, Beckett has made several changes amd cuts from the original play version in order to simplify his Krapp and to concentrate even more on that which seems to Beckett today to be most essential in the play. In addition further changes and simplifications were made during the course of rehearsals. Beckett wanted everything 'superfluous' removed from the play. The only exceptions were: all that which causes 'a necessary disorder' on stage. Finally, the play was also adapted to the nature of the present actor, Rick Cluchey.

In the following paragraphs we give a list of all changes in the order of their appearance in the play for comparison with the original play version.

Costume and make-up are considerably simplified. Krapp is wearing a dark bath-robe with only one small breast pocket, black baggy pants which are too long (Beckett's comment: 'the old Krapp has shrunk'). He is wearing simple black slippers. Because the pocket watch is superfluous, it has been eliminated.

The worn-out bath-robe which Rick dug up at a second-hand shop meets with Beckett's immediate approval: it is made out of terrycloth with large black and dark-grey stripes, a prison outfit.

Krapp's make-up now is a realistic reproduction of an old face whose life colours have been replaced with a sallow-grey. The hands ought to correspond to that in age and colour. Rather than two big bananas Beckett wants the two halves, with stems, to be shown visibly. Their length should correspond exactly to the quantity of three normal bites. The whole banana business is simplified and rhythmically structured.

Krapp now goes into the den without having a first drink, bringing back to the table with a quick pace the ledger, a stack of tins (old version: cardboard boxes) containing the tapes and the tape recorder. The seven biscuit tins from which the paper has been removed are tied together with a black ribbon: ('mourning crepe') as Beckett explains since Krapp always gets them out on his birthday.

Since, according to Beckett, Krapp only owns one room, the den forms a small part of that room, separated by a curtain. The curtain is hung on a rod with heavy metal rings to make a clattering noise when opened. The curtain stays open throughout the entire play. The den is lit, the faint light stays visible until the blackout.

The Stage Set

He dislikes the motor noise of the curtain, but he thinks that the big (stage) curtain is an echo to the den's curtain and furthermore it is good to have the light curtain open in front of the dark stage. This would also allow Krapp to get on and off stage unnoticed by the audience.

When the stage curtain opens, Krapp is sitting at an empty black table under a small conical black lamp which throws a cold light onto the table.

The table has only one drawer which is opened on the left side of the table without a key.

The light-dark principle

Beckett desires that his basic principle in Krapp be clearly recognisable: 'Everything bringing out this effect is good'. Krapp's obsession with the idea of light and shadow, his decision against the body and or the mind is symbolised in this production with multiple light-dark effects. It begins with the black curtain hung onstage where the conical lamp cuts white light out of the shadows. It is illustrated with the shadow-play on the back wall in the den when Krapp is taking his drinks. With the costume: black robe, black pants, white shirt; with the make-up as well as with the props. It is important to Beckett that the tape-recorder and the microphone show this effect also.

And it goes without saying that this principle is omnipresent in the text, explicitly and implicitly. There is the lamp which the 39-year-old Krapp got himself for his birthday, 'the new light above my table', which makes his solitude easier to bear 'with all this darkness round me'. There is Bianca who lives on Kedar Street (anagram of dark.) Or the black plumage of the vidua bird – 'Krapp is the vidua bird'. The 'dark nurse' all in starched white with a black perambulator. The little white dog with the small black ball, etc.

Also, the importance which Beckett attaches to the 'eye' in the play has to do with the light-dark principle, the returning emphasis on 'her eyes', 'the eyes she had' etc. Beckett: 'The eye is the organ of interruption between light and dark, therefore it is important.' Likewise are Krapp's 'two completely different voices' an expression of this basic principle — utmost bitterness, disgust and utmost tenderness, warmth. For example when he is dreaming about her eyes where he finds 'all the light and darkness' of this old muckball.

In the play Krapp's two irreconcilable worlds are represented with the change from violent noise to absolute stillness, immobility to motion. Therefore, instead of the first version's cardboard boxes, tins for the spools which fall to the floor with a clatter; a drawer which closes with a bang; heavy metal rods for the curtain's suspension; a heavy dictionary whose pages of the last quarter are glued together to allow for an effective closing, etc.

Furthermore, the stillness is symbolised through two identical echo-actions of Krapp, this too in addition to the first version: Hain. In his working plan Beckett describes the Hain-play and explains it as Krapp's 'sensation of a presence behind him in the shadow': the sudden interruption of the action of the tape-recorder. Krapp's immobility, his gaze into the darkness behind are striking variations of the light-dark motif. Krapp senses the presence of death and conveys its eeriness and proximity by his action. With this expression borrowed from the '*Hainbund*', Beckett refers to the romantic image of a beautiful, friendly death (for example: death and the maiden), Krapp's longing for ultimate peace.

It is important to Beckett that the den's curtain be of completely opaque, black material, closing tightly on all sides: this ensures the surprise effect of the sudden shining light backstage when Krapp opens the curtain.

All the elements enumerated here — voice and visual appearance, echo effect, noise and stillness, light and motion — are coordinated by Beckett as director in precise detailed work and joined together to the stage sculpture of 'Krapp'.

Excerpts from the Rehearsal Diary

The studio stage of the *Akademie der Künste* a few days before the première.

Meanwhile the stage has been carefully set in every detail, but economically. After several changes Beckett is now satisfied with Krapp's costume. The text stands, the transitions from live-monologue to taped voice as well as the pauses in the mime play are fixed generally. 'Krapp' is ready in the wider outlines.

Today and during the remaining rehearsals Beckett wants to join the parts still tighter together. Before the run-through, he speaks again about the play's rhythmical structure and musical quality. 'We have to try to bring rhythm into every detail.' Also in the banana business. Krapp's walk from the table to the forestage where he paces back and forth becomes a little concert of shuffling steps. Quite a bit of experimenting took place during rehearsals up to this point: Krapp's slippers turned 'musical' with the aid of sandpaper, metal pieces, finally with solid leather soles. Beckett was not satisfied with any of these solutions. Today he brought his own slippers for Krapp: worn black-leather slippers with a soft sole. Rick tries them out — the right tone has been found. Beckett explains Krapp's pace: 'His walk is unstable yet stiff. When he leaves his table he walks as if he were moving out into the rough sea, with a careful yet paradoxically rhythmical pace.' Krapp has to practise the same number of steps and rhythm for the banana business — each time eight little steps with seven shuffling noises, expressing at the same time Krapp's routine and his stiffness caused by age. Same rhythm again for his walks to the den and between the table and the den, but twice the speed. Krapp finally remembered what he was looking for, the year with the girl in the boat, impatience spurs him on.

A number of explosive, forceful sounds ought to be a contrasting musical element to this subdued rhythm, which concentrates the general solitude around Krapp even further: in the banana business Krapp is to close the drawer with a loud bang. Beckett says: 'After the silence of the beginning, the closing of the drawer ought to sound like gunfire.' Krapp should open the curtain to the den with a strong clattering noise — therefore the heavy rod, the heavy metal rings hitting a metal stop. The ledger, the stack of tins and the tape-recorder ought to be put down on the table with a bang. Before Krapp sits down again, he claps his hands once.

Beckett wants an additional comical effect: the ledger should be filled with talcum powder to cause a cloud of dust to rise when dropping it on the table and slamming it shut. Krapp uses the ledger once a year . . .

A clear rhythmical sequence for the business with the tins: they are taken individually from the stack and put down on the table with emphasis. Likewise the lid of box No. 3. After Krapp has taken spool 5 out of it, he puts the tin box on the ledger at the right-hand side of the table: both fall to the floor with a lot of noise. After that Krapp sweeps the remaining boxes vehemently to the floor — 'this should be a true explosion'. In the intervals (and always in the same rhythm) fall Krapp's three curses, his fist hitting the table and the clicking noise when the tape recorder is switched on or off (this Beckett wants to hear clearly throughout the whole play). Following this crescendo, the silence returns and out of it comes only Krapp's hushed voice.

A word on the Hain moment. Here also Beckett desires rhythm through precise accentuation of five distinct moments: 1. Freeze 2. Slow turn 3. Hold gaze backstage 4. Return position to stagefront 5. Resume rewinding spools. Rick ought to clarify the shock of the 'presence'. Beckett gives the cue by clapping his hands. 'You hear something behind you and react instantly. Absolute immobility of hands and head while turning slowly without any haste.'

Again, rhythm for Krapp's drinks in the den, here too action in 5 sections:

1. Simple clink of the bottle and the glass
2. Setting down of bottle on table
3. Silence while Krapp drinks (with his shadow visible on the back wall)
4. Krapp's gasp of satisfaction
5. Setting down of glass

With the second drink, this action is modified somewhat. Krapp's shuffling to the den is notably slowed down, he serves himself the double amount of whisky. Thus the pouring and drinking take more time. Instead of the gasp only a drinker's cough. 'Not too much, Rick, it should not be realistic but stylised.'

This is one of the numerous echo effects in 'Krapp' that Beckett works out. As the second drink repeats the first one in an echo, so is the closing of the dictionary after the last phrase ('the vidua-bird!') an echo to the ledger which Krapp closes noisily after 'love'. Krapp drops both books on the table in the same manner.

Again a few explosive sounds in the second half of the play before returning to absolute silence in the end. The microphone, which Krapp brings from the den after the second drink, is placed loudly on the table. The drawer which Krapp opens to get out a new tape is again forcefully closed. The two reels, which Krapp just recorded, he then dashes to the floor.

A few days back Rick had caused the lamp to swing wildly during this violent action. While the lamp was swinging, Krapp's head was alternately in the light and shadow while he carefully puts the old reel back on: the swinging stopped as Krapp becomes immobile for the final position. 'Try to keep that', Beckett asks. He thought that this play of light and dark, motion and silence was 'superb'.

Rick takes his seat on the stool at the table for the starting positon. Once more the content and working condition of the drawer are checked. A shutter is placed over the lamp above the table to reduce the cone of light even further — a light blue gel gives the desired 'coldness'. Beckett stands in the auditorium and observes the closing of the curtain. After initial hesitation he has decided to use the stage curtain.

Today, for the first time, the runthrough begins with the curtain. It opens, the lamp above the table and the three additional spots to augment the light of the table area are softly fading up, while Krapp's face, immobile and lost in a far away dream, emerges slowly out of the dark. Krapp begins his short endgame — war with himself.

Director's notes: Beckett comes up onstage to the table with a few quickly jotted down observations, he speaks with a hushed, concentrated voice. A few notes about the banana business. Beckett wants Rick to hold the banana halves in his left hand clearly visible by the stem and to peel them in that position. His face ought to show the anticipated enjoyment of the bananas. A change in the action: Up until now Beckett had Krapp catch the peels of the second banana in the air. Now he wants Krapp to drop them like the first banana peels, increase his pace, stop, remembering his mishap with the first peel, bend down, pick them up and throw them upstage.

To clarify the shift of mood from the interiority of the lyrical passage, with the little white dog and the small black ball, Beckett suggests a change in the action from the original version: Rick should turn the tape off after 'Ah well', glance whisky-thirsty to the den, get up, look back to the tape and decide then to listen to the tape after all — an interrupted interruption. Krapp is wavering between his appetite for a drink and his desire to finally find the passage with the girl in the boat again. What Krapp hears then — in the excited, feverish intonation of the 39-year-old — makes him lose his temper. Beckett explains: everything he has heard from the tape concerning other people in his life is 'acceptable material' for him. What he cannot bear in his present state 'as a wash-out' is the reminder of his personal business, his spiritual adventures, 'all that business of the vision'.

Beckett wants Krapp's positions set apart and more precisely defined:

Krapp's opening and identical final position are marked by the weight of the reminiscences — upright posture, the hands flat down on the table, the eyes open with a remote gaze, 'deadly silent'.

Krapp's listening position expresses the effort of listening, the tension of the face muscles, the left hand on the switch, always reacting to what is being heard, in constant readiness to switch the machine on or off, 'a communicative tension'. Krapp's face is right above the tape-recorder in order not to miss a single word.

Dreaming position: Krapp is caught in his memories, his fantasies, he 'sees' again situations from his past or his imagination, always connected with the women he once knew, women he dreamed about like Effie, their faces, their eyes. His attitude here is an interruption of the listening position, without a change in the posture of his hands. Halfway to the opening position, Krapp stops, day dreaming, his eyes opened and his face relaxed.

Beckett isn't satisfied yet with the transitions. He wants specific rhythm, connecting Krapp's world of memories and his occupation with the concrete objects of his habitation: the gaze lowered after the opening position; before Krapp looks at the drawer where the bananas are; after the dreaming position, before his eyes move to the den which again prepares him for his walk there, etc.

A few notes to the transitions between positions: Rick is to separate them neatly, not to mix the different moods.

Then Beckett works in detail on Krapp's life-monologue. 'For your entire life you have been drowned in dreams', Beckett says. Here, the 69-year-old Krapp returns from his bitter hopelessness to his fantasies. 'It has to come out clearly that he constantly interrupts himself, he has interrupted himself his entire life.'

'You should keep it as small, simple and monotone as possible. Try to bring out the immobility, no intensity, no colour except for a few specific moments where you will use both intensity and colour. The eye action will help you with that. And above all: don't force the tone.' Then Beckett begins a detailed critique of the lines.

'The voice! Jesus!' this echo-effect Beckett wants emphasised. Rick should use the tone and voice of the tape voice on 'The eyes she had!'. The right hand grasps the note paper, interruption, drops on the table, short dreaming position. '. . . the ages!' — Beckett insisting: 'Don't speak that too loudly otherwise no one will hear it.'

'Nothing to say, not a squeak' — here, an exception to the rule that action and word are never to coincide: Krapp is to crumple the piece of note paper and to flick it away on 'squeal'. Here again clear rhythm: the note paper falls on the floor and the hand falls on the table — 'What's a year now?' 'Seventeen copies sold' Beckett says this is an intensification of absurdities crowned by 'getting known' which Krapp is to embellish with a smile. Then his expression turns into a grimace.

The Effie passage. Beckett explains: 'Krapp is wrapped up in this dream — up there on the Baltic with the pine trees — and then its absurdity overwhelms him. His face lights up and then — "could I?" — the light extinguishes. You see what is happening: he just said "last fancies" and right away he is in the midst of his dreams again.' A short pause before 'Effie' which Krapp says slowly with warmth and accentuation.

'And she' — at the peak of absurdity, Krapp drops his clenched fists on the table and bows his head.

Fanny. The dream passes over into the reality of the old Krapp: his voice expresses how far he is removed from Effie. The passage is spoken quickly, bitterly, contemptuously. A movement of the head on 'she said' the first and only time in the play.

'Sometimes wondered in the night if a last effort mightn't . . .' Beckett wants Krapp to only imply the last word. 'Maybe you can clarify the interruption, cut the word off, a further self-interruption. He is constantly torn between these fruitless fantasies and cold reality. This is one of his fantasies here whose absurdity overwhelms him immediately.'

The second 'leave it at that' Rick is to speak with final emphasis, his head bowed.

Following this is the very lyrical, rhythmical and detached passage beginning with, 'Lie propped up in the dark'. In the dreaming position spoken in a balanced tone. Rick ought to visualise the images of his memory while speaking, set clear pauses.

'And so on' — continues with this rhythm, each word has its own weight.

'Be again, be again': 'be' held, a vibrato like the ringing of the bells Krapp wants to hear again.

'All that old misery' should begin quietly. If 'misery' becomes too loud, then the dramatic effect of 'once wasn't enough for you' would be lost. Because unexpected, the sudden intensity gives this sentence its necessary effect. 'The more unexpectedly the sentence is said, the better it is.' Krapp flings the sentence while throwing his head vehemently to the left. 'Lie down across her' — Krapp turns his head into the dreaming position, speaks with an excited 'interior voice' before his rage overwhelms him; furiously he rips the new tape off the machine and dashes it to the floor. With the utmost care he puts the old tape back on — the bearer of his memories — listens and then becomes immobile in his final position. The silence takes him back. After the blackout the empty tape continues to run and only the light of a little lamp Beckett had mounted on the tape recorder stays visible for a few seconds; a white light from the darkness of the stage before the curtain closes.

Appendices

BECKETT DIRECTS PINGET

Beckett's active participation in the production of his own works increased from his first attendance at the rehearsals of *En attendant Godot*. His growing interest in the mechanics of the practical theatre led to his helping Pierre Chabert direct Robert Pinget's *l'Hypothèse* in 1966, the one occasion on which Beckett has directed a work by another playwright.

In 1962 Beckett's English 'adaptation' of Pinget's *La Manivelle* (*The Old Tune*) had been published in *New Writers II* (London, John Calder). Beckett also knew and liked *l'Hypothèse*, which Pinget had written for the actor Jean Martin who played 'Lucky' in Roger Blin's original production of *Godot*. When Chabert was directing *l'Hypothèse* and playing the role of Mortin, Beckett attended rehearsals at the invitation of Pinget, became interested in the play and ultimately agreed to assist in directing.

l'Hypothèse is a one act play of 33 pages in the *Éditions de Minuit* text. It has one actor and a series of cinematographic projections of his image. The single character, Mortin, is in his sparsely furnished room in formal attire; a manuscript is in front of him on a table; he is preparing a lecture. Although the text is in front of him, he tries to repeat it by heart as if to an imaginary audience. From time to time, however, he is forced to refer back to the text. The main action of the play is Mortin's monologue in which he hypothesises about the origin of a manuscript apparently discarded at the bottom of a well, and its author's motivation for writing and abandoning it. Mortin's struggle with this hypothesis by means of a series of pseudo-logical and delerious conclusions and the final burning of his text closely parallels the predicament of the imaginary author of the manuscript.

The following account by Pierre Chabert shows Beckett in his first independent role as a stage director using stage space, gesture, and lighting in ways he was to employ later when he assumed full responsibility for directing his own plays.

Beckett's *l'Hypothèse*

In 1966 I was doing Robert Pinget's *l'Hypothèse* for the Paris *Biennale*. I was both directing and acting. Naturally that was quite difficult. Then one day Pinget brought Beckett by to see what I was doing. Beckett said he thought he could add something. He really liked the play. He came back to make suggestions. We worked a long time together, very minutely. Then when I did it again at the Odéon as part of a bill including Beckett's *Comédie*, and Ionesco's *La Lacune* and *Délire à Deux*, Beckett reworked it with me.

It is a play that is difficult to dramatise because it is a monologue interrupted by a cinematographic image of the central character, Mortin, which is projected on the wall. The film had already been made before Beckett arrived. It is an image of Mortin's own face which appears five times. In the first appearance the face is twice the actual size and each time it begins with a single image of the face and then it is joined by a second identical face and finally a third.

As it grows in size, the projection also remains visible longer and grows more voluble. The first appearance is for only ten seconds and the image is silent. The second projection remains longer while Mortin is at first unaware of it; it too is silent. In the third projection the face begins to move its lips but there is no audible speech. By the fourth appearance, the image murmurs words which are at first indistinct, but as this murmur grows to a crescendo and Mortin turns his attention to it, the words become clear and the image begins a monologue which is a parody, a derisory inversion of what the character has just recounted. In the fifth and final projection the voice of the image replaces that of Mortin who reads inaudibly from his manuscript. Mortin's few audible passages grow shorter as the triple image takes over a long section, speaking louder and louder and faster and faster. Pinget wants it delivered with a 'ferocious expression'. Beckett was completely satisfied with the cinematographic projection.

He did have a very definite suggestions about the lighting for the projection. Every time the image appears on the wall, the light has to change in order for the cinematographic image to be seen. As soon as the image appears there has to be a drop in intensity of the stage lighting. There is still some light, we still see the character, there is a confrontation between him and the image. This change in lighting can be done two ways: the light can go rapidly from bright to dim while passing through all the decreasing stages of intensity (as on a dimmer) or it can go from bright to dim instantaneously (by using a switch). Beckett wanted the light to change instantaneously in a very brusque manner as if a kind of night had descended upon the character like a sudden blow, and then we receive the shock of the image. But when the image disappears, the light goes up more slowly. When I recently saw *Godot* directed by Beckett, I discovered the same lighting effect — the lighting drops suddenly just after Pozzo and Lucky's exit when night falls.

When he had seen the runthroughs, Beckett realised that the production lacked something concrete to dramatise Mortin's monologue. The whole idea of the play is of course the relationship of a man to his manuscript, and Beckett found the way to visualise this relationship and make it concrete. Instead of having the manuscript on the table as Pinget indicated, the character is always working with a portion of it, and every time he gets up from the table he takes it with him. That is to say he has a physical rapport with this large stack of paper. It was a wonderful idea not only intellectually but visually. Throughout the play, pages are falling all over the stage and he's picking them up again. For example, when the face appears on the wall, he lets the whole pile fall all over the stage. At the end when he is going to throw it in the fire, there is only a single page left on the table (the rest of the manuscript is spread all over the floor), so finally he makes the long walk from the table to the stove to throw this great manuscript in, and there it is — one page.

But not only was there the visualisation of the pages spread all about, there was the sound. When he is going to throw the last leaf in the fire, Beckett insisted that he hear the sound of the character walking through the leaves that have fallen on to the floor, and he insisted that we hear the clacking of the stove — he slams it shut with a loud clack.

He also made changes in the stage directions for the set which helped give a visual dramatic structure. Pinget's set called for a room with a bookshelf on the right, the stove at the back against a blank white wall, and a table on the left. Beckett moved the stove downstage left, then the table to stage right, and backstage centre is the wall where the projected image appears. This created a sense of three distinct areas, each with its own importance, which helped give a special quality to Mortin's action in each of the spaces. For example, Beckett insisted upon a physical rapport between the character and the table. The story of *l'Hypothèse* is of a rather pompous pedant preparing a lecture, and he relies very much on the manuscript. It is a little bit the same with the table: at the moment that Mortin doesn't have his text any more he runs to the table. He has practically an umbilical relationship to it. When I did *Krapp* with Beckett I found the same relationship with the table.

He made other changes that added dramatic intensity to Mortin's action. In Pinget's text Mortin aims a revolver at the image, and the second time it appears he shoots, whereupon the image disappears. Pinget has him calmly clean the revolver and return it to the drawer of the table. Beckett has him drop the revolver so that in the fourth appearance of the image, when it is giving Mortin its account of the tender relationship of the father and his daughter, exactly opposite to Mortin's own account of a sadistic relationship, Mortin runs across the stage and grabs the pistol. He is just ready to shoot again, but before he can fire, the image disappears. In the Pinget text after Mortin has heard the story he runs to the bookshelf and throws the books one at a time all over the stage, but for the purpose of rhythm and a single rapid gesture, Beckett had the books placed in a special way so that they would all fall at once. He wanted this whole action to have a single rapid rhythm. It is at once very violent but very clean and precise. Then when the image appears for the fifth time and it is at last telling him the whole truth, he is seated at the table, his back to the image. He puts his hands over his ears. Beckett wanted this done very gradually so that his face would disappear as he lowers his head down on the table.

Beckett pays enormous attention to details, gestures, the intonations of the words. He asked me to find particular gestures for key words — for example the word 'well', the place where the original author left his manuscript — is very important in the text. He asked me to find a specific gesture that would prolong, punctuate, underline this word. And with every enumeration — 'first', 'second', 'third' — Mortin taps on the table. We divided some words into syllables. I'd already done that, but it seemed to correspond to something deep in Beckett. For example, *'l'in-a-ni-té'*, *'l'hy-po-thèse'*.

He had me use a variety of rhythms throughout the text. We worked on rhythm musically. The text goes very very fast, then all of a sudden it will stop. There will be a silence so that a word will come out. One phrase that was emphasised was '*l'auteur, l'auteur, où se trouve l'auteur?*' which is repeated three or four times. This phrase: 'the author, the author, where is the author?' is a kind of key to the play and probably its fundamental theme: his failure to find his identity, even through writing. Thus, the act of discarding the manuscript at the bottom of the well in the lecture is repeated in Mortin's burning of his own manuscript at the end of the play. Beckett asked me to emphasise the word 'author' as if he were 'the author of the world'.

Beckett has a sense of the form of the whole play. There are certain sections which are evident as units in the play itself. Some of them divide it into movements. For example when Mortin is at different places — at the table, at the stove. When Mortin has completely destroyed his manuscript, the tone changes entirely. The language becomes simpler — the tone becomes subdued. There is a kind of *rallentando*. Beckett did a very interesting thing at the end; when Mortin has thrown away his manuscript he begins to disrobe and then Beckett said to assume a rather broken attitude. Mortin is completely destroyed at the end, no longer in the middle of the room as in the original, but completely over to the left side next to the stove, so we achieved a complete decentralisation of the character, as if he too had been exhausted, like the manuscript.

(Interview, 1976)

ELMAR TOPHOVEN: TRANSLATING BECKETT

My first experience of working directly with Beckett was in Karlsruhe in 1952 when we went over my translation of *En attendant Godot*. Then later I went during several afternoons to his little studio in the *rue des Favorites*. I read my translation aloud to him and he pointed out what needed changing. At one place Gogo suggests that Pozzo's watch '*ist stehengeblieben*' ('. . . it has stopped'); earlier Didi had said '*Die Zeit steht*' ('Time has stopped'). Beckett wanted the two verbs to coincide, either: '*Die Uhr ist stehengeblieben*', '*Die Zeit ist stehengeblieben*' or '*Die Uhr steht*'; '*Die Zeit steht*'. There are twenty pages between those two passages in the text. A kind of light went on in my head when I realised the importance to him of the echoes and repetition of words and phrases which work like leitmotifs throughout the play.

At the beginning I wasn't quite so aware of his subtle

precision. In my first translation of *Godot* I translated, '*enfin*' ('at last'), as '*Endlich*' ('finally', 'at last') but of course that doesn't have the same value as '*na, ja*' ('ah, yes'). No one pointed that out to me then. Beckett's special awareness of the possibilities of language has become clearer to me as we have worked together. *Lösigkeit, Lessness* in English, in his own title. It is a creation that the German language offers, but one that doesn't actually occur in normal usage. '*Heimatlösigkeit*' ('homelessness') yes, but not just *Lösigkeit* by itself. There you can see Beckett's mind at work! He took the responsibility, the possibility existed and he took advantage of it.

His verbal precision has led me to ask questions about German that I had never asked before. For example, the difference between '*Jetzt*' and '*Nun*' both rendered by 'now' in English. But in German if someone asked me '*Wie alt bist du jetzt?*' ('How old are you now?') I might answer, '*Drei und fünfzig Jahre, zwei Monaten, zwanzig Tage, und vier Stunden*' ('Fifty-three years, two months, twenty days and four hours'. That would be '*jetzt*'. If someone asked me '*Wie alt bist du nun?*' I would give a less definite answer like '*Drei und Fünfzig*' (fifty-three'). We discuss this sort of thing; I ask questions and he gives answers. In our work we discuss the linguistic details of the text almost exclusively. He never gives interpretations, explains the characters or anything like that with me. In this respect I sometimes have the feeling of being thrown in the deep end, sink or swim.

When I begin a translation he gives me the text. I work slowly and patiently. (*Godot* was the easiest: I did it in three weeks. Sometimes, as with *Watt*, it takes years.) Then I go to him with my translation. We sit down face to face. He has the original, I have my German version. I read slowly, trying to capture his reactions. Sometimes now I record my translation on a tape cassette and play it for him. That way I can watch his face for those places where he isn't perfectly satisfied. At certain points he may interrupt because something is not exactly right. Then we try to find a solution together. It might, for example, be an allusion, hidden or modified. The question will be how to render that. Once I was reading my translation of *Malone stirbt* (*Malone Dies*). he stopped me and said: 'I was thinking of a phrase from Grillparzer. It was from *Das Meeres und der Liebe Wellen: "der Tag wird kommen und die stille Nacht, der Herbst , der Lenz, das langen Sommers Freuden"*.' The citation appears in the text without any without any indication that it is from Grillparzer: '*die Blätter* . . . *die des langen sommers Freuden hinter sich haben* . . .' (Suhrkamp *Werkausgabe* p. 137) ('. . . old leaves that have known the long joys of summer . . .') (Grove. page 231). Later in my notes to the Suhrkamp edition, I did reveal that it was a citation from Grillparzer, but Beckett did not want to include anything that would make that explicit upon first reading.

One thing that has become very important for me is that my German translations have frequently followed Beckett's own French or English translations. I have to deal with a kind of 'authorised interpretation' which he wants taken into account in the German version. I have to compare my text with the French or English to learn the most recent state of the work. In the case of *Lösigkeit* I had both the French and the English original. At first I was alone with the text. Later he gave me a key. But at first I was alone trying to work out the assonances, underscoring certain syllables just to get the proper proportion of repeated sounds in each phrase. The possibility of repetition of consonants in French is not the same as in German, so I had to determine the frequency of a word in the text to know how important it was. I had to find the right degree of verbal echoes and the ways of establishing them. I wrote each phrase in French at the top of a card and the English at the bottom. Then in the middle between the two 'originals' I wrote the German. It was indispensable for me to see the English to grasp a certain sense of the phrase and also to know if I was missing the precise structure of it.

There are some things you can do in one language but not in another. In the German text we were unable to retain either the sense of the traditional English toast, 'Happy Days', or the refrain of the popular song, 'Happy days are here again'; both are lost in '*Glückliche Tage*'. We just had to let that go. On the other hand, there are places where an equivalency can be found, if you work for it — when the two languages can be made to overlap so to speak. In *Happy Days* Winnie mentions a Mr. Shower who might have been called Mr. Cooker. Since Beckett derived the name Shower from the German 'schauen' ('to look') and the name Cooker from 'küchen' ('to peer') the process could be reversed in the translation. In the German version Winnie remembers a Herr Pierer perhaps called Herr Stärer from the English verbs 'to peer' and 'to stare'. The names retain their puzzling associations in both languages. And in some cases the language you are translating in offers compensatory opportunities. The leitmotif of the verb *'gehen, ging, gegangen'* (go, went, gone') could be given even greater emphasis in our German text of *Endspiel* because German has a large number of phrases containing the verb *'gehen'*.

Different texts offer different problems. I mentioned the allusions in *Watt*. Allusions were a great problem in *Glückliche Tage (Happy Days)*. *Glückliche Tage* was the hardest. In this one case Beckett first tried to make the corrections in the German text by himself to find the correspondences and verbal echoes I had missed. Then we worked together. The phrase *'genug von Erdenparadise* for example, is only eight syllables. For an English ear, 'paradise enow' is enough to evoke the whole world of Omar Khayyám, but not for a German. 'That's too hard', I said. In German all of Winnie's recollections of lines from the classics can at best only be emphasised through unusual sentence constructions and words. When he was going to direct the play in Berlin we went over the text together and read various German translations of *Paradise Lost*, Shakespearian plays, etc., to find the best for our purposes and then made our selections. A typical example of how we solved the problem is a citation by Winnie from Dante's *Inferno* (XXIX, 64). The passage involves an ant. The normal German word for ant is *'Ameise'*, but instead we had Winnie use the archaic word *'Emse'*. In English she uses *'Emmet*. Neither word is current in either language, but the kind of insect can be understood from the action of the play and both these archaisms appear in the English and German translations of Dante so that it is possible to make the link to the allusion since the words stand out; they invite the audience to sense a connection.

Comment C'est was a very special problem. It consists of aggregates of words which must be both heard and read. The rhythm of these words plays a very important part. But because it is printed, the line endings add new caesuras. This creates a difficulty in the reader's perception. I discussed this with him. One solution might have been to have marked each line of the text and to have requested the publisher to provide a text in which each line of print ends with a complete aggregate. But he didn't do that. The one thing that was clear to both us, however, was how much the reception depended upon the integrity of the essentially auditory units and the difficulty created by the printed medium. In his own French translations of *Eh Joe* and *Not I*

Beckett has tried to compensate for the fact that a French phrase usually contains more syllables than its English equivalent by keeping some sort of correspondence in the relatively consistent length of the aggregates in the originals. These things are important to him and I try to take them into account in my translation.

The more recent play *Footfalls* presents some typical problems. The title itself is hard. Beckett's first suggestion was *Schritte* (*Steps*), but that has overtones of *fortschritte* (*progress*). And it is also very important that these steps are heard. So we came to *Tritte*. I have also had some difficulties translating the game 'Lacrosse'. I tried to find a game to preserve the sense of something outmoded. I remembered that my mother used to play croquet when she was young. But the word 'Cross' is prominent in the English. Also there is the problem of keeping the notion of movement in the sport. Jumping rope would have retained that sense of motion, but the reference to the cross is lost. This is a question which I will discuss with him to find out what we should do. It's the kind of thing I like to leave up to him, which of the connotations are most important to preserve.

In most cases, though, our attention is on the structural details of the shape of a sentence, its rhythm, the interplay of sounds which play such a large part in establishing the leitmotifs. In *Fragment du Théâtre I* (*Theatre I*), for example, there is a phrase '*Il n'y a plus de mystère*'. I translated that as '*Es gibt kein Rätsel mehr*'. The word '*Rätsel*' corresponding to '*mystère*' changes place to the interior of the phrase. The German ended with the word '*mehr*'. The problem was how to maintain the accent at the end of the sentence. It finally became '*Es gibt nichts mehr zu rätzeln*'. I think Beckett appreciates the attention to these little things. He wants to retain rhythms as exactly as possible. That was something we had to work out when he was going to direct *Glückliche Tage* (*Happy Days*) in Berlin — how to keep the same sense of abruptness of the original in Winnie's monologue.

This kind of perfecting of the texts is constantly going on. His works are evolving and later works are being written. We have taken advantage of each occasion of a new edition or a new production to add things, change things — make little modifications, and since there is a kind of unity among all the translations, we now deal with correspondences between earlier works and ones written later. If, for example, you include the words '*Wie es ist*' in a later work, you set up a resonance with the novel *Comment C'est, Wie es Ist*.

Beckett was satisfied with my first translation of *Godot* and it was the beginning of our long relationship as author and translator, but before going to the Schiller-Theater in Berlin in 1975 to direct *Warten auf Godot* he reviewed the entire text. I realised at one point that he had memorised all the roles. He had learned it by heart and could quote it to me without looking at the book. I had also reviewed the text and made some changes; we met twice to incorporate our alterations.

Our work together on *Godot* gives a rather good idea of the kind of things we do when we go over a text. Consonance is always a paramount consideration — the consistent choice of one German word for its equivalent in the original where the language will allow it. I had translated the opening line, '*Rien à faire*' as '*Nichts zu machen*' ('Nothing to be done'), but throughout the text I had sometimes used '*tun*' and sometimes '*machen*' to render the French '*faire*' (English 'do'). Beckett did not want a difference between '*tun*' and '*machen*' in the latest version of the play. For me '*machen*' has a greater sense of actually doing something concrete — overtones of creating something. '*Tun*' is more abstract. Beckett wanted '*machen*' throughout. So, for example, when Vladimir originally asked '*Was haben wir gestern Abend getan?*' at Berlin he asked '*Was haben wir gestern Abend gemacht?*' ('Now what did we do yesterday [evening]?').

Then there is the refinement of the verbal details. The English version of the play appeared after my first translation. We took advantage of that to introduce the same kind of alliteration in the duel of insults between Gogo and Didi. 'Cretin' and 'Critic' both begin with C, but not in German or French. So I asked myself what I should do to achieve a similar result to make the duel more effective. I tried to replace insults of 2 syllables with those of 3 syllables — 'bum, bum, bum' and to find insults more wounding towards the end. The duel begins rather innocuously at first and grows more intense. I hadn't done that in the beginning.

I also tried to express the aggressiveness in explosive consonants: '*Pestbeula*' ('plague-boil') '*Parasite*' ('parasite'). In my first translation I replaced the word '*architecte*' in the French with the word '*Oberkellner*' ('head-waiter'). '*Ober*' is typically German: '*Oberforster*'. Then it became '*Ober . . . forstinspector*' ('Head forest inspector'). The purpose was to give a sense of authority of the state. It had worked for 22 or 23 years but now I replaced it with a word beginning with 'P', '*Paleolitiker*'. I had another reason for that too. At one point Estragon says '*Hör mir auf mit deinen Landschaften. Sag mir lieber, wie es drunter aussieht*' (literally 'Leave off about your landscapes. Tell me about what's underneath!'). In Beckett's own English translation it's 'You and your landscapes. Tell me about the worms!' (Grove p. 39). The word '*Paleolitiker*', 'old stone-age man', strengthened that theme of something underlying everything. But at rehearsals the actors still preferred '*Oberforst-inspector*', and Beckett agreed to leave it that way. When it comes to the demands of the stage he is very flexible. In the text it remains '*Paleolitiker*'.

As we reworked the text for the Berlin production we reduced the number of composite words. '*Dichköpfig*' ('thickheaded') was changed to '*stör*' ('stubborn'). I wouldn't say that we made an effort to change every composite word to a 'simplex', but the tendency was in that direction. It helped maintain a certain unity of rhythmic tone in the language in keeping with the sparseness of the whole play.

Some of the changes we made gave a sharper definition or a heightened sense to the action. One important change in the Berlin version is that Pozzo never uses the familiar '*Du*' or other forms. A certain distance between him and the other characters is always maintained. Beckett also changed the song which Vladimir sings to Estragon as he tries to go to sleep. It was '*Ei ya po pia*' in my original — that was my suggestion, probably something I remembered from my childhood. In Berlin, Vladimir sings the well-known '*Schlafe mein Prinzchen, schlaf ein*'. It is less individualised, more marked.

He suggested several seemingly small changes — at times only of one word — which reinforce the major themes of the play. *Godot* is full of pairs of characters and objects which are inseparable, complementary but nevertheless ill-suited to each other. One of Gogo's fine boots fits, the other is too small. He struggles to remove one boot. He doesn't need Didi's help with the other. So Beckett changed Gogo's '*Hilf mir die Dreckschuhe* [plural 'boots'] *aus zu ziehen*' (in English and French simply 'Help me!', '*Aide-moi*') to the singular, '*Dreckschuh*' ('boot').

If the pairs always are in some way mismatched, they do remain inextricable and dependent upon one another. Didi suggests in the original that repentance might be a solution: '*Wenn wir es bereuen würden*' ('Suppose we repented'). Beckett added '*beiden*' ('both'). A little later Didi refers to the thieves crucified with '*dem Erlöser*' ('The Saviour'). Gogo asked in my original translation *'Mit dem was?'* ('With the what?') Beckett wanted the 'our' which is in his English 'Our what?' but not in the French (*'Le Sauveur'*). Gogo now asks *'Mit unserem was?'* This has two meanings, the general idea of one Saviour for all but also it introduces the idea that a release from their own predicament is feasible.

The work is careful and purposeful, but certainly not humourless. Beckett likes the light parts too. The Englishman who shows up in Gogo's brothel joke is just 'drunk' in the French original. I had made him *'Ein Englander, der mehr als gewöhnlich getrunken hat'* ('An Englishman who had drunk more than usual'). Beckett's English translation makes its own humorous comment on the drinking habits of the English. There it's 'An Englishman having drunk a *little* more than usual.' To bring out the joke in German, Beckett had me add *'etwas'* ('somewhat', 'a little') — *'Ein Englander des etwas mehr als gewöhnlich getrunken hat.'* At the point in Act Two where Didi asks the boy about Godot's beard, he wants to know if it is white or black. This last time Beckett added red. It used to be *'Trägt er einen Bart der Herr Godot? Blond oder . . . schwarz?'* we added *'Oder Rot?'* There is a note of whimsy. Why not red? Everything is possible.

My manuscript of *Godot* is full of changes made over a period of more than 20 years — too many to go through all of them. You can see from these examples, though, how we work. From the first it had been this continuing process of making the translation approach more closely what one thinks or experiences from the original. Beckett doesn't like to speak about what can be found in the text itself. Always we work to perfect the text so that it makes its own statement in translation just as it does in the original French and the author's English translation, and to incorporate the changes which have occurred to Beckett as he has reviewed the text and worked on it in production.

(Interview 1976)

Notes

Preface

1. Letter to Alan Schneider, 11 January, 1956. *Village Voice* 19 March, 1958.
2. Authors' interview Simone Benmussa, London, June 1978.
3. Authors' interview, Paris, June, 1978.

Chapter 1

1. Authors' interview with Maureen O'Brien Flegg, 1967.
2. Authors' interview with Georges Pelorson, 1976.
3. These letters and Corneille's response, the judgement of the Academie and Voltaire's footnote commentary on the controversy are contained in *Œuvres Complètes de Pierre Corneille*, Firmin Didot Frères, 1843, Vol. 2, p. 545 ff. Ms. Rina Kampes of York University (Toronto) pointed out this connection and supplied the documentation.
4. Authors' interview with Maureen O'Brien Flegg, 1976.
5. Authors' interview with Maureen O'Brien Flegg, 1976.
6. T.C.D. *A College Miscellany*, 26 February, 1931.
7. This information is from an interview, June 16, 1982, with the Dublin actress, Rachel Burrows who was enrolled in Beckett's 1931 lectures. On that occasion she also provided a photocopy of her class notebook. A copy of that notebook is also in Trinity College Dublin Library.
8. A typescript of 'Dream of Fair to Middling Women' is at Baker Library, Dartmouth College, New Hampshire, USA. The excerpt is reprinted in *Disjecta*, ed. Ruby Cohn, John Calder Ltd., London 1983, p. 46.
9. The project is discussed fully by Ruby Cohn in *Just Play*, Princeton 1980, pp. 143ff.
10. Deirdre Bair, *Samuel Beckett*, New York 1978, p. 254.
11. It is published in *Disjecta*, ed. Ruby Cohn, John Calder Ltd., London, 1983. It was performed at Beckett's suggestion at the University of Texas Beckett Symposium, *Beckett Translating/Translating Beckett*, 1984.
12. Beckett has generously made his text available by allowing access and photocopies of the 136 page typescript in French first through Baker Library at Dartmouth College, New Hampshire and more recently The Humanities Research Center of University of Texas, and the Samuel Beckett Archives at Reading University, England. The original of the 136 page typescript and a preceding holograph draft are at Texas. The other copies of the typescript are identical facsimiles. Parenthetical page references are to the typescript. English translations are by the authors with assistance of Marie-Thérèse Dow, Prof. Emeritus, Duke University.

Chapter 2

1. Arnold Geulincx, *Ethica* in *Sämtliche Schriftlichen*, ed. H.J. Vleeschawer, Stuttgart 1968. Band III. This translation is by Ronald Begley, Department of Classics, University of North Carolina at Chapel Hill. Beckett almost certainly used the more rare *Antverpiensis opera philosophica recognovit J P N Land. Sumptibus providerunt sortis. Spinozanae curatores. Volumen tertium idque postremum.* Hagae comitum apud martinum nijhoff MDCCCXCIII acquired by Trinity College in 1906. This volume places Geulincx in the context of Spinoza.
2. Beckett to Alec Reid. Alec Reid, 'Beckett and the Drama of Unknowing', *Drama Survey*, Fall 1962, p. 130.
3. Jack MacGowran, 'MacGowran on Beckett'. (Interview by Richard Toscan, *Theatre Quarterly*, July-Sept, 1973), p. 16.
4. Samuel Beckett, *Werke*. Band II. Suhrkamp Verlag, Frankfurt am Main, 1976, p. 383.
5. Roger Blin in Ruby Cohn, ed. *Casebook on Waiting for Godot*. Grove Press, New York, 1967, p. 26.
6. Beckett to Alan Schneider. Alan Schneider, 'Waiting for Beckett, A Personal Chronicle', *Beckett at Sixty*, Calder and Boyars, 1967, p. 38.
7. Colin Duckworth, ed. *En attendant Godot*, London, 1966, p. 1.
8. Duckworth, p. LXV.
9. 'MacGowran' p. 17.
10. 'MacGowran' p. 17.
11. Alan Schneider, 'Anyway you like Alan: Working with Beckett' *Theatre Quarterly*, 1975, IV(19), p. 26.
12. Duckworth, p. LXIII.
13. Duckworth, p. LXIII.
14. Duckworth, pp. LX, LXI.
15. Duckworth, p. LXII.
16. Duckworth, p. CIV.
17. Duckworth, p. 99.
18. Duckworth, p. LXIII.
19. Duckworth, p. 96.
20. Jack MacGowran in Derek Malcolm, 'The Day the Malt Fused', *The Guardian*, 30 December, 1964, p. 7.
21. 'MacGowran' p. 17.
22. Authors' interview with Donal Donnelly, 1978.
23. 'MacGowran' p. 17.
24. The drawing is in the copy of the first French edition that Beckett used at rehearsals, now in the possession of John Calder. A photocopy is available at Reading University.
25. Authors' interview with Jean Martin, 1976.
26. Photocopy in Reading University Library, (RUL MS 1485/1).
27. Deirdre Bair. *Samuel Beckett: A Biography*, New York, 1978, pp. 428-429.
28. Letter to Alan Schneider, 15 October, 1956. 'Beckett's letter on Endgame' *Village Voice Reader* p. 183.
29. Alan Schneider to John Lahr, TV interview 1971. Videotape recording at Theatre Library, the Julliard School, New York City.

30. Alan Simpson, *Beckett and Behan*, Kegan Ltd., London, 1962, pp. 131-132.
31. Peter Bull, *I Know the Face But...* London, 1959, p. 179.
32. Beckett to Paul Danemann, 'The Long Wait', *Times Literary Supplement*, 5 May, 1961, p. 277.
33. Alan Schneider, 'Any Way You Like, Alan', *Theatre Quarterly*, XIX. p. 31.
34. Beckett to Charles Marowitz, 'Paris Log' *Encore*, March-April, 1962,p. 42.
35. Duckworth, p. LXXXI.
36. Marowitz, p. 44.
37. Authors' interview with Matias, 1976.
38. Marowitz, p. 44.
39. Authors' interview with Deryk Mendel, 1976.
40. Schneider, 'Any Way You Like, Alan', p. 32.
41. Authors' Interview, 1976
42. Anthony Page, 'Working with Beckett', interview with Ronald Hayman, *The Times,* 19 January, 1973, p. 13.
43. John Fletcher, 'Acting and Play', *Modern Drama*, December 1966, p. 248.

Chapter 3

1. Jean Reavey, unpublished journal in her possession.
2. Translated and adapted by the authors from *Materialen zu Samuel Beckett, Warten auf Godot (Zweiten Band) Herausgegeben von Hartmut Englehardt und Dieter Mettler*. Suhrkamp Verlag, Frankfurt-am-Main, 1979.
3. This information based upon authors' attendance at rehearsals and discussions with Walter Asmus, the actors, and production staff.

Chapter 4

1. Interview, Patrick Magee, 1976.
2. Interview and letter, Roger Blin, 1976.
3. Interview by Richard Toscan, 'MacGowran on Beckett', *Theatre Quarterly*, July-Sept, 1973.
4. 'Is This The Person To Murder Me?' *Sunday Times* (colour magazine) March 1, 1964, pp. 17-22, Clancy Sigal is a journalist and author who attended rehearsals as an observer but had no part in the production.
5. From *Materialen zu Beckett's 'Endspiel'*, Suhrkamp, Frankfurt, 1968. Translated by Britta von Diezelski, copyright 1984.
6. From *Materialen zu Beckett's 'Endspiel'*. Authors' translation.

Chapter 5

1. Typescript in Baker Library, Dartmouth College, USA, photocopy at Reading University Library.
2. In working with Marcel Mihalovici on the text for his opera *Krapp*, Beckett acknowledged that Krapp's recordings were like a photograph album evoking memories of central moments of his past.
3. The holograph *Magee Monologue* is at Reading University (RUL MS 1227/7/7/1), the typescripts are at the Humanities Research Center, University of Texas, Austin.
4. At Reading University (RUL 1396/4/16)

5. Volker Canaris, 'Auf die Stille haben wir gesetzt' *Das letzt Band, Regiebuch*, Frankfurt 1970, p. 119.
6. Reproduced from Clas Zilliacus, *Beckett and Broadcasting*, Abo (Finland), 1976, pp. 204-205.

Index

329